W9-CIP-435

THE QUALITY OF GROWTH IN AFRICA

INITIATIVE FOR POLICY DIALOGUE AT COLUMBIA:
CHALLENGES IN DEVELOPMENT AND GLOBALIZATION

THE QUALITY
OF GROWTH
IN AFRICA

EDITED BY

Ravi Kanbur, Akbar Noman,
and Joseph E. Stiglitz

COLUMBIA UNIVERSITY PRESS

NEW YORK

Columbia University Press
Publishers Since 1893
New York   Chichester, West Sussex
cup.columbia.edu

Library of Congress Cataloging-in-Publication Data
A complete CIP record is available from the Library of Congress.
ISBN 978-0-231-19476-1 (cloth : alk. paper)
ISBN 978-0-231-55098-7 (e-book)

Columbia University Press books are printed on permanent
and durable acid-free paper.
Printed in the United States of America

Cover image: Lost Horizon Images/Cultura/Getty Images

INITIATIVE FOR POLICY DIALOGUE AT COLUMBIA: CHALLENGES IN DEVELOPMENT AND GLOBALIZATION

JOSÉ ANTONIO OCAMPO AND JOSEPH E. STIGLITZ, SERIES EDITORS

The Initiative for Policy Dialogue (IPD) at Columbia University brings together academics, policy makers, and practitioners from developed and developing countries to address the most pressing issues in economic policy today. IPD is an important part of Columbia's broad program on development and globalization. The Initiative for Policy Dialogue at Columbia: Challenges in Development and Globalization presents the latest academic thinking on a wide range of development topics and lays out alternative policy options and tradeoffs. Written in a language accessible to policy makers and students alike, this series is unique in that it both shapes the academic research agenda and furthers the economic policy debate, facilitating a more democratic discussion of development policies.

The *quality* of economic growth has been at the center of global debates in recent years. This book focuses on how those concerns pertain to and are reflected in Africa (mainly South of the Sahara). Several research and policy issues around the quality of growth have arisen in the region after the resumption of economic growth in the 1990s following a long period of stagnation or decline in much of it.

The authors in this volume examine a range of interrelated concerns that fall under the general heading of the *quality of growth*. These include: (i) the distribution of the income gains from growth; (ii) the translation of economic growth into nonincome dimensions of wellbeing such as employment, health, education and security; (iii) the structural transformation of the economy so that the sources of growth and employment are diversified away from dependence on low-productivity primary commodities and informal activities towards modern manufacturing (including "industrialized agriculture") and services; (iv) managing the urbanization process so it enhances the quality of life; and (v) environmental sustainability.

CONTENTS

ACKNOWLEDGMENTS

This volume reflects the work of the Africa Task Force of the Initiative for Policy Dialogue at Columbia University supported by the Japan International Cooperation Agency (JICA). The papers presented here reflect the central themes of the discussions at meetings of the Task Force held in New York and Nairobi. In addition to the authors of chapters in this collection, several other participants at the meetings made valuable contributions to the work of the Task Force. Notable among them were Yaw Ansu, Elizabeth Asiedu, William Baah-Boateng, Naohiro Kitano, and Celestin Monga, who made their own presentations as well as served as discussants and commentators. We would like to express our gratitude to them.

JICA's support went beyond a generous financial contribution and included substantive support not only in the form of contributions to this collection but also active participation by JICA staff and consultants in the deliberations of the Task Force. We are most grateful for this support.

The assiduous work of the following notetakers, who recorded and wrote up the discussions at the meetings, is greatly appreciated: Natasha Ardiani, Btissam Benkeroum, Maurice Jackson, Olivia Marra, and Laila Staudinger Pedroza. In organizing meetings, managing, and financial accounting first Jiaming Ju and then for the most part Gabriela Plump played a vital role with exemplary dedication. Others who deserve our gratitude for their help include Hannah Assadi, Debarati Ghosh, and Kristen Grennan.

Finally, Nicole Pope did a superb job of copyediting and managing the publication process on behalf of the Task Force. We are most grateful for her efforts, as we are for the valuable help and guidance of Christian Winting and Marisa Lastres at Columbia University Press.

THE QUALITY OF GROWTH IN AFRICA

INTRODUCTION

THE QUALITY OF GROWTH IN AFRICA: AN OVERVIEW

Ravi Kanbur, Akbar Noman, and Joseph E. Stiglitz

In the postwar years, the world has seen rapidly increasing gross domestic product (GDP) per capita, economic growth like never before. It had taken one thousand years up to 1950 for income per capita to rise by a factor of fifteen. It took only six more decades for it to multiply by a factor of four. Between 1000 CE and 1978, China's per capita GDP increased by a factor of two, but it multiplied sixfold over the next thirty years. India's per capita income increased fivefold in the seventy years since its independence, having increased a mere 20 percent in the previous millennium. The 2008 economic crisis caused a major dent in this long-term trend, but it was just that—a dent. Even allowing for the sharp decreases in output as a result of the crisis, postwar economic growth is spectacular compared with what was achieved in the previous thousand years. Overall, the world has seen considerable improvements in nonincome dimensions of economic development, such as health and education levels, which are valuable both intrinsically and as instruments for further progress.

The quality of growth, however, has emerged as an issue of considerable concern, all over the world, especially since the 2008 crisis, the long shadow of which still lingers. Death by suicide in the United States rose by nearly 30 percent between 1999 and 2016, during which time nearly 45,000 Americans committed suicide and another 42,000 died from opioid overdoses. These and other manifestations of distress and despair, such as a decline in the life expectancy of white American males, are widely attributed to a deterioration in the quality of economic growth, reflected in growing inequalities and insecurities.[1]

Writing in 2018, Stiglitz says,

in the beginning of this century I wrote *Globalization and Its Discontents* . . . to explain the unhappiness with globalization . . . in so many countries in the developing world. . . . The unhappiness was greatest in Sub-Saharan Africa. . . . Its rich human and natural resources have been stolen from it for centuries. . . . Now globalization's opponents are joined by those in the middle and lower classes of the advanced industrial countries . . . the fact . . . is that large segments of the population in advanced countries have not been doing well. (2018, xv–xvi)

He adds, "but we should not lose sight of its benefits . . . the post–World War II global economic order, of which globalization is a part . . . has contributed to creating the fastest rate of economic growth ever . . . with hundreds of millions moving out of poverty" (2018, xix). The discontent regardless is because "globalization has been mismanaged" (2018, xix).

As a result, notwithstanding the background of spectacular achievements at the global level, there is much to stop us from declaring a victorious past on human progress. Good global average trends, although they are to be welcomed, can hide alarming countertendencies. Countries in Africa that are mired in conflict do not have any growth to speak of, and indeed, they often are in decline. For African countries for which we have data, although the percentage of people in poverty has been falling, the absolute number of people living in poverty has risen by almost one hundred million in the past quarter century because of population growth.

A similar conflicting tale confronts us when we look at global income inequality. Income inequality among all individuals in the world can be viewed as made up of two components. The first is inequality between average incomes across countries—the gap between rich and poor countries. The second is inequality within each country. Given the fast growth of large poorer countries like India and China relative to the growth of richer countries like the United States, Japan, and those in Europe, inequality between countries has declined. Within-country inequality displays a more complex picture, but sharp rises in inequality (reflected in any of a number of measures) in the United States, Europe, and China and India means that overall within-country inequality has increased Combining the two measures using one standard metric, the Gini coefficient, we find that world inequality has in fact declined overall by at least some accounts. However, on some of the adjustments made to the data to take account of the understatement of income of the richest decile in household surveys much of the decline in inequality disappears (Lakner and Milanovic 2016). In the unadjusted data, the importance of between-nation inequality has fallen from a contribution of four-fifths of global inequality a quarter century ago. But its contribution is still not lower than three-quarters of total world inequality. These two features—rising within-nation inequality especially in large developing countries (with a few notable exceptions, most importantly Brazil) and the still-enormous role of between-nation inequality—are the other side of the coin from the good news of developing country growth on average in the past three decades.

Moreover, income growth, if it comes at the expense of the environment, mismeasures improvement in human well-being. Particulate pollution has increased by 10 percent over the past quarter century, bringing all its related health implications. The global population experiencing water stress has almost doubled in the past half century, and global forest area has declined steadily over the same period. Global greenhouse gas emissions have increased from less than forty gigatons to almost fifty gigatons in the past quarter century. On present trends, global warming is projected to reach around 4 degrees Celsius by 2100, well above the safe warming level of 1.5 degrees Celsius. The consequences of global warming have already begun to appear as increases in severe weather.

Thus, the past seven decades have indeed been golden ones for economic development. But all is not golden. The trends hide some worrying tendencies, which will shape the landscape of development going forward. One worry is whether the growth that we have seen is sustainable. The manufacturing export-led growth model that worked so well in East Asia, and that more recently seems to have played a role in Africa (notably in Ethiopia), may be coming to an end, both because of growing protectionism and because manufacturing, as a share of global output and employment, is in decline.

This book focuses on a range of interrelated concerns that fall under the general heading of the *quality of growth*. These include (1) the distribution of the income gains from growth; (2) the translation of economic growth into nonincome dimensions of well-being, such as employment, health, education, and security; (3) the structural transformation of the economy, so that the sources of growth and employment are diversified away from dependence on low-productivity primary commodities and informal activities toward modern manufacturing (including "industrialized agriculture"[2]) and services; (4) management of the urbanization process so that it enhances the quality of life; and (5) environmental sustainability.

All of these concerns about the quality of growth are present in Sub-Saharan Africa (henceforth Africa for short). On average, African growth was significantly faster during the first years of the new millennium. Annual growth approached 5 percent during this century, with six of the ten fastest-growing economies in the world during 2000–2010[3] being in the region as it came out of its "lost quarter century," which commenced on the eve of the 1980s. This growth, however, was uneven both across and within countries. Many countries were mired in conflict and insecurity, hindering public and private investment and growth. In many of the countries that experienced growth, it was based on high global demand for commodities driven by Chinese growth. Most countries in the region lacked the structural transformation that is the hallmark of high-quality growth. There were, however, notable exceptions, especially Ethiopia and Rwanda. Throughout Africa, jobs lagged behind growth and behind the demographic explosion, raising the prospect of rising unemployment, especially for youth. The attendant insecurities weighed heavily on the quality of the growth.

Income inequality within these growing countries was as likely to go up as come down, raising the question of which policy differences explained the divergence.[4] Investment in education and health also lagged behind exploding needs. Rapid urbanization added its own pressures, drawing policy makers' attention to investment in megacities and small towns, which were absorbing this exodus from rural areas, as well as to appropriate investment in agriculture to stem the flow and make it more manageable. And despite not having caused climate change, Africa has borne, and will continue to bear, the burden of adaptation to address its consequences.

Thus, aside from issues of equity, sharing the benefits of growth, especially by generating jobs, and of sustainability, this volume pays particular attention to another important concern: the quality of urban development. As the world's most rapidly urbanizing region, with the urban population projected to rise from around four hundred million in 2010 to about eight hundred million by 2030 and nearly 1.2 billion by 2050, the livability of cities will have an important bearing on Africans' quality of life. Running through much of this volume is a concern with more and better jobs given the demographic explosion underway in the region. Sub-Saharan Africa's labor force is projected to increase by 2.1 billion between 2010 and 2100, accounting for more than 100 percent of the increase in the world's labor force of 2.0 billion, this aspect of the quality of growth assumes exceptional importance.

For all of these reasons, the quality of growth is at the forefront of African policy discourse. The chapters in the volume elaborate on different dimensions of the quality of growth in Africa, combining diagnosis with prescription. This volume is divided into five parts. Part I focuses on issues of measurement of growth and of equity and employment. Parts II and III focus on different aspects of the structural and economic transformations that are crucial for sustaining growth, including, importantly, the "industrialization" of agriculture. Part IV is devoted to the environment and part V to urbanization.

The first of the chapters in what follows is by Lorenzo Fioramonti, who takes a critical look at GDP[5] as a measure, particularly from an African perspective. Fioramonti argues that "a new approach to the measurement of prosperity is indispensable to devise policies that improve the quality of growth in Africa." GDP estimates tend to altogether neglect or seriously underestimate (1) activities outside the formal economy, and (2) the services of the ecosystem and the depletion of both physical and natural capital in the process of production. The latter is of particular importance for Africa, where many countries are heavily dependent on the production and export of nonrenewable minerals and metals, such as oil, copper, iron, gold, and diamonds. Fioramonti cites World Bank estimates of natural capital depletion, indicating that "African countries have been losing their wealth to the tune of about 1.2 percent a year over the past decade or so." Other inadequacies of the GDP measure that Fioramonti emphasizes include its neglect of distributional considerations, of insecurity, and of the costs of pollution.

Following the Commission on the Measurement of Economic Performance and Social Progress, Fioramonti calls for a dashboard to measure the quality of growth in Africa with three dials indicating "social well-being," "real economy," and "natural welfare." Notwithstanding the inadequacies of GDP, it remains a vital metric, even for Africa, as Ebrahim Patel, South Africa's economy minister, emphasized in meetings of the Organisation for Economic Co-operation and Development (OECD) High-Level Expert Group (HLEG) on the Measurement of Economic Performance and Social Progress (HLEG 2015).

A related issue is that of the capacity of statistical agencies to generate the data requirements of any of the elements of a dashboard. The weakness of such capacity in most of Africa is widely recognized. The use of GDP has the advantage of not only familiarity but also a widely used methodology for estimating it, albeit often used badly. Both better estimates of GDP and the generation of new or reasonably reliable data of other metrics that would populate a dashboard to assess the quality and quantity of growth require the strengthening of statistical capacity in African countries. There are inevitable trade-offs, including whether to devote resources to improving estimates of national accounts or GDP itself and other indicators.

The quality of data across many developing countries, not just those in Africa, leaves much to be desired. This point is emphasized in the careful empirical analysis that Andy McKay's chapter undertakes. Chapter 2 seeks to assess the quality of growth in Africa during the quarter century of 1990–2015, focusing on poverty reduction, equity, and issues of political fragility or sustainability. McKay refers to the recent proposal of Mlachila, Tapsoba, and Tapsoba (2016) for measuring the quality of growth, comprising "six main aspects, four relating to growth fundamentals (strength, volatility, sectoral composition, and demand composition) and two relating to social outcomes (education and health)." What McKay seeks to do is not to derive some overall measure of the quality of growth but to carefully examine the economic growth record during 1990–2015 and assess its interactions with social outcomes, equity, and political stability. The last is related to the concern with fragility of states that is such a key issue for sustainability of growth in some African countries.

McKay presents a set of clear and compelling graphs and tables on the growth story as well as on trends in poverty, equity, and fragility, albeit with inevitable gaps in country and time coverage. Over the fifty-five years between 1960 and 2015, three phases are distinguished: (1) from 1960 to the early to mid-1970s, a period characterized by a booming world economy and commodity prices, during which per capita GDP grew at a rate of 2.4 percent a year; (2) from the early to mid-1970s to the early to mid-1990s, a period dominated by conditionality and reforms under the International Monetary Fund (IMF) and World Bank–supported programs, and soft commodity prices, when incomes contracted sharply with per capita GDP growth averaging a rate of –1.4 percent a year; and (3) from 1994 to 2015, when per capita GDP growth averaged 1.8 percent per year, although it slowed down during 2013–2015. Per capita income did not recover to its mid-1970's peak until the early twenty-first century, which, along with other trends such as deindustrialization, led to the period being referred to as Africa's "lost quarter century" (Noman and Stiglitz 2012).

McKay then disaggregates the SSA growth experience first during 1990–2015 and second during 2006–2015 to the individual country level, finding a wide diversity of growth performances. Fast growers—that is, the fourteen countries in the region whose per capita GDP grew at a faster rate than 2.5 percent a year during 1990–2015—were generally resource-rich countries (especially those with new hydrocarbon discoveries), with Ethiopia and Rwanda being the most notable exceptions. At the other extreme, ten countries in the region experienced falling per capita GDP in that period, many of which were affected by conflict or political instability.

In the latest and most successful growth phase of 2006–2015, four countries had per capita GDP growth of more than 5 percent a year, and another nineteen countries had growth between 2.5 percent and 4.9 percent a year, whereas at the other extreme six countries experienced negative per capita growth. There was also considerable year-to-year variability in many countries, with only five countries in the region not having any years of negative per capita growth and six having ten or more such years. McKay observes that again "conflict or instability is a common factor in high growth volatility, but all too often so is high commodity dependence."

On the impact of growth on poverty reduction in Africa, McKay argues that the use of data available in international sources such as World Development Indicators (WDI) and PovcalNet is fraught with difficulties. Accordingly, he relies mainly on "careful and broadly comparable country case studies" conducted in sixteen of the largest twenty-four countries in Africa by Arndt, McKay, and Tarp (2016). The countries are classified into four groups: (1) good performance on both growth and poverty reduction (Ethiopia, Ghana, Malawi, Rwanda, and Uganda); (2) good growth but limited poverty reduction (Burkina Faso, Mozambique, Nigeria, Tanzania, and Zambia); (3) poor growth and poverty reduction (Cameroon, Cote d'Ivoire, Kenya, Madagascar, and South Africa); and (4) insufficient data for clear conclusions (Democratic Republic of Congo).

Using WDI data for the same twenty-four countries, McKay reports a statistically significant association between rate of poverty reduction and rate of per capita GDP growth as well as "quite a lot of scatter about the line—cases of low poverty reduction despite reasonable growth and the opposite." Indeed, out of ten countries in the sample that had good growth performance, only half also exhibited good performance in reducing income poverty. Although explanations about the relationship between growth and poverty reduction vary, one factor that emerges is the association between good performance in agriculture and poverty reduction.

McKay points out that many countries now have reasonably good quality household survey data for the purposes of measuring poverty, but such surveys are "much less successful at measuring the consumption or income of the rich," who are often, if not invariably, left out in such surveys. Hence, measuring inequality is much more problematic in developing countries, where the data typically rely on household surveys. Nonetheless, McKay utilizes the inequality data provided in WDI with a further caveat about the quality of the data: "in several cases, the changes in inequality (chiefly cases of reductions) they imply over relatively short periods are simply not plausible." There are thirty-seven African countries for which WDI show estimates of Gini coefficients at two or more points between 1990 and 2015. McKay tabulates the frequency distribution of the Gini coefficients for the latest year for which they are available, which shows that three countries, all in Southern Africa, have extremely high inequality by international standards, with a Gini coefficient greater than 60 (South Africa, Namibia, and Botswana) and another five have very high inequality, with Gini coefficients between 50 and 60 (Zambia, Lesotho, Swaziland, Guinea-Bissau, and Rwanda). Conversely, there are seven countries that have fairly low inequality, with Gini coefficients between 30 and 35. This data set also suggests that a number of countries would seem to have reduced their Gini coefficients significantly over the periods considered but in several cases the magnitude of reduction in the Gini coefficient is hard to believe in the absence of a clear country-specific explanation. Moreover, the WDI data set suggests that the "level of inequality or its change seems not to be significantly associated with growth in a bivariate cross-country comparison."

The last part of McKay's chapter is concerned with political stability or fragility. McKay reports that analysis using an index of fragility finds that "more fragile countries do grow more slowly on average; but much more strikingly, they have much more volatile growth rates." McKay also finds that more fragile countries have both higher poverty levels and slower progress in poverty reduction.

The last of the three chapters in part I is on the quality of jobs and growth in SSA. Moazam Mahmood begins by distinguishing three categories of countries in the region: thirty-two least developed countries (LDCs) with a per capita income under $1,000; ten low- and middle-income countries (LMICs) with per capita incomes between $1,000 and $4,000, and six emerging economies (EEs) with per capita incomes ranging from $4,000 to $12,000. Mahmood documents growth trends over the periods 2000–2007 and 2008–2016. His description is broadly consistent with that of McKay, but Mahmood adds information on some important characteristics of the growth experience, notably a reliance on primary exports (especially extractives) and services, and he discusses the deindustrialization that saw the share of manufacturing in GDP between 2000 and 2015 decline from 9.3 percent to 7.3 percent in LDCs and from 13.4 percent to 11.7 percent in EEs, while rising modestly from 8.4 percent to 8.9 percent in LMICS. For SSA, the share of manufacturing in this period declined from 10.9 percent to 9.5 percent.

Noting that open unemployment and employment growth are not good metrics to assess labor market outcomes in developing countries with large subsistence and informal sectors—the poor cannot afford to be wholly unemployed—Mahmood focuses on the quality rather than the quantity of jobs. The working poor, defined as those below the poverty line of purchasing power parity (PPP) $1.90 per capita a day, accounted for some 54 percent of Africa's labor force in 2000, and this share fell substantially to 36 percent in 2015. For LDCs in Africa the decline was from 63.9 percent to 41.1 percent, for LMICs it was from 42.9 percent to 31.6 percent, and for EEs it was from 17.5 percent to 5.5 percent.

What is more salient is that wage and salaried workers, typically viewed as the least vulnerable form of employment, saw their share of the labor force rise from about 25 percent to nearly 30 percent over the decade and a half from 2000 to 2015. Mahmood points out that Africa's pattern of growth, with its heavy reliance on low productivity services and primary exports of low labor intensity, has implied "weaker labor market outcomes in terms of productivity, incomes, and . . . transformation from vulnerable forms of employment to waged employment" with higher productivity and improved working conditions, such as social protection, rights, and access to national legislation on workers' rights. He concludes that a "strategy toward productive transformation is much needed."

Parts II and III of this volume are devoted to issues of such a productive transformation, which is vital not only for generating decent jobs but also for the sustainability of growth. Before turning to this set of issues, it would be apposite to emphasize the enormity of the employment challenge and opportunity facing Africa. The region is experiencing a demographic explosion with a projected increase in its labor force of

2.1 billion during 2010–2100, an amount exceeding the combined total of the increase of 2 billion in the world's labor force. Africa's share of the world's working age population is projected to rise from under 13 percent in 2010 to some 41 percent by 2100. Whether this turns out to be a demographic dividend or disaster depends on what happens to employment. The importance of the matter cannot be overstated, particularly given the implications of a demographic disaster with vast numbers of unemployed or underemployed youth presenting a challenge to political stability in Africa with ramifications for the rest of the world—all the more so, given the politically toxic turn that the issue of immigration has taken in Europe and North America.

In chapter 4, Antonio Andreoni, Ha-Joon Chang, and Isabel Estevez state that for their purposes "quality of growth is understood to be a growth process led by production transformation and collective capabilities development that results in the creation of quality jobs and sustainable structural change." The objective of their chapter is to critically examine how global rules constrain the ability of developing countries, particularly in Africa, to improve the quality of their growth and how these rules need to be reformed. They begin the chapter by tracing the evolution of global rules since the nineteenth century and observe that the new global regime that emerged post–World War II and postcolonialism put "only mild restrictions" on the ability of developing countries to pursue the sort of industrial and trade policies that Japan and the much-vaunted East Asian success stories pursued in achieving high-quality growth. Beginning in the mid-1990s, however, global rules started to become more constraining. The General Agreement of Tariffs and Trade (GATT) was succeeded by a more restrictive World Trade Organization (WTO), and Free Trade Agreements (FTAs) and Bilateral Investment Treaties (BITS) that tended to be even more restrictive proliferated. FTAs increased from some 50 in the mid-1990s to more than 250 and BITs from less than 500 at the beginning of the 1990s to more than 2,000 by the end of the decade.

The chapter documents the shrinking of the policy space for developing countries, inhibiting their ability to employ several "policy instruments, which had been widely used to achieve quality of growth in today's developed countries." They add that bilateral agreements "have become the major factor shrinking countries' policy space," generally encroaching more on that space than multilateral agreements, such as the WTO. The consequences have been most severe for least developed or low-income countries, which predominate in Africa and are exempted from many restrictions in the multilateral agreements. They add that "the political-institutional mechanisms established in global trade and investment rules . . . have enabled dominant economic groups . . . to erect barriers to entry and to appropriate their shares of the value generated in global production and exchange, whether or not they have actually produced it." They list as critical in this regard, four mechanisms pertaining to (1) intellectual property rights and copyrights, (2) international standards, (3) liberalization of trade and capital flows, and (4) investor–state dispute settlement.

In applying their framework to Africa, the authors begin by mapping the relationship between some of the Sustainable Development Goals (SDGs), particular SDGs 8 and 9 that bear most closely on the quality of growth, highlighting the constraints imposed by global rules as well as the creative mechanisms that can be used to circumvent them. SDG 8 is concerned with promoting "sustained, inclusive and sustainable economic growth, full and productive employment and decent work for all," while SDG 9 aims to "build resilient infrastructure, promote inclusive and sustainable industrialization and foster innovation" (United Nations 2015). They state that "in the belief that the best way to design policy is on the basis of experience," they sketch a list of ten policy measures drawn from "successful diversification and industrial upgrading experiences," which they match to SDGs 8 and 9. They then analyze how these policies are affected by current global rules. The upshot is that "it is difficult to generalize . . . because countries have widely varying commitments" under the proliferating trade and investment agreements, and the impact of such WTO-plus arrangements on restricting policy options "must not be underestimated." Nonetheless, the authors note that several policies remain at the disposal of policy makers.

In their priorities for reforms, the authors identify the following: (1) revising the global rule targets in the SDGs (they point to several inconsistencies in the stated objectives of the SDGs and the corresponding reforms to global rules that are identified); (2) giving urgency to reforming rules pertaining to intellectual property rights; (3) extending the time frame for infant-industry protection; (4) reforming investor–state dispute settlement; and (5) limiting bilateral and regional trade agreements. This last priority is all the more important because developing countries often sign these agreements under the pressures of a nexus of trade, aid, financial, and investment relationships with donor countries. Moreover, they often are hampered by the paucity of relevant experts to negotiate or modify complex agreements that encompass not only trade but also a host of other provisions.

The chapter concludes that there is much to be gained from expanding the policy space for the pursuit of high-quality growth but that "many countries neglect to use the policy space that is available to them, not only out of fear of economic retaliation [but] also . . . an ideological environment that instills . . . a distrust of industrial policy, even in the face of the cold, hard evidence provided by experience. In this sense, it might be said that the most fundamental reform that is needed is ideological." This is the ultimate triumph of the Washington Consensus: although it has now been widely discredited among academics and policy makers in developed countries, many of those working in or on developing countries cling to variants of the Washington Consensus ideology.

In chapter 5, Jomo Kwame Sundaram picks up on the theme of learning from successful historical experiences, especially of the East Asian countries that Andreoni, Chang, and Estevez emphasize. He also touches on the issue of how global rules affect the feasibility of African countries emulating today what East Asia did yesterday under the earlier framework of global rules. Jomo undertakes sweeping reviews of East Asian experiences and then asks whether these East Asian experiences are still relevant and feasible for Africa. His overview of East Asia touches on major controversies on the interpretation of the causal links between public policies and the outcomes that determine the quality of growth. He comes out firmly on the side of those who emphasize the importance of activist, unorthodox policy interventions in the East Asian outcomes, notably industrial policy, including in agriculture where the green revolutions are said to have been dependent on a host of government interventions, in contrast to Africa where the withdrawal of the state from agriculture ignored important lessons from the Green Revolution in Asia. Conversely, he is highly critical of the Washington Consensus reform programs in Africa under the aegis of the IMF and the World Bank in the 1980s and 1990s, with their focus on liberalization and privatization deemed to be inappropriate and too premature or rapid.

Jomo argues that supporters of the Washington Consensus continue to deny that the poor economic performance of Africa and elsewhere in the world, can be directly attributed to their policies as well as policy advice and conditionalities since the 1980s. He claims that there is still considerable relevance of the East Asian experience for Africa, notwithstanding the significant changes in context, including the spread of globalization, expansion of global value chains, and changes in global rules. Among the policies that he advocates are those that pay particular attention to encouraging domestic investment (partly because savings are not independent of investment as the East Asian experience shows, where powerful incentives to invest led businesses to save more). He echoes Andreoni, Chang, and Estevez in saying, "although the policy space has been reduced, room exists to use some policies, which can be combined with the remaining industrial policy instruments . . . many useful lessons can be drawn from the varied experiences of the East Asian economies."

Chapter 6, by Akio Hosono, is titled "Economic Transformation for High-Quality Growth: Insights from International Cooperation." Hosono begins with an overview of the growing concern with and current policy debates related to transformation and quality of growth in academic writings as well as in international and regional organizations and think-tanks, including notably the African Union, the UN Economic Commission for Africa, and the African Development Bank. He quotes a report of the African Center for Economic Transformation (ACET) that to "ensure that growth is sustainable and continues to improve the lives of many, countries need to vigorously promote economic transformation" (ACET 2014, 1). Hosono points to an emerging literature emphasizing that development is about transforming the productive structure of the economy and accumulating the requisite capabilities. He adds that learning capacity, infrastructure, and institutions, along with the standard factor endowments, are critical determinants of dynamic comparative advantage.

Hosono then identifies strategies for enhancing learning capacity, infrastructure, and institutions, in particular by providing examples of programs and projects, many supported by Japan International Cooperation Agency (JICA).

Hosono discusses the following successful cases in some detail.

1. Raising the quality of Science and Mathematics education (JICA supported projects in Africa based on the idea that in-service teacher training can improve the skills, motivation, and output of teachers)
2. Capacity to learn by "learning by doing" (several capacity-building programs such as "life improvement program" aimed at rural women's ability to improve the quality of their lives, given income; the One Village One Product programs involving learning by doing; and

    kaizen programs (which aim to raise productivity through organizational and quality control measures requiring little or no investment)

3. Programs to improve the quality of roads
4. Schemes to strengthen institutions aiming to build capacity of small and midsize enterprises
5. Strategies for sequential/catching-up transformation (the so-called flying geese pattern)
6. Approaches to facilitating regional networks and integration through development corridors, and for transformation through integration with global value chains and innovation-led transformation
7. Establishing sustainable and inclusive agroforestry in tropical rainforests
8. Strategy for business-led transformation using "inclusive business models" (e.g., along the lines introduced by the joint venture of Grameen Bank and Danone in Bangladesh, which produced affordable yogurt for low-income families fortified by micronutrients and delivered at home by women in their neighborhoods)

Hosono concludes by explaining that his discussion of these strategies and case studies indicates that the quality of growth is intertwined with transformation. He comments that the enhancement of endowments and transformation are essentially endogenous processes but need to be catalyzed by industrial strategies and policies.

Part III of the volume begins with Christopher Cramer and John Sender's deliciously titled chapter, "Oranges Are Not Only Fruit." Cramer and Sender begin by noting that, notwithstanding rapid growth in many African countries, there are doubts and concerns about the sustainability and quality of growth on account of limited economic transformation and the nexus of poverty and inequity. In their words, the chapter

> contributes to the discussion of quality of growth by showing the importance of disaggregating the category of industry or manufacturing. . . .
> The categorical distinctions among manufacturing, agriculture, and services have broken down as these activities have seeped across the boundaries of traditional classification systems. . . . At the heart of this process are both "servification" (of manufacturing and agriculture) and what we call the industrialization of freshness.

This is important for countries, such as the typical African ones, "because of the huge scope" for growth of productivity, exports, and employment in industrialized agriculture and "because it should lead to a reassessment of the scope of and priorities for industrial policy." Cramer and Sender mainly draw on examples from Ethiopia and South Africa based on primary research to show how "export-oriented agricultural production increasingly involves the insertion of an intricate nexus of inputs and steps between a crop and the final consumption good."

Cramer and Sender provide a succinct but rich overview of Ethiopia's economic performance in the past two decades or so. They point out that despite being just about the fastest-growing non-oil economy in the world (about the same growth rate as China since 2004) and showing an impressive reduction in head count poverty, Ethiopia faces concerns about the quality of growth. These concerns pertain to equity—including regional and ethnic—and the adverse impact on the poorest of high food price inflation. Although Ethiopia has not been deindustrializing, the speed of transformation as measured by the rise in the share of manufacturing in GDP and employment has been rather modest.

After a brief critique of the "deindustrialization" discourse, including of Dani Rodrik (2016), which emphasized the tendency for the share of manufacturing in total output and employment to peak at lower levels of income, and which even on its own terms Cramer and Sender find to be too pessimistic (there is considerable variance and scope for policy-induced differences), their chapter turns to a more profound critique. Thus, to "make claims about the pattern and prospects of industrialization or deindustrialization . . . involves a categorical fallacy that is growing increasingly problematic for economics" and that reflects the "industrialization of freshness" discussed earlier. They argue that agriculture, "particularly globally traded agricultural production is increasingly not merely 'like' industry, it is industry." This is not only true for processing agro-industry but also for the production and trade of fresh fruit, vegetables, and flowers. "This. . . . is partly a function of the technological inputs into modern global agriculture, which have extended out of the factory and onto the farm, and it is partly a function of industrial process and organization."

Cramer and Sender illustrate the point not only by discussing oranges but also by providing several examples in the production of such items as flowers, blueberries, avocados, and coffee. These examples are drawn from Ethiopia and South Africa. The authors observe that " 'just-in-time' industrial organization, famously developed in Japanese manufacturing, is now fundamental to the competitive success of international agriculture." Moreover in contrast to "industrialization concentrated in urban factories . . . agro-industrialization has enormous scope for employment creation." As one example of the "employment effects of the industrialization of freshness in Ethiopia is the dramatic growth of towns like Ziwau . . . with large inward migration from quite distant rural areas . . . attracted by employment opportunities in and linked to the town's floriculture concentration (and more recently wine production)." Cramer and Sender hypothesize that "the greater the intricacy of the nexus between producer and final consumption good . . . the greater the scope for employment creation and better jobs."

Cramer and Sender's conclusions include the following: first, given that the key to long-term economic development and catching up involves avoiding growth collapses as much as generating spells of fast growth and converting growth spurts into long-lasting growth and change, the fact that recent growth in Sub-Saharan Africa has often been dependent on a few primary commodities is a cause for concern. It is even more disturbing for development economists to confront the possibility that classic industrialization may not be the engine of growth, employment and structural change that it once was.

Second, the "concerns about the quality of recent growth, specifically in Ethiopia are real enough but . . . maybe overblown . . . the industrialization (and servification) of agriculture globally is nothing new. But the extent to which this trend is reaching into globalized production of commodities in which many developing countries have high levels of productive potential has not been sufficiently acknowledged." Thus, the scope for economic transformation that it provides is not adequately appreciated. Third, there are challenges for policy makers "still often trapped in an outdated imaginary of a linear transition away from primary commodity production in rural areas to urban industrial factories. Policy makers need to consider incentives in the light of the overall capacity of economic activities . . . to generate productive dynamism, technical learning and change, and employment." Fourth, although this requires the development of policy-making capabilities, "there is no reason to believe" that they cannot be acquired "through 'policy learning by doing,' even if this involves learning by failing."

Both as a contrast and a complement to Christopher Cramer and John Sender's chapter, the subsequent one by Haroon Bhorat, Ravi Kanbur, Christopher Rooney, and Francois Steenkamp focuses on the structural characteristics of Africa's manufacturing sector or more precisely its "economic complexity." Like Cramer and Sender, an important aspect of the authors' motivation is the concern with employment in the face of the dramatic demographic expansion that Africa is undergoing. Like Jomo, the authors of chapter 8 also join the debate "over the prospects of Africa following in the economic footsteps of East and South Asia . . . and the pursuit of manufacturing-led structural transformation, and thereby creating jobs for a young and growing labor force." They do so by going beyond the manufacturing sector at the aggregate level to provide "a more granular product-level analysis of SSA's evolving manufacturing sector with the Asian experience serving as a counterpoint, . . . aided by the tools of complexity analysis."

They sketch the demographic trends in SSA, elaborating on those we outlined earlier by noting that the region is to account for some 75 percent of the world's population increase and an even higher proportion of the labor force increase so that its share of the world's labor force is projected to rise from some 10 percent in 2015 to almost 40 percent in 2100. They point to considerable intercountry variance and note that the overall demographic trends represent both opportunities and risks. Like several other contributors, they note the revival of growth in the past couple of decades as well as the concern with lack of structural transformation, and they provide an overview of sectoral productivity and employment changes in Africa and Asia from 1975 to 2010. Although both regions saw a decline in the share of agriculture, Asia saw a shift to manufacturing, whereas Africa saw a shift to low-productivity services typically generated in the informal sector.

In part this occurred because "it is becoming increasingly difficult to industrialize." The authors present data showing that early industrializers saw peak manufacturing employment of 30 percent of total employment. The next wave of industrializing economies, mainly in East Asia, saw peaks well below that, whereas most Latin American and African countries began experiencing deindustrialization when the peak share of manufacturing employment was in the 13–17 percent range. Nonetheless, the authors argue, "manufacturing remains the best hope for SSA to generate a large number of good jobs and reduce the prospects of political and social instability" (Cramer and Sender would agree if manufacturing includes the "industrialization of freshness.")

Bhorat and colleagues refer to the literature that provides insight into the extent to which African countries can industrialize and generate manufacturing jobs.[6] They note, however, that these analyses focus on the manufacturing sector at an aggregate level, whereas their analysis provides product-level insights into the evolution of the sector with the aim of providing "nuance to the existing debate through a granular method of analysis." They do so by using "economic complexity analytics to provide product-level insights into Sub-Saharan Africa's development path in comparison with that of the Eastern and Southern Asian regions."

After a conceptual discussion of complexity and connectedness, the chapter provides a fairly detailed empirical analysis focused, in particular, on a comparative product-level analysis of the evolution of export structure for the two regions. We shall not attempt to summarize the chapter's rich empirical findings here but jump to the upshot. It concludes that the authors' analysis shows "a Sub-Saharan Africa productive structure that is disconnected and that is characterized by products with low levels of economic complexity, [Thus] limited productive capabilities. Furthermore . . . these productive capabilities are distant from those needed to produce increasingly complex manufactured products. . . . In contrast to the productive structure in the East and South Asian region that is connected and complex." And, they add, "This ability to shift has implications for the extent to which manufacturing sector can generate employment" and explain that the "nature of the African manufacturing sector points to limited employment opportunities. The relatively high employment relative to economic complexity elasticity for Africa offers hope . . . if Africa is to generate jobs through manufacturing-led industrialization, it needs to accumulate productive capabilities that will allow it to do so."

That complexity is good for employment may appear to be counterintuitive because a more complex manufacturing tends to be more capital intensive. A more complex manufacturing sector, however, has greater scope for development and potential for transformation and hence for employment. The dynamics dominate the static effect of any higher capital intensity of more complex manufacturing.

To build the productive capabilities that Bhorat and colleagues call for, Antonio Andreoni suggests one approach in chapter 9 titled "A Generalized Linkage Approach to Local Production Systems Development in the Era of Global Value Chains, with Special Reference to Africa." Andreoni opens with the observation that since "the mid-1990s, the African continent has experienced an increasing backward and forward integration into global value chins (GVCs), mainly led by the penetration . . . of transnational corporations (TNCs)." He explains, however, that "in the majority of the African economies, this new industrialization model (i.e., integration into

GVCs) has not led to increasing domestic value addition . . . [and has] failed to create any significant transformation of the local production systems (LPS)." Hence, his paper aims to refocus "the industrial policy debate in Africa from GVC integration to LPS development." According to Andreoni, the quality of growth in Africa depends critically on "the 'cumulative' processes of increasing value addition, collective learning, and linkage development in the LPSs. These processes must be coupled with strategic integration into regional value chains and GVCs."

Andreoni provides a fairly detailed critique of what he terms "the GVC-led industrialization model" as usually practiced in Africa and finds the quality of resulting growth wanting. In sum, this is because (1) "the produced value might be concentrated and retained by TNCs"; (2) the tendency for integration into sectoral value chains that are "not those with high-value opportunities or margins for manufacturing"; (3) production locked into "low-value segments"; (4) specialization "in limited or isolated tasks" with little learning; (5) vertical linkages "in silos without horizontal linkages"; and (6) in some political economy contexts, the possibility of "entrenching power even more upstream and . . . an incentive structure biased towards importers more than producers."

For an alternative, Andreoni turns to Albert Hirschman's concept of "linkage," particularly as elaborated in Hirschman (1977), where he defined the "linkage effect" as "investment generating forces that are set in motion through input–output relations" and delineated a taxonomy of linkages. Andreoni argues that this taxonomy "suggests the need to understand production transformation from a multilinkages generalized perspective. . . . that is, the LPS. More specifically, an LPS can be defined as the *structural configuration of multiple types of linkages in a given economy*."

Andreoni sketches stylized facts about LPS in Africa and proposes moving from "a GVC-led industrialization model to a generalized linkage approach to LPS development." He argues, "this approach stands on two fundamental ideas. First, the incremental and cumulative processes of increasing value additions and linkage development in the LPS, coupled with strategic integration into regional . . . and global . . . value chains can deliver quality of growth. Second, the LPS will never develop without shifting incentives from importers and rentiers to productive organizations, while also disciplining rents allocation and reducing rent chains and power concentration." An important way to shift incentives along these lines would be the pursuit of industrial policies (not just for manufacturing but also for modern agriculture and services).[7]

Reducing rents and power concentration feature prominently in chapter 10 by Simon Roberts, who "considers the shaping of markets and competition concerns through the example of food production in southern Africa." He argues that the "nature of competitive rivalry and the identity of market participants are central to the quality of growth. . . . A key challenge to economic development is to *generate* competition and competitors." Roberts's chapter, with its attention on food production and processing as a route to industrialization and employment, also complements the chapter by Christopher Cramer and John Sender.

Roberts points to the change in consumption patterns in SSA resulting from rapid urbanization, with fast-growing demand for processed and packaged foods and the associated expansion of supermarkets. He adds, "meeting growing demand for food in African cities is one of the most critical industrial development challenges." It is thus central to whether premature deindustrialization can be reversed.

The main thrust of his chapter, which draws on a range of recent research on regional value chains and markets in southern Africa, is how lack of competition and associated monopolistic practices are hindering the development of both agriculture and the processing of its products. He points to the fact that Africa is a substantial net importer of food. The low agricultural productivity, in important measure, reflects extremely scant use of fertilizer. A notable reason for this is the high prices for fertilizer because of a combination of oligopolistic markets and collusion among producers of that input.

Roberts provides a pithy overview of the different types of fertilizer and their production, marketing, and logistical characteristics. He observes, "although notionally markets appear to be contestable, the markups that are applied along the supply chain reflect the importance of control over these facilities . . . . The prices of fertilizer in SSA countries have been significantly above benchmark world prices." Perhaps the most startling is the case of urea for which the data for 2012–2014 show the retail prices in Malawi, Tanzania, and Zambia were usually well over double the FOB price in the Arabian Gulf. Depending on the country and time, the difference ranged from about 50 percent to more than 500 percent.

Roberts attributes the high prices of fertilizers to several international and local factors, including (1) export cartels (although not for urea); (2) national and regional collusive arrangements between the main suppliers; and (3) a combination of restrictions on transport, storage, and trading that have supported incumbents. He adds, "Although anticompetitive conduct is part of the picture, it is unclear how effective enforcement by national authorities can be against regional and international arrangements" and that "businesses have a strong incentive to lobby for rules and regulations which bolster their position and keep rivals out." Roberts also examines the noncompetitiveness of markets in sugar, confectionary, poultry, and animal feed and their assorted adverse implications for both domestic producers and consumers. He then looks at the phenomenon of the rapid growth in supermarkets, which, while yielding benefits, has also had some costs, such as constraints on access by local suppliers to shelf space and on small-scale domestic retailers. According to Roberts, the "issue is how supermarkets can be partners in regional industrial development for increased trade so that they may build capabilities. . . . This possibility holds the prospect of moving the southern Africa region as a whole from being a net processed food importer to a net exporter of food products."

Roberts's concluding remarks call for going beyond addressing discrete anticompetitive conduct through the conventional instruments of competition agencies to "frame the agenda in terms of the ways in which industrial policy and economic regulation can reshape markets to generate competition." Its requirements include a better understanding of "the regional scope of actual and potential linkages. . . . Big businesses are integrating their activities across the region, but they are not necessarily doing so to build productive capabilities for competitive production." It also requires that we "understand how the regional value chains are governed and the extent of market power and its exertion by large firms . . . to earn rents and exclude local rivals. . . . A competition policy agenda that links to industrial policy is essential to generate competitive markets and stimulate dynamic rivalry built on investments in improved capabilities."

Part IV of this volume is devoted to climate change and the quality of growth, which is also the title of Ben Orlove's contribution. Orlove begins with a review of the various assessments of the impact of climate change in Africa, noting at the outset "experts agree that Sub-Saharan Africa has already experienced significant climate change and is likely to experience additional impacts, many of them even more severe, during this century."

Thus, the latest and Fifth Assessment Report of the Intergovernmental Panel on Climate Change (IPCC) finds a significant warming trend in Africa and notes that this trend will continue with particularly sharp rises in average temperatures in the more arid region. Orlove points to the "very strong agreement" that temperatures will rise by more than 2°C over much of Africa toward the end of this century under medium emission scenarios and between 3°C and 6°C under high emission scenarios.

Orlove also sketches a number of other assessments of various dimensions of the impact of climate change in Africa, including by the World Bank, United Nations Development Programme, the Network of African Science Academies, and the Center for International Governance Innovation. There is widespread agreement on the adverse effects in various arenas, including agriculture, water, health, and overall economic performance, with implications for conflict and migration attendant upon the social stresses. The chapter also looks at the relative evaluations and rankings of countries on the counts of vulnerability and preparedness. One worldwide index by the Notre Dame Global Adaptation Initiative combines these two dimensions and includes forty-nine African countries. The top three in the world on this measure (least vulnerable/most prepared) are Norway, New Zealand, and Finland. In contrast, the top three in Africa, Mauritius, the Seychelles, and Botswana, are ranked fifty, ninety-one, and ninety-three, respectively, in the global order.

Orlove states that "a broad examination of effects of climate change on the quality of growth in Africa shows five areas of importance: reduced rates of growth, shocks, deterioration of natural capital, inadequate provision of basic needs, and cascading impacts."

Moving from adaptation to mitigation, Orlove focuses on the energy sector, adding that although "mitigation is largely the responsibility of developed and emerging economies," Africa should also take it seriously "both because the continent's emissions are growing and low-carbon energy sources represent major opportunities," particularly given the great potential of hydropower and solar power.

Go Shimada's chapter reinforces earlier conclusions of the magnitude of adverse effects of climate change on Africa, but his main focus is not so much on adaptation as mitigation. He presents data showing that natural disasters in SSA, mainly in the form of floods and droughts, gradually increased in the 1990s and did so at an accelerated pace in the 2000s. Concomitantly, the number of people displaced by such disasters has been rising. The data he presents also show that air quality in major African cities is much worse than what World Health Organization guidelines propose. Although data are lacking on water pollution, Shimada hypothesizes that it is also a significant and growing problem.

Shimada explores the possibilities of green industrial policy in African countries as an instrument to reduce emissions contributing to climate change. Because "it is likely that environmental issues will affect Africa more severely than other continents," Africa's imperative of structural transformation raises the question of how to make that transformation environmentally sustainable. The chapter looks at some of the studies showing that environmental regulations either did not adversely affect or even enhance the competitiveness of industries in some developed countries. In particular, he looks at the case of the Japanese automobile industry and how seeking to meet more stringent environmental standards spurred innovation and enhanced competitiveness. Although generalizability to Africa is limited, Shimada attempts a first cut at examining whether there is a reasonable probability that it also could enhance competitiveness in the region. He looks at the correlation between an "environmental governance indicator," measuring the performance of environmental policies and their implementation, on one hand, and total factor productivity (TFP), on the other. This correlation is positive for all of the countries covered in the data and "although the sample size for African countries is limited, positive correlation can indeed be observed. . . . It is possible to say that environmental policy does not necessarily make industry less competitive."

Shimada then undertakes a tentative analysis that suggests that stricter environmental policies do not necessarily discourage foreign direct investment in Africa. He ends with some suggestions of what the international community could do to assist Africa's pursuit of green industrial policy. His conclusions include (1) "[compatible] protection of the environment and economic development"; (2) "[implementation of] green industrial policies"; and (3) help from donor countries "to introduce existing environmental technologies."

In the past, Africa has made minimal contributions to greenhouse gas emissions and is primarily on the receiving end of the adverse effects of climate change; however, the notion that African countries not focus exclusively on adaptation but also contribute to mitigation has emerged as a concern in the region. For example, Ethiopia's ambitious Climate Resilient Green Economy (CRGE) strategy aims to achieve rapid economic growth without an increase in greenhouse gas emissions, in principle, although its practical targets envisage a modest increase. The case for such technological leapfrogging is based partly on the consideration that the enormous needs of the region require a rapid expansion of activities, particularly energy generation, which can have significant emissions, and partly on the availability of green alternatives, such as hydropower in Ethiopia and solar energy in many countries. Another argument that has been made is that leapfrogging could have wider payoffs in advancing technological development in Africa and may sometimes be cost effective, especially on some projections of the declining costs of clean technologies. The primary concern in dealing with climate change in Africa remains adaptation and, hence, for financing such adaptation, including foreign assistance as envisaged in the Paris Agreement.

To start part V, Takyiwaa Manuh and Edlam Abera Yemeru turn to the topic of urbanization and the quality of growth in Africa (including North Africa, although the focus is mainly on SSA). They observe that around half of Africa's population will be living in urban areas by 2035, and with an annual growth rate of 3.5 percent, the continent is experiencing the fastest increase of urban population in the world. At the outset, Manuh and Yemeru note the theoretical and historical association between urbanization and structural transformation, adding that their "chapter argues that the manner in which urbanization is planned and managed today will play a crucial role in the quality of growth in Africa . . . and in particular the achievement of structural transformation through industrialization."

They broadly endorse the importance attached by several other contributors to this volume to structural transformation for high-quality growth in Africa. They do so, however, from an urban development lens and hence with different nuances. Manuh and Yemeru also paint a picture of poverty, equity, and employment trends, with particular attention given to their urban dimension, which is broadly consistent with those of McKay and other contributors who have commented on these trends in this volume. More distinctively, Manuh and Yemeru introduce reference to a gender inequality index—derived from rates of maternal mortality and adolescent births as well as differentials in shares of parliamentary seats, educational attainment, and labor force participation: Africa's poor rating in this index adds another aspect to concern with quality of growth.

Manuh and Yemeru sketch the urban transition, taking place in Africa on a scale unprecedented in history . . . [with] almost 900 million new urban dwellers in the next 35 years. By 2050 Africa is projected to have an urban population of 1.48 billion (and some 1 billion rural dwellers). They distinguish four dimensions to this transition: demographic, economic, social, and environmental and disaggregate some of them to subregional and country levels. A selection of their finding and comments follows.

Broadly, an inverse relationship exists between the level of urbanization and the rate of urbanization, and in several countries, secondary cities are growing more rapidly than the biggest metropolis, which they see as promising for the development of agriculture-related industries. Like Roberts, they note the rapid growth in consumption and imports of processed food in urban areas and the potential that it provides for import-substituting industrialization. Realizing that potential is the more important because of the need for structural transformation and the generation of urban jobs, they emphasize the following: "Delinked from high productivity and job-intensive activities, such as manufacturing, African cities face high unemployment, underemployment, and the prevalence of informal employment." In fact, they continue, "66 percent of nonagricultural employment . . . is informal." Manuh and Yemeru concur with Christopher Cramer and John Sender in commenting, "agricultural modernization . . . is a top priority for the region." In apparent contrast to Cramer and Sender, they seem to focus on "agricultural processing and agriculture-based industries" rather than on Cramer and Sender's idea of "industrialization of freshness," a natural difference given their focus on urbanization.

On the social dimension, Manuh and Yemeru lament the "poverty, inequality, and informality" that characterizes urbanization in the region, noting that "more than half of . . . [the] urban population . . . lives in slums." They emphasize the need for urban land reforms that provide legality and greater security of tenure for the urban poor. Not entirely unrelated to that is the fact that urban population with access to piped water connection declined from 40 percent in 2000 to 33 percent in 2015; less than half have access to electricity and less than 60 percent of the paved roads are recorded to be in "good condition." The chapter also points to the adverse impacts of environmental pollution and lack of solid waste management, and safe water, on health. In addition, these cities are becoming more vulnerable to disasters, with "thirty-seven cities of Africa with populations exceeding one million . . . [exposed] to ensuing sea-level rise, coastal erosion, storms, and floods."

It is not all doom and gloom. On the contrary, Manuh and Yemeru see urbanization as having a "particularly important role to play in ensuring the quality of economic growth . . . although considerable challenges are associated with urbanization. . . . With the right planning and foresight, urbanization can deliver profound dividends." Also urbanization can facilitate a more rapid demographic transition with a decline in fertility rates. Manuh and Yemeru then turn to what they call "policy anchors" for urbanization for quality growth. In sum, "economic and urban or spatial planning need to be linked at the national, regional, and local levels through an approach that combines subsector targeting and industrial policies with spatial targeting and urban and regional policies." The chapter ends with a call: "It is imperative for African states to unleash the potential of their cities by fusing economic and urban policy in a holistic manner, thereby reaping synergies" that will deliver higher and better growth.

The main themes of Manuh and Yemeru are reflected in the examples of "hotly debated" issues of urbanization cited by Luc Christiaensen, Joachim De Weerdt, Bert Ingelaere, and Ravi Kanbur: (1) the association and two-way causal relation between urbanization and growth; (2) the question of whether African urbanization is "different"; (3) the associations and two-way causal relation among employment, poverty reduction, and urbanization; (4) the relationship between urbanization and formalization; and (5) the attainment of the benefits of agglomeration.

Although these issues are generally debated at the aggregate level, the authors' "central contention is that the composition of urbanization could be as important for employment generation and poverty reduction as is the overall aggregate rate" (the composition they refer to pertains to city sizes). Again Manuh and Yemeru are not entirely unmindful of this consideration, paying some attention to the "small" versus the "big" city distinction as they trace urbanization trends. Christaensen and colleagues' distinctive contribution is to report "on a line of research and policy analysis focused on Tanzania, which highlights the role of secondary towns in migration and poverty reduction." This shows that "migration to secondary towns contributes more in aggregate to poverty reduction than migration to big cities, even though the typical move from a rural area to a town reduces poverty less than the typical move from a rural area to a city." This is true because many more people move from rural to (smaller) towns than to (big) cities.

They solve the seeming puzzle of why that should be, particularly given that a move to the big city is so beneficial by introducing "distance" and "migration" costs "not only in the physical sense (transport) but also in the sense of information, uncertainty, and contacts." The authors conclude with the hope that "these insights from Tanzania will lead to further research on small towns and their role in migration and poverty reduction, and that this role will increasingly be factored into policy analysis and decision making."

The last chapter is by Gabriella Y. Carolini, and it also picks up on the theme of how urban development affects the poor. She points out that almost 60 percent of urban dwellers in SSA live in slums. Furthermore, this proportion "has steadily grown over the past three decades . . . [and] if no action is taken, the slum population in African cities is expected to continue on this growth trajectory." Carolini argues for greater attention to meeting the basic needs of this majority of the urban population. To this end, she focuses on reforms in the areas of municipal finance, infrastructure development, and urban planning, with particular attention to the case of Maputo (the capital of Mozambique).

Carolini notes that " property tax is one of the major untapped revenue sources" in Africa and argues that updating "property valuation and increasing the levels of collected [property tax] represent a significant opportunity—and political challenge—for cities like Maputo." She makes some detailed proposals for revenue-raising reforms in Maputo, arguing that they have wide relevance in African cities. Carolini adds that "infrastructure development that benefits the wide urban populace calls for good urban planning" and notes that "broad-based and local support and a wide distribution of project benefits must be part of the plan. This means, for example, that rather than considering displacement an unfortunate but necessary and unavoidable outcome of major urban infrastructure development, public policy makers can do more to enhance alternative planning, augment contingency budgets that include fair compensation for displaced households, and actively seek out and incorporate input from affected households in the *initial* phases of infrastructure planning." Carolini lauds some fairly recent initiatives in SSA to build capacity for urban planning and slum renewal programs, such as the network of planning programs across universities (the Association of African Planning Schools), which now includes fifty-five different urban planning programs. Such capacity-building efforts are welcome and need further support and strengthening to improve the quality of urbanization.

The chapters in this volume cover a wide range of issues bearing on the quality of growth in Africa. The growing concern with the relationship between economic growth and human well-being that motivates this collection of essays calls for greater and more systematic attention to sustainable growth whose benefits are widely shared. Because Africa has left its "lost quarter century" well behind and has been recording reasonable growth, with some countries emerging as among the fastest growers of GDP, the countries of the region are now well poised to do so. As noted at the outset, this is not only an issue for Africa or developing countries but also the most affluent countries need to pay more attention to the quality of growth. The widespread discontent in much of the world, rich and poor alike, is giving rise to populist movements not entirely unlike those that wreaked such havoc in the world during the 1930s era of depressions, war, and upheavals. These are indeed "interesting times," in the sense of the proverbial Chinese curse. Perhaps this collection of essays can inform public policies and help make some African countries among the global leaders in ensuring not just that GDP is increasing but also that there is "quality" growth—that is, shared and sustainable growth that improves the well-being of the vast majority of the population.

NOTES

1. See, for example, Richard Wilkinson and Kate Pickett, *The Inner Level: How More Equal Societies Reduce Stress, Restore Sanity and Improve Everyone's Well-being* (London: Allen Lane, 2018).

2. This notion is elaborated in chapter 7 in this volume by Christopher Cramer and John Sender, "Oranges Are Not Only Fruit: The Industrialization of Freshness and the Quality of Growth" and is summarized later in this overview.

3. In Angola, Chad, Ethiopia, Mozambique, Nigeria, and Rwanda, average annual growth exceeded 7.5 percent over the decade; with the notable exceptions of Ethiopia and Rwanda, the growth was based on booming commodity prices and new discoveries of hydrocarbons.

4. Note, however, that expenditures on education and health do not translate quickly into increases in income, and most measures of inequality focus on inequalities in private incomes and consumption and do not include public expenditures.

5. For a broader critique, see Joseph E. Stiglitz, Amartya Sen, and Jean-Paul Fitoussi, *Mismeasuring Our Lives: Why GDP Doesn't Add Up* (New York: New Press, 2010); and Joseph E. Stiglitz, Jean-Paul Fitoussi, and Martine Durand, eds., *For Good Measure: Advancing Research on Well-being Metrics Beyond GDP* (Paris: OECD Publishing, 2018).

6. In particular, see Margaret McMillan, Dani Rodrik, and Íñigo Verduzco-Gallo, "Globalization, Structural Change and Productivity Growth, with an Update on Africa," *World Development* 63 (2014): 11–32; see also Dani Rodrik, "Premature Deindustrialization," *Journal of Economic Growth* 21, no. 1 (2016): 1–33.

7. See, for example, Akbar Noman and Joseph E. Stiglitz, eds., *Industrial Policy and Economic Transformation in Africa* (New York: Columbia University Press, 2015).

REFERENCES

African Centre for Economic Transformation (ACET). 2014. *Africa Transformation Report: Growth with Depth.* Washington, DC: ACET.

Arndt, Channing, Andy McKay, and Finn Tarp, eds. 2016. *Growth and Poverty in Sub-Saharan Africa.* UNI-WIDER Studies in Development Economics. Oxford: Oxford University Press.

High-Level Expert Group on the Measurement of Economic Performance and Social Progress. 2015. Proceedings from the Measurement of Wellbeing and Development in Africa, a conference organized by the government of South Africa, Columbia University, and Cornell University, Durban, South Africa, November 12–14, 2015. Accessed March 17, 2019, https://www.oecd.org/statistics/measuring -economic-social-progress/HLEG%20workshop%20on%20measurement%20 of%20well%20being%20and%20development%20in%20Africa%20agenda.pdf.

Hirschman, Albert O. 1977. "A Generalized Linkage Approach to Development, with Special Reference to Staples." *Economic Development and Cultural Change* 25 (Suppl.): 67–98.

Lakner, Christoph, and Branko Milanovic. 2016. "Global Income Distribution: From the Fall of the Berlin Wall to the Great Recession." *The World Bank Economic Review*, 30 (2): 203–232.

McMillan, Margaret, Dani Rodrik, and Íñigo Verduzco-Gallo. 2014. "Globalization, Structural Change and Productivity Growth, with an Update on Africa." *World Development* 63: 11–32.

Milanovic, Branko. 2016. *Global Inequality: A New Approach for the Age of Globalization*, Cambridge, MA: Belknap Press of Harvard University Press.

Mlachila, Montfort, Rene Tapsoba, and Sampawende J. Tapsoba. 2016. "A Quality of Growth Index for Developing Countries: A Proposal." *Social Indicators Research* 134 (2): 675–710.

Noman, Akbar, and Joseph E. Stiglitz. 2012. "African Development Prospects and Possibilities." In *The Oxford Companion to the Economics of Africa*, ed. E. Aryeetey, S. Devarajan, R. Kanbur and L. Kasekende. New York: Oxford University Press.

——. 2012. "Strategies for African Development." In *Good Growth and Governance in Africa: Rethinking Development Strategies*, ed. A. Noman, K. Botchwey, H. Stein, and J. E. Stiglitz. Oxford: Oxford University Press.

——, eds. 2015. *Industrial Policy and Economic Transformation in Africa.* New York: Columbia University Press.

Rodrik, Dani. 2016. "Premature Deindustrialization." *Journal of Economic Growth* 21 (1): 1–33.

Stiglitz, Joseph E. 2018. *Globalization And Its Discontents Revisited.* New York: Norton.

Stiglitz, Joseph E., Amartya Sen, and Jean-Paul Fitoussi. 2010. *Mismeasuring Our Lives: Why GDP Doesn't Add Up.* New York: New Press.

Stiglitz, Joseph E., Jean-Paul Fitoussi, and Martine Durand, eds. 2018. *For Good Measure: Advancing Research on Well-being Metrics Beyond GDP.* Paris: OECD Publishing, https://doi.org/10.1787/9789264307278-en.

United Nations. 2015. *Transforming Our World: The 2030 Agenda for Sustainable Development.* Accessed March 17, 2019, https://sustainabledevelopment.un.org/content /documents/21252030%20Agenda%20for%20Sustainable%20Development% 20web.pdf.

Wilkinson, Richard, and Kate Pickett. 2018. *The Inner Level: How More Equal Societies Reduce Stress, Restore Sanity, and Improve Everyone's Well-being.* London: Allen Lane.

PART I

Gross Domestic Product, Equity, and Employment

CHAPTER 1

Beyond Gross Domestic Product

MEASURING THE QUALITY OF GROWTH IN AFRICA

Lorenzo Fioramonti

If African countries are to achieve sustainable and equitable growth, they will need a different set of metrics of economic performance from those available at present. In particular, the chief measure of economic performance, the gross domestic product (GDP), is inadequate to assess the quality of growth, especially in the so-called developing countries.

GDP, indeed, is not a measure of *all* economic activities. It not only focuses exclusively on "flows," thus disregarding the state of the "stocks," but also imposes specific boundaries as to which types of flows count for economic performance. It measures mostly (and, at times, only) what is transacted in the formal economy, which means that other economic activities occurring in "informal" sectors as well as a variety of services made available free of charge, from household and community-based production to the services provided by natural ecosystems, are either poorly represented or completely discounted as part of the economy. This generates evident paradoxes. Take the case of a country in which natural resources are considered common property and are made available for public access, people exchange goods and services through informal structures (e.g., barter markets, secondhand markets, community-based exchange initiatives, time banks), and most people produce what they consume (e.g., through small-scale or family farming, off-the-grid systems of energy distribution). Although this country's economy may be vibrant and people may enjoy a high level of individual and social well-being, GDP would probably be quite low and therefore the country's economy would be considered underdeveloped or in distress. By contrast, a country that depletes its resources, cuts down its forests, replaces green spaces with concrete, and exploits the people to the point of social collapse may very well be regarded as having a strong and healthy economy.

The United Nations Development Programme (UNDP) has identified at least five types of "undesirable" GDP growth: (1) *jobless growth*, which occurs when the economy grows with increased buying and selling of goods and services but without creating more jobs, let alone good and dignified jobs; (2) *voiceless growth*, when an apparently successful economy rides on the back of the suppression of civil rights and democracy, as has occurred in many dictatorships (notoriously good achievers in terms of GDP growth); (3) *ruthless growth*, which is characterized by high or rising inequality, conspicuous consumption, and increasing tensions and stress in society; (4) *rootless growth*, which underscores the socially and culturally destructive effects, for instance, of rampant industrialization and economic globalization; and (5) *futureless growth*, indicating the unsustainable consumption of natural capital and the negative effects of pollution on a finite planet (UNDP 1996).

All these issues matter a great deal for Africa's present and future development. Indeed, many economies in this continent are largely informal, communal property mechanisms are more prevalent than market-based private property, and even the limited industrial production achieved thus far has already had significant negative impacts on social dynamics, ecosystems, and natural resources. As indicated in the report of the Commission on the Measurement of Economic Performance and Social Progress, "what we measure affects what we do; and if our measurements are flawed, decisions may be distorted" (Stiglitz, Sen, and Fitoussi 2009, 8). The information provided by GDP statistics can be misleading for development policy in Africa, because it may provide a superficial sense of "rising income," neglecting the hidden costs of industrial policies, exploitation of natural resources, and inequality thereof. In turn, this may give politicians, businesses, and consumers the wrong incentives. The fact that African countries are developing at a time of increasing scarcity, evolving climate change, and rising social tensions makes it even more compelling to take this issue seriously. In particular, the Sustainable Development Goals (SDGs) provide a road map for future development, which must be different from the divisive, exploitative, and belligerent process followed by many so-called developing nations in the past.

This chapter argues that a new approach to the measurement of prosperity is indispensable to devise policies that improve the quality of growth in Africa. It begins with an overview of the flaws of GDP as a measurement of economic performance and explains how they relate to the African context. Then it proposes possible ways forward to develop a different set of measurements to help policy makers and societies at large achieve sustainable and equitable development.

THE NEED TO MOVE BEYOND GDP

GDP is a sum of market flows, which means that whatever is exchanged outside the market (e.g., within households, in the informal economies) is either miscounted or completely ignored as part of the economy, let alone for its growth. One may even say that GDP is "gross" not only because it does not include the depreciation of assets utilized in the production process (such as machineries, tools, vehicles) but also because it is blind to a wide range of "costs" generated by the process of industrialization, which is what economist Simon Kuznets, the father of the national accounts, termed the "reverse side of income," that is, the wearing out of people through industrial production and consumption (Fioramonti 2013, 55). GDP also disregards the value of stocks consumed by the economy, especially natural resources, which are obtained free of charge from nature. Moreover, it does not consider the consequences of pollution and environmental degradation, which are obvious negative effects of industrial development. At the global level, research has shown that the economic values of ecosystem services and natural capital, which are preconditions for any form of human production and consumption, exceed the value of global GDP by at least three times (Costanza et al. 1997). Their loss not only would be disastrous for development but also impossible to replace, even if the global economy was to grow much faster than it has ever done in history. Yet, this is what most countries do every day with a view toward increasing their GDP. Studies conducted in China and India, among other countries, show that the cost of pollution is actually eroding these countries' real income and wealth (Mallet 2013). A leading report on the social and economic impacts of poor health known as the Global Burden of Disease demonstrates that pollution-related conditions are causing a human catastrophe in China and that their costs are likely to curtail economic prosperity, too (Lozano et al. 2010). A project led by the Chinese government in 2006 and followed up in 2013 aimed to deduct environmental costs from GDP, and found that ecological degradation is costing at least 8 percent of GDP every year and is on the rise (Fioramonti 2013). GDP not only omits important contributors to prosperity but also counts as positive drivers of growth a number of expenditures that are quite "uneconomic," that is, they add no utility to consumers and society at large. Take military expenses, for instance, which add to GDP although they are at best a "necessary" evil, as Kuznets himself recognized (Fioramonti 2013).

GDP is a not just *a* metric among many others, but it is a profoundly institutionalized indicator: it is used to decide which policies to adopt, what reforms to introduce, and what economic sectors to reward. Its uncritical adoption may thus introduce perverse incentives that can easily trigger poor policy decisions at the local, national, and international level (Fioramonti 2017). For instance, Africa's natural resources account for the most significant share of GDP growth in the continent, with peaks of more than 40 percent in the more resource-rich countries (Lundgren, Thomas, and York 2013). Without an understanding of stock depletion and the negative effects on the environment (which are a real cost to society), the blind exploitation of such resources may win African countries the appreciation of multinational corporations and foreign investors, but almost invariably this comes with the consequence of undermining the structural transformation of the economy while leading to environmental degradation and social tensions (Africa Progress Panel 2013).

Given that this economic "performance" is based on the exploitation of nonrenewable natural capital, most of the "growth" we have seen in the past few years may very well be the result of a short-term and self-defeating statistical mirage. What would the picture look like if such losses were discounted from the continent's wealth? The World Bank has introduced an indicator of genuine savings, which complements GDP by taking into account the negative effects of natural capital depletion, while also measuring the positive contribution of human capital (mostly through education). Its overall picture is that African countries have been losing their overall wealth to the tune of about 1.2 percent a year over the past decade or so. Rather than growing, most African economies have been shrinking. In 2013, for instance, Sierra Leone experienced net losses of about 20 percent, Angola of 40 percent, Chad of 50 percent, and the Democratic Republic of Congo of more than 57 percent (World Bank 2013). It is important to emphasize that the World Bank's net savings calculation is a rather conservative measurement of sustainable development. It is a measure of weak sustainability that allows for compensating a loss in natural wealth with any form of investment in produced or built capital. This means that the overall loss of natural capital in Africa would be far greater if one adopted strong sustainability approaches, which by contrast do not see different types of capital as substitutable.

Another crucial issue pertains to the distribution of income generated by economic growth. GDP is indeed blind to the extent to which income is shared across society, yet this is essential to gauge the health of an economy, as Kuznets, Stiglitz, and others have pointed out over many decades (Stiglitz 2015). An increase of wealth at the top could easily offset a loss of income at the bottom, while still showing positive growth on average. Moreover, in the absence of corrective and redistributive policies, growth can generate significant inequalities, especially in developing countries. This is due to the fact that common resources and assets must be brought under the institutional control of either the state or the market to become part of the economy proper, and a fee or price must be charged for their use to be counted as part of GDP, which inevitably leads to the exclusion of communities that previously accessed those resources and assets for free. In many cases, elites are better positioned to capture the value of the monetization of what were once open-access resources, thus increasing the likelihood of inequality. This is why Kuznets discouraged the use of GDP in non-industrial nations (Lundberg 1971).

African economies are already among the most unequal in the world. In the absence of metrics to capture distributional effects, there is little hope that policy makers will be in a position to tackle and diminish inequality.

African people do not seem to be impressed by official GDP statistics. For instance, the Afrobarometer, Africa's largest public opinion survey, shows widespread dissatisfaction with the continent economic trajectory of the past decade, despite its comparatively faster growth than in other continents (Dulani, Mattes, and Logan 2013). Across the thirty-four countries surveyed by the research, a majority of respondents (53 percent) rate the current condition of their national economy as "fairly bad" or "very bad," whereas just 29 percent offer a positive assessment. Only one in three Africans thinks economic conditions have improved and most respondents (more than 70 percent) believe governments have done a "fairly bad" to "very bad" job at improving living standards and narrowing income gaps. According to the survey team, "lived poverty" remains pervasive across the continent, suggesting that if real growth is occurring, then "its effects are not trickling down to the poorest citizens" and "income inequality may be worsening." Alternatively, actual growth rates may simply "not match up to those being reported" (Dulani, Mattes, and Logan 2013, 1).

GDP estimations of household services and the informal economy are done poorly, with limited resources, and often these contributions are not included at all (Jerven 2013). This is problematic, especially in the African context where there is a clear need to measure the overall quality of informal production as well as how it affects the poorest. This not only skews our understanding of the volume of goods and services really produced but also limits our ability to recognize the special role that informal economies perform: without the innumerable free-of-charge functions rendered at the household level (from child and elder care to education), and without the exchanges performed informally, which are often the only sources of income and jobs for many people, the formal market economy would arguably grind to halt. This is not only the case in Africa, where household and community-based production are proportionally larger and economies are less formalized than in other continents, but also in the so-called developed world. For instance, in the United States, official estimates indicate that household services may have provided the equivalent of one-third of the national economic output since the mid-1960s (Bridgman et al. 2012). In postcommunist societies, informal work accounts for about a third of all economically valuable activities, whereas in the world's richest countries, about 15 percent of all transactions belong to the "shadow" economy, with countries such as Greece and Italy showing the largest informal working sectors, at 30 percent and 27 percent, respectively. In a high-income country like Denmark, which routinely tops a variety of global prosperity ranks, the informal economy's share of total labor doubled during the 1980s and 1990s, from about 8 percent to more than 15 percent. Similar trends have been registered in other high-income countries like Germany and France (Schneider and Enste 2002).

Because GDP does a poor job capturing informal economies, the economic contribution of subsistence farming, noncommercial agriculture, and other localized forms of production and consumption are measured incorrectly or are completely neglected in Africa (Jerven 2013). Similarly, disregarding the input of natural resources just because they are provided for free by nature makes us forget that economic growth is only possible because of a continuous provision of capital from our ecosystems. When these resources are depleted, however, we risk endangering not only economic progress but also the natural equilibrium that makes life possible.

GDP establishes the boundaries of the assets and productions that count as economically relevant. Through GDP, our model of growth becomes a sum of market consumption, regardless of whether what is consumed is good for society, for the environment, and, as a consequence, for the economy itself. GDP is not just an indicator. As a performance assessment coupled with rewards and sanctions, whether through preferential loans by institutions like the International Monetary Fund and the World Bank, foreign direct investment or rating upgrades or downgrades, it influences policy makers, businesses, and society at large, determining what is considered to hold value for the economy and what activities create prosperity, thus generating incentives to take certain decisions and adopt certain behaviors (Fioramonti 2017). If we are to improve the quality of growth in Africa by making it more sustainable and inclusive, then we need different metrics of economic development. Otherwise, we will not be able to effectively gauge what activities to encourage through policy and what to discourage. Just like a good manager would alter the performance assessment tools of its company to ensure that employees work differently, policy makers require different indicators to assess and incentivize different modes of production and consumption in the economy at large.

NEW METRICS FOR A NEW ECONOMY

The quality of existing statistics in Africa has been subjected to scrutiny (Jerven 2013). The measurement of GDP, in particular, presents numerous challenges because it is a cumbersome and time-consuming process. Data are often patchy and incomplete, and the informality of many productive systems makes this measurement even less relevant, thus undermining any easy generalizations about the overall economic performance of the continent. If the continent is to invest in equipping itself with a statistical apparatus that is fit for purpose in the twenty-first century, it should invest in developing new metrics and data collection techniques rather than continue to pursue an obsolete accounting framework.

For most of the 1970s and 1980s, various economists attempted to define ways of correcting or replacing GDP, for instance by subtracting work-related spending (e.g., commuting expenses) and the costs associated with environmental degradation or by adding the value of non-market outputs, many of which are produced within the household (Nordhaus and Tobin 1971; Eisner 1989). Moreover, since the 1990s, an increasing number of ecological economists have been trying to measure the economic value of natural and ecosystem services with a view toward informing policy makers about the critical importance of these assets (Costanza et al. 1997), while the United Nations has introduced indicators such as the Human Development Index (HDI), which complements income with measures of education and health. The best-known attempt at integrating macroeconomic, social, and environmental data into a comprehensive measure of economic welfare is the genuine progress indicator (GPI). The GPI considers the current flow of services to humanity from *all* sources as relevant to economic welfare, not just the output of marketable goods and services (Daly and Cobb 1994). This indicator takes into account such dimensions as leisure, public services, unpaid work (e.g., housework, parenting and care giving), the economic impact of pollution, insecurity (e.g., car accidents, unemployment, and underemployment), family breakdown, and economic losses associated with resource depletion and environmental damage. Recent research shows that although global GDP and GPI followed a similar trajectory between the early 1950s and the late 1970s, since 1978, the world has increased its GDP at the expense of social, economic, and ecological well-being (Kubiszewski et al. 2013).

In the past decade, the World Bank has introduced new measures of "total wealth," drawing inspiration from the ideas of the classical economists, who viewed land, labor, and produced capital as the primary factors of production, which the United Nations followed with its Inclusive Wealth Index. In 2009, a commission led by Nobel Prize winners Joseph Stiglitz and Amartya Sen and French economist Jean-Paul Fitoussi brought new life to efforts to identify alternative measures that policy makers could use to replace or at least complement GDP. In its final report, the commission recommended creating a "dashboard," rather than one single indicator, to include measures of unpaid work, health, education, governance, social connections, and sustainability (Stiglitz, Sen, and Fitoussi 2009). Taking its cue from their work, the Skoll World Forum launched the Social Progress Index in 2013, which—along with the Better Life Index developed by the Organisation for Economic Co-operation and Development—is one of the most advanced dashboard experiments to date.

In 2014 and 2015, my research team convened a number of meetings with African statisticians to discuss a possible way forward for a beyond-GDP process in the continent. We reached general consensus that GDP has been improperly used as a measure of economic progress, as it is designed only to measure levels of formal production and consumption. Statisticians agreed that African economies should complement GDP with measures of sustainability, informal economic systems, income inequality, and fiscal flows, including how much wealth produced in Africa eventually leaves the continent. Ultimately, governments should devise their policies and strategies based on a dashboard of indicators, possibly standardized at the regional level among African countries willing to experiment with a new form of accounting. A regional collective approach would strengthen the impact of the initiative, lower the transaction costs of change compared to countries moving beyond GDP on their own, and increase relevance for global economic governance (as it would be felt as a united effort by pioneering African countries). Many statistical offices across Africa already collect valuable information on human development (e.g., investment in knowledge generation and education, infant mortality, enrollment rates, doctors-to-population ratio), quality of the environment (e.g., air quality, material flows, land use, ecosystems, pollution, and waste), decent work (e.g., labor force surveys, standardized across African countries, in partnership also with the International Labour Organization), and social inclusion and social capital (e.g., time use and household production). Yet, this information is not connected to central accounts and is often left to the margins, with limited resources available. With more support, statisticians could (1) provide better data on land cover change and water stress, (2) conduct systematic and timely household surveys, (3) map social connections and participation in community-based productive activities, and (4) use measures of skills development to assess the extent to which education is aligned with sustainable development policies.

Taking stock of these various experiences, what lessons can be applied to rethinking GDP in the African context? I suggest that a post-GDP dashboard should focus on three pillars: the real economy, social well-being, and natural welfare. In the following sections, I discuss each pillar in detail.

THE "REAL" ECONOMY

Although GDP sees economic value only in those activities we perform in exchange for money within the market economy, the real economy is much broader. Many activities that make economic growth possible and support progress are performed free of charge, as part of human beings' natural predisposition to provide for one another. People of all demographics carry out vital unpaid work for relatives and for the wider community. Volunteering, caring for the elderly or disabled, supporting community based-groups, assisting migrants, training sport teams, and the like all deeply contribute to economic progress. In a nutshell, the real economy considers much more than mere monetary income.

In many ways, households are the cornerstone of the real economy, yet they have been neglected by mainstream economic thinking, despite the fact that they are the primary locations where individuals provide care for one another (Folbre 2001, 2008). Even though it is not directly monetized, this unpaid work represents implicit income (Becker 1965). Across the world, 24 percent of total time is spent on unpaid work and leisure, 46 percent is spent on personal care (including sleeping and eating), and only 19 percent of a person's time is spent on paid work and formal studies (Ahmad and Koh 2011).

As African countries strive to modernize, however, a substantial part of household-based production and services (e.g., food, clothing, and caring activities) is transferred to the market and formally purchased by families. In turn, external household consumption pushes up volumes of transported goods and centralizes systems of production, which contribute to overproduction and waste, ultimately taking a toll on the environment.

GDP treats such a shift from the household to mass production as progress, which gives a false impression of improving living standards. Economies of scale may make goods and services cheaper, but they do so only because our pricing mechanisms do not take into account the full cost of negative externalities, including waste disposal, transportation, and pollution. This is also true at the microlevel of family life, in Africa and beyond. Parents with enough free time to take care of their children and perform other household-based functions often enjoy a higher disposable income than families with slightly higher gross income but in which both parents work full time and must purchase all of these services from the market (Frazis and Stewart 2011). Ignoring household economies may bias not only measures of inequality and poverty but also measures of sustainability (Abraham and Mackie 2005). If household production and services were to be included in official estimates, for instance, the U.S. economy would be surpassed by a number of European countries (Miranda 2011). In China, for example, GDP per capita relative to the United States improves by 50 percent when all household production of nonmarket services is included (Ahmad and Koh 2011). It would be interesting to see what effects that may have on perceptions of development and progress across Africa, too.

These community practices are not marginal or irrelevant: rather, they are the precondition for the sustainable functioning of whatever society, because they build interpersonal trust and social capital. For instance, children are the future workers and taxpayers of a country. The level of care that goes into raising them is a public good benefiting society as a whole: investing time in them at the family and community level offers a significant payback to all participants in the economy. This is particularly important in a continent like Africa, which has the world's largest young population and it expected to add about 1.3 billion people by 2050 (United Nations 2015). According to a study conducted by the World Bank in a number of developed and developing countries, social capital is not only an essential pillar of the economy (Hamilton, Helliwell, and Woolcock 2016) but also has a direct and irreplaceable monetary value. It accounts for more than 20 percent of the value of all goods and services produced (with peaks of 28 percent in the members states of the Organisation for Economic Co-operation and Development), making it the most valuable industry any country can boast.

Despite the collective benefit that society derives from thriving communities and households, national income accounts have treated it as irrelevant in the assessment of economic performance. This has provided a statistical incentive for policies that neglect households, voluntary activities, and civil society. Moreover, GDP-enhancing policies often limit the amount of time individuals spend in social activities or within the household, as these are considered to be a loss for the economy. For GDP, the perfect society is that in which parents spend all of their waking time at work and pay their entire take-home salary to a domestic servant or nanny to produce the services they no longer are able or willing to provide. As full-time workers and simultaneously as employers, they would contribute twice to GDP growth.

In many African countries, where a process of chaotic urbanization and marketization of the economy actively undermines free-of-charge social activities, households and communities are under threat. Migrant work has weakened family structures and many social services are either under-resourced or privatized, which makes households particularly vulnerable.

Against this backdrop, it is crucial that such information about household services, community-based activities, and informal economic processes is integrated into the dashboard with a view toward producing a more comprehensive picture of the real economy.

SOCIAL WELL-BEING

There are hundreds of new indicators and approaches to measure well-being and the quality of life (OECD 2014). In North America, attempts at monitoring the social costs of GDP growth and its impact on well-being have been made by the Fordham Index of Social Health, by the Index of Economic Well-Being, and the Canadian Index of Well-Being. The OECD has launched the Better Life Index, which looks at education, health, life satisfaction, housing, environment, safety, and several other key dimensions integrated into one dashboard. In South Africa, the Institute for Race Relations produced a specific development index in 2011, with a view toward assessing progress in six domains, namely, the economy, education, health, living conditions, gender, and crime. The Institute found that while literacy and education attainments improved and crime diminished, all other sectors experienced a downward trend compared with the late 1990s. The Living Conditions Survey by Statistics South Africa (2014) already includes important information such as the availability, affordability, and quality of services used by households. In many other African countries, similar information already exists, although not always complete and often marred by significant time lags. This information should be complemented through data from the general household surveys on access to food, quality of housing, household sources of energy, health-care provision and quality of care, social cohesion, school attendance, and educational attainment. The Social Progress Index reports enough information on social well-being around the world, including many African countries. Ongoing opinion polls like the World Values Survey and the Afrobarometer can help a great deal.

People's well-being is directly affected by how they use their time, particularly in so far as how they organize their lives and how they set personal, social, and professional priorities (Dasgupta 2001; Dasgupta and Serageldin 2001). A society in which people have little time to devote to the real economy and to build social connections can hardly be a society founded on well-being. This brings us to the central issue of the quality of work.

Employment is an important component of human and social progress and certainly is a crucial aspect of Africa's present and future development, particularly given the demographic explosion we will see in the coming years throughout Africa. Yet, per se, it does not tell us anything about the type and quality of work that a country seeks for its own citizens. If we want African economies to successfully transition to a sustainable growth path, we need to rethink work and how we measure it. According to the ILO's website, decent work is that which provides "opportunities for women and men to obtain decent and productive work in conditions of freedom, equity, security and human dignity" (see also ILO 1999). A precondition of decent work is good earnings and a balance between worked hours and leisure. For the ILO, excessive hours and atypical hours can be detrimental to physical and mental health. To this, one must add the stability and security of work: changing jobs disrupts the process of human capital accumulation. The balance between work and family life is also crucial for sustainable growth, as it connects the formal economy (e.g., work) with community-based activities (e.g., household, family, community). It is therefore important to measure the extent to which formal jobs allow people to manage the work–life balance appropriately, as caring for the family and the community is a fundamental public good for society and should not be seen as a privilege or a loss of productivity.

Many African economies are divided into a first economy of formal working relations (and modern establishments), and a second dark economy consisting of a range of precarious and vulnerable forms of work. Yet, this distinction is often metaphorical: the dark economy is an integral part of the national economy and it would be incorrect to see it merely as a set of survival activities performed by the poor and marginalized (Webster et al. 2008). In their Decent Work Deficit Index for South Africa, for instance, Webster and his team show how some traditionally productive sectors, such as mining and commercial farming, are largely sustained by a web of formal and informal jobs characterized by very low labor rights and work insecurity (Webster et al. 2008). To assess the quality of jobs, not just the amount, African countries need to complement their data on employment and earnings with information about the quality of work and how it affects the management of time for the working population. The ILO has produced a set of indicators to measure decent work, which have been adopted in a number of African countries. Moreover, lessons could be learned from the country of Bhutan, where regular surveys monitor trends in time use, community vitality, and social capital.

Finally, metrics of well-being must include indicators of inequality in the distribution of income and, ideally, of wealth. In most cases, the Gini coefficient can be used as an interim measure of inequality, but it would be preferable to develop more accurate measures based on tax data (Piketty 2014).

NATURAL WELFARE

Since the Rio+20 summit of 2012, accounting for natural resources has become an imperative in economic governance. Natural capital adds to economic progress and well-being in multiple ways, which are systematically neglected by official GDP statistics (Fioramonti 2014). Because human welfare is a function of much more than the consumption of formal goods and services, the fundamental role played by nature cannot be disregarded, especially in Africa, a continent whose natural wealth has been traditionally exploited by colonizers first, and multinational corporations later. When we plot time-series data of genuine savings based on World Bank data, it emerges clearly that Africa is the continent with the most worrying downward trend in terms of sustainable use of natural resources, with the costs of natural capital depletion far outweighing the benefits of growth and human capital investment since at least the early 2000s (when the genuine savings rate was below zero as a percentage of national income).

A research and policy initiative on "the economics of ecosystems and biodiversity" (commonly known as TEEB) argues that "Nature is the source of much value to us every day, and yet it mostly bypasses markets, escapes pricing and defies valuation. This lack of valuation is [. . .] an underlying cause for the observed degradation of ecosystems and the loss of biodiversity" (European Union 2008, 4).

The World Bank has launched the Wealth Accounting and Valuation of Ecosystem Services (WAVES), a global partnership to measure the economic value of natural resources, which is already being rolled out in a number of African countries, from Botswana to Rwanda and Madagascar. The World Bank asserts that "in poorer countries, natural capital is more important than produced capital," thus suggesting that the careful management of natural resources should become a fundamental component of development strategies, "particularly since the poorest households in those countries are usually the most dependent on these resources" (World Bank 2006, xvi). In 2012, the UN Statistical Commission adopted the first international standard for the valuation of natural capital, the System of Environmental-Economic Accounting, and the UN University published the Inclusive Wealth Report, which provided further information on the state of natural capital in regard to human and produced capital in more than 20 countries (UN Statistical Commission et al. 2012).

These indicators look at nature as "capital," which poses the inevitable problem of finding acceptable methodologies to monetize the contribution of natural resources to economic performance (Fioramonti 2014). Other indicators look at nature as having an intrinsic value and simply measure its capacity to sustain itself as well as human well-being. One of these is the ecological footprint produced by the Global Footprint Network since the 1990s. The footprint accounts, now available for almost all countries around the world, are based on data from, among others, the Food and Agriculture Organization, the UN Statistics Division, and the International Energy Agency (Ewing et al. 2010). Footprint data are currently available for more than forty African countries. An interesting attempt to combine measures of welfare with ecological impact is the Happy Planet Index developed by the UK-based New Economics Foundation in 2006 (NEF 2009). The index complements the ecological footprint with life satisfaction and life expectancy, thus rejecting income or GDP as a guiding parameter. Ever since its creation, the index has consistently shown that high levels of resource consumption do not necessarily produce comparable levels of well-being, and that it is possible to achieve high levels of satisfaction (as measured in conventional public opinion polls) without excessive consumption of the Earth's natural capital. In 2010, the UN University launched a Human Sustainable Development Index, by simply adding a new dimension (per capita carbon footprint) to the three dimensions of the HDI, which are income, education, and health (Togtokh and Gaffney 2010). The results show, among others, that developed countries such as the United States and Canada, which enjoy relatively high human development, do so at a huge environmental cost to themselves and humanity. To the contrary, middle-income countries such as Costa Rica and Uruguay are among those achieving the highest level of human development with a much more acceptable footprint, which is a fraction of that generated by the most industrial nations. In general, African policy makers may gain critical insights by exchanging notes with these more efficient economies rather than the more wasteful developed world.

A DASHBOARD TO MEASURE AFRICA'S QUALITY OF GROWTH

The various components outlined thus far should be integrated into a dashboard to measure the quality of growth. Different countries may opt for different combinations of the various dimensions making up each

Social Well-Being

Education, health, work-life balance, decent work

Real Economy

Paid and unpaid work, social cohesion, household production/consumption, integrated reporting for public and private enterprises

Natural Welfare

Natural resource use, biodiversity, ecological/carbon footprint, ecosystem preservation

pillar, but it would be useful to keep at least the three main dials: real economy, social well-being, and natural welfare. The conceptual structure of the dashboard may follow that represented in the text box above.

What would then happen to GDP? Note that a significant component of national income would already be included in the central dial of the dashboard—that is, the real economy, which captures monetary income by measuring paid work as well as a number of additional contributions. Another option would be to simply add GDP as a fourth component to the dashboard, thus giving it a more central role as a measure of income and market production, bearing in mind all its limitations (as described in this chapter).

Another important consideration regards the possibility combining the dashboard into a composite index, which we will call the Quality of Growth Index (QGI). This index would have the advantage of providing both results: the multidimensional information of the dashboard, on one hand, and the aggregated score, on the other (as is the case in GDP).

Such a process of aggregation obviously presents challenges and methodological problems, including the need to express all dimensions (or most of them) in equivalent terms, such as monetary or other similar units (e.g., time, labor). At the same time, there may be good policy reasons for doing it. First, it can be useful to capture the inevitable trade-offs between formal economic transactions and the dimensions discussed in this chapter. Second, it would allow policy makers to get a simplified picture of the overall state of the economy and how it is contributing to the quality of growth. In a sense, the QGI would present a snapshot of the net economic contribution of all dimensions, following the total wealth approach promoted by the World Bank, various UN agencies, and others, such as the genuine progress indicator.

The QGI could be expressed as follows:

$$QGI = f(R, S, N),\qquad\qquad(1.1)$$

where: R = Real Economy contribution,
S = Social Well-being contribution, and
N = Natural Welfare contribution.

How these four elements combine to produce QGI is important. They should not be linear combinations: all of them are indeed crucial to the quality of growth and the absence of even one of these factors would immediately push the QGI to zero. The relationship should be seen as multiplicative, but an overall "limiting factor" may help policy makers understand that the best effects result not from the maximization of all components, which would be impossible (given the inevitable trade-offs), but from their optimization. For example, it is clear that increases in material standards make a major difference to the quality of growth in poorer countries where many people lack basic necessities, yet as countries get richer, further increases in material standards make increasingly less difference and can easily endanger the other dimensions, thus negatively affecting the overall QGI. Such interconnectedness may be represented as follows:

$$QGI = L_{max} \times (R/(k_r + R)) \times (S/(k_s + S)) \times (N/(k_n + S),\qquad(1.2)$$

where: L_{max} = the maximum achievable QGI when all factors are simultaneously at their maximum;
k_r = the half saturation constant of R, that is, the value of R where the result of this term achieves half its maximum value;
k_s = the half saturation constant of S; and
k_n = the half saturation constant of N.

A dual approach that keeps both the dashboard components as distinct and an aggregate index for policy synthesis can be quite useful. By combining both the intrinsic value of the real economy, social well-being, and natural welfare with their narrow econometric impact on QGI, we may be able to design policies that are respectful of the inherent complexity of social and natural dynamics, while also producing numbers that would be useful to understand whether the type of economic growth we achieve is genuinely green and financially sound.

Moreover, this would allow societies to set nonmonetary thresholds on all dimensions. For instance, countries could agree that R, S, and N cannot fall below a certain physical value, regardless of their combined contribution to the QGI. This would mean introducing early warning systems for each dimension, such that policy makers and societies at large are alerted when they reach critically low levels. In this vein, the goal of economic policy would become to create value (or growth) by optimizing the interaction of the various dimensions above the minimum safeguarded margins.

CONCLUSION

This chapter discussed the fallacies of GDP as a measurement of economic performance, arguing that a transition to sustainable development and better quality growth in Africa would imply rethinking how we measure prosperity and growth. For this, we need new metrics, ideally combined in a dashboard presenting different levels of aggregation and disaggregation. The dashboard could include a variety of dimensions clustered around three main dials: real economy, social well-being, and natural welfare. If useful for the purpose of policy making and communication, an overall aggregate index could be generated by taking into account trade-offs and limiting factors. It is crucial, however, that the dashboard be capable of showing the complex interactions behind the key drivers of prosperity: a multifaceted process that cannot be managed efficiently and responsibly by looking only at one dial.

African countries are at a crossroads in their development trajectories. Their quest for prosperity has been long in the making, but inequalities, social tensions, and environmental degradation have had a significant impact on the quality of growth. Moreover, their future development aspirations will need to be framed in a global context in which sustainable and equitable prosperity is more important than ever. To manage policies designed to improve the quality of growth, they need a different approach and new measurements. The relative underdevelopment of statistical capacity is an opportunity to leapfrog to a beyond-GDP approach to national income, in line with the current global debate. In this regard, the continent could become a pioneer in the redesign of economic development at a time in which conventional growth approaches seem increasingly ineffective. From a policy perspective, an innovative approach to development statistics can be realized with the support of a number of agencies in the continent, from the African Centre for Statistics at the UN Economic Commission for Africa (for expertise and coordination) to the African Union Commission (for political support and coordination), the African Development Bank (for infrastructural and economic support), and various subregional organizations, including the Southern African Development Community, the East African Community, and the Economic Community of West African States, whose mandate includes promoting sustainable and equitable development on the continent.

REFERENCES

Abraham, Katharine G., and Christopher Mackie. 2005. *Beyond the Market: Designing Nonmarket Accounts for the United States*. Washington, DC: National Academies Press.

Africa Progress Panel. 2013. *Equity in Extractives. Stewarding Africa's Natural Resources for All*. Geneva: Africa Progress Panel.

Ahmad, Nadim, and Seung-Hee Koh. 2011. "Incorporating Estimates of Household Production of Non-Market Services Into International Comparisons of Material Well-Being." Statistics Directorate, Working Paper No. 42. OECD Publishing, Paris.

Becker, Gary S. 1965. "A Theory of the Allocation of Time." *Economic Journal* 75 (299): 493–517.

Bridgman, Benjamin, Andrew Dugan, Mikhail Lal, Matthew Osborne, and Shauna Villones. 2012. "Accounting for Household Production in the National Accounts, 1965–2010." *Survey of Current Business* 92 (5): 23–36.

Costanza, Roberto, Ralph d'Arge, Rudolf de Groot, Stephen Farber, Monica Grasso, Bruce Hannon, Karin Limburg, et al. 1997. "The Value of the World's Ecosystem Services and Natural Capital," *Nature* 387 (May 15): 253–270.

Daly, Herman E., and John B. Cobb. 1994. *For the Common Good: Redirecting the Economy toward Community, the Environment and a Sustainable Future*. 2nd ed. Boston: Beacon Press.

Dasgupta, Partha. 2001. *Human Well-Being and the Natural Environment*. Oxford: Oxford University Press.

Dasgupta, Partha, and Ismail Serageldin, eds. 2001. *Social Capital: A Multifaceted Perspective*. Washington, DC: World Bank.

Dulani, Boniface, Robert Mattes, and Carolyn Logan. 2013. "After a Decade of Growth in Africa, Little Change in Poverty at the Grassroots." Policy Brief No. 1. Centre for Democratic Development, Accra, Ghana.

Eisner, Robert. 1989. *The Total Incomes System of Accounts.* Chicago: University of Chicago Press.

European Union. 2008. *The Economics of Ecosystems and Biodiversity. An Interim Report.* Brussels: European Commission. Accessed January 26, 2019, http:// ec.europa.eu/environment/nature/biodiversity/economics.

Ewing, Brad, David Moore, Steven Goldfinger, Anna Oursler, Anders Reed, and Mathis Wackernagel. 2010. *Ecological Footprint Atlas 2010.* Oakland, CA: Global Footprint Network.

Fioramonti, Lorenzo. 2013. *Gross Domestic Problem: The Politics Behind the World's Most Powerful Number.* London: Zed Books.

———. 2014. *How Numbers Rule the World: The Use and Abuse of Statistics in Global Politics.* London: Zed Books.

———. 2017. *The World After GDP: Economics, Politics and International Relations in the Post-Growth Era.* Cambridge: Polity Books.

Folbre, Nancy. 2001. *The Invisible Heart: Economics and Family Values.* New York: New Press.

———. 2008. *Valuing Children: Rethinking the Economics of the Family.* Cambridge, MA: Harvard University Press.

Frazis, Harley, and Jay Stewart. 2011. "How Does Household Production Affect Measured Income Inequality?" *Journal of Population Economics* 24 (1): 3–22.

Hamilton, Kirk E., John F. Helliwell, and Michael Woolcock. 2016. *Social Capital, Trust and Well-being in the Evaluation of Wealth.* Washington, DC: World Bank. Accessed July 26, 2017, http://www-wds.worldbank.org/external/default /WDSContentServer/WDSP/IB/2016/06/20/090224b0843e2438/1_0/Rendered /PDF/Social0capital0evaluation0of0wealth.pdf.

International Labour Organization (ILO). 1999. *Decent Work Agenda.* Geneva: ILO.

Jerven, Morten. 2013. *Poor Numbers: How We Are Misled by Africa's Development Statistics and What to Do About It.* Ithaca, NY: Cornell University Press.

Kubiszewski, Ida, Robert Costanza, Carol Franco, Philip Lawn, John Talberth, Tim Jackson, and Camille Aylmer. 2013. "Beyond GDP: Measuring and Achieving Global Genuine Progress." *Ecological Economics* 93 (2013): 57–68.

Lozano, Rafael, Mohsen Naghavi, Kyle Foreman, Stephen Lim, Kenji Shibuya, Victor Aboyans, Jerry Abraham, et al. 2010. "Global and Regional Mortality from 235 Causes of Death for 20 Age Groups in 1990 and 2010: A Systematic Analysis for the Global Burden of Disease Study 2010." *The Lancet* 380 (9859): 2095–2128.

Lundberg, Erik. 1971. "Simon Kuznets' Contribution to Economics." *Swedish Journal of Economics* 73 (4): 444–459.

Lundgren, Charlotte J., Alun H. Thomas, and Robert C. York. 2013. *Boom, Bust or Prosperity? Managing Sub-Saharan Africa's Natural Resource Wealth.* Washington, DC: International Monetary Fund.

Mallet, Victor. 2013. "Environmental Damage Costs India $80 bn a Year." *Financial Times,* July 17. Accessed January 26, 2019, https://www.ft.com /content/0a89f3a8-eeca-11e2-98dd-00144feabdc0.

Miranda, Veerle. 2011. "Cooking, Caring and Volunteering: Unpaid Work around the World." OECD Social, Employment and Migration Working Papers No. 116. OECD Publishing, Paris.

New Economics Foundation (NEF). 2009. *The Happy Planet Index 2.0: Why Good Lives Don't Have to Cost the Earth.* London: NEF.

Nordhaus, William D., and James Tobin. 1971. "Is Growth Obsolete?" Reprinted from *The Measurement of Economic and Social Performance,* ed. Milton Moss. Special issue of *Studies in Income and Wealth* 38 (1973): 509–532.

Organisation for Economic Co-operation and Development (OECD). 2014. *Wiki-Progress.* Accessed January 26, 2019, www.wikiprogress.org.

Piketty, Thomas. 2014. *Capital in the 21st Century.* Cambridge MA: Belknap Press.

Schneider, Friedrich, and Dominik Enste. 2002. "Hiding in the Shadows: the Growth of the Underground Economy." Economic Issues No. 30. International Monetary Fund, Brussels.

Statistics South Africa. 2014. *What Is the Living Conditions Survey (LCS)?* Accessed January 26, 2019, http://www.statssa.gov.za/LCS/lcs.asp.

Stiglitz, Joseph E. 2015. *The Great Divide: Unequal Societies and What We Can Do About Them.* New York: Norton.

Stiglitz, Joseph E., Amartya Sen, and Jean-Paul Fitoussi. 2009. *Report by the Commission on the Measurement of Economic Performance and Social Progress.* Accessed January 26, 2019, http://library.bsl.org.au/jspui/bitstream/1/1267/1/Measurement_of_economic_performance_and_social_progress.pdf.

Togtokh, Chuluun, and Owen Gaffney. 2010. *2010 Human Sustainable Development Index.* Accessed January 26, 2019, http://ourworld.unu.edu/en/the-2010 -human-sustainable-development-index.

United Nations. 2015. *World Population Prospects. 2015 Revision.* New York: Department of Economic and Social Affairs.

United Nations Development Programme (UNDP). 1996. *Human Development Report 1996.* New York: Oxford University Press.

United Nations Statistical Commission et al. 2012. *System of Environmental-Economic Accounting.* New York: United Nations. Accessed January 26, 2019, https://seea .un.org/.

Webster, Edward, Asanda Benya, Xoliswa Dilata, Catherine Joynt, Kholofelo Ngoepe, and Mariane Tsoeu. 2008. "Making Visible the Invisible: Confronting South Africa's Decent Work Deficit." Sociology of Work Unit, University of the Witwatersrand, Johannesburg. Accessed January 26, 2019, http://www.labour.gov.za/DOL /downloads/documents/research-documents/webster.pdf.

World Bank. 2006. *Where Is the Wealth of Nations? Measuring Capital for the 21st Century.* Washington, DC: World Bank.

——. 2013. *Little Green Data Book 2013.* Washington, DC: World Bank. Accessed January 26, 2019, http://data.worldbank.org/products/data-books /little-data-book/little-green-data-book.

CHAPTER 2

Recent African Growth Experience

POVERTY, EQUITY, AND POLITICAL STABILITY

Andy McKay

The growth recovery experienced by Sub-Saharan Africa (SSA) over the period from around 1994 to 2014, in part supported by favorable commodity prices, is well known, although concerns about growth rates slowing have emerged subsequently. This chapter assesses the quality of growth experienced over this period. Such an analysis faces two particular challenges. First, although it is widely accepted that growth is a means to other ends rather than an end in its own right, a clear understanding of what precisely quality of growth means is lacking. Second, there are significant challenges about the quality of the data to inform such an analysis, including both the actual growth data and the data to capture aspects of the quality of growth.

An important early initiative in thinking about quality of growth was a World Bank study by Thomas et al. (2000). Among other things, this report argued that inadequate attention had hitherto been devoted to assets the poor rely highly on, in particular human and natural capital. Natural capital does play a key role in the livelihoods of many poor people; land is one such important natural asset, but poor people often also rely heavily on common property natural resources, which are commonly overexploited and not prioritized in policy. Although there has been for a long time a strong focus on human capital, the emphasis on this in relation to poorer households has often been weaker.

The report identified four neglected actions in relation to economic growth, specifically: improving the distribution of opportunities, sustaining natural capital, dealing with global financial risks, and improving governance and controlling corruption. These themes then form the main chapters of the report. The importance of global financial risks became obvious only seven years later with the 2007–2008 global financial crisis, which certainly had a major impact on the poor. The poor almost certainly suffer most in relative terms from a failure to sustain natural capital; and a continued policy focus on gross domestic product (GDP) growth neglects this issue. It is often the case that the poor suffer most from poor governance and corruption, particularly given that richer people are often better able to protect their position from any adverse effects. Without doubt, the distribution of opportunities is a key dimension of the quality of growth.

Later work has focused on the role of fiscal policy in supporting a better quality of growth (Lopez, Thomas, and Wang 2010). This is a key factor given the importance of the availability of many key public goods for social outcomes; it is also a key mechanism of redistribution and a key means of seeking to regulate environmental degradation. A lack of an agreed understanding of what the quality of growth means, however, still remains. Mlachila, Tapsoba, and Tapsoba (2016) recently developed a measure of the quality of growth, which takes account of six main aspects: four relating to growth fundamentals (strength, volatility, sectoral composition, and demand composition) and two relating to social outcomes (education and health). It remains unclear how these different elements can be measured and combined. Here we do not seek to measure quality of growth in SSA. Rather, we focus on examining the growth record of the past twenty-five years to assess the ability of growth to translate into improved social outcomes, as well as its distributional pattern; and we seek to assess the extent to which growth may be sustainable taking account of the stability of the political environment, a key issue in many SSA countries. Unfortunately, sufficiently reliable data are not available to sufficiently judge the impact of growth on environmental sustainability, another important aspect of the quality of growth.

A second key issue is the quality of available data to assess not just the growth record but also its outcomes. The reliability of national accounts data has been subject to substantial critique based on the work of Jerven (2010, 2013, among others); this has been most emphasized in relation to national accounts data and, inter alia, to the reliability of available estimates of economic growth. The quality of available data on some aspects of social outcomes, derived from household surveys of different types, may be better, but even here the indicators that can be easily measured are not always the most important ones—for example, school attendance rather than learning outcomes. International data sets such as World Development Indicators (WDI) and PovcalNet, offer an easily useable source of information on different data on growth and social outcomes, but the data they contain may be subject to significant question, in particular because of a lack of information about sources and consistency of definition.

In this chapter, we nonetheless mainly make use of WDI data to assess growth and social outcomes across all SSA countries. This is one of the few currently practical ways to make comparisons across all countries, given that variables are meant to be defined in the same way in all cases. It is important always to maintain a critical perspective throughout, remaining aware of the potential limitations of this data. In some places in this chapter, we draw on evidence from more carefully conducted country studies, which were undertaken on a largely comparable basis.

This chapter is structured as follows. A detailed discussion and analysis of the SSA growth record is presented in section 2. Section 3 then focuses on the extent to which growth has been associated with progress in reducing income (strictly usually consumption) poverty, as well as its association with a wider range of social outcomes. Section 4 focuses on inequality, a major issue in SSA, often regarded as the world region with the second-highest level of inequality following Latin America. Section 5 concentrates on political sustainability, by looking at fragility, after which Section 6 offers some conclusions and discusses next steps.

THE GROWTH RECORD IN SUB-SAHARAN AFRICA

Many different measures of GDP are available in international data sets. In considering growth in SSA in this chapter, our main focus is on growth in per capita GDP, reflecting the fact that the significance of a given rate of growth is highly dependent on the extent of population growth. When comparing levels of GDP across countries, we necessarily need to focus on constant U.S. dollar values, now in 2010 values; but in considering growth rates, we can instead focus on local currency values to avoid the complexity of exchange rate conversions. The focus on GDP rather than gross national income (GNI) reflects a choice to focus on production at the country level—the normal concept for growth—although for some purposes, income may also be of interest.

The evolution of the average per capita GDP for SSA in aggregate from 1960 to 2015 is presented in figure 2.1. This chart shows three main phases. From 1960 to the early 1970s, the early postindependence years for many countries, growth performance was reasonably strong. This was a period over which commodity prices were increasing and also when the

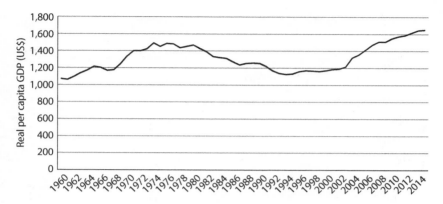

Figure 2.1   Growth of real per capita GDP (2010 U.S. dollars) in Sub-Saharan Africa, 1960–2015

Source: Computed from World Bank (2016).

world economy was performing relatively well. Over this period, per capita GDP grew at an average of 2.4 percent per year. Then from the early to mid-1970s to the early to mid-1990s, SSA experienced twenty years of stagnation and decline, with an average growth rate of –1.4 percent between 1974 and 1994. This reduced growth rate reflected adverse movements in commodity prices and was also the period during which many SSA countries were required to undertake stabilization and structural adjustment programs. Since the mid-1990s, however, SSA has experienced a growth recovery, with an annual average growth rate of 1.8 percent between 1994 and 2015 (and higher rates within subperiods). This was also a period of generally increasing commodity prices, although the growth recovery reflects much more than this factor (Radelet 2010). In addition both commodity-producing and non-commodity-producing countries often shared equally in the growth recovery.

Although the SSA growth is obviously welcome, it is also important to consider this growth in comparison with other world regions. Figure 2.2 presents growth of the major world regions over the 1990–2015 period, again based on WDI data, and table 2.1 summarizes average growth rates for these regions for this period and subperiods. What this comparison immediately reveals is that growth in SSA has been significantly below the developing country average and substantially below what has been achieved in East Asia and the Pacific and South Asia. Between 2006 and

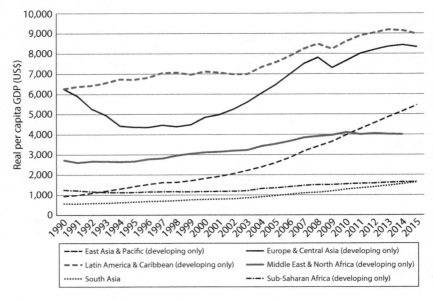

Figure 2.2   Growth of real per capita GDP (2010 U.S. dollars) by world region, 1990–2015

Source: Computed from World Bank (2016).

2015, the average growth rate in SSA was 2.0 percent, whereas it was 5.3 percent over the same period in South Asia and 7.7 percent in East Asia and the Pacific. The cumulative effects of these convergent growth rates are obvious in figure 2.2.

Table 2.1 also shows that the growth rates appear to be lower in the past three years than they have been before in both SSA and across the developing world. The high growth that had been achieved in the first decade of the 2000s, in particular (with the interruption of the world financial crisis), does not seem to have been sustained into the second decade of the 2000s.

We now consider the growth experience at the individual country level in the period from 1990 to 2015. We focus on country growth rates, which are now based on local currency GDP values and therefore are not affected by exchange rate changes. Table 2.2 classifies countries based on the average growth rate of their per capita GDP over the 1990–2015 and 2006–2015 periods. This classification highlights the diversity of growth experiences. Only two countries, Equatorial Guinea and Cabo Verde, had an average growth rate of per capita GDP above 5 percent over the

Table 2.1   Average Growth Rates for Major World Regions (% per Year)

	1990–2015	2006–2015	2013–2015
East Asia and Pacific (developing only)	7.2	7.7	6.0
Europe and Central Asia (developing only)	1.2	2.6	0.6
Latin America and Caribbean (developing only)	1.4	1.7	-0.2
Middle East and North Africa (developing only)	1.9	1.4	-0.5
South Asia	4.3	5.4	5.3
Sub-Saharan Africa (developing only)	1.1	2.0	1.3
All developing countries	3.0	4.2	2.9

Source: Computed from World Development Indicators (2016).

1990–2015 period, but another twelve countries had average growth rates over this twenty-five-year period of between 2.5 percent and 4.9 percent. Among this latter group, not all are commodity rich economies, like, for example, Ethiopia or Rwanda. At the same time, ten countries had a negative growth in per capita GDP over this period. Among these are many countries affected by conflict or political instability. This analysis

Table 2.2   Frequency Distribution of Average Annual Growth Rates in Per Capita GDP for African Countries

1990–2015	
≥5%	Equatorial Guinea, Cabo Verde
2.5% to 4.9%	Mozambique, Mauritius, Mali, Ethiopia, Rwanda. Uganda, Nigeria, Sudan, Ghana, Lesotho, São Tomé and Principe, Botswana
1.0% to 2.4%	Burkina Faso, Chad, Tanzania, Namibia, Malawi, Angola, Zambia, Eritrea, Swaziland, Benin, Mauritania
0.0% to 0.9%	Kenya, Sierra Leone, South Africa, Congo, The Gambia, Togo, Djibouti, Guinea, Gabon, Guinea-Bissau, Côte d'Ivoire
-1.5% to -0.1%	Cameroon, Niger, Liberia, Comoros, Madagascar, Zimbabwe, Burundi
< -1.5%	Somalia, Democratic Republic of Congo, South Sudan
2006–2015	
≥5%	Ethiopia, Mali, Angola, Rwanda
2.5% to 4.9%	Ghana, Mozambique, Sudan, Zambia, Lesotho, Mauritius, Djibouti, Uganda, Tanzania, Cabo Verde, Nigeria, Namibia, Sierra Leone, São Tomé and Principe, Liberia, Botswana, Malawi, Mauritania, Kenya, Democratic Republic of Congo
1.0% to 2.4%	Burkina Faso, Côte d'Ivoire, Congo, Benin, Niger, Cameroon, Chad, Togo, South Sudan
0.0% to 0.9%	Gabon, Guinea-Bissau, Swaziland, Senegal, Zimbabwe, Burundi, The Gambia
-1.5% to -0.1%	Madagascar, Comoros, Guinea, Eritrea
< -1.5%	Equatorial Guinea, South Sudan
Missing	Somalia

Source: Computed from World Development Indicators (2016).

Note: GDP = gross domestic product.

highlights the wide diversity of growth experiences in SSA, which the aggregate data presented in figure 2.1 hide. There have been cases of very fast growth as well as a large number of cases of either indifferent or negative growth.

Table 2.2 also includes an equivalent analysis for the 2006–2015 period, which was a faster growth period overall, as reflected in the classification. Although some countries' classifications change, this shows the same diversity of experience. Over this period, four countries had average per capita growth rates above 5 percent; among these, Angola is resource rich, but Ethiopia and Rwanda are less so. Another nineteen countries experienced growth rates of between 2.5 percent and 4.9 percent. But even over this period, six countries experienced negative average growth rates and seven experienced average growth rates, which were positive but less than 1 percent.

A focus on average growth rates at the country level does not take account of within-country variability. Looking at the period of renewed growth from 1995 to 2015, only five SSA countries had no years of negative growth; by contrast, six had ten or more years in which growth was negative, the latter often being countries affected by conflict or political instability. The standard deviation of the growth rate over the 1995–2015 period exceeded 10 percent in South Sudan and Sierra Leone, and it was in excess of 7 percent in Equatorial Guinea, Zimbabwe, and Angola. Again conflict or instability is a common factor in high growth volatility, but all too often so is high commodity dependence.

In summary, SSA has performed substantially better in growth terms in the period since the mid-1990s. But it is important to remember that some other world regions, especially in Asia, have performed substantially better over the same period. Additionally, growth in SSA has shown substantial variability across countries and over time within many countries.

THE ASSOCIATIONS AMONG GROWTH, POVERTY, AND OTHER SOCIAL OUTCOMES

A central question in considering the quality of growth is the extent to which economic growth delivers improved social outcomes, in particular, poverty reduction. This section first focuses on income poverty. An extensive body of literature highlights the importance of growth in bringing about poverty reduction, and plenty of empirical evidence indicates that economic growth can be effective for poverty reduction. At the same time, this is not necessarily the case, and there are plenty of examples of a country experiencing good growth performance but with only limited poverty reduction. Although growth may have been said to be "good for the poor" (Dollar and Kraay 2002; Dollar, Kleineberg, and Kraay 2016), it is not inevitable that growth translates into poverty reduction, and the one-to-one relationship between growth and poverty reduction has been widely challenged (Foster and Székely 2008). For this reason, important policy foci have developed to look at pro-poor growth (Besley and Cord 2007; Grimm, Klasen, and McKay 2007) and, more recently, at inclusive growth.

What is the record in SSA of growth translating into poverty reduction? One way to consider this is to use poverty data available in international sources, such as WDI and PovcalNet, which report poverty headcounts relative to the international $1.90 or $3.10 lines and sometimes relative to national lines. The problem with using these sources is understanding whether the data they present really are comparable between one year and another within countries. Meaningful poverty comparisons require that consistent approaches be used in the poverty calculations for each year, and typically these sources do not come with enough documentation to be able to judge this. In some countries, different surveys are known not to be comparable, but this frequently is not reported. In addition, if the comparisons are based on dollar-denominated poverty lines, then conclusions may reflect changes in exchange rates over the period. In analyzing poverty changes over time, it is therefore much safer to rely on poverty relative to national poverty lines, as long as the same line is consistently applied for the different points in time being compared.

Given the problems with poverty data from WDI and PovcalNet, we only briefly consider changes in poverty headcounts relative to national poverty lines based on WDI. A much more careful country-level analysis is desirable in considering changes in poverty. For the purposes of this chapter, we draw on a study of growth and poverty reduction coordinated by Arndt, McKay, and Tarp (2016), which was based on careful and broadly comparable country case studies conducted in sixteen of the largest twenty-four countries in SSA through a project coordinated by UNU-WIDER. The studies were generally carried out by leading poverty researchers from the countries concerned working with international country experts; and a broadly similar approach to looking at growth and changes in poverty (relative to a comparable national poverty line) was carried out in each study.

Data from this study on changes in poverty for each country are reported in table 2.3. These poverty figures are comparable overtime

Table 2.3 Reduction in National Poverty Headcounts (% Rates of Poverty Headcounts)

Countries with Good Growth and Good Poverty Reduction		
Ethiopia	2000	46.8
	2005	46.0
	2011	23.8
Ghana	1991–1992	51.7
	1998–1999	39.5
	2005–2006	28.0
	2005–2006 (updated)	31.9
	2012–2013	24.2
Malawi	2004–2004	47.0
	2010–2011	38.6
Rwanda	2000–2001	58.9
	2005–2006	56.7
	2010–2011	44.9
Uganda	2005–2006	42.3
	2009–2010	38.1
	2010–2011	37.0
	2011–2012	35.9
	2012–2013	31.5
Countries with Good Growth with Limited Poverty Reduction		
Burkina Faso	1994	55.5
	1998	61.8
	2003	47.2
	2003 (revised)	46.3
	2009	43.9
Mozambique	1996–1997	69.4
	2002–2003	54.1
	2008–2009	54.7
Nigeria	Official	
	1996	61.6
	2004	54.4
	2010	69.0
	World Bank	
	2010–2011	35.2
	2012–2013	33.1
Tanzania	1992	38.6
	2001	35.7
	2007	33.5
	2007 (revised)	34.2
	2012	28.2
Zambia	1996	69
	1998	73
	2004	68
	2006	63

Table 2.3 (*Continued*)

Countries with Poor Growth and Poverty Reduction		
Cameroon	1996	53.3
	2001	40.2
	2007	39.9
Côte d'Ivoire	1988	18
	1993	34
	1998	22
	2002	22
	2008	31
Kenya	1994	40.2
	1997	54.3
	2005–2006	45.9
Madagascar	2001	57.8
	2005	59.1
	2010	61.7
South Africa	1993	56
	Late 2000s	54
Countries with Insufficient Data		
Democratic Republic of Congo		

Source: Based on a study by Arndt, McKay, and Tarp (2016).

within each country, but they are not comparable between countries because they use national poverty lines. In their analysis, Arndt at al. (2016) classified the countries into four groups: five countries that had good growth performance accompanied by good poverty-reduction performance; five countries with good growth but limited poverty reduction; five countries with poor growth and poverty-reduction performance; and one country without enough data to draw clear conclusions.

It is important to remember that results for consumption poverty can be quite sensitive to the points in time when surveys are conducted, as consumption can be quite volatile over time. For instance, the results for the $1.90 poverty headcount from the 2013–2014 survey in Rwanda as reported in WDI would suggest that poverty did not fall in the three years following the end point of the country chapter included in the project. But whether or not this is the case, the point remains that of the ten cases of good growth performance, only half of them were associated with good performance in reducing income poverty. Half were not. The country studies all present a detailed explanation for the observed factors; however, one factor that is common to several cases is the performance of the agricultural sector. Good performance of the agricultural sector was

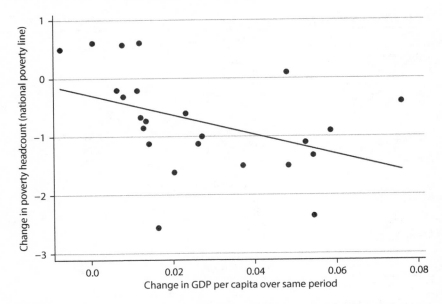

Figure 2.3   Annualized poverty reduction (national poverty line) against annual rate of GDP per capita growth

Source: Computed from World Bank (2016).

associated with good poverty reduction in Ethiopia and Malawi; poor performance of the agricultural sector was associated with limited poverty reduction in Mozambique and Tanzania.

To the extent that the poverty data in WDI can be trusted, figure 2.3 presents a scatterplot of the changes in national poverty between the earliest and latest available years for each of twenty-six SSA countries and the growth of per capita GDP over the same period. This shows a statistically significant association between the annualized percentage rate of poverty reduction in a country and the annual percentage rate of growth of per capita GDP. It also shows quite a lot of scatter about the line—cases of low poverty reduction despite reasonable growth and the opposite. This supports the message from the previous more careful country study approach that demonstrates the variability with which growth translates into income poverty reduction.

The country studies in Arndt et al. (2016) also showed that most countries did make good progress in improving many social indicators over the periods considered, notably indicators of education and health.

South Africa for instance, which made little progress in reducing income poverty, made significant progress in reducing multidimensional poverty, which in part was a consequence of important public policy actions. Consistent with this progress, Alkire and Housseini (2017) have shown that measures of multidimensional poverty reduced to a statistically significant extent in fifteen of the seventeen countries they considered.

The social outcomes, such as school enrolment or under-five mortality rates, typically are less strongly linked to growth. Public spending and the effectiveness of its delivery are potentially more important factors affecting these outcomes, although faster growth could enable this if it generates more tax revenue and if the tax revenue is used for this purpose (one or both of these assumptions may not apply). Improving health knowledge and practices can be associated with reduced child mortality. Figure 2.4 presents a scatterplot of annualized changes in the under-five mortality rate (which fell in almost every African country) and the average annual growth rate of per capita GDP over the same period. The negative association is significant, but the fit is much weaker than for

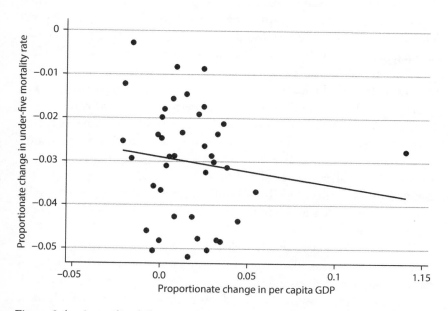

Figure 2.4   Annualized changes in under-five mortality against annual rate of GDP per capita growth

Source: Computed from World Bank (2016).

income poverty. There is significant variation in the rate of reduction of under-five mortality among the many countries that grew in the range of –1 percent to 3 percent, for instance.

GROWTH, INEQUALITY, AND ITS CHANGES

The data for estimating income poverty are now relatively good, with many countries having reasonable quality household survey data, which are suitable for the purpose. These surveys are designed to relatively accurately estimate the consumption of the poor and those who are close to the poverty line. But they are likely to be much less successful at measuring the consumption or income of the rich, even if richer households choose to participate in the survey (they often do not). The quality of available estimates of inequality is then open to significant question.

This is unfortunate because, first, SSA is commonly regarded as the world region with the second-highest level of inequality outside Latin America, and some countries in southern Africa have the highest Gini coefficients in the world. But second, inequality is directly relevant to the issues being considered in this chapter. If growth has not been associated with much poverty reduction, then it is highly likely that this growth was distributionally unequal and thus may have contributed to increases in inequality. A higher level of inequality in a country, even if it does not increase, also means that growth will be less effective in generating poverty reduction. In addition, a growing body of empirical evidence also suggests that high inequality may have adverse effects for growth.

In the Arndt et al. (2016) study, the focus was more on poverty reduction, so it did not have the same systematic consideration of inequality in the country studies. For the purposes of this chapter, we will consider the inequality data available in WDI, even if in several cases, the changes in inequality (chiefly cases of reductions) they imply over relatively short periods are simply not plausible in the absence of a convincing explanation.

The WDI also have a much higher number of estimates of Gini coefficients for countries than the number of poverty statistics based on national poverty lines, even if the same survey is presumably used for both calculations. Thirty-seven countries have estimates of Gini coefficients at two or more points in time between 1990 and 2015, thus enabling consideration of changes in inequality.

For these thirty-seven countries, table 2.4 presents a frequency distribution of the level of the Gini coefficient in the latest year. Three countries, all in Southern Africa, have Gini coefficients about 0.60, and another five—again three of which are in Southern Africa (as well as Guinea-Bissau and Rwanda)—have a Gini coefficient above 0.50. These represent high levels of inequality on an international scale. Conversely, seven countries have Gini coefficient below 0.35, which is relatively low among developing countries.

Plots of the annualized rate of change in the Gini coefficient between the earliest and latest years in the data or of the level of the Gini coefficient in the latest year against the average annual rate of per capita GDP growth over the same period do not show any statistically significant relationships. The level of inequality or its change seems not to be significantly associated with growth in a bivariate cross-country comparison.

These statistics concern income (strictly consumption) inequality, but inequality is an equally important issue in relation to social outcomes. It is hard to define Gini coefficient measures for these outcomes. If, however, one considers social indicators obtained from the Demographic and Health Surveys (DHS), the variation of social outcomes can be considered by asset quintile. Table 2.5 reports the ratio of under-five mortality in the poorest asset quintile to that in the richest asset quintile, reporting this in the earliest and latest DHS surveys for twenty-nine countries. What this shows is that this measure of inequality has increased in seventeen of the twenty-nine countries and has fallen in twelve. The impressive progress in social outcomes is seen in all asset quintiles, but often the rate of progress at the bottom of the distribution is lower than that at the top

Table 2.4   Frequency Distribution of Latest Gini Coefficients for Different African Countries

>60	South Africa, Namibia, Botswana
50–60	Zambia, Lesotho, Swaziland, Guinea-Bissau, Rwanda
45–50	Congo, Kenya, The Gambia, Cabo Verde, Cameroon, Malawi, Togo, Mozambique
40–45	Djibouti, Benin, Chad, Côte d'Ivoire, Nigeria, Ghana, Angola, Madagascar, Democratic Republic of Congo, Uganda, Senegal
35–40	Tanzania, Mauritius, Burkina Faso
30–35	Niger, Sierra Leone, Guinea, Burundi, Mali, Mauritania, São Tomé and Principe
Not available	Comoros, Equatorial Guinea, Gabon, Liberia, Somalia, South Sudan, Sudan

Source: World Bank (2016).

Table 2.5 Trend in Ratio of Under-Five Mortality Rate in Lowest Asset Quintile to Highest Asset Quintile

Country	Survey	Under-Five Mortality Rate, per 1,000 Live Births	Ratio of Q1 to Q5
Benin	2011–2012 DHS	70	2.00
Benin	1996 DHS	166	1.89
Burkina Faso	2010 DHS	129	1.80
Burkina Faso	1993 DHS	187	1.27
Cameroon	2011 DHS	122	2.56
Cameroon	1991 DHS	125	2.45
Chad	2014–2015 DHS	133	1.17
Chad	1996–1997 DHS	194	0.99
Comoros	2012 DHS	50	1.30
Comoros	1996 DHS	104	1.48
Congo	2011–2012 DHS	68	1.65
Congo	2005 DHS	117	1.59
Congo, Democratic Republic	2013–2014 DHS	104	1.54
Congo, Democratic Republic	2007 DHS	148	1.90
Cote d'Ivoire	2011–2012 DHS	108	1.50
Cote d'Ivoire	1994 DHS	150	1.96
Eritrea	2002 DHS	93	1.54
Eritrea	1995 DHS	136	1.48
Ethiopia	2011 DHS	88	1.59
Ethiopia	2000 DHS	166	1.08
Gabon	2012 DHS	65	1.50
Gabon	2000 DHS	89	1.69
Ghana	2014 DHS	60	1.44
Ghana	1993 DHS	119	2.08
Guinea	2012 DHS	123	2.54
Guinea	1999 DHS	177	1.73
Kenya	2014 DHS	52	1.21
Kenya	1993 DHS	96	2.08
Lesotho	2014 DHS	85	1.10
Lesotho	2004 DHS	113	1.38
Liberia	2013 DHS	94	1.31
Liberia	2007 DHS	110	1.18
Madagascar	2008–2009 DHS	72	2.21
Madagascar	1997 DHS	159	1.93
Malawi	2015–2016 DHS	63	1.38
Malawi	1992 DHS	234	1.47
Mali	2012–2013 DHS	95	1.84
Mali	1995–1996 DHS	238	1.76
Mozambique	2011 DHS	97	1.42
Mozambique	1997 DHS	201	1.91
Namibia	2013 DHS	54	2.16
Namibia	1992 DHS	84	1.47
Niger	2006 DHS	198	1.31
Niger	1998 DHS	274	1.53
Nigeria	2013 DHS	128	2.60
Nigeria	1990 DHS	193	2.00
Rwanda	2014–2015 DHS	50	2.10

Table 2.5   (*Continued*)

Rwanda	1992 DHS	151	1.06
Senegal	2014 DHS	54	3.29
Senegal	1997 DHS	139	2.59
Sierra Leone	2013 DHS	156	1.29
Sierra Leone	2008 DHS	140	1.47
Tanzania	2015–2016 DHS	67	1.07
Tanzania	1996 DHS	136	1.43
Togo	2013–2014 DHS	88	2.61
Togo	1998 DHS	146	1.73
Uganda	2011 DHS	90	1.71
Uganda	1995 DHS	147	1.70
Zambia	2013–2014 DHS	75	1.72
Zambia	1996 DHS	197	1.56
Zimbabwe	2015 DHS	69	1.96
Zimbabwe	1994 DHS	77	1.52

Note: DHS = Demographic and Health Surveys, various years as indicated in table.

Source: Computed from DHS surveys.

of the distribution, even if mortality rates are already much lower at the top of the distribution.

Although this issue is probably less about growth and more about the effectiveness of public spending, it remains an important public policy concern. Better education and health outcomes are likely to be essential for future growth.

FRAGILITY, GROWTH, AND SOCIAL OUTCOMES

One key issue linked to the quality of growth is the ability to maintain a sustained rate of growth for a significant period of time. Four important countries with poorer growth performance and also high growth volatility (Côte d'Ivoire, Democratic Republic of Congo, Madagascar, and Zimbabwe) were all affected by political instability or conflict. If countries are not able to attain sustained growth, it will be difficult for them to achieve better development outcomes, in particular linked to poverty reduction.

The political stability of a country is another key aspect of the quality of growth. In international discussions, SSA countries have been well represented among countries identified as fragile or even failed states as well as among conflict-affected states.

Rather than an essentially arbitrary division between fragile and nonfragile states, it is more helpful to think about degrees of fragility

(McKay and Thorbecke, 2019). Two important recent initiatives, which have sought to measure the degree of fragility of countries, are the Fragile States Index (FSI), developed by the Fund for Peace, and the State Fragility Index, developed by the Center for Systemic Peace. Both are based on judgments of degrees of fragility of different countries. The FSI considers four dimensions of social outcomes (demographic pressures, refugees and internally displaced persons, group grievances, human flight), two of economic outcomes (uneven development, poverty and economic decline) and six political and military outcomes (legitimacy of the state, public services, human rights, security apparatus, factionalized elites, external interventions). Each of these twelve domains is scored from 0 (best) to 10 (worst), and the scores are added to give an overall index ranging from 0 to 120. Time-series data for this index are available each year from 2005 to 2016. The State Fragility Index instead looks separately at effectiveness and legitimacy in each of four domains—security, political, economic, and social—and scores all countries from zero (least fragile) to three (most fragile) in these eight areas. Adding these up gives the State Fragility Index, which takes values from 0 to 25. Time-series data for this index are available from 1995 to 2014.

In practice, these two indices are highly correlated over the ten years for which both are available, and so we focus here on the FSI. Table 2.6, taken from McKay and Thorbecke (2019), shows that among the ten most fragile countries in the world, six are from SSA. SSA also includes twenty-one of the top thirty most fragile countries. Thus, SSA is overrepresented among the most fragile states.

Table 2.7, also taken from McKay and Thorbecke (2019), shows the distribution of SSA countries by fragility quartile. The presence of many of the most fragile countries is very much as expected, but it is also notable that two good performers in terms of growth and poverty reduction, Ethiopia and Rwanda, are found in the second-highest quartile of fragility.

McKay and Thorbecke (2019) constructed an amended version of the FSI, dropping three components that they regarded more as outcomes of fragility rather than direct dimensions of fragility (demographic pressures, uneven development, growth and poverty reduction) and then looked at the correlations between this amended index and different measures of growth performance and deprivation, including average and standard deviation of growth, poverty and its change, inequality, and different social outcomes. A strong positive association exists between the

Table 2.6 Ten Most Fragile Countries in 2016 According to Fragile States Index

Fragile States Index 2016	Total	Demographic Pressures	Refugees and IDPs	Group Grievance	Human Flight	Uneven Development	Poverty and Economic Decline	Legitimacy of the State	Public Services	Human Rights	Security Apparatus	Factionalized Elites	External Intervention		2006 Ranking
Somalia	**114.0**	9.7	9.7	9.4	9.5	9.3	9.0	9.5	9.0	9.7	9.7	10.0	9.5	1	Sudan
South Sudan	**113.8**	9.9	10.0	9.9	6.6	9.0	9.3	9.7	10.0	9.7	10.0	9.7	10.0	2	Dem. Rep. Congo
Central African Republic	**112.1**	8.7	10.0	9.3	7.2	9.9	8.6	9.8	10.0	9.9	9.2	10.0	9.5	3	Cote d'Ivoire
Sudan	**111.5**	9.0	10.0	9.8	9.1	7.6	8.7	9.8	9.1	9.3	9.2	10.0	9.9	4	Iraq
Yemen	**111.5**	9.5	9.6	9.5	7.5	8.4	9.4	9.4	9.3	9.4	10.0	9.5	10.0	5	Zimbabwe
Syria	**110.8**	8.4	10.0	10.0	8.6	7.4	7.8	10.0	8.9	9.8	10.0	9.9	10.0	6	Chad
Chad	**110.1**	9.9	9.8	8.5	8.9	9.3	8.0	9.2	9.8	9.3	9.1	9.8	8.5	6	Somalia
Dem. Rep. Congo	**110.0**	9.1	9.7	9.7	6.8	8.9	8.1	9.3	9.7	10.0	9.2	9.8	9.7	8	Haiti
Afghanistan	**107.9**	9.5	9.5	8.6	8.4	7.5	8.5	9.1	9.6	8.7	10.0	8.6	9.9	9	Pakistan
Haiti	**105.1**	9.2	7.9	6.7	9.0	9.5	8.9	9.4	9.4	7.7	7.9	9.6	9.9	10	Afghanistan

Source: McKay and Thorbecke (2019).

Table 2.7   Distribution of Sub-Saharan African Countries by Quartile of the Revised Fragile States Index

Lowest Fragility	Second	Third	Highest Fragility
Tanzania	Zambia	Cameroon	Guinea
South Africa	Comoros	Congo	Chad
Madagascar	Burkina Faso	Burundi	Dem. Rep. Congo
São Tomé and Principe	Mozambique	Mali	Somalia
Mauritius	Sierra Leone	Rwanda	Zimbabwe
Botswana	Togo	Uganda	Central African Republic
Namibia	Senegal	Eritrea	Sudan
Gabon	Malawi	Niger	Nigeria
The Gambia	Djibouti	Liberia	South Sudan
Cabo Verde	Equatorial Guinea	Kenya	Côte d'Ivoire
Ghana	Angola	Mauritania	Guinea-Bissau
Benin		Ethiopia	

Source: Computed by McKay and Thorbecke (2019) based on the components on the FFP-FSI (Fund for Peace-Fragile States Index) measure.

level of fragility and the volatility of the growth rate; and a much weaker, although still just significant, negative association exists between the average growth rate and fragility. More fragile countries do grow more slowly on average; but much more strikingly, they have much more volatile growth rates.

The amended fragility index is strongly positively associated with the level of the $1.90 poverty headcount in each country. The extent of poverty reduction, based on the national poverty line, is significantly negatively associated with fragility. More fragile countries have higher poverty levels and appear to have made less progress in poverty reduction. This is likely to be linked to their slower and more volatile growth performance. Other social outcomes are more strongly negatively associated with fragility, including under-five mortality and lower secondary enrolment. Unsurprisingly more fragile states appear to be much less successful at providing health and education services to their populations.

Perhaps surprisingly, however, McKay and Thorbecke (2019) do not find inequality to be significantly correlated with fragility. This probably reflects the fact that several of the countries with lower levels of fragility also are highly unequal countries, such as Botswana and South Africa.

It is clear from this analysis that fragility is an essential factor underlying poor performance in both growth and social outcomes, and it is an extremely important dimension of the quality of growth to be considered.

CONCLUSION

This chapter has examined the quality of growth in SSA over the twenty-five years from 1990 to 2015. Although there has been an impressive growth recovery from the mid-1990s until recently, growth may now be slowing down to some extent; and SSA's overall growth performance does not compare favorably with, in particular, the Asian experience. It is also quite clear that there has been a high diversity of growth experience within SSA, both across countries and over time in many countries. Fragility appears to be an important factor associated with growth volatility and sometimes with slower growth performance, but two-way causality certainly is at work. Without doubt, addressing this is an important policy priority in many countries where high levels of fragility are present, and it is important to note that many good growth performers in SSA also display relatively high levels of fragility, which raises a sustainability concern.

In countries where growth performance has been weak, there has also been limited progress in income poverty reduction. This again supports the view that growth is potentially important for poverty reduction. If there is not much growth, then there is not much to talk about in relation to quality of growth. But the analysis also shows that, in many cases, growth led to limited poverty reduction. Growth and poverty reduction do not have an automatic association. In countries that achieved growth but had limited poverty reduction, this may reflect the pattern of growth. In general, countries in which the agricultural sector made an important contribution to growth also achieved better poverty reduction, and conversely. Of course, where growth has been associated with increasing inequality, poverty reduction has been limited; and poverty reduction also will be more limited in countries that had higher inequality to start.

In other cases, good growth performance was associated with a good record on poverty reduction, at least for the periods of time that were considered. A broad-based pattern of growth appears to be an important common factor.

Many nonincome dimensions of poverty improved significantly in most countries over the period considered in this study. So, for instance, many multidimensional poverty indices showed impressive progress in these domains. The association with growth is likely to be less important, but the extent and effectiveness of public spending is an important factor here; so, in some areas, are improvements in health practices or technology.

Fragility is again seen to be an important correlate of better social outcomes; although progress has been made in many fragile countries, the rate of progress is much slower than has been achieved in less fragile environments. Again tackling fragility seems to be a key factor in addressing not just the quality of growth but also the quality of outcomes of public spending.

REFERENCES

Alkire, Sabina, and Bouba Housseini. 2017. "Multidimensional Poverty in Sub-Saharan Africa: Levels and Trends." Chap. 5 in *Poverty Reduction in the Course of African Development*, ed. M. Nissanke and M. Ndulo. Oxford: Oxford University Press.

Arndt, Channing, Andy McKay, and Finn Tarp. 2016. *Growth and Poverty in Sub-Saharan Africa*. WIDER Studies in Development Economics. Oxford: Oxford University Press.

Besley, Tim, and Louise J. Cord, eds. 2007. *Delivering on the Promise of Pro-Poor Growth: Insights and Lessons from Country Experiences*. Washington, DC: World Bank and Palgrave Macmillan.

Dollar, David, and Aart Kraay. 2002. "Growth Is Good for the Poor." *Journal of Economic Growth* 7 (3): 195–225.

Dollar, David, Tatjana Kleineberg, and Aaart Kraay. 2016. "Growth Is Still Good for the Poor." *European Economic Review* 81: 68–85.

Foster, James E., and Miguel Székely. 2008. "Is Economic Growth Good for the Poor? Tracking Low Incomes Using General Means." *International Economic Review* 49 (4): 1143–1172.

Grimm, Michael, Stephan Klasen, and Andrew McKay. 2007. *Determinants of Pro Poor Growth: Analytical Issues and Findings from Country Cases*. New York: Palgrave Macmillan.

Jerven, Morten. 2010. "Random Growth in Africa? Lessons from an Evaluation of the Growth Evidence on Botswana, Kenya, Tanzania and Zambia, 1965–1995." *Journal of Development Studies* 46 (2): 274–294.

———. 2013. *Poor Numbers: How We Are Misled by African Development Statistics and What to Do About It*. Ithaca, NY: Cornell University Press

Lopez, Ramon E., Vinod Thomas, and Yan Wang. 2010. "The Effect of Fiscal Policies on the Quality of Growth." Evaluation Brief No. 9. Independent Evaluation Group, World Bank, Washington, DC.

McKay, Andy, and Erik Thorbecke. 2019. "The Anatomy of Fragile States in Sub-Saharan Africa: Understanding the Inter-Relationship Between Fragility and Deprivation." *Review of Development Economics*. https://doi.org/10.1111/rode.12578.

Mlachila, Montfort, Rene Tapsoba, and Sampawende Tapsoba. 2016. "A Quality of Growth Index for Developing Countries: A Proposal." *Social Indicators Research* 134 (2): 675–710.

Radelet, Steven. 2010. *Emerging Africa: How 17 Countries Are Leading the Way.* Washington, DC: Center For Global Development.

Thomas, Vinod, Mansoor Dailimi, Ashok Dhareshwar, Daniel Kaufmann, Nalin Kishor, Ramon Lopez, and Yan. Wang. 2000. *The Quality of Growth.* Washington, DC: World Bank. http://documents.worldbank.org/curated /en/756531468780293668/The-quality-of-growth.

World Bank. 2016. *World Development Indicators.* Washington, DC: World Bank.

CHAPTER 3

The Quality of Jobs and Growth in Sub-Saharan Africa

Moazam Mahmood

This chapter looks at jobs, growth, and poverty reduction in Sub-Saharan Africa (SSA). It argues that weaknesses in growth find their way into weaknesses in jobs in the region. Policy to improve jobs and poverty outcomes cannot be restricted solely to the labor market and must be based on a general equilibrium analysis of both jobs and growth. So, although growth is dealt with extensively in other parts of this volume, this chapter recaps and draws out the linkages between patterns of gross domestic product (GDP) growth and patterns of job growth.

The SSA region includes thirty-two of the world's forty-seven least developed countries (LDCs), whose per capita income falls just below $1,000. This low per capita income reflects their development and structural challenges, as outlined by a number of global initiatives, preeminent among them the United Nations Istanbul Program of Action and goals established in 2011 (International Labour Organization [ILO] 2011b). SSA also counts a number of higher-income countries—including ten low- and middle-income countries (LMICs), with a per capita income between $1,000 and $4,000 per capita, and six emerging economies (EEs), with a per capita income between $4,000 and $12,000—and therefore should not be defined only by the structural parameters and opportunities of LDCs. This chapter finds that SSA is tightly constrained in the quality of its growth, employment, and poverty outcomes.

WEAKNESSES IN THE QUANTUM AND QUALITY OF GROWTH

An examination of the trajectory of GDP growth for SSA over the past decade and a half, from 2000 to 2016, reveals a weakness in the quantum of growth. Compared with other regions, growth in SSA has been at the

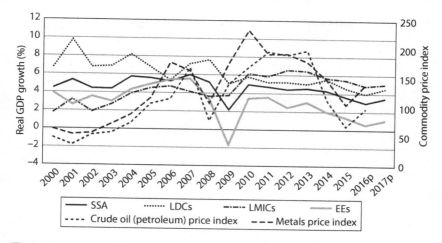

Figure 3.1   Real GDP growth and commodity prices in Sub-Saharan Africa

Note: p = projected estimates; SSA = Sub-Saharan Africa; LDC = least developed countries; LMIC = low- and middle-income countries; EE = emerging economies.

Source: Author's estimates, based on data from the International Monetary Fund (2017).

lower end of the global range, and it has been volatile and subject to fluctuations, as figure 3.1 shows.

Underlying the weakness in the quantum of growth has been a weakness in the quality of growth and in its nature. Table 3.1 shows that a major weakness in the nature of growth in SSA has been its great reliance

Table 3.1   Macroeconomic Determinants of Growth as a Percentage of GDP

	Consumption			Investment			Government Expenditure		
	2000	2007	2015	2000	2007	2015	2000	2007	2015
SSA	61.7	68.0	69.8	14.9	17.2	20.1	15.9	14.1	14.3
LDCs	64.3	60.9	70.8	19.2	20.5	23.2	20.2	14.0	15.1
LMICs	60.5	77.5	76.5	10.7	11.6	17.1	10.7	10.7	9.2
EEs	61.5	61.6	59.5	16.8	21.4	21.5	18.7	18.0	20.8

	Exports			Imports		
	2000	2007	2015	2000	2007	2015
SSA	37.4	35.8	24.0	29.9	35.1	28.2
LDCs	42.4	48.0	28.5	46.1	43.4	37.6
LMICs	44.9	32.5	15.8	26.8	32.3	18.6
EEs	28.3	32.4	31.9	25.3	33.4	33.7

Source: Author's estimates based on data from the International Monetary Fund (2017).

Note: GDP = gross domestic product; SSA = Sub-Saharan Africa; LDC = least developed countries; LMIC = low- and middle-income countries; EE = emerging economies.

Table 3.2   Annual Growth Rate, by Sector, Period Average (%)

	Agriculture, Value		Industry, Value Added		Manufacturing, Value		Services, Value Added	
	2001–07	2008–15	2001–07	2008–15	2001–07	2008–15	2001–07	2008–15
SSA	8.2	4.6	5.1	2.9	5.1	4.3	7.5	5.9
LDCs	5.5	3.8	11.3	5.0	5.7	4.7	9.5	7.4
LMICs	11.1	5.2	5.0	4.2	6.9	9.4	11.3	8.6
EEs	0.6	2.5	3.3	0.4	3.9	0.4	4.7	2.8

Source: Author's estimates based on data from the International Monetary Fund (2017).

Note: SSA = Sub-Saharan Africa; LDC = least developed countries; LMIC = low- and middle-income countries; EE = emerging economies.

on exogenously determined drivers of growth, such as exports, rather than on domestically determined drivers of growth, such as investment.

Furthermore, growth in SSA has been based not on an expansion of manufacturing but rather on extractives. Disaggregating SSAs' reliance on extractives into income groups (LDCs, LMICs, and EEs), table 3.2 shows that LDC growth was led by extractives rather than by manufacturing. In LMICs and EEs, growth was led more or equally by manufacturing. As a result of this growth trajectory based on services and extractives, SSA, led by LDCs, has deindustrialized in the past decade and a half.

Table 3.3 shows that for SSA the share of the manufacturing sector in GDP declined from an already low 11 percent to 9.5 percent between 2000 and 2015.

Disaggregating the region into the three income groups, the deindustrialization has been led by LDCs, which already had a low share of GDP in manufacturing (9 percent) in 2000. By 2015, it had dropped by 2 percentage points to 7 percent. LMICs kept their share of manufacturing constant at about 9 percent of GDP over this period. EEs had the highest share of GDP in manufacturing in 2000 (just over 13 percent), but by 2015, this share had reduced by 1 percentage point to 12 percent.

Deindustrialization and growth led by commodities and extractives explain the high volatility in growth in SSA, as GDP growth in SSA effectively follows commodity prices (figure 3.1). The vulnerabilities in the quantum and quality of growth in SSA over the past decade and a half have had a strong impact on its labor market, jobs, incomes, and welfare, as will be discussed in the following sections.

Table 3.3   Value-Added Sectoral Share of GDP

		2000	2007	2015
SSA	Agriculture	14.4	15.9	15.7
	Industry	29.8	26.9	23.2
	Manufacturing	10.9	9.8	9.5
	Services	44.9	47.4	51.6
LDCs	Agriculture	33.4	27.7	24.1
	Industry	20.9	25.2	24.0
	Manufacturing	9.3	7.9	7.3
	Services	36.4	39.2	44.7
LMICs	Agriculture	20.9	23.9	21.2
	Industry	34.2	26.4	21.6
	Manufacturing	8.4	7.4	8.9
	Services	36.5	42.3	48.4
EEs	Agriculture	2.8	2.2	2.3
	Industry	29.7	28.2	25.3
	Manufacturing	13.4	13.2	11.7
	Services	54.1	56.3	60.7

Source: Author's estimates based on data from the International Monetary Fund (2017).

Note: GDP = gross domestic product; SSA = Sub-Saharan Africa; LDC = least developed countries; LMIC = low- and middle-income countries; EE = emerging economies.

THE LABOR MARKET IN SSA

Labor market outcomes in SSA, observed over the past decade and a half, have to reflect the growth path followed, in terms of the quantum of GDP growth achieved as well as the nature of that growth. This chapter finds that they do. Before elaborating, we will address a methodological caveat in the choice of metric used to evaluate labor market outcomes.

Conventional labor market metrics are arguably better suited for advanced economies (AEs) with more registered workers and lower levels of informality. In developing countries (DCs), as in most of SSA, the lack of social protection, especially for the poor, compels people to work under any conditions and leads to the phenomenon of the working poor. As a result, the metrics of employment growth and unemployment levels are moot, which disqualifies them as the best indicators of labor market outcomes. For labor markets in developing countries, job quality has proved to be a better indicator of success and distress.

Newer metrics adopted to better discern labor market outcomes more accurately reflect weaknesses in the SSA growth path, in terms of the quantum and the quality and nature of growth. Weaknesses in the quantum of growth, in GDP growth, and in the high volatility of this growth undermine the rate of improvement in job quality. The fact that growth is driven mainly by exogenously determined exports—a major weakness in the quantum of growth—subjects both growth and jobs to more volatility and to fluctuations in the rate of job quality improvements. Similarly, the fact that growth is led by the services sector, which is perceived to be lagging technologically—another significant weakness in the quantum of growth—has been shown to dampen labor productivity levels and their growth over time, and therefore per capita incomes. Deindustrialization has weakened progress and the ability to catch up in terms of productivity and incomes. It also accounts for slower progress in generating better forms of employment, such as wage jobs, to replace more vulnerable forms of employment, such as unpaid family labor, which burden women in particular. These labor market outcomes have strong implications for welfare and poverty reduction, as discussed in the following sections.

EMPLOYMENT AND UNEMPLOYMENT

Employment, unemployment, and the real wage are the conventional indicators of labor market outcomes. The ILO benchmarks these labor market metrics globally for 180 or so countries on a quarterly basis, using a partial equilibrium econometric model, based precisely on Okun's law correlating employment to output.

The ILO has recognized that the metrics of employment and unemployment are apt indicators of the labor market for AEs, whose labor force is largely registered and entitled to social security. For DCs with large parts of their labor force unregistered and not covered by any effective social security, however, these metrics of employment and unemployment are not relevant indicators of labor market outcomes. Given the lack of any significant coverage by social security floors, the poor cannot afford to be unemployed (Mahmood 2018).[1] They are simply too poor to not work. Being compelled to work forces the poor to accept or undertake any work, no matter how unfavorable the working conditions in terms of productivity, remuneration, working hours, hazards, occupational safety, and health as well as weak rights.

Effectively, if the poor cannot find decent work in the formal economy, they will accept or undertake work in the informal unregistered economy,[2] even if it involves a large decent work deficit. This gives rise to the phenomenon of the working poor.

The working poverty phenomenon and its significance have two major implications for the employment and unemployment metrics. One, in countries with large shares of the labor force working in the unregistered informal economy, a significant proportion of the working poor implies that employment growth will approximate labor force growth. The behavioral logic, which suggests that the poor are compelled to work under any conditions, implies that most of the labor force works. Any surplus labor, those who are unable to find formal jobs in the registered economy, will be compelled to find jobs or self-employment in the informal economy. Hence, employment growth will approximate labor force growth.

The working poverty phenomenon then equates employment growth with labor force growth, which is supply-led by demographics. Employment growth is no longer determined by demand for output and employment, and therefore, it is not a good indicator to gauge success or distress in the labor market.

Two, in countries with large proportions of the labor force working in the informal economy, a significant share of the working poor implies that the unemployment rate will not be a good indicator of demand in the labor market. According to the logic of the working poverty phenomenon, the fact that the poorest are compelled to accept work in less than decent conditions depresses and disguises unemployment. Lack of social protection means the poor cannot be unemployed, and they are compelled to accept any work.

When the working poverty phenomenon accounts for a significant proportion of the employed in a country, it implies that both the employment growth rate and the unemployment rate are not the best indicators of demand in the labor market. Therefore, they are not good outcome metrics of success or distress.

In SSA, too, the metrics of the employment growth rate and the unemployment rate are not the best indicators of labor market outcomes. The unemployment rate is a better indicator for higher-income countries with a less significant proportion of the working poor employed in the informal economy.

Table 3.4 and Figure 3.2 show that employment growth in SSA between 2000 and 2015 ranged from 3.1 percent to 3.2 percent and largely approximated labor force growth.

Figure 3.2 illustrates this approximation between employment growth and labor force growth quite well. For SSA as whole and for each of its income groups, the employment growth curve tracks the labor force

Table 3.4 Labor Force Growth and Employment Growth

Labor Force Growth (%)	2000	2001	2002	2003	2004	2005	2006	2007	2008	2009	2010	2011	2012	2013	2014	2015
SSA	3.1	2.8	2.8	2.6	2.6	3.1	2.9	2.9	3.2	2.9	2.9	2.9	2.9	3.2	3.1	3.2
LDCs	3.3	3.1	3.2	3.2	3.2	3.3	3.1	3.1	3.2	3.3	3.3	3	2.9	3.2	3.3	3.4
LMICs	3.0	2.4	2.3	2.3	2.2	2.4	2.5	3.0	3.0	3.0	3.0	2.9	3.0	3.0	2.9	3.0
EEs	2.3	2.1	1.7	-0.5	-1.2	4.3	3.2	0.4	3.4	-1.4	-0.9	1.4	2.4	3.4	2.1	2.1
Asia Pacific	1.6	1.7	1.5	1.7	1.6	1.6	0.8	0.8	0.7	0.7	0.6	1.0	0.9	1.1	1.0	1.1

Employment Growth (%)	2000	2001	2002	2003	2004	2005	2006	2007	2008	2009	2010	2011	2012	2013	2014	2015p
SSA	3.4	2.3	3.0	3.0	3.0	3.0	3.0	2.9	3.3	2.9	2.9	3.0	2.8	3.3	3.4	3.0
LDCs	4.0	2.3	3.6	3.5	3.3	3.2	2.9	3.4	3.3	3.3	3.2	3.0	3.0	3.4	3.2	3.3
LMICs	2.9	2.2	2.3	2.7	2.8	2.4	2.9	2.2	3.5	3.0	3.2	3.1	2.4	3.1	4.1	2.5
EEs	0.9	2.9	0.1	-0.5	1.6	5.3	5.0	0.7	2.4	-2.2	-1.8	1.4	2.2	3.5	1.8	1.8
Asia Pacific	1.7	1.7	1.4	1.7	1.6	1.5	1.0	1.2	0.4	0.6	0.9	1.1	0.9	1.1	1.1	1.1

Source: Author's estimates based on data from the World Bank (2016) and the ILO Trends Unit (2016).

Note: p = projected estimates; SSA = Sub-Saharan Africa; LDC = least developed countries; LMIC = low- and middle-income countries; EE = emerging economies.

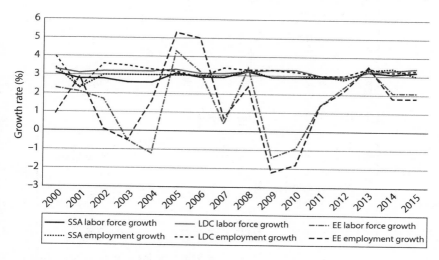

Figure 3.2   Labor force growth and employment growth

Note: SSA = Sub-Saharan Africa; LDC = least developed countries; EE = emerging economies.
Source: Author's estimates based on data from the World Bank (2016) and International Labour Organization Trends Unit (2016).

growth curve. Because labor force growth is determined by demographics, so, too, is employment growth. In SSA, employment growth is largely determined by labor supply, rather than by labor demand, and therefore, it is not the best metric to gauge labor market outcomes.

Table 3.5 shows that the unemployment rate is a better gauge for SSA than employment growth, but it often is an ambiguous indicator of success or distress in the labor market. The table gives the unemployment rate for SSA as a whole, and for its income groups for the period from 2000 to 2017.

For the pre-financial crisis boom period in SSA, when GDP growth peaked, the unemployment rate should have declined. Table 3.5 shows that the aggregate unemployment rate for SSA dropped from 8.2 percent of the labor force in 2000 to 7.6 percent of the labor force by 2008. The sharp impact of the crisis on GDP growth in SSA, and the subsequent lower growth during the recession, also should be reflected in increases in the unemployment rate. The decline in GDP growth, however, did not register in the unemployment rate in 2009 or onward, with the unemployment rate in fact inching down. The youth unemployment rate did show a slight uptick from 11.5 percent in 2008 to 11.8 percent by 2010, after which it fell again.

Table 3.5 Overall, Youth, and Adult Unemployment Rates

Overall (%)

	2000	2001	2002	2003	2004	2005	2006	2007	2008	2009	2010	2011	2012	2013	2014	2015p	2016p	2017p
SSA	8.2	8.7	8.5	8.2	7.8	7.8	7.8	7.7	7.6	7.6	7.6	7.5	7.6	7.5	7.2	7.4	7.5	7.5
LDCs	6.1	6.8	6.4	6.2	6.1	6.2	6.4	6.1	6.0	6.0	6.1	6.1	6.0	5.8	5.9	6.0	6.0	6.0
LMICs	8.1	8.2	8.3	7.9	7.5	7.5	7.1	7.8	7.4	7.4	7.2	7.1	7.6	7.5	6.4	6.9	7.1	7.2
EEs	25.4	24.9	26.1	26.1	24	23.2	21.9	21.6	22.5	23.1	23.7	23.7	23.9	23.9	24.1	24.3	24.6	24.7
Asia Pacific	4.7	4.7	4.9	4.8	4.8	4.8	4.6	4.2	4.5	4.6	4.4	4.3	4.4	4.4	4.4	4.4	4.3	4.3

Youth (%)

	2000	2001	2002	2003	2004	2005	2006	2007	2008	2009	2010	2011	2012	2013	2014	2015p	2016p	2017p
SSA	12.2	13.2	12.9	12.4	11.7	11.9	11.8	11.6	11.5	11.7	11.8	11.4	11.5	11.3	10.9	11.1	11.2	11.2
LDCs	9.7	10.7	9.9	9.4	9.3	9.3	9.9	9.3	9.2	9.3	9.7	9.5	9.4	9.0	9.2	9.3	9.4	9.4
LMICs	13.2	13.6	14.0	13.0	11.8	12.6	11.4	12.3	12.1	12.8	12.0	11.3	12.3	12.2	10.6	11.3	11.6	11.7
EEs	42.3	47.9	50.0	52.2	48.6	46.1	44.1	43.1	43.7	45.7	47.8	47.2	48.6	48.6	48.2	47.3	46.9	46.3
Asia Pacific	11.0	10.8	11.3	11.2	11.1	11.3	11.1	10.0	10.8	11.0	10.8	11.0	11.1	11.7	11.5	11.5	11.6	11.6

Adult (%)

	2000	2001	2002	2003	2004	2005	2006	2007	2008	2009	2010	2011	2012	2013	2014	2015p	2016p	2017p
SSA	6.7	6.9	6.7	6.5	6.2	6.2	6.1	6.2	6.0	5.9	6.0	6.0	6.1	6.0	5.8	6.0	6.1	6.1
LDCs	4.6	5.1	4.8	4.6	4.6	4.7	4.8	4.6	4.5	4.5	4.5	4.5	4.4	4.3	4.4	4.5	4.5	4.5
LMICs	6.4	6.5	6.4	6.2	6.0	5.8	5.7	6.3	5.8	5.6	5.7	5.7	6.1	6.1	5.2	5.5	5.7	5.8
EEs	22.0	20.2	21.1	20.7	19.0	18.5	17.2	17.1	17.9	18.5	19.1	19.5	19.6	19.7	20.1	20.5	21	21.3
Asia Pacific	3.1	3.1	3.2	3.2	3.2	3.2	3.1	2.8	3.1	3.2	3.0	3.0	3.0	3.0	3.0	3.1	3.1	3.1

Source: Author's estimates based on data from the World Bank (2016) and ILO Trends Unit (2016).

Note: p = projected estimates; SSA = Sub-Saharan Africa; LDC = least developed countries; LMIC = low- and middle-income countries; EE = emerging economies.

The argument that working poverty vitiates the metrics of employment growth and the unemployment rate is based on the significance of the proportion of people in the unregistered economy. This share can be expected to drop as per capita incomes rise, reintroducing the efficacy of employment growth and the unemployment rate as metrics. This effect also holds for the disaggregated unemployment rates for LDCs, LMICs, and EEs in SSA.

Table 3.5 shows that the unemployment rates of LDCs in SSA are the most sluggish in response to GDP booms and busts; the LMIC unemployment rates fare a bit better, and the EE unemployment rates are quite responsive. LDC unemployment, before the crisis, during the crisis, and in the ensuing recession, remained on trend at about 6 percent of the labor force. LMIC unemployment rates come down in the precrisis boom, from 8.1 percent to 7.4 percent of the labor force, but then it kept dropping despite the crisis and the recession. EE unemployment rates, however, dropped significantly in the precrisis boom, from 25.4 percent to 21.6 percent of the labor force. With the crisis and the recession that followed, unemployment rates rose to 24.3 percent by 2015, and they were projected to approach 25 percent by 2017. The very high unemployment rate for EEs is driven by the very high unemployment rate in South Africa, which trends at around a quarter of its labor force.

The youth unemployment rate for EEs is similarly responsive to the precrisis GDP boom and subsequent bust. The youth unemployment rate in EEs fell from about 50 percent to 43 percent of the youth labor force in the precrisis boom, and it increased with the crisis and the recession to 49 percent by 2014. Similarly, the adult unemployment rate in EEs followed a declining trend in the precrisis boom, from 22 percent to 17 percent of the adult labor force, and then it rose again in the ensuing bust period to reach 20 percent by 2014.

Ergo, the two quantum indicators of labor market outcomes perform with varying degrees of success in SSA. Employment growth approximates labor force growth, which is given demographically. Employment growth is driven more by labor supply, and therefore, it is not the best indicator of labor demand.

At the aggregate level of all of SSA, the unemployment rate also is sluggish in response to GDP growth. The unemployment rate responds to long-run booms quite well, decreasing slowly, but it is not as good at registering the impact of a crisis. Disaggregated unemployment rates register both booms and busts more accurately. The youth unemployment rate is a more responsive metric to GDP growth. In higher-income groups, LMICs and especially EEs, unemployment rates also are more responsive to GDP growth. As the significance of the unregistered and unprotected working poor employed in the informal economy declines with increases in country incomes, the unemployment rate becomes a better metric.

If the quantum indicators of employment growth and the unemployment rate are not good metrics to gauge labor market outcomes for low-income countries, better metrics are needed for LDCs, which make up two-thirds of SSA. Better labor market indicators shift from measuring job quantity to measuring job quality.

METRICS FOR JOB QUALITY

The selection of qualitative metrics of unemployment, as better indicators of labor market outcomes, emerges from the logic that impairs quantitative metrics in the first place. A better labor market metric should be more responsive to GDP growth than the more sluggish quantitative indicators seen above. Okun's law should hold, with demand for output implying demand for employment. Yet SSA data for the past 15 years of booms and busts show that in LDCs, and to some extent in LMICs, unemployment rates responded sluggishly, if at all.

Consider the problem posed in figure 3.3. The labor demand curve, DL1, normally slopes downward. A formal economy's effective real wage of w1 demands N1 employment in the formal economy. Assume that this real wage includes the money wage, plus the monetized costs of using registered labor, which include social protection and all other compliance costs entailed by national laws and workers' rights (e.g., dismissal costs, occupational safety and health, other working conditions, and other transaction costs). Hence, it becomes the effective real wage paid in the formal economy.

Labor demand in the formal economy of N1 has to be met by a labor supply of N1. Assume, however, that the labor force is much larger, say Nf. Then the labor supply at w1 will be perfectly elastic. That is, at w1, a lot more labor can be supplied than is demanded. This gives a flat, perfectly elastic supply curve for labor SL1, which results in a formal economy wage of w1, employing N1 labor and producing the formal economy demand curve for labor, DL1. Okun's law then applies this rule to the formal economy, with the demand for output reflected in the demand for labor of N1. This demand should result in an unemployment rate of N1Nf, and this unemployment rate would be a good metric for labor market outcomes.

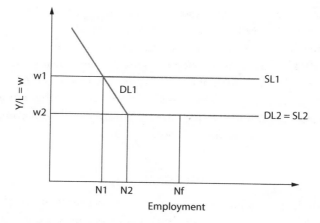

Figure 3.3   A non linearity in the demand for labor across formal and informal labor markets

Source: Author's estimates for this study.

What impairs Okun's law is the existence of surplus labor N1Nf, which has not found formal employment, enjoys no social protection, and is too poor to be unemployed. In this case, this surplus labor is willing to accept a cut in the effective real wage w1 and to offer its services in the unregistered, informal economy, at w2—with w2 being significantly lower than w1 because it is a lower money wage and entails none of the monetized costs of using registered labor, including social protection, rights, occupational safety and health, other working conditions, and other transaction costs. At w2 then, Say's law (supply creates its own demand) would appear to operate, with the supply of surplus labor N1Nf creating its own demand. The demand curve for labor becomes flat and perfectly elastic, DL2. At w2, all of the surplus labor N1Nf obtains employment. These are the working poor. They impair Okun's law because they reduce the unemployment rate to Nf, and Nf is sluggish in good times and bad, because the working poor need to work in all circumstances.

Therefore, Okun's law is vitiated in low-income countries with large informal economies because of a kink or non linearity in the labor demand curve. The formal economy has a normal downward sloping segment, whereas the unregistered informal economy has a perfectly elastic flat segment, which works at a significantly lower effective real wage.

This non linearity in the labor demand curve makes the unemployment rate a more applicable metric to countries with a smaller share of the informal sector. What, then, are the metrics for the informal economy, N1Nf? The answer is revealed in figure 3.3, as shown in the effective real wage w2. In the informal economy, we need to observe the cut not only in the money wage offered but also in the lack of other employment costs. Because the number of jobs, being supply-led, do not count as significantly, job quality becomes the key metric.

INDICATORS OF JOB QUALITY

The first indicator of job quality has to be an estimate of N1Nf, the size of the working poor population. In fact, this becomes a complement to the employment rate N1, which applies to the formal economy. If we assume full employment of the labor force, then N1Nf gives the working poor; and the labor force Lf, minus N1Nf, will give N1, as follows:

$$Lf = N1 + N1Nf. \qquad (3.1)$$

The size of the working poor population thus becomes a shortcut method used to estimate the size of the informal economy. This is a convenient proxy, because estimating the informal economy based on the ILO's (2013b) correct methodology requires a head count of employment in both formal and informal enterprises.

Returning to figure 3.3, what separates the formal sector's effective real wage, w1, from the informal sector's effective real wage of w2, is a basic difference between formal and unregistered employment—that is, the ability for workers to earn a wage rather than contribute to family work, which is typically unpaid labor. Furthermore, this form of employment introduces a strong gender bias, with women making up much larger shares of contributing family workers in many countries (ILO 2016). Hence, contributing family workers are considered to be vulnerable, and this form of employment becomes important to estimate.

Another form of vulnerable employment is self-employment, which can cover a broad range of workers, including rich as well as poor workers. In low-income countries, the majority of self-employed workers will include the poor. Self-employed and contributing family workers are both unlikely to have stable incomes and also are less likely to have access to basic worker rights provided under national legislation. Therefore, self-employment becomes another important form of employment to estimate.

Waged employment has several advantages compared with vulnerable forms of labor. A waged income will tend to be more stable, secure, and accessible than a family enterprise income at the lower end of the income scale. Waged employment will always have some rights attached to it, by definition, which improves access to national legislation for workers compared with contributing family work or self-employment. Waged work also has higher productivity and therefore higher remuneration compared with contributing family work and self-employment. These key metrics of job quality estimate a reduction in the size of N1Nf and an improvement in w2 going toward w1. They are proxy indicators for Okun's law and show movement toward Okun.

JOB QUALITY IN SSA

The working poor are defined as those workers whose per capita incomes fall below the internationally agreed poverty line, now established by the World Bank at $1.90 for extreme poverty (see ILO 2016). Their inability to meet a required dietary allowance (RDA) of 2,250 calories per day for themselves, let alone for their dependents, compels them to work at any effective real wage offered or self-employed remuneration possible.

Table 3.6 shows that in 2000, 54 percent of SSA's labor force fell into the category of the working poor, compared with just over a third for the Asia-Pacific region. Over time, GDP growth reduced the share of the working poor in SSA's labor force, pushing it down by 18 percentage points to 36 percent by 2015. In comparison, the Asia-Pacific region reduced its share of working poverty in the labor force by 28 percentage points, bringing it down to just under 10 percent from 2000 to 2015.

One-third of the labor force in SSA appears compelled to work for less than formal economy real wages, even in the absence of effective social protection and access to national legislation on workers' rights, which result in poor working conditions. At about 1.1 percent per year over the past decade and a half, the rate of reduction of working poverty has been much lower than the rate of GDP growth, which has been 4 percent and higher for SSA. In comparison, in the Asia-Pacific region, the working poor's share of the labor force has declined at a rate of nearly 2 percent per year.

Decomposing the working poor by income groups, by 2015, they made up 41 percent of the labor force in LDCs, 32 percent in LMICs, and just 6 percent in EEs. A reduction in the share of the working poor

Table 3.6 Percentage of the Working Poor (at US$1.90 PPP Poverty Line)

	2000	2001	2002	2003	2004	2005	2006	2007	2008	2009	2010	2011	2012	2013	2014	2015p
SSA	54.3	54.3	53.1	52.1	49.2	47.6	46.6	45.4	44.4	43.9	42.5	41.2	39.9	38.7	37.3	36.3
LDCs	63.9	63.0	62.3	61.0	58.7	56.2	55.1	53.4	52.1	51.6	49.9	47.6	45.6	44.1	42.4	41.1
LMICs	42.9	42.0	42.3	41.3	37.0	37.0	36.5	36.2	35.8	35.0	33.8	34.0	34.0	33.1	32.2	31.6
EEs	17.5	17.0	16.1	15.1	13.8	12.5	11.4	9.0	7.5	7.0	6.8	6.5	6.2	5.8	5.7	5.5
Asia Pacific	38.2	36.6	34.6	31.2	28.1	25.1	23.9	21.9	21.1	19.3	17.6	14.6	12.6	11.4	10.4	9.6

Source: Author's estimates based on data from the World Bank (2016) and ILO Trends Unit (2016)

Note: PPP = purchasing power parity; p = projected estimates; SSA = Sub-Saharan Africa; LDC = least developed countries; LMIC = low- and middle-income countries; EE = emerging economies.

population over time did not show any deceleration because of the crisis and ensuing recession. This category appears to be too broad for the impact to have affected the labor market. Then, specific forms of employment emerge as the category most sensitive to GDP change. Among these forms of employment, the vulnerable employment category, including contributing family workers, self-employed, and own-account workers, is the largest. The reciprocal to these vulnerable forms of employment is wage employment.

Table 3.7 shows that vulnerable employment accounted for 73 percent of the labor force in SSA in 2000. By 2015, this share had only dropped by 3 percentage points. Although GDP growth helped reduce the vulnerable in the labor force, vulnerable employment did not decline unequivocally over time, experiencing small reversals in some years. From 2000 to 2003, the share of vulnerable workers increased slightly, coinciding with a 1 percentage point drop in GDP growth in SSA. Subsequently, GDP growth picked up, as did the reduction of vulnerable workers as a share of the labor force. The crisis then lowered GDP growth in 2009, and the share of the vulnerable in the labor force increased slightly. In subsequent years, GDP growth picked up, and again the share of vulnerable employment in the labor force dropped. Finally, in 2014–2015, GDP growth fell with the end of the commodities supercycle of high prices, and the share of vulnerable workers in the labor force stopped declining.

Vulnerability therefore proves a surprisingly good metric of labor market outcomes linked to GDP changes. Both categories of vulnerable employment—contributing family workers and the self-employed—reflect reversals in their declining trends, with women more affected by these reversals than men.

Table 3.8 decomposes total employment into its major forms. Between 2000 and 2007, the overall reduction in vulnerable employment involved a drop in the share of self-employed workers but a 0.5 percentage point increase in the share of contributing family workers. Projections for 2017 by the ILO showed that the shares of both contributing family workers and self-employment dropped.

Within vulnerability, the contributing family workers category appears to be quite sensitive to labor market outcomes. It does not display an inexorable reduction over time and also has shown reversals. A key reason for the sensitivity of this category may be its strong gender bias.

Table 3.7 Percentage of Vulnerable Employment, Total

	2000	2001	2002	2003	2004	2005	2006	2007	2008	2009	2010	2011	2012	2013	2014	2015p
SSA	73.3	73.5	73.6	73.4	72.3	72.4	72.0	72.2	71.7	72.0	71.6	71.2	70.9	70.9	69.8	69.8
LDCs	83.5	83.5	83.0	82.6	81.7	82.1	81.8	81.8	81.2	81.4	81.0	80.5	80.1	80.3	79.3	79.2
LMICs	64.4	65.3	65.9	65.5	64.1	63.9	63.6	63.6	63.9	63.7	62.7	62.3	61.9	61.6	60.1	60.2
EEs	18.2	18.0	18.0	18.0	14.9	14.5	14.4	15.6	11.1	11.9	12.0	11.9	11.8	11.2	11.2	11.2
Asia Pacific	65.6	65.3	64.8	64.7	63.9	63.5	63.1	62.2	60.3	59.5	59.1	58.0	56.9	56.4	55.7	55.4

Source: Author's estimates based on data from the World Bank (2016) and ILO Trends Unit (2016).

Note: p = projected estimates; SSA = Sub-Saharan Africa; LDC = least developed countries; LMIC = low- and middle-income countries; EE = emerging economies.

Table 3.8 Percentage Share of Status in Employment

	2000				2007				2017p			
	Wage and Salaried Workers	Employers	Own-Account Workers	Contributing Family Workers	Wage and Salaried Workers	Employers	Own-Account Workers	Contributing Family Workers	Wage and Salaried Workers	Employers	Own-Account Workers	Contributing Family Workers
SSA	25.1	1.5	47.1	26.3	26.2	1.6	45.3	26.9	29.9	2.0	44.7	23.4
LDCs	15.3	1.2	52.6	30.9	16.8	1.3	49.1	32.7	17.2	1.5	50.6	30.7
LMICs	33.6	1.9	42.2	22.3	34.4	2.1	43.5	20.1	43.6	2.4	40.0	14.0
EEs	79.2	2.6	17.1	1.2	81.9	2.5	14.7	0.9	84.4	4.8	9.7	1.1
Asia Pacific	32.3	2.2	40.4	25.2	36.2	1.6	43.1	19.1	48.5	1.7	39.9	9.9

	Change 2000–2007				Change 2007–2017p			
	Wage and Salaried Workers	Employers	Own-Account Workers	Contributing Family Workers	Wage and Salaried Workers	Employers	Own-Account Workers	Contributing Family Workers
SSA	1.0	0.1	-1.8	0.6	3.8	0.3	-0.6	-3.5
LDCs	1.5	0.1	-3.5	1.8	0.4	0.1	1.5	-2.0
LMICs	0.7	0.1	1.3	-2.2	9.3	0.3	-3.5	-6.1
EEs	2.7	-0.1	-2.3		2.5	2.3	-5.0	0.2
Asia Pacific	3.9	-0.5	2.7	-6.1	12.3	0.1	-3.2	-9.2

Source: Author's estimates based on data from the World Bank (2016) and ILO Trends Unit (2016).

Note: p = projected estimates; SSA = Sub-Saharan Africa; LDC = least developed countries; LMIC = low- and middle-income countries; EE = emerging economies.

Table 3.9 decomposes the major forms of employment in SSA by gender. In 2015, 17 percent of the male labor force and 35 percent of the female labor force were contributing family workers. Overall, some 77 percent of the female labor force was in vulnerable employment, compared with 66 percent for males.

Table 3.9 also shows a reversal in the decline of the share of contributing family workers between 2000 and 2007, which largely reflected a reversal that affected women rather than men. The increase in the women's share of contributing family workers was double that of the men. Furthermore, during the crisis and ensuing period, between 2007 and 2015, the women's share in the other category of vulnerable employment, own-account work (i.e., self-employment) actually increased by 1.5 percentage points.

The reciprocal of vulnerability is waged employment, which offers better and more stable remuneration and working conditions and rights. As shown in table 3.8, by 2017, just under 30 percent of SSA's labor force was in waged employment. This compares to just under half of the labor force in waged employment in the Asia-Pacific region. Over the past decade and a half, SSA increased its share of waged employment by 5 percentage points, whereas this share went up by 17 percentage points over this period in the Asia-Pacific region.

The metrics of labor market outcomes have to be capped by the productivity levels reached and incomes earned in SSA. Productivity and incomes are key links between the growth path chosen by SSA and its labor market outcomes.

In the Lewis model (1954), and SSA's variant of it, development proceeds with a shrinking value added in agriculture and the transfer of workers to higher productivity industry and services. Services in low-income DCs have a strong refuge element, with surplus labor from agriculture and the formal industry crowding into services and weakening productivity growth.

First, in SSA, in the past decade and a half, growth has been led by services, and SSA's productivity levels and growth were seen to be weak. This also produces weak growth in per capita incomes, with SSA growing at 3 percent per year in the precrisis period, in line with the Asia-Pacific region's growth, but slumping to 1 percent per year in the crisis and ensuing recessionary period, whereas the Asia-Pacific region continued its 3 percent growth trend.

Second, over this period, SSA's growth has been led by sectoral commodities and extractives, rather than by manufacturing, whose share has

Table 3.9 Percentage Share of Status in Employment Segregated by Gender

	2000				2007				2015p			
	Wage and Salaried Workers	Employers	Own-Account Workers	Contributing Family Workers	Wage and Salaried Workers	Employers	Own-Account Workers	Contributing Family Workers	Wage and Salaried Workers	Employers	Own-Account Workers	Contributing Family Workers
Share of status in employment, male												
SSA	29.9	2.1	50.3	17.8	31.2	2.2	48.5	18.1	34.0	2.5	46.5	17.0
LDCs	17.9	1.7	59.6	20.8	19.7	1.9	56.6	21.7	23.1	2.0	54.1	20.8
LMICs	41.6	2.6	40.0	15.8	43.0	2.8	39.7	14.5	46.9	2.7	38.1	12.3
EEs	79.7	2.8	16.8	0.8	83.1	2.3	13.9	0.7	83.1	6.8	9.3	0.8
Asia Pacific	35.1	2.8	48.0	14.1	37.8	2.1	49.2	10.8	43.0	1.7	48.6	6.7
Share of status in employment, female												
SSA	19.4	0.8	43.2	36.6	20.2	0.9	41.6	37.3	21.4	1.2	42.5	34.9
LDCs	12.3	0.6	44.7	42.4	13.6	0.7	40.7	45.1	14.9	0.8	42.1	42.2
LMICs	22.5	1.0	45.2	31.2	23.3	1.1	48.4	27.3	25.3	1.9	48.2	24.5
EEs	78.6	2.3	17.5	1.7	80.3	2.8	15.8	1.2	84.9	2.4	11.1	1.6
Asia Pacific	27.9	1.1	28.5	42.5	33.5	0.8	33.3	32.4	43.9	0.6	36.1	19.4

Source: Author's estimates based on data from the World Bank (2016) and ILO Trends Unit (2016).

Note: p = projected estimates; SSA = Sub-Saharan Africa; LDC = least developed countries; LMIC = low- and middle-income countries; EE = emerging economies.

decreased. This deindustrialization has robbed SSA from the benefits of a sector well acknowledged to promote technological change and enable the domestic economy to catch up through learning by doing. This deindustrialization has weakened outcomes for productivity and per capita income in SSA.

Third, exports of commodities and extractives, rather than investment and consumption, have been major drivers of SSA's growth. Reliance on such exports has made growth more volatile and more exogenously driven. Exports of commodities and extractives, in particular, tend to be capital-intensive, with low employment and weak links to the rest of the domestic economy. Higher value added in domestic manufacturing produces stronger employment outcomes and creates stronger links to the rest of the economy. Better employment outcomes enabled by manufacturing also allow for a greater transformation of the forms of employment to waged employment with higher productivity, higher incomes, and improved working conditions and rights.

SSA's growth path has therefore given weaker labor market outcomes in terms of productivity, incomes, and the lack of transformation from vulnerable forms of employment to waged employment.

POVERTY, JOBS, AND GROWTH: THE PRIMARY POLICY AGENDA FOR SSA

Given the growth path that SSA has taken and its labor market outcomes, it is important to determine the outcome for poverty. This has been examined by estimating the number of working poor. But the working poor population comprises only a part of the total population in poverty, since the working poor population comprises only those workers who are unable to reach the poverty line of $1.90 per day themselves. It does not include their dependents, who, by definition, would fall under the poverty line. Therefore, a broader estimate of the population in poverty in SSA is needed.

The policy agenda for poverty reduction has to be based on identifying the poor and estimating their income gaps. The two kinds of income gaps for the poor include (1) gaps in jobs and incomes for the working poor and the unemployed, and (2) gaps in income for those who cannot work.[3]

The working poor and the unemployed need better jobs and more work, with higher remuneration. The population of poor who cannot work needs transfers. This economic assessment can then lead to a policy debate on the feasibility of filling these gaps.

Poverty in Africa declined from 48 percent of the population in 2005 to 41 percent by 2012 (ILO 2016). Six important characteristics have emerged in the identification of the poor population in SSA.

Table 3.10 decomposes the entire population of SSA into poor and non-poor, based on the extreme poverty threshold at $1.90. Among the population of the poor, some 48 percent, the largest share, were dependents under fifteen years of age. There is a glaring gap with the non-poor population, which had a much lower share (38 percent) of dependents under fifteen years of age. Adding to these young dependents were the elderly, who accounted for 4 percent of the poor population, which was the same as the non-poor population.

Supporting the concept of the poor being compelled to work, table 3.10 shows that the share of unemployed poor was only 1 percent, in significant contrast with the non-poor population, which had nearly 3 percent unemployed.

When we account for the young, the elderly, and those out of work, we are left with the working poor. Because of the high demographic drag, only 30 percent of the poor population was employed compared with 35 percent of the non-poor population.

Among the poor, less than 3 percent had waged employment, revealing a wide gap compared with the non-poor population, 10 percent of which had waged work. The poverty rate among the total population of waged workers was the lowest among all forms of employment at 16 percent, demonstrating that waged work, indeed, offers much higher productivity and remuneration.

The poor relied more heavily on contributing to family work, at nearly 9 percent, whereas the share of non-poor contributing to family work was close to 7 percent. Both the poor and non-poor populations were almost equally reliant on self-employment, at around 17 percent.

Among contributing family workers, the poverty rate was close to 50 percent, the highest among all forms of employment. The poverty rate among the self-employed population was the next highest at 41 percent, confirming observations that these two forms of employment are indeed vulnerable.

Table 3.10 Extreme Poverty in 2012, by Population Group and Labor Status (%)

		Total	Under 15	Total	Wage and Salaried Workers	Employers	Contributing Family Workers	Own-Account Workers	Others	Unemployed	Inactive	Elderly
SSA LDCs	Poor	100	49.76	34.32	2.94	0.65	11.81	18.9	0.01	0.77	11.78	3.37
	Non-poor	100	42.71	37.08	6.39	1.17	10.02	19.44	0.05	1.24	15.45	3.52
SSA LMICs	Poor	100	45.93	26.77	2.26	0.07	6.41	17.68	0.35	0.93	21.73	4.64
	Non-poor	100	37.13	35.52	9.87	0.63	5.22	19.26	0.54	2.27	20.24	4.84
SSA EEs	Poor	100	40.54	9.01	7.01	0.01	0.21	1.79	0.00	10.24	36.35	3.85
	Non-poor	100	27.14	28.17	24.33	0.04	0.22	3.58	0.00	9.18	30.12	5.40
SSA	Poor	100	47.64	29.89	2.77	0.36	8.87	17.72	0.17	1.18	17.31	3.98
	Non-poor	100	38.38	35.29	10.12	0.80	6.74	17.38	0.25	2.68	19.33	4.32
Asia Pacific (LDCs, LMICs, EEs)	Poor	100	32.74	30.96	9.38	0.93	4.24	16.41	0.00	0.56	30.83	4.91
	Non-poor	100	20.47	38.25	20.90	1.61	3.37	12.37	0.00	1.48	33.76	6.03
Poverty Rates												
SSA LDCs		44	47.45	41.77	26.28	30.2	47.74	42.97	17.32	32.47	37.15	42.61
SSA LMICs		43	48.6	36.55	14.91	7.93	48.42	41.23	33.16	23.88	45.08	42.27
SSA EEs		17	22.89	5.98	5.42	2.45	15.5	9.03	3.53	18.15	19.34	12.43
SSA		41	46.43	37.16	16.03	23.84	47.88	41.59	32.03	23.6	38.47	39.16
Asia Pacific (LDCs, LMICs, EEs)		15	22.15	12.59	7.40	9.26	18.30	19.10	0.47	6.27	13.98	12.65

Source: Estimates by Florence Bonnet for the ILO (2017).

Note: SSA = Sub-Saharan Africa; LDC = least developed countries; LMIC = low- and middle-income countries; EE = emerging economies.

Table 3.11   Percentage of Poverty, by Broad Economic Sector, 2012

Extreme Poverty	Total		Agriculture		Industry		Services	
	Poor	Non-Poor	Poor	Non-Poor	Poor	Non-Poor	Poor	Non-Poor
SSA LDCs	100	100	79.79	51.63	5.18	8.70	15.03	39.68
SSA LMICs	100	100	59.98	31.10	8.97	10.56	31.05	58.34
SSA EEs	100	100	45.86	10.33	13.95	24.86	40.19	64.81
SSA	100	100	68.85	34.60	7.31	12.14	23.84	53.27
Asia Pacific (LDCs, LMICs, EEs)	100	100	63.34	41.62	20.49	22.39	16.17	35.99
Poverty Rate								
SSA LDCs	47		58.09		34.80		25.36	
SSA LMICs	39		55.31		35.30		25.46	
SSA EEs	6		21.58		3.36		3.70	
SSA	39		55.87		27.69		22.16	
Asia Pacific (LDCs, LMICs, EEs)	15		21.35		14.03		7.42	

Source: Estimates by Florence Bonnet for the ILO (2017).

Note: SSA = Sub-Saharan Africa; LDC = least developed countries; LMIC = low- and middle-income countries; EE = emerging economies.

Table 3.11 takes the total population of the poor and non-poor who were employed, and decomposes them by sector. Of the employed poor, 69 percent were concentrated in agriculture, whereas in glaring contrast, just under 35 percent of the non-poor were concentrated in agriculture.

A lower proportion of the poor, 7 percent, was employed in industry, compared with 12 percent of the non-poor. A far lower proportion of the poor, 24 percent, were employed in services, compared with 53 percent of the non-poor. The poverty rate in agriculture—that is, those working in agriculture who were poor—was 56 percent, compared with 28 percent in industry and 22 percent in services.

Table 3.12 takes the total employed populations for the poor and non-poor and decomposes them into detailed sectors. The most obvious differences between the poor and the non-poor are evident in manufacturing and trade. In manufacturing, the population of employed poor was 6 percent, compared with the non-poor at 10 percent, whereas in trade, the poor population's share was 7 percent, compared with 14 percent for the non-poor. These characteristics of SSA poverty neatly connect elements of a growth, jobs, and poverty strategy.

Table 3.12 Percentage of Poverty, by Detailed Economic Sector, 2012

		Total	Agriculture	Construction	Education	Electricity, Gas, and Water	Financial Intermediation	Health and Social Work	Hotels and Restaurants
SSA LDCs	Poor	100	80.56	1.22	0.69	0.03	0.05	0.32	0.41
	Non-poor	100	52.65	2.10	3.98	0.16	0.58	1.55	1.38
SSA LMICs	Poor	100	56.61	0.84	1.62	0.23	0.21	0.35	4.33
	Non-poor	100	41.81	1.77	3.66	0.39	0.57	0.92	1.86
SSA EEs	Poor	100	45.55	6.09	0.23	0.36	1.87	0.03	0.07
	Non-poor	100	10.27	5.24	0.58	0.64	9.06	0.13	0.12
SSA	Poor	100	66.35	1.08	1.21	0.15	0.17	0.33	2.64
	Non-poor	100	39.90	2.42	3.26	0.37	1.93	0.98	1.44
Asia Pacific (LDCs, LMICs, EEs)	Poor	100	63.33	10.82	0.68	0.17	0.2	0.17	0.78
	Non-poor	100	41.63	8.43	3.14	0.83	2.38	1.31	2.11
Poverty Rate									
SSA LDCs		100	57.40	33.89	13.33	12.79	6.58	15.49	20.87
SSA LMICs		100	46.20	23.19	21.91	27.31	18.5	19.38	59.57
SSA EEs		100	21.57	6.73	2.37	3.35	1.26	1.22	3.68
SSA		100	50.52	21.58	18.61	20.09	5.03	17.31	52.84
Asia Pacific (LDCs, LMICs, EEs)		100	21.33	18.62	3.70	3.47	1.49	2.30	6.19

		Manufacturing	Mining and Quarrying	Other Services	Public Administration	Transport, Storage and Communications	Wholesale and Retail Trade	Not Classifiable
SSA LDCs	Poor	3.67	0.68	2.30	0.55	0.70	8.64	0.17
	Non-poor	5.96	0.81	7.51	2.33	2.60	18.19	0.21
SSA LMICs	Poor	7.28	0.05	6.42	1.22	1.68	17.43	1.74
	Non-poor	10.77	0.32	8.21	2.81	3.06	21.90	1.95
SSA EEs	Poor	6.82	0.59	16.13	4.33	1.70	15.57	0.67
	Non-poor	13.97	4.84	10.26	17.99	5.38	20.90	0.62
SSA	Poor	5.77	0.32	4.87	0.99	1.28	13.76	1.07
	Non-poor	9.90	1.18	8.33	5.10	3.30	20.67	1.24
Asia Pacific (LDCs, LMICs, EEs)	Poor	8.49	0.94	2.92	1.29	3.20	6.89	0.13
	Non-poor	11.85	1.18	4.25	4.55	4.76	13.43	0.15
Poverty Rate								
SSA LDCs		35.11	42.72	21.23	17.34	19.11	29.49	41.74
SSA LMICs		29.99	9.03	33.17	21.55	25.90	33.54	36.08
SSA EEs		2.94	0.75	8.88	1.47	1.92	4.42	6.24
SSA		26.37	14.27	26.41	10.68	19.20	29.01	34.71
Asia Pacific (LDCs, LMICs, EEs)		11.33	12.40	10.91	4.80	10.68	8.38	12.95

Source: Estimates by Florence Bonnet for the ILO (2017).

Note: SSA = Sub-Saharan Africa; LDC = least developed countries; LMIC = low- and middle-income countries; EE = emerging economies.

ESTIMATING INCOME GAPS TO RAISE THE POOR OUT OF POVERTY

On the basis of these estimates and decompositions of the poor population, the ILO (2016, chap. 2) was able to estimate the income gap that
needs to be filled to raise the extreme poor out of poverty.

This income gap has two parts. The first is the gap to be filled by
income transfers to the poor who are unable to work, including dependents, below and above the working age, and the disabled. The second is
the gap to be filled by the labor market through more work and higher
remuneration. The demographic and labor market profile of each poor
household enables us to estimate these two gaps. Table 3.13 presents estimates for SSA, showing that the region has a total income gap of $38
billion per year to raise its extremely poor out of poverty. This represents
2.4 percent of its GDP. Of this 2.4 percent of GDP, the largest share,
1.2 percent, is needed for poor children, with another 0.1 percent needed
for the elderly. These would be pure income transfers.

Of the 2.4 percent income gap, another 0.7 percent would be needed
to increase employment and incomes for the working poor, and another
0.5 percent would be needed to generate employment or to provide social
protection for the inactive and unemployed. Although these income gaps
are daunting shares of GDP, they represent an even higher share, 13 percent, of government expenditure, or an extremely challenging 69 percent
share of social protection expenditure, as shown in table 3.14.

The challenge increases as incomes fall. For LDCs, the income gap
amounts to nearly a quarter of government expenditures and represents more than the share of current social protection expenditures. For
LMICs, the income gap amounts to 16 percent of government expenditure and accounts for 87 percent of current social protection expenditures. For EEs, the income gap remains below 1 percent of government
expenditure and accounts for 3 percent of current social protection
expenditures.

A POLICY AGENDA FOR THE WAY FORWARD
IN POVERTY, JOBS, AND GROWTH IN SSA

The characteristics of poverty in SSA have a near symmetry with the
region's weaknesses in labor market outcomes and weaknesses in growth.
What ails the poor in the region is also what ails the labor market,
growth, and the macro-economy. A growth and employment strategy that

Table 3.13 Poverty Income Gap, by Population Group and Labor Status, 2012

	Children	Employed			Unemployed	Inactive	Older Persons	Total Gap
		Total	Wage and Salaried Workers	Self-Employed				
Total Income Gap as a Percentage of GDP								
Extreme Poverty (<US$1.90 PPP Per Capita Per Day)								
SSA								
African LDCs	2.6	1.7	0.1	1.6	0.0	0.5	0.2	5.1
Other low- and lower-middle income	1.1	0.6	0.0	0.6	0.0	0.5	0.1	2.3
Other upper-middle income	0.1	0.0	0.0	0.0	0.0	0.1	0.0	0.3
Total	1.2	0.7	0.1	0.7	0.0	0.4	0.1	2.4
Asia Pacific (LDCs, LMICs, EEs)	0.1	0.1	0.0	0.0	0.0	0.1	0.0	0.2
Extreme and Moderate Poverty (<US$3.10 PPP Per Capita Per Day)								
SSA								
African LDCs	9.0	6.3	0.5	5.8	0.1	1.9	0.6	18.0
Other low- and lower-middle income	3.5	2.1	0.2	1.9	0.1	1.4	0.4	7.4
Other upper-middle income	0.5	0.1	0.1	0.0	0.1	0.4	0.0	1.1
Total	4.0	2.6	0.2	2.3	0.1	1.3	0.3	8.3
Asia Pacific (LDCs, LMICs, EEs)	0.5	0.5	0.1	0.4	0.0	0.5	0.1	1.5

(continued)

Table 3.13 (Continued)

Total Income Gap, US$ Million, Current

Extreme Poverty (<US$1.90 PPP Per Capita Per Day)

SSA							
African LDCs	11,225	7,455	572	6,884	153	2,315	736	21,884
Other low- and lower-middle income	7,035	3,992	278	3,715	126	3,106	720	14,979
Other upper-middle income	483	98	76	22	126	403	41	1,151
Total	18,743	11,546	925	10,621	404	5,823	1,497	38,014
Asia Pacific (LDCs, LMICs, EEs)	9,151	7,982	2,137	5,846	134	9,219	1,196	27,683

Extreme and Moderate Poverty (<US$3.10 PPP Per Capita Per Day)

SSA							
African LDCs	39,193	27,263	2,120	25,143	536	8,242	2,698	77,931
Other low- and lower-middle income	15,075	9,071	861	8,210	337	6,263	1,534	32,279
Other upper-middle income	1,952	502	399	103	522	1,637	206	4,818
Total	56,220	36,835	3,379	33,456	1,395	16,141	4,438	115,029
Asia Pacific (LDCs, LMICs, EEs)	65,511	65,377	17,295	48,082	1,277	62,555	9,689	204,409

Source: Estimates by Florence Bonnet for the ILO (2017).

Note: GDP = gross domestic product; PPP = purchasing power parity; SSA = Sub-Saharan Africa; LDC = least developed countries; LMIC = low- and middle-income countries; EE = emerging economies.

Table 3.14   Global Income Gap, by Region and Level of the Poverty Line, 2012

	Income Gap (% GDP)		Income Gap (% Government Expenditure)		Income Gap (% Social Protection Expenditure)	
	US$1.90 PPP	US$3.10 PPP	US$1.90 PPP	US$3.10 PPP	US$1.90 PPP	US$3.10 PPP
SSA						
African LDCs	5.1	18.0	23.0	85.4	110.8	414.8
Other low- and lower-middle income	2.3	7.4	15.7	48.9	86.6	277.3
Other upper-middle income	0.3	1.1	0.8	3.6	2.7	11.9
Total	2.4	8.3	13.4	45.5	69.4	238.1
Asia Pacific (LDCs, LMICs, EEs)	0.2	1.5	0.7	5.8	9.2	73.5

Source: Estimates by Florence Bonnet for the ILO (2017).

Note: GDP = gross domestic product; PPP = purchasing power parity; SSA = Sub-Saharan Africa; LDC = least developed countries; LMIC = low- and middle-income countries; EE = emerging economies.

prioritizes increases in incomes, employment, and growth of the poor, also provides the most pragmatic approach to a broader policy agenda.

Beginning with the employed, and setting aside the demographic drag and entailed transfers for the concluding fiscal arguments, the primary causal factor of poverty in SSA is a lack of waged employment. A much higher rate of transformation from low-productivity self-employment to higher productivity and remunerated waged employment (Lewis 1954) is needed.

The poor, lacking waged employment, are concentrated in contributing family work and self-employment, which have the highest poverty rates among all forms of employment.

The transformation from contributing family work and self-employment to waged employment requires a sectoral change or productive transformation. The poor are concentrated in lower productivity agriculture, which is largely based on self-employment. Poverty rates are much lower in higher productivity and better remunerated industry and services, which tend to be based on waged employment. SSA has had a low rate of productive transformation from agriculture to industry and services. Thus, an investment strategy toward productive transformation is much needed.

Within industry, the poor have had the least access to employment in manufacturing and trade, which have the lowest poverty rates among large-scale forms of employment. SSA has based its GDP growth on service and extractive industries, while manufacturing has decreased.

Compared with extractive industries, manufacturing has a higher capacity to generate employment. Because it reduces unemployment, its value added better links it to the rest of the domestic economy. It is also a technology leader, and allows the economy to catch up through learning by doing. From the micro to the macro levels, all arguments show that SSA's deindustrialization has been damaging and needs to be reversed.

SSA needs to achieve a better balance among its macro drivers of growth. Its major driver of growth has been exports, which are largely exogenously determined, especially when based on low in-country value added exports, such as commodities and extractives. Figure 3.4 illustrates this argument for a more balanced "sweet spot" among the three major drivers of growth: exports, investment, and consumption. Relative to consumption-led growth, exports tend to depress consumption, while enhancing productivity; relative to investment-led growth, exports tend to depress investment, while enhancing productivity; and relative to consumption-led growth, investment tends to depress consumption. A move towards a sweet spot in the middle of the hyperplane of these three macro drivers of growth is indicated.

We next consider the ability to fill the largest income gap—for dependents, young and old—through income transfers. This income gap of 1.3 percent of GDP per year is clearly a heuristic device to focus policy

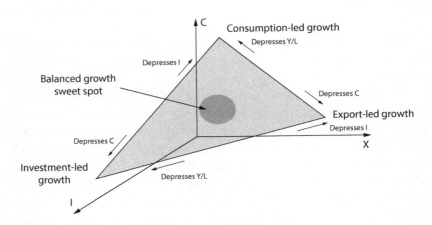

Figure 3.4   Balance among determinants of growth

Source: Mahmood (2018).

by estimating the size of the problem. Filling this gap may be out of the immediate reach for LDCs and LMICs because it requires at least doubling their social protection budgets. But poverty reduction policy must logically prioritize dependents, who are the least able to help themselves, and also avoid child labor, which would damage both the children and the economy.

NOTES

Research assistance provided by Maria Martha Sarabia and Aimal Tanvir.

1. See also the ILO's *Global Employment Trends* reports: *Global Employment Trends 2011: The Challenge of a Jobs Recovery* (Geneva: International Labour Office, 2011a); *Global Employment Trends 2012: Preventing a Deeper Jobs Crisis* (Geneva: International Labour Office, 2012); *Global Employment Trends 2013: Recovering from a Second Jobs Dip* (Geneva: International Labour Office, 2013a); and *Global Employment Trends 2014: The Risk of a Jobless Recovery* (Geneva: International Labour Office, 2014).

2. The International Conference of Labour Statisticians defines the informal economy as unregistered work, without access to any social protection. In effect, lack of any social protection becomes the criterion for the definition of informal work; see International Labour Organization, *Final Report of the 17th International Conference of Labour Statisticians* (Geneva: International Labour Office, 2004).

3. This conceptualization is based on the author's work with Florence Bonnet; see International Labour Office, *World Employment and Social Outlook 2016: Transforming Jobs to End Poverty* (Geneva: International Labour Office, 2016), chap. 2.

REFERENCES

Ball, Laurence, Daniel Leigh, and Prakash Loungani. 2013. "Okun's Law: Fit at 50?" Working Paper No. 13/10. International Monetary Fund, Washington, DC.

International Labour Organization. 2004. *Final Report of the 17th International Conference of Labour Statisticians*. Geneva: International Labour Office.

——. 2011a. *Global Employment Trends 2011: The Challenge of a Jobs Recovery*. Geneva: International Labour Office.

——. 2011b. *Growth, Productive Employment and Decent Work in the Least Developed Countries*. Geneva: International Labour Office.

——. 2012. *Global Employment Trends 2012: Preventing a Deeper Jobs Crisis*. Geneva: International Labour Office.

——. 2013a. *Global Employment Trends 2013: Recovering from a Second Jobs Dip*. Geneva: International Labour Office.

——. 2013b. *Measuring Informality: A Statistical Manual on the Informal Sector and Informal Employment*. Geneva: International Labour Office.

——. 2014. *Global Employment Trends 2014: The Risk of a Jobless Recovery*. Geneva: International Labour Office.

——. 2016. *World Employment and Social Outlook 2016: Transforming Jobs to End Poverty.* Geneva: International Labour Office.

——. 2017. Estimates by Florence Bonnet for the International Labour Office , Geneva: International Labour Office.

——. Forthcoming. "The Beveridge Curve Shifts." Unpublished manuscript. ILO Research Department, Geneva.

International Labour Organization Trends Unit. 2016 *Trends Econometric Models.* Geneva: International Labour Office.

International Monetary Fund. 2017. *World Economic Indicators.* Washington, DC: International Monetary Fund.

Lewis, W. Arthur. 1954. "Economic Development with Unlimited Supplies of Labour." *The Manchester School* 22 (2): 139–91.

Mahmood, Moazam. 2018. *The Three Regularities in Development: Growth, Jobs and Macro Policy in Developing Countries.* London: Palgrave Macmillan.

World Bank. 2016. *World Development Indicators.* Washington, DC: World Bank.

PART II

Structural Transformation
for Quality Growth

CHAPTER 4

New Global Rules, Policy Space, and Quality of Growth in Africa

Antonio Andreoni, Ha-Joon Chang, and Isabel Estevez

As other chapters in this book show, many factors limit the ability of African countries to generate growth and ensure its quality. Among these factors, the most difficult to change are the global rules that determine how the global economy works and how individual countries can operate within it.

In this chapter, we discuss how these global rules currently restrict the ability of developing countries, especially those in Africa, to enhance the quality of their growth, and how we need to reform these rules. We address this topic in three parts.

In the first section, we situate the current global rules in their historical context, by discussing their evolution since the nineteenth century. We argue that, although the current global rules are less punishing for developing countries than those under colonialism and imperialism, they are far more restrictive than the rules that prevailed between the end of World War II and the 1970s.

We next analyze the ways in which the new global rules that have emerged in the past few decades have negatively affected the quality of growth in developing countries. We discuss two aspects to this issue.

In the second section, we introduce a new framework distinguishing two related processes, whereby countries' "policy space" is constrained. Although the debates on policy space and developmental state have focused mainly on the "direct" impact of global rules on countries' policy space, we also highlight the "indirect" impact that such global rules have on the policy space by favoring increasing concentration and value capture in global economic structures, both at the geographic and sectoral levels.

In the third section, building on our policy space framework, we show how today's global rules reduce the policy space that developing countries have in pursuing quality of growth. In this respect, quality of growth is understood to be a growth process led by production transformation and collective capabilities development that results in the creation of quality jobs and sustainable structural change (Andreoni and Chang 2017). We discuss the issue of policy space with concrete references to the UN Sustainable Development Goals (SDGs) that we think are more closely related to our definition of quality of growth and highlight the contradictions between development goals and policy space in today's global development discourse.

In the fourth section, we make proposals as to how global and regional rules may be reformed to address some of their worst effects on the quality of growth. We specifically highlight those global rules that are related to intellectual property rights (IPRs), infant industry provision, investor–state dispute settlement, and global standards. Finally, with respect to regional rules, specifically the Continental Free Trade Agreement (CFTA), we highlight the need for a step-by-step strategic approach in which regional integration does not end up exacerbating existing intra-Africa structural imbalances.

GLOBAL RULES: OLD AND NEW

Since its emergence in the sixteenth century, the global economy has been organized and run according to the will of the leading capitalist economies. The most extreme examples are all the countries that were colonized by the more powerful countries. The colonies were made to do whatever suited the colonizing country and the settlers, and the few rules that existed were set without any regard for or consultation with the subjugated native population. From the nineteenth century, however, more formal arrangements that took the form of "treaties" between nations began to emerge.

The first of these treaties developed when the Latin American countries became independent from Spain and Portugal and thus gained sovereignty. These countries were forced into "unequal treaties" that regarded them as second-class nations. They were, for example, forced to accept extraterritoriality, which meant they were not allowed to try the citizens of the stronger nations and, instead, had to deport them to their home countries, on the ground that their legal systems were not satisfactory.

More relevant for this chapter, these treaties deprived these countries of the right to set their own tariffs (i.e., "tariff autonomy") and allowed them to impose only a low (3–5 percent) and uniform rate of tariff for revenue, which naturally made it impossible for them to use infant industry protection. These treaties also introduced the concept of "most favored nation" (MFN), which enabled all of the countries that signed a(n) (unequal) treaty with a weaker country to get more favorable treatment if any one of them managed to extract a concession.

Over the next several decades, unequal treaties were imposed on weaker countries outside Latin America, because the country concerned could not easily be colonized (e.g., China, the Ottoman Empire, Persia, Japan), because the treaty could be a prelude to full colonization (e.g., Korea), or because it was in the strategic interests of the powers concerned not to let it become the colony of a particular country (e.g., Siam, Ethiopia).

By the 1880s, the unequal treaties for the Latin American countries had expired, but in other parts of what is today considered the developing world, few countries were not colonies or semi-independent countries subject to unequal treaties.

The tide of colonialism and unequal treaties started to recede slowly from the 1920s, with the expiry of the unequal treaties for Turkey in 1923 (following the dissolution of the Ottoman Empire in 1922) and China in 1929 and the rise of anticolonial resistance around the globe. Starting from the mid-1940s, former colonies (e.g., Lebanon, 1943; Korea and Vietnam, 1945; British India, 1947) started gaining independence, and imperialist countries significantly loosened their grips on what the developing countries could and could not do.

The new global regime of economic rules that emerged after the end of World War II, represented by the General Agreement on Tariffs and Trade (GATT), put only mild restrictions on the trade and industrial policies of developing countries. The policy space for developing countries started shrinking in the 1980s, with the introduction of the Structural Adjustment Program (SAP) by the International Monetary Fund (IMF) and the World Bank, which imposed conditionalities on their loans that demanded the dismantling of interventionist policies, but the post–World War II global rules remained largely in place until the mid-1990s.

Things started changing in the mid-1990s. In 1995, GATT expanded into the World Trade Organization (WTO), which is much more restrictive of what developing countries can do. Bilateral and regional free trade agreements (FTAs) proliferated. The most symbolic of these agreements was the 1994 signing of the North American Free Trade Agreement (NAFTA) between the United States, Canada, and Mexico, which was the first significant FTA formed between developed and developing countries. Bilateral and regional FTAs multiplied—for example, bilateral FTAs numbered around fifty in the mid-1990s but more than two hundred fifty currently exist. Bilateral investment treaties (BITs) have also seen a huge increase in numbers: from less than five hundred at the beginning of the 1990s, to more than two thousand by the end of the decade (Tucker 2017, 36, figure 1).

The more accommodating nature of the early post–World War II global rules for the developing countries is best understood by discussing the five most significant changes introduced since the mid-1990s.

First, in the WTO, the principle of "single undertaking" means that member countries have to sign up to all agreements. By contrast, in the GATT, countries could choose to reject agreements that they did not want (the so-called pluri-lateralism).

Second, the new global rules cover many more areas. Issues like regulation on foreign direct investment (FDI), IPRs, and trade in services have been brought into the fold of the WTO and other trade and investment agreements.

Third, the rules have been tightened. The use of tariffs has become more circumscribed. Many (although not all) developing countries have been compelled to put ceilings on their tariffs (i.e., "tariff binding"), while it has become more difficult to use emergency tariffs on the grounds of balance of payments. The rules on the use of subsidies also have been significantly tightened: subsidies tied to local contents in production and export subsidies have been banned (except for the least developed countries [LDCs]), whereas other subsidies have become more subject to challenge.

Fourth, completely new rules have been introduced. The most significant of these rules is the increasing adoption of the investor-state dispute settlement (ISDS) mechanism in international agreements on trade and investment, which allows foreign investors to sue governments directly for reducing profits through regulation. Once an obscure arrangement adopted in a small number of BITs, this mechanism has been incorporated into most of the investment treaties adopted since the 1990s and has generated a major shift in the balance of power between national (especially developing country) governments and global corporations, in favor of the latter.

Fifth, less devastating but still important is the introduction of various product "standards," including sanitation and phytho-sanitation, which are expensive to meet. These rules are unilaterally set, through a non-transparent process, by governments and other actors, including private companies, in rich countries. These standards act as entry barriers in particular, although not exclusively, against developing countries.

In the following sections, we analyze how the new global rules that have emerged since the 1990s are limiting the ability of developing countries to meet their development challenges and how these rules should be reformed to allow those countries to achieve higher quality growth.

THE POLICY SPACE FRAMEWORK: THE "DIRECT" AND "INDIRECT" IMPACT OF THE NEW GLOBAL RULES ON QUALITY OF GROWTH IN AFRICA

The policy space debate traditionally has been centered on the constraining role of global rules on developing countries, in particular with respect to their industrial and trade policies (Amsden 2001; Chang 2002, 2007; Wade 2003; Gallagher 2005; Mayer 2009) and to the adoption of developmental macroeconomic policies (Ocampo and Vos 2008). Building on the Listian idea of "kicking away the ladder," these contributions adopt a linear framework linking global rules, that is, multilateral and bilateral agreements, to policy space. In doing so, the policy space debate has mainly focused on the "direct" impact of global rules on developing countries' policy space.

Since the mid-1990s and increasingly in the 2000s, however, changes in the geopolitical and regional settlement, as well as the increasing concentration in global economic structures, have unleashed new pressures—both "direct" and "indirect"—on developing countries' policy space. Figure 4.1 provides a conceptual framework to analyze these two different, although related, constraining dynamics.

If we focus on the direct impact of global rules on the policy space, bilateral agreements, including regional trade agreements (RTAs), have become the major factor shrinking countries' policy space, even more than traditional multilateral agreements, which allow for certain technology and trade policies. Alongside this increasing direct pressure on developing countries' policy space, both multilateral and bilateral agreements have played a key role in preserving existing global economic structures and facilitating further concentration of economic power in the hands of powerful corporations (this is represented by the arrow above the policy space in figure 4.1).

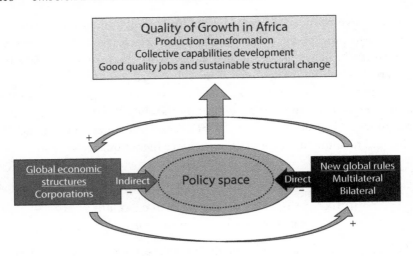

Figure 4.1 Policy space framework

Source: Authors' creation.

In certain economic sectors, the consolidation of multinational corporations, in particular, their capacity to capture value in global production networks and markets, has resulted in greater concentration. Barriers to entry, large-scale production, price competition and dumping practices, control by multinational corporations of entire supply chains, and prices and standards all have limited opportunities for productive organizations in developing countries to learn and catch up in both domestic and international markets. This is the "indirect" impact of global rules on developing countries' policy space.

In turn, this growing power concentration has increased corporations' ability to exercise political pressure on national governments and international organizations, to introduce and enforce global rules that favor them (this is represented by the arrow below the policy space in figure 4.1). This is evident in the context of the trade-related aspects of intellectual property rights (TRIPS) and trade-related investment measures (TRIMS), but also ISDS and international standards.

As a result of these two related and reinforcing dynamics, developing countries' policy space has been increasingly shrinking, and governments have found it more difficult to implement industrial and trade policies in support of their productive sector. To assess the political space of today's developing countries, in particular with respect to the African continent, the next sections examine both the direct and indirect impact of global rules and provide evidence of the two dynamics described in our framework.

NEW GLOBAL RULES AND POLICY SPACE

Policy space has been gradually restricted by new global rules, with a significant acceleration since the mid-1990s. In particular, the political-institutional dynamics of value appropriation that characterized the colonial era have been recast in more sophisticated political-institutional mechanisms (e.g., IPR systems, principle of national treatment, ISDS, and international standards). Despite this increasing sophistication, unless developing countries have signed bilateral agreements with rich countries or stringent regional agreements, they still enjoy a certain amount of "policy space" to implement industrial policies. Against this complex scenario, the quality of growth of today's developing countries critically depends on their capacity to (1) fully exploit the policy space left within multilateral agreements; (2) learn how to navigate the insidious new political-institutional mechanisms that reduce their policy space, both within multilateral and bilateral agreement; and (3) refrain from signing (or have the capacity to revise) stringent bilateral trade agreements constraining their policy space.

In 1995, with the establishment of the WTO, developing countries witnessed the introduction and proliferation of new multilateral agreements alongside the GATT. These included the Agreement on Subsidies and Countervailing Measures (SCM), the TRIMS , the General Agreement on Trade in Services (GATS), and the TRIPS. Each of these multilateral agreements redesigned the geopolitical settlement and constrained developing countries' policy space in specific areas of industrial, technology, investment, and trade policies. Specifically, three policy instruments, which had been widely used to achieve quality of growth in today's developed countries, were no longer allowed under the new WTO regime.

First, the use of tariffs became constrained by the introduction of a "binding" mechanism: WTO members were forced to sign a Schedule of Commitments under which tariff upper-bound limits were settled for a large number of products and sectors. Against this new system, a number of developing countries have since undergone a process of "unilateral liberalization" (Baldwin 2010), that is, they have applied tariffs at a much lower level than allowed within their own Schedule of Commitments (for a review of bound and applied tariffs, see Chang, Hauge, and Irfan 2016, 119).

This reduction in the policy space was partially due to various rounds of "tariff rationalization" processes promoted by the IMF and backed by other international organizations such as the World Bank and WTO. In particular, the WTO has systematically attempted to reduce further the policy space countries could use to raise their tariffs within the upper-bound limits.[1] In spite of these limitations, some instruments are still available to developing countries within GATT. Under special conditions, the "Government Assistance to Economic Development" and the "Balance of Payments" provisions allow tariffs to be raised to promote specific industries and permit quantitative restrictions to be introduced.

Second, under the SCM multilateral agreement, sector-specific subsidies, especially those for export promotion and those related to local content in manufacturing, were banned. SCM constrained the use of indirect subsidies in the form of intra–private sector transfers and set strong enforcement conditions, including the right of the importing country (often a developed country) to impose countervailing duties to offset the effects of subsidies on the price of products.

Developing countries (in particular LDCs and countries with a per capita income of less than $1,000), however, can use subsidies until they cause adverse effects, and even when they are challenged, countervailing actions might take up to three years to be implemented and may require proactive government action. In countries that are potentially hampered, corporations would lobby the government to take these actions to protect their markets from imports.

The SCM regime does not constrain the use of subsidies to promote research and development (R&D), especially in support of depressed regions and green technologies. Although these subsidies leave important areas for technology policies in developing countries, R&D investments are hard to translate into industrial innovation, commercialization, and increasing market competitiveness, precisely because these countries lack productive industrial organizations. Having said that, targeted R&D subsidies in the form of production and technology services can reduce firms' costs (indirect subsidy) and improve their industrial competitiveness.

Third, TRIMS and GATS have curbed countries' policy space with respect to the imposition of performance requirements and other conditionalities on foreign investors. These include the imposition of export requirements, the use of local content policies favoring domestic insourcing of locally manufactured inputs and the employment of local workers, and foreign exchange or trade balancing measures. As is the case with tariffs, the "development" provision within the GATT leaves some policy space to developing countries. Also, other regulatory investment measures are allowed, including investment policy instruments, such as joint ventures maintenance, technology transfer, and conditions on foreign equity ownership.

All of these instruments are critical for the development of the local production system and diffused technical skills (see chapter 9, in this volume). In fact, they are so critical that all countries make use of them in various disguised forms (Andreoni 2016) and exceptions are introduced in various preferential and bilateral trade agreements (Chang, Hauge, and Irfan 2016). For example, under the U.S. African Growth and Opportunities Act (AGOA) trade regime between Africa (excluding North Africa) and the United States, the Rules of Origin requirements are specified in such a way that certain products qualify for a certain proportion of local contents under preferential treatment.[2]

Currently, with respect to trade in services regulated under GATS, countries have retained significant policy space, including the use of procurement requirements. The fact that trade in goods and manufacturing investments have been more severely controlled highlights the fact that these are critical sectors, which also are perceived as the main threat to developed countries. Given the development of service industries in countries like India, however, the current WTO Doha Development Round has opened the way to further binding regulations under the GATS.

Fourth, technology transfer and IPRs have been framed within the TRIPS, with a view toward providing global protection to innovators of knowledge. Although a number of ambiguities are inherent in the definition of "invention," the TRIPS has been successful in protecting multinational corporations by imposing minimum IPR standards on developing countries. In particular, patents and copyrights have given multinational corporations powerful tools to protect "their" inventions across WTO countries. The latter are bound to protect patents and not to discriminate among IPR holders. The use of technologies by third parties is protected for twenty years and expensive royalty systems are enforced (Chang 2001, Rasiah 2005).

The TRIPS holds significant implications for technology transfer and diffusion among developing countries. While emerging economies like China have been able to bypass some of these IPR constraints by introducing creative national legislation and offering access to corporations that wish to penetrate the Chinese economy, the majority of African countries continue paying significant royalties. The only exception in which developing countries have managed to retain the power to issue compulsory licenses for registered patents is related to health emergencies.

Despite these restrictions on industrial policy instruments, unless developing countries have signed stringent bilateral agreements with rich countries (or RTAs), they still have a certain amount of "policy space," including the following:

- targeted infrastructural investments;
- targeted skills development;
- worker training requirements;
- the use of public technology intermediaries, R&D disguised subsidies, and the promotion of university-industry linkages;
- state-led strategic mergers;
- tax benefits and exemptions;
- accelerated depreciation allowances;
- exemptions of small and medium enterprises (SMEs) from certain regulations (e.g., the U.S. exemption of SMEs from the ban on export cartel; the German exemption of SME successors from inheritance tax); and
- preferential treatment of national firms in government procurement.

Within the multilateral WTO system, two types of bilateral agreements are recognized that deviated from the WTO's MFN principle. These are preferential trade agreements (PTAs), such as the Generalized System of Preferences (GSP) adopted by the European Union and other developed countries or the U.S. AGOA PTA, and the RTAs, such as the Common Market for Eastern and Southern Africa (COMESA) and the Economic Community of West Africa States (ECOWAS) in Africa.

PTAs are nonreciprocal tariff preferences that developed countries (usually donor countries) have unilaterally granted to developing countries (usually aid recipients) to allow exported products from developing countries to access markets in developed countries with lower tariffs. These preferences are generally MFN plus, that is, the tariffs applied on eligible products are lower than the donor country's applied MFN rates. To qualify for such PTAs, developing countries are asked to commit to follow various trade and nontrade issues, such as labor standards, technical standards, environmental regulations, and stricter rules on FDI regulation and protection. They also must commit to liberalization in the form of privatization, deregulation, and restrictions on government preferential procurement (Chang, Hauge, and Irfan 2016).

PTAs might have different impacts on developing countries' policy space. For example, the EU's GSP Plus (GSP+) extends lower tariffs to fifteen vulnerable countries, which implement at least twenty-seven international conventions on labor and environmental standards as well as good governance. The conditions imposed by the United States on developing countries under PTAs are even more pervasive, and they are distinctively aimed at protecting U.S. corporations operating in these countries (e.g., ownership protection or banning taxes resulting in businesses expropriation) or at utilizing their tangible and intangible assets (e.g., patents, trademarks, or other IPR protection). PTAs might even be used to compel developing countries to adhere to other WTO multilateral agreements and to prevent developing country governments from using those policy instruments, which are still allowed under WTO (see section "Which Policies That Help Enhance the Quality of Growth Are Allowed Under the New Global Rules?").

The use of PTAs has become increasingly common among African countries. Given their bilateral nature, combined with a unilateral enforcement of the agreement, developing countries are ultimately trapped in binding PTAs without flexibilities or provisions and that depend on conditions settled by the donors. The nonreciprocity of PTAs, while appearing to be benevolent concessions, has been effectively used as a mechanism to extort strict conditions far beyond the WTO multilateral setting, in which countries are at least equally constrained and can rely on external dispute resolution mechanisms. Moreover, when developing countries sign a PTA, voluntary exit from a preferential regime might become difficult, in particular if governments come under political pressure from domestic private business interests.

Until 2016, no country has made a voluntary request to opt out of a PTA (Chang, Hauge, and Irfan 2016). Note, however, that in response to the mounting criticism against PTAs and a number of controversial negotiations, the European Union has moved away from PTAs and has advanced a new form of North-South RTA called the economic partnership agreement (EPAs).

Unlike PTAs, RTAs are reciprocal agreements under which countries accord the same tariff preferences, either in the form of FTAs or a customs union (CU). Depending on the countries involved, RTAs can take the form of North-North, North-South, and South-South agreements. All African countries currently are involved in multiple South-South intracontinental RTAs and North-South RTAs with the United States and the European Union. The desperate need for harmonization has pushed ahead the idea of a CFTA, the implementation of which raises significant challenges, especially with respect to the increased structural imbalances that this continental trade arrangement could potentially generate (more on this in the fourth section).

North-South RTAs generally are the most constraining, and among them, those involving the United States are particularly problematic, because they tend to impede the use of duty drawbacks or impose heightened patent protection via "pipeline protection" (Thrasher and Gallagher 2008). The inherent problem of these North-South FTAs is that developing countries have much lower bargaining power than they have in multilateral negotiations. Additionally, the trade benefits for developing countries are limited because of their backward industrial structure and limited diversification.

In both multilateral and bilateral trade agreements, firms from developing countries have been asked to comply with increasingly demanding product and process international standards. Standards are critical coordination devices along the supply chains as well as important means of transmitting information about the products (and processes) to consumers. Standards have become central to the debates on the structure and governance of global supply chains. In particular, the way developed country governments and corporations are able to control standards development, specifically "the scope of specific standards, the manner by which compliance is verifiably monitored" (Nadvi 2008, 6) has been highlighted. Because developed countries control the standards agenda and the enforcement mechanisms, standards tend to reflect the needs and interests of their corporations (i.e., the "standard setters") and can be used to exercise control over developing countries (i.e., the "standard takers") or can even create barriers to entry. Indeed, given that the process under which standards are settled is not fully accountable and that a number of these standards remain opaque and present inconsistencies, developed countries might use them to protect their domestic markets and companies from imports. The fact that no mechanisms are available to resolve conflicts— buyer companies or countries decide on "standard conformance"—puts developing countries in an even less favorable situation.

Alongside these North-South FTAs, a number of developing countries in Africa recently signed BITs, although several of these countries (e.g., South Africa) already have reacted to them by revoking signed BITs. Table 4.1 provides an overview of BITs in Africa today.

Table 4.1   Bilateral Investment Treaties in Africa

Partner Economy	African Countries Involved	BIT Signed but Not Yet in Force *or* Other Type of Investment Agreement Signed
United States	Cameroon, Congo, DRC, Mozambique, Rwanda, Senegal	Ghana—Investment Development Agreement
Canada	Cote d'Ivoire, Mali, Senegal, Nigeria, Cameroon, Tanzania, Benin, South Africa	
European Union	Individual European countries have signed bilateral agreements with several African countries; 271 BITs are in force presently that involve European and African countries (UNCTAD)	
India	Mauritius, Mozambique, Senegal	Djibouti, Ethiopia, Ghana, DRC, Seychelles, Sudan, Zimbabwe
Japan	Mozambique	
High-income developing economies (including South Korea, China, Singapore, Taiwan, Malaysia, Turkey)	83 bilateral agreements with individual African countries are reported with this group	
Israel	South Africa, DRC, Ethiopia	
China	Benin, Botswana, Cape Verde, Cameroon, Chad, DRC, Congo, Cote d'Ivoire, Djibouti, Equatorial Guinea, Ethiopia, Gabon, Ghana, Guinea, Kenya, Madagascar, Mali, Mauritius, Mozambique, Namibia, Nigeria, Seychelles, Sierra Leone, South Africa, Sudan, Tanzania, Uganda, Zambia, Zimbabwe	
Russia	Angola, Equatorial Guinea, Namibia, Ethiopia	
Brazil	0	
African countries (excluding North Africa)	72 BITs are in force between and among African countries (excluding North African countries)	

Source: Chang, Hauge, and Irfan (2016).

Note: BIT = bilateral investment treaty; DRC = Democratic Republic of Congo; UNCTAD = UN Conference on Trade and Development.

BITs promoted by the United States are aimed primarily at protecting corporations' interests in countries where investor rights are not fully protected, penetrating developing countries' markets, and pushing for the adoption of promarket reforms. These BITs also constrain developing countries' policy space far beyond the WTO regime, from macroeconomic policies (e.g., restricting capital controls) to industrial policies. In particular, these treaties give corporations increased powers, including the right to binding arbitration of disputes related to agreement violations and the possibility of demanding and enforcing compensation at the World Bank's International Centre for the Settlement of Investment Disputes (ICSID) (Gallagher 2005). BITs promoted by the European Union, Japan, Canada, and China tend to be more flexible and less pervasive. For example, they allow for balance-of-payments temporary safeguards or some forms of capital controls.

GLOBAL POWER CONCENTRATION, ENDOGENOUS ASYMMETRIES, AND POLICY SPACE: THE INDIRECT IMPACT ON QUALITY OF GROWTH

The political-institutional mechanisms established in global trade and investment rules—largely a product of the political lobbying of major transnational corporations—have enabled the dominant economic groups (i.e., corporations and those who serve them, such as international law firms and international consulting companies) to erect barriers to entry and appropriate their shares of the value generated in global production and exchange, whether or not they have actually produced that value. The following four mechanisms have been particularly critical in this respect:

- **IPRs and copyrights:** acting as mechanisms for extracting rents and as barriers to entry
- **International standards:** acting as increased barriers to entry or as a mechanism to control innovation
- **Liberalization of trade and capital flows:** facilitating the expansion of markets for oligopolistic firms and global speculative operations
- **ISDS:** helping powerful firms to extract resources from developing countries

At the same time, the fact that the new global rules have not constrained other mechanisms to appropriate value created through the use of collectively provided inputs—for example, "tax havens"—further proves the way global rules preserve (and even support) power concentration in global economic structures, and in turn, how corporations are able to control global economic rules setting.

Defining and gathering evidence on global power concentration are difficult tasks. At the most fundamental level, defining concentration requires a theory of competition beyond the neoclassical "quantity theory of competition" (Weeks 2012). The quantity theory of competition is built on (1) a purely theoretical construction of perfect competitive markets and (2) the idea that more competition is always associated with welfare improvements. In 1967, John Kenneth Galbraith's *New Industrial State* dismantled both positive and normative pillars of the neoclassical theory of competition. He pointed to the complex manifestations and processes of power concentration in several kinds of corporations in the United States and beyond (point 1) (see Galbraith 1967, chap. 7). He also debunked the myth of benign competition, as pointed out by Schumpeter and Marx before him, by highlighting the role of planning and the imperatives of technologies in modern corporations (see Galbraith 1967, chaps. 1–3).

In gathering evidence on global power concentration, and building on a more historically grounded theory of competition, we must recognize how concentration manifests in multiple ways. We also must understand that its measurement is made difficult by limited data availability and by a number of inherent biases of different concentration indices.

First, global power concentration might manifest as a form of "geographic concentration" when the big winners in global markets are monopolistic and oligopolistic corporations, which almost without exception are situated in the Global North (Nolan 2001, 2012).

Second, economic sectors might show different levels of "sectoral concentration." For example, the world economy might experience declining levels of concentration in certain sectors and increasing levels in others. Therefore, if sectoral concentration increases exactly in those sectors where developing countries are attempting to build up their industries, barriers to entry might be even higher than average concentration indices would suggest.

Third, concentration might be increasing within countries or regions (let's say the African continent), while declining at the global level (or vice versa), depending on the relevant markets in which companies operate.

Fourth, in measuring concentration, depending on their availability, we might use different data (e.g., revenues, value added, employment) as well as different indices (four-firm concentration, eight-firm concentration, Herfindahl–Hirschman) (Freund and Sidhu 2017). Each of these indices presents inherent biases that might lead to over- (or under-) estimations of concentration and may miss qualitative aspects of global production organization across different stages of the value chain.

Indeed, fifth, today's global economic structures are characterized by the existence of "endogenous asymmetries" in global production networks (Milberg and Winkler 2013, chap. 4). Thus, in many sectoral value chains, we have oligopolistic lead firms at the top and competitive markets among the lower-tier suppliers, although concentration has been increasing at the level of first-tier global suppliers as well. As a result of this concentration at the top, global lead firms (often system integrators) benefit from a high degree of markup pricing power and are able to capture value generated in long and complex supply chains. At the lower levels of the global value chains, there is evidence of persistently high levels of dispersion, and increasingly so as developing countries try to enter lower-level tasks in manufacturing and services industries (see also chapter 9, in this volume). Concentration at the top allows lead firms and first-tier suppliers to squeeze subcontractors often located in the Global South.

The evidence available on geographic concentration is quite telling. If we look at the Fortune Global 500 companies in 2016, they controlled 37 percent of world GDP, equal to US$27.7 trillion, and around US$1.5 trillion of profits. They employ sixty-seven million workers and are represented by thirty-four countries. Among them, the United States hosts 132 companies (including Walmart, the largest global company with a revenue of US$485 billion in 2016), while in 2016, China saw the number of its headquartered companies in the Fortune Global 500 rise to 109. It is striking that no company in the Fortune Global 500 is headquartered in Africa. According to the Africa Report Top 500 (2016) companies, not only is Africa not represented among the Fortune Global 500, but the continent also shows intracontinental levels of high geographic concentration. On the basis of 2014 company results, more than half of the turnover was concentrated among companies in Southern Africa (almost exclusively South Africa).

Evidence on sectoral concentration is more difficult to gather and different studies show different results, according to the different concentration indices used. For example, Furman and Orszag (2015) used the fifty-firm concentration ratio in thirteen broad economic sectors to find that concentration increased on average by 4 percent between

1997 and 2007. More recently, Freund and Sidhu (2017) examined how global industrial concentration changed between 2006 and 2014 with the rise of China. The study analyses change in the top-four firms' shares of total revenues to find that, according to this concentration ratio, global concentration has in fact declined on average by 4 percent, and that three-quarters of the eighty-four industries have recorded a decrease in concentration.

Aside from several acknowledged potential biases in the concentration ratios used, this paper highlights two other critical issues. First, the rise of China and other emerging markets may have played a critical role in increasing global competition, although when Chinese state-owned enterprises (SOEs) dominate the sector, industry competition rises from 3 to 6 percent points. In fact, although Chinese companies have risen dramatically in the ranks of the Fortune Global 500, in certain sectors, disparities in business power persist between firms from developed and developing countries. In some instances, numerous leading global firms have "gone into" China and have retained corporate governance and control over technologies (Nolan 2012). In other cases, China has managed to develop its own national champions, and its oligopolistic firms have taken control of important tradable sectors (Zhou, Lazonick, and Sun 2016).

Second, and more important, sectors in which concentration is declining most rapidly tend to be the nontradable services (only one manufacturing industry—electronics—presents fast-increasing competition because of China's rise). In other sectors, such as mining, civil engineering, oil, gas, and beverages, concentration has been increasing. These sectors are critical for the African continent, particularly given its resource abundance and need for infrastructure development. In all of them, African countries are facing powerful oligopolistic corporations whose interests are increasingly protected by bilateral agreements (see table 4.1).

Since 2005, mergers and acquisitions (M&A) have boomed. Of the thirty largest deals in history, almost half occurred in the past ten years, including national mergers, such as the one between Dow Chemicals and DuPont, and global cross-border mergers, such as the one between Anheuser-Busch Inbev and SAB Miller. M&A and takeovers have been critical mechanisms leading to increased industrial concentration (Singh 1971, 2014). In fact, as forcefully pointed out by the late Ajit Singh, "A large body of research on mergers indicates that mega-mergers have the potential of increasing market dominance and reducing contestability. Discouraging such mergers would therefore enhance global contestability, competition, and economic efficiency, while at the same time being distributionally more equitable" (2014, 3).

SURFING THE NEW WAVE OF GLOBALIZATION: NEW GLOBAL RULES AND THE POLICY SPACE IN SUB-SAHARAN AFRICA

In the preceding section, we introduced a theoretical framework for thinking about the relationships among global rules, policy space, and quality of growth. We now apply the framework to the case of Sub-Saharan Africa. In doing so, we conceptualize quality of growth as a development process of "production transformation led by the expansion of collective capabilities and resulting in the creation of good quality jobs and sustainable structural change" (Andreoni and Chang 2017, 173).

We begin by mapping the relationship between two Sustainable Development Goals (SDGs), which we use as proxies for different dimensions of "quality of growth," and the policies required to reach these goals (figure 4.2).[3] In particular, we focus on SDG8 and SDG9, which are most closely related to our definition of quality of growth. Next, we examine the extent to which the current regulatory environment allows for the implementation of these policies in Sub-Saharan Africa, highlighting the limits imposed by new global rules as well as the creative mechanisms that can be used to circumvent them.

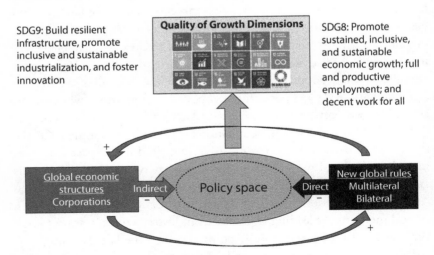

Figure 4.2 Policy space framework and Sustainable Development Goals

Source: Authors' creation.

As discussed, global rules affect quality of growth through "indirect" mechanisms in addition to the more direct effect of their curtailment of development policy space. These mechanisms facilitate the concentration of market power by oligopolistic firms and induce the transfer of value from developing to developed countries. These "indirect" mechanisms, however, are mediated by sector-, value chain–, and location-specific concentration dynamics, so they cannot be discussed in greater detail without reference to specific sectors. Therefore, in this section, we focus on the "direct" impact of global rules on policy space.

We make the case that any genuine commitment on behalf of the international community to improve the quality of growth in Sub-Saharan Africa, and other developing countries, must include reforms of, at the least, certain critical global rules.

QUALITY OF GROWTH TARGETS AND THE POLICIES REQUIRED TO MEET THEM

An exhaustive mapping of the relationships among the various dimensions of quality of growth and the policies required to attain this quality is a large-scale undertaking that falls well outside the scope of this chapter. Instead, we present an example of how this essential exercise could be carried out by global or national policy makers seeking to better understand the complex relationships between global economic rules and the quality of growth.

In our example, we have selected the two SDGs that most directly serve as proxies for quality of growth: SDG8 and SDG9. The aim of SDG8 is to "promote sustained, inclusive and sustainable economic growth, full and productive employment and decent work for all," while SDG9 aims to "build resilient infrastructure, promote inclusive and sustainable industrialization and foster innovation" (United Nations 2015).[4]

In the belief that the best way to design policy is on the basis of experience, we have constructed a list of policies drawn from successful diversification and industrial upgrading experiences. Note that we have omitted many of the effective policies that were implemented by early industrializers—namely, Europe and the United States (see the first section; also see Chang 2002)—because these fall too far outside the spectrum of the politically feasible for today's developing countries (e.g., unbridled theft of intellectual property).

Of the ten policy measures that we have matched to SDG8 and SDG9, all were successfully implemented by at least some of the first-tier newly industrial economies (NIEs) (i.e., South Korea, Taiwan, Singapore, Hong Kong). South Korea and Taiwan used every single one of these measures in their productive transformation strategies. Singapore also adopted many of these policies and, to this day, has one of the largest SOE sectors in the world at 22 percent of GDP (Chang 2007). The second-tier NIEs (i.e., Malaysia, Indonesia, Thailand, and China) have likewise implemented many of these measures. China, for example, protected and supported the industries targeted in its five-year plans through tariff and nontariff barriers, including local content requirements, and provided them with subsidized loans from state "policy banks," with SOEs receiving the lion's share of these loans. Transnational corporations (TNCs) were induced to form joint ventures with domestic companies to promote technology transfer (Andreoni 2016).[5] Likewise, Malaysia has used sophisticated industrial targeting, using a range of mechanisms, from FDI regulation and protections for import substitution to incentives for exports, R&D, and local content incorporation for export products.[6] Thailand and Indonesia also have embraced many of these policies, with their own variations and specificities.[7]

Policies Required to Achieve Quality of Growth Proxies

SDG8 and SDG9—Sustained Growth and Industrialization Dimensions

Selected Targets for SDG8 and SDG9

SDG8. Decent work and economic growth:

- Target 8.1. Sustain [. . .] at least 7 percent gross domestic product growth per annum in the least developed countries.
- Target 8.2. Achieve higher levels of economic productivity through diversification, technological upgrading and innovation, including through a focus on high-value added and labor-intensive sectors.

SDG9. Industry, innovation, and infrastructure:

- Target 9.2. Promote inclusive and sustainable industrialization and, by 2030, significantly raise industry's share of employment and gross domestic product, in line with national circumstances, and double its share in least developed countries.
- Target 9.5 Enhance scientific research, upgrade the technological capabilities of industrial sectors in all countries [. . .].

Policies to Achieve SDG8 and SDG9

Following are some of the key measures that have been effectively used historically or that are being used currently to achieve these objectives:

1. **Targeted investments in infrastructure, training, education, and R&D** to increase productivity and promote high-value-added industries
2. **Coordinated investments** in complementary sectors to promote high-value-added industries and government-mediated mergers to achieve scale economies and reduce inefficient competition
3. **Subsidies for key industrial sectors** to promote high-value-added industries and exports
4. **Creation of SOEs** to kick-start new, high-value added industries
5. **Infant industry protections**, such as tariffs, quotas, and market reservations for domestic industrial producers
6. **Capital controls and capital outflow taxes** to prevent capital flight and encourage savings to remain in the country, facilitating productive investments, including investments in R&D
7. **Government allocation of foreign exchange**, giving top priority to capital goods imports and least priority to luxury consumption goods imports
8. **Performance requirements**, such as requirements on foreign investors to incorporate local content and workers or to engage in joint ventures and technology transfer
9. **Procurement policy** through preferential treatment of domestic firms or of foreign providers willing to transfer technology or accept high (and rising) levels of local content

The success of the NIEs in the use of the policies highlighted in the text box strongly suggests that these are useful measures for achieving sustained per capita economic growth. More critically, these measures are useful for enhancing the quality of growth, defined in terms of structural transformation of the production system and collective capabilities development.

Depending on how many of these quality-of-growth dimensions policy makers aim to address, multiple additional SDGs and their subcomponents could be matched to specific corresponding policies (e.g., one related to sustainable structural change, specifically in relation to environmental sustainability).

Having mapped some of the dimensions of quality of growth and their corresponding policies, we can now begin to analyze how these policies are affected by global rules.

WHICH POLICIES THAT HELP ENHANCE THE QUALITY OF GROWTH ARE ALLOWED UNDER THE NEW GLOBAL RULES?

Of the nine key policies that have proven to be effective in fostering sustained per capita growth (Target 8.1), several remain available to policy makers, largely unrestricted by the global economic regulatory framework. It is difficult to generalize on this point because countries have widely varying commitments under the ever-growing number of trade and investment agreements that regulate economic flows and the permitted role of the state in their management.

In the case of Sub-Saharan Africa[8], all but eight of the forty-seven countries in the region are full members of the WTO, whose constitutive agreements include the broadest set of global rules on trade and investment. Under the current set of WTO agreements, countries are largely free to use several of the policies corresponding to SDG Target 8.1. They are allowed to make investments in R&D, training, and infrastructure; to make coordinated investments and government-mediated mergers; and, in many cases, to use SOEs and government procurement policies to stimulate technology transfer and to kick-start domestic industries (see policies 1, 2, 4, and 9). Countries are also free to use less ambitious measures, such as tax benefits, worker-training requirements, and export taxes, to discourage the export of raw materials and to encourage value-added production.[9]

WTO agreements, however, do impose varying degrees of restrictions on several other policies matched to Target 8.1 (table 4.2). Most of these policies can be generally considered to be somewhat restricted—namely, infant industry protections, capital outflow taxes, certain performance requirements, and the use of SOEs—whereas others can be considered to be mostly restricted—namely, most subsidies and some other performance requirements.

We can think of WTO restrictions as a "baseline" of policy space restriction, beyond which additional agreements, such as BITs, the ill-named FTAs, EPAs, PTAs, and megaregional agreements (e.g., the Transpacific Partnership), introduce further restrictions on policy space. We will refer to these kinds of agreements collectively as "WTO plus" (WTO+) agreements.[10]

WTO+ agreements have proliferated in the past two decades, partly in response to the stagnation of the Doha Round of WTO trade negotiations in the mid-2000s. This stagnation, in turn, was largely the result of strong resistance from developing countries to further curtailment of their policy autonomy. Faced with this staunch opposition, developed countries shifted strategies and began to pursue their goals outside the confines of the WTO. Thus, although they have continued to diplomatically pay lip service to the Doha negotiations, they have devoted the better part of their energies to the pursuit of even more ambitious agreements of the sort listed previously.

Table 4.2[11] provides a snapshot of some of the ways in which WTO and WTO+ agreements have restricted the policies we have identified as useful for advancing sustained growth and the industrialization dimensions of quality of growth. Although it is safe to assume that any WTO+ agreement can only be expected to impose additional restrictions to those agreed upon within WTO, some agreements do allow for greater flexibilities than others. For example, even though performance requirements on foreign investors are tightly restricted in the WTO's Agreement on TRIMS, it is possible to circumvent some of these restrictions in the services sector under the WTO's GATS, as most developing countries have made few commitments related to the (restraints on) regulation of FDI. Although WTO+ agreements are far less permissive, even countries that have made commitments of this sort can carve out policy space in unexpected places with some creativity and political courage. For example, despite the draconian restrictions on local content requirements, many countries still use them and have yet to be challenged in the WTO

Table 4.2   Impacts of Global Rules on Quality of Growth Proxies

Sustainable Development Goals 8 (SDG8) and 9 (SDG9): Sustained Growth and
Industrialization Dimensions

Policies to achieve quality of growth proxies SDG8 and SDG9	Global rules that affect policies
1. Targeted investments in infrastructure, training, education, research and development (R&D)	Not directly affected by World Trade Organization (WTO) or WTO+ agreements
2. Coordinated investments and government-mediated mergers	Not directly affected by WTO or WTO+ agreements
3. Subsidies for key industrial sectors	The WTO's Agreement on Subsidies and Countervailing Measures considers subsidies trade-distorting measures and prohibits any sector-specific subsidies, as well as those for export promotion and for enforcing the use of local content in manufacturing. It also prohibits indirect subsidies through intra–private sector transfers brought about by government regulation. In practice, however, subsidies can be used until they are challenged or countervailed.
	Subsidies for R&D, regional balances, and environmentally friendly technologies are "actionable" but have seldom been disputed, in part because developed countries often use them. Least developed countries are permitted to use export subsidies under certain conditions but are not exempted from countervailing measures from trading partners.
4. Creation of state-owned enterprises (SOEs)	The use of SOEs is not directly affected by WTO agreements. However, tariff cuts in the General Agreement on Tariffs and Trade (GATT) and market-access and national treatment requirements in the General Agreement on the Trade of Services (GATS)—Mode 3 (commercial presence) can be fatal for SOEs, limiting the potential to use them as industrial policy tools (e.g., a state-owned telecom company buying from local handset makers) or to supply services to locally owned industries at a subsidized rate (e.g., state-owned electricity companies giving concessional rates to designated industries or "industrial zones").
	Service sector commitments apply only to the sectors that countries agree to include, but developing countries are being pressured to expand and deepen their commitments in the Doha Round of WTO negotiations. WTO+ agreements are effectively used to achieve these aims despite the stagnation of the WTO's Doha Round or negotiation.

Table 4.2 *(Continued)*

5. Infant industry protections	WTO member countries are all required to bind at least some of their tariffs at an upper limit. In the Doha Round of Non-Agricultural Market Access negotiations, industrial countries are pushing to bind and slash all unbound tariffs. The GATT (Art. XVIII) allows developing countries with low standards of living to temporarily raise tariffs to promote the establishment of a particular industry, but this requires difficult negotiations, approval of WTO members, and compensation through other tariff reductions. Furthermore, the time frame allowed (eight years) is very short relative to historically effective time frames for infant-industry protections (Chang 2003, 268).
6. Capital controls and capital outflow taxes	Under the GATS and Trade-Related Investment Measures (TRIMS) regulations, restrictions on capital controls exist, but violations of the rules can be challenged in a dispute only if a member country initiates state-state arbitration. WTO+ agreements are much more restrictive. U.S. Bilateral Investment Treaties, for example, require that U.S. firms be allowed to freely transfer payments in and out of host countries without delay.
7. Government allocation of foreign exchange	Not directly affected by WTO or WTO+ agreements (or IMF)
8. Performance requirements	The WTO's TRIMS Agreement constrains local content requirements, but not conditions for joint venture and transfer of technology. The activities covered by the GATS-Mode 3 (services delivered through commercial presence) are subject to fewer restrictions than those covered by the TRIMS. WTO+ agreements, increase restrictions on performance requirements (e.g., U.S. BITs strictly prohibit all performance requirements; signatories in Sub-Saharan Africa include Cameroon, Congo, DRC, Mozambique, Rwanda, and Senegal).
9. Procurement policy	The WTO Agreement on Government Procurement restricts these measures, but most developing countries are not signatories. Some WTO+ trade and investment agreements restrict these measures (e.g., EU economic partnership agreements [EU-EPAs] categorically prohibit them). Cameroon, Côte d'Ivoire, Mauritius, Seychelles, and Zimbabwe are among the Sub-Saharan African countries that have in force EU-EPAs or are working toward them.

(e.g., Malaysia, Brazil, Trinidad and Tobago, India, Kazakhstan, Nigeria, Norway, United Kingdom). Subsidies for R&D, regional balances, and environmentally friendly technologies are in theory challengeable (i.e., "actionable" in the WTO jargon), but they are seldom disputed, in part because they are the subsidies that are often used by developed countries. Even tariff and quota restrictions can be circumvented with the strategic deployment of such measures as technical regulations and rules of origin, which can function as nontariff barriers to imports.

The drastic nature of the policy restrictions encoded in WTO+ agreements and the consequent impacts on quality of growth must not be underestimated. Even ostensibly benign agreements, such as PTAs, in which developed countries give unilateral tariff preferences to developing countries, ironically, are aggressively restrictive of their policy autonomy. PTAs are used not only to compel developing countries to make concessions on issues that lack consensus in the WTO (e.g., stricter investor rights protections, restrictions on government procurement) but also to coerce countries into making commitments that have little or nothing to do with trade, such as pursuing privatization and domestic deregulation. The U.S. AGOA, for example, requires various standards for qualification, including a commitment not to impose any taxes or operational conditions that could be interpreted as expropriation or taking control of U.S. firms. The act also requires that countries not "fail to work towards the provision of adequate and effective provision of intellectual property rights" (U.S. Trade Representative 2013; Chang, Hauge, and Irfan 2016, 131), which requires an enormous dedication of resources. Because developing countries are dependent on developed country markets, it is hardly an exaggeration to view these agreements as economic blackmail. Although it can sometimes be necessary for developing countries to make these kinds of concessions in exchange for access to developed country markets, they must be careful when evaluating the trade-offs, especially when it comes to policy autonomy.

GLOBAL RULES: PRIORITIES FOR REFORM

THE IMPORTANCE OF REVISING THE GLOBAL RULES TARGETS IN THE SUSTAINABLE DEVELOPMENT GOALS

It is encouraging that the Agenda for Sustainable Development recognizes the need for developing countries to work toward productive transformation, protect worker's rights, and aim for a host of other objectives that advance the quality of growth. Unfortunately, the few SDGs that address the need to reform global rules reveal some misunderstanding of the relationship between these global rules and the quality of growth. This should be rectified if the SDGs are to guide the reform of the global regulatory framework.

Table 4.3 highlights the inconsistency between the stated objectives of several SDGs and the reforms to global rules they identify as targets and indicators. For example, one of the indicators for SDG17 implicitly aims to lower the worldwide tariff average, which is antithetical to development if this is achieved at the expense of developing countries' tariff autonomy. Similarly, SDG3 Target 3.b correctly affirms the right of developing countries to use TRIPS flexibilities on intellectual property to achieve good health and well-being, but its indicator measures only net development assistance for medical research, rendering the intellectual property component of the target effectively toothless. A revision of these global rules–related targets in the spirit of what we propose in table 4.3 is an important task for the international community to pursue.

THE URGENCY OF IPR REFORM

The neglect of intellectual property in the SDGs is especially unfortunate when one considers the profound impact of IPRs on quality of growth. We have noted the implications of the TRIPS and WTO+ agreements for access to life-saving medication and agricultural livelihoods, but IPRs have even broader implications for quality of growth. They limit access to educational materials—indispensable for building human capabilities— and make patented technologies prohibitively expensive, hindering productivity growth. They also impose unnecessary strains on the limited public resources of developing countries, as a result of strong enforcement requirements, and they permeate all policy areas that are relevant for industrialization measures. For example, the European Union's EPAs not only include an entire chapter on intellectual property but also introduce IPR-related measures in the chapters on agricultural market access (i.e., expanding protection of geographical indications) and government procurement. These agreements go as far as forbidding countries from applying technological licensing requirements to foreign providers as a condition to participate in tendering processes.

Table 4.3   Global Rules in the Agenda for Sustainable Development

SDGs, Targets, and Indicators (Quality of Growth Proxies) that Address Global Rules Directly	Analysis of Global Rules Measures Proposed in the Agenda for Sustainable Development
2. End hunger, achieve food security and improved nutrition, and promote sustainable agriculture Target 2.b Correct and prevent trade restrictions and distortions in world agricultural markets, including through the parallel elimination of all forms of agricultural export subsidies [. . .] (Indicator 2.b.1 Producer Support Estimate; Indicator 2.b.2 Agricultural export subsidies).	Obligations to reduce agricultural export subsidies should be limited to developed countries, which could still be allowed to retain some subsidies for food sovereignty purposes. Developing countries should not be subjected to the restrictions. The global rules identified for SDG8 and SDG9 (see table 4.3) are far more relevant for achieving SDG2. **Alternative indicator:** Proportion of trade and investment agreements that do not restrict policies identified in SDG8 and SDG9.
3. Ensure healthy lives and promote well-being for all at all ages Target 3.b Support the research and development of vaccines and medicines [. . .] in accordance with the Doha Declaration on the TRIPS Agreement and Public Health, which affirms the right of developing countries to use to the full the provisions in the TRIPS Agreement regarding flexibilities to protect public health, and, in particular, provide access to medicines for all. (Indicator 3.b.2 Total net official development assistance to medical research and basic health sectors).	Target 3.b is consistent in affirming the right to developing countries to use TRIPS flexibilities. This would also imply recommending that countries do not sign on to WTO+ agreements that restrict these flexibilities. **Alternative indicator:** A more relevant indicator than 3.b.2 would be the number of revoked free trade agreements and bilateral investment treaties that restrict TRIPS flexibilities.
10. Reduce inequality within and among countries Target 10.a Implement the principle of special and differential treatment for developing countries [. . .] (Indicator 10.a.1 Proportion of tariff lines applied to imports from [. . .] developing countries with zero-tariff).	Target 10.a correctly identifies the need to implement the principle of special and differential treatment (SDT), but the indicator should be revised. **Alternative indicator:** proportion of trade and investment agreements that apply SDT and do not restrict policies identified in SDG8 and SDG9.

Table 4.3   (Continued)

17. Strengthen the means of implementation and revitalize the global partnership for sustainable development Target 17.10 Promote a universal, rules-based, open, nondiscriminatory and equitable multilateral trading system [. . .] (Indicator 17.10.1 Worldwide weighted tariff-average) Target 17.12 Realize timely implementation of duty-free and quota-free market access [. . .] for all least developed countries (Indicator 17.12.1 Average tariffs faced by developing countries, least developed countries and small island developing states)	Target 17.10 and its corresponding indicator are problematic and potentially inconsistent with target 10.a, which endorses special and differential treatment rather than the nondiscrimination proposed in 17.10. The objective should not be to lower worldwide average tariff, as implied by the indicator. Target 17.10.12 is helpful, but the policies and global rules identified for in SDG8 and SDG9 are far more relevant for SDG17. **Alternative indicator**: proportion of trade and investment agreements that apply SDT and do not restrict policies identified in SDG8 and SDG9.

Source: Authors. Targets and indicators from United Nations (2015).

Although the broad-ranging implications of IPRs for quality of growth render them the single most important priority for reform, the dispersion of IPR restrictions over countless agreements and their subcomponents makes this a difficult challenge to tackle. At the very least, countries should avoid making additional commitments to those already enshrined in the WTO agreements. If developing countries are able to collaborate within the framework of the WTO, they also can protect the flexibilities afforded by the TRIPS. In WTO+ agreements, developing countries should be especially careful to ensure that additional IPR restrictions are not included in new and unexpected places (e.g., government procurement, where they still have autonomy).

EXTENDING THE TIME FRAME FOR INFANT INDUSTRY PROTECTIONS TO SAFEGUARD INDUSTRIAL POLICY MEASURES

Like intellectual property, "infant industry protections" can cover a host of policy areas related to quality of growth, from tariffs to subsidies. Rather than trying to reform the plethora of individual rules that impinge on the capacity of countries to use tried-and-true industrial policy measures (see the text box and table 4.2), a simple way to endow developing countries with greater policy autonomy is to extend the number of years during which infant industry protections, in general, are allowed. With few exceptions, the current WTO allowance of eight years pales in comparison to the periods of protection that historically have been required for the development of new industries (e.g., several decades for the Japanese and Korean auto industries and nearly two decades for Finland's Nokia). Developing countries could push for this reform within the framework of the WTO, invoking the Agenda for Sustainable Development's call for the application of the principle of special and differential treatment. Should such a scenario fail to materialize, individual countries (or blocs, like the African Union) could refrain from making further concessions on this front. In so doing, they would ensure that any agreement they sign preserves the eight-year infant industry period granted by the WTO.

REFORMING INVESTOR-STATE DISPUTE SETTLEMENT TO FIGHT REGULATORY CHILL AND PROTECT STATE SOVEREIGNTY

When considering "global rules," it can be easy to forget the impact of how they are enforced. This enforcement can have far-reaching consequences for quality of growth, as evidenced by the outcomes of the rise of ISDS in recent decades. Although spaces like the World Bank's ICSID have been around for decades, WTO+ agreements (especially BITs) have greatly expanded the capacity of firms to use these spaces.

Aside from the problematic cession of jurisdictional sovereignty, ISDS has been particularly detrimental to developing countries, which find it difficult to defend themselves in international arbitration because of limited resources and weak geopolitical positions. Furthermore, the threat of ISDS has proven effective in inducing "regulatory chill," dissuading countries from implementing even the most commonsense quality-of-growth measures. One well-known example is Philip Morris's threats to Togo over proposed plain-packaging regulations for tobacco. Togo, which has a GDP of US$4 billion, received a letter from Philip Morris, with revenues of close to US$80 billion, warning of an "incalculable amount of trade litigation"[12] if the country chose to proceed, on the grounds that plain packaging would be considered a violation of the company's IPRs. Unsurprisingly, the threat was effective.

LIMIT BILATERAL AND REGIONAL TRADE AGREEMENTS

In today's global economy, bilateral and regional trade and investment agreements are among the most powerful threats to developing countries' policy space. We claim that a progressive logic of trade should challenge the damaging effects and legitimacy of certain BITs and RTAs within the WTO. We should allow developing countries to pull out of the most damaging agreements or at least reconsider the terms of these agreements. More important, both North-South and South-South regional agreements, like the CFTA, should move away from placing excessive faith in the benefits of indiscriminate market integration and instead should consider its real impact, especially when integration involves countries with extremely unequal productive structures and capabilities.

In the section "Global Power Concentration, Endogenous Asymmetries, and Policy Space," we identified the ways in which FTAs and RTAs like EPA can hamper the industrialization of African countries. With respect to South-South regional agreements in Africa, the CFTA is the most ambitious plan of continental integration that African countries have undertaken. The establishment of the CFTA would create a continental market of more than a billion people and a GDP of more than US$3 trillion. Despite its potential, in its current format, tariff liberalization under the CFTA will lead to further structural imbalances between countries in the continent and will exacerbate and potentially accelerate existing problems, in particular, fiscal revenue imbalances and deindustrialization.

The principle informing the redesign of these agreements should balance both demand-side pull dynamics (market integration) and supply-side bottlenecks (lack of industrial capabilities and weak production structure). To capture opportunities offered by trade integration, developing countries should be given more policy space and support in other industrial and investment policies (beyond trade policies), which will counterbalance the negative impacts of integration during the early stages of industrialization.

CONCLUSION

The reform of global rules is undoubtedly a fundamental component of any serious agenda to improve quality of growth, whether it is global, regional, or national. Global reform, however, is ultimately a geopolitical power game and, for developing countries, this means that the reforms they require can be achieved only through the cooperation of citizens in developed countries (e.g., ISDS reform) or through the formation of regional or transregional power blocs capable of countering the pressures of the global powers (e.g., in WTO and WTO+ negotiations). In this sense, African countries have much to gain from the consolidation of the African Union.

Even if regional divisions outstrip the willingness to cooperate for the common good, developing countries can benefit from taking a more careful, measured, and courageous approach to the management of policy space. Much can be gained from devoting resources to creatively carving out policy space, attenuating the most stringent restrictions, and devising new measures that have effects similar to those that have been proscribed[13] as well as from fully exploiting the considerable policy autonomy that remains. Many countries neglect to use the policy space available to them, not only out of fear of economic retaliation but also as a result of an ideological environment that instills in policy makers an instinctive distrust in industrial policy, even in the face of the hard evidence provided by experience. In this sense, it might be said that the most fundamental reform that is needed is ideological.

NOTES

1. For example, in the Doha Development Round, as part of the proposed Non-Agriculture Market Access agreement, countries were asked to bind all the remaining unbound tariffs and then slash them using the so-called Swiss Formula for all products (according to the six-digit Harmonized System of classification); see Ha-Joon Chang, Jostein Løre Hauge, and Muhammad Irfan, *Transformative Industrial Policy for Africa* (Addis Ababa, Ethiopia: UN Economic Commission for Africa, 2016, 120).

2. Within the AGOA PTA, textile and apparel manufactured in Africa qualify for duty-free access export to the United States. The raw materials used in the production of these garments, however, must be insourced domestically or from the United States. In the case raw material is imported from third countries, a cap on exports applies.

3. These are consistent with the objectives of the African Union's Agenda 2063.

4. We include only a small selection of the corresponding targets and indicators. For a full list, see the UN Economic and Social Council, "Report of the Inter-Agency and Expert Group on Sustainable Development Goal Indicators" (New York: UN Economic and Social Council, 2016).

5. For further detail on China's industrial policy, as well as that of Singapore, South Korea, and others, see Ha-Joon Chang, Antonio Andreoni and Ming-Leon

Kuan, *International Industrial Policy Experiences and Lessons for the UK* (London: UK Government Office for Science, 2013).

6. For further detail on Malaysia see, Ha-Joon Chang, Jostein Løre Hauge, and Muhammad Irfan, *Transformative Industrial Policy for Africa* (Addis Ababa, Ethiopia: UN Economic Commission for Africa, 2016).

7. For detail on these experiences of Thailand and Indonesia, see Michael T. Rock, "Selective Industrial Policy and Manufacturing Export Success in Thailand" and "Making the Case for the Success of Industrial Policy in Indonesia" in *Southeast Asia's Industrialization: Industrial Policy, Capabilities and Sustainability*, ed. Jomo Kwame Sundaram, *Studies in the Economies of East and Southeast Asia* (Basingstoke, UK: Palgrave, 2001).

8. We include all countries in the geographic region of Sub-Saharan Africa, including those of North Africa that belong to the Arab League.

9. For more details on both the tariff commitments of Sub-Saharan countries in the WTO and the policies allowed under WTO commitments, see Ha-Joon Chang et al., *Transformative Industrial Policy for Africa*.

10. Technically, WTO+ agreements build on those already agreed to in the WTO's multilateral agreements.

11. Further detail on most of these policy restrictions can be found in Ha-Joon Chang et al., *Transformative Industrial Policy for* Africa, 117–142. These tables draw heavily on the legal analysis in this report.

12. See Chuck Idelson, "Trade Deals Should Come with Their Own Warnings for Public Health," National Nurses United, February 18, 2015, http://www.nationalnursesunited.org/blog/entry/trade-deals-should-come-with-their-own-warnings-for-public-health/.

13. For instance, although subsidies are prohibited, development banks can lend at preferential rates to nascent industries.

REFERENCES

The Africa Report. 2016. Top 500 Companies. http://www.theafricareport.com/Top-500-Companies-2016.html.

Amsden, Alice H. 2001. *The Rise of "the Rest": Challenges to the West from Late-Industrializing Economies*. Oxford: Oxford University Press.

Andreoni, Antonio. 2016. "Varieties of Industrial Policy: Models, Packages and Transformation Cycles." In *Efficiency, Finance and Varieties of Industrial Policy*, ed. Akbar Noman and Joseph Stiglitz, 245–305. New York: Columbia University Press

——. 2019. "A Generalized Linkage Approach to Local Production Systems Development in the Era of Global Value Chains, with Special Reference to Africa." Chap. 9 in *The Quality of Growth in Africa*," ed. Ravi Kanbur, Akbar Noman, and Joseph E. Stiglitz (this volume). New York: Columbia University Press.

Andreoni, Antonio, and Ha-Joon Chang. 2017. "Bringing Production and Employment Back into Development: Alice Amsden's Legacy for a New Developmentalist Agenda." *Cambridge Journal of Regions, Economy and Society* 10 (1): 173–187.

Baldwin, Richard. 2010. "Unilateral Tariff Liberalisation." NBER Working Paper 16600, December. National Bureau of Economic Research, Cambridge, MA.

Chang, Ha-Joon. 2001. "Intellectual Property Rights and Economic Development: Historical Lessons and Emerging Issues." *Journal of Human Development* 2: 287–309.

———. 2002. *Kicking Away the Ladder: Development Strategy in Historical Perspective.* London: Anthem Press.

———. 2003. *Globalisation, Economic Development, and the Role of the State.* New York: Zed Books

———, ed. 2007. "State-Owned Enterprise Reform." National Development Strategies—Policy Notes. UN Department of Social and Economic Affairs, United Nations, New York.

Chang, Ha-Joon, Antonio Andreoni, and Ming-Leon Kuan. 2013. *International Industrial Policy Experiences and Lessons for the UK.* London: UK Government Office for Science.

Chang, Ha-Joon, Jostein Løre Hauge, and Muhammad Irfan. 2016. *Transformative Industrial Policy for Africa.* Addis Ababa, Ethiopia: UN Economic Commission for Africa.

Fortune. (2017). "Global 500." October 27. http://fortune.com/global500/.

Freund, Caroline, and Dario Sidhu. 2017. "Global Competition and the Rise of China." Working Paper No. 17–3. Peterson Institute for International Economics, Washington, DC.

Furman, Jason, and Peter Orszag. 2015. "A Firm-Level Perspective on the Role of Rents in the Rise in Inequality." Presentation at "A Just Society" Centennial Event in Honor of Joseph Stiglitz, October 16, Columbia University, New York.

Galbraith, John Kenneth. 1967. *The New Industrial State.* Princeton, NJ: Princeton University Press.

Gallagher, Kevin P. 2005. *Putting Development First: The Importance of Policy Space in the WTO and International Financial Institutions.* London: Zed Books.

Idelson, Chuck. 2015. "Trade Deals Should Come with Their Own Warnings for Public Health." National Nurses United, February 18. http://www.nationalnursesunited.org/blog/entry/trade-deals-should-come-with-their-own-warnings-for-public-health/.

Mayer, Jörg. 2009. "Policy Space: What, for What, and Where?" *Development Policy Review* 27: 373–395

Milberg, William, and Deborah Winkler. 2013. *Outsourcing Economics: Global Value Chains in Capitalist Development.* Cambridge: Cambridge University Press.

Nadvi, Khalid. 2008. "Global standards, Global Governance and the Organization of Global Value Chains." *Journal of Economic Geography* 8 (3): 323–343.

Nolan, Peter. 2001. *China and the Global Economy: National Champions, Industrial Policy, and the Big Business Revolution.* New York: Palgrave.

Nolan, Peter. 2012. *Is China Buying the World?* Cambridge: Polity Press.

Ocampo, Jose Antonio, and Rob Vos. 2008. *Uneven Economic Development.* London: Zed Books.

Rasiah, Rajah. 2005. "Trade-related Investment Liberalization under the WTO: The Malaysian Experience." *Global Economic Review* 34: 453–471.

Rock, Michael T. 2001. "Selective Industrial Policy and Manufacturing Export Success in Thailand." In *Southeast Asia's Industrialization: Industrial Policy, Capabilities and Sustainability*, ed. Jomo Kwame Sundaram. Studies in the Economies of East and Southeast Asia. Basingstoke, UK: Palgrave.

Rock, Michael T. 2001. "Making the Case for the Success of Industrial Policy in Indonesia." In *Southeast Asia's Industrialization: Industrial Policy, Capabilities and Sustainability*, ed. Jomo Kwame Sundaram. Studies in the Economies of East and Southeast Asia. Basingstoke, UK: Palgrave.

Singh, Ajit. 1971. *Take-Overs: Their Relevance to the Stock Market and the Theory of the Firm.* Cambridge: Cambridge University Press.

——. 2014. "Competition, Competition Policy, Competitiveness, Globalisation and Development." Working Paper 460. Centre for Business Research, University of Cambridge.

Thrasher, Rachel D. and Gallagher, Kevin. 2008. "21st Century Trade Agreements: Implications for Long-Run Development Policy." The Pardee Papers, No. 2. Frederick S. Pardee Center for the Study of the Longer-range Future, Boston University.

Tucker, Todd N. 2017. "The Sustainable Equitable Trade Doctrine. Building Progressive International Cooperation to Counter Right-Wing Economic Authoritarianism." Roosevelt Institute. http://rooseveltinstitute.org/wp-content/uploads/2017/03/The-Sustainable-Equitable-Trade-Doctrine.pdf.

United Nations. 2015. *Transforming our World: The 2030 Agenda for Sustainable Development.* New York: United Nations.

United Nations Economic and Social Council. 2016. "Report of the Inter-Agency and Expert Group on Sustainable Development Goal Indicators." New York: UN Economic and Social Council.

United Nations Economic Commission for Africa. 2015. *Economic Report on Africa 2015: Industrializing Through Trade.* Addis Ababa, Ethiopia: UN Economic Commission for Africa.

U.S. Trade Representative. 2013. "Seventh Report to the Congress on the Operation of the Andean Trade Preference Act as Amended." Accessed March 19, 2017, https://ustr.gov/sites/default/files/USTR%202013%20ATPA%20Report.pdf.

Wade, Robert. 2003. "What Strategies Are Viable for Developing Countries Today? The World Trade Organization and the Shrinking of 'DEVELOPMENT Space.' " *Review of International Political Economy* 10 (4): 621–644.

Weeks, John. 2012. "The Fallacy of Competition: Markets and the Movement of Capital." In *Alternative Theories of Competition*, ed. Jamee K. Moudud, Cyrus Bina, and Patrick L. Mason, 35–48. London: Routledge.

Zhou Yu, William Lazonick, and Yifei Sun. 2016. *China as an Innovation Nation.* Oxford: Oxford University Press.

CHAPTER 5

What Should Africa Learn from East Asian Development?

Jomo Kwame Sundaram

After a quarter century of stagnation from the end of the 1970s, growth in many countries in Sub-Saharan Africa (SSA) finally picked up early this century. Both internal and external factors—particularly growing demand associated with high growth rates in some large Asian emerging economies, higher commodity prices, and new resource exploitation opportunities—contributed to this acceleration. Even with this growth, average real per capita income is still barely higher than it was in 1980, and compared with other regions, the continent has lost ground on most development and welfare indicators.

During this lost quarter century from the late 1970s until 2000, real income growth failed to keep pace with population growth in SSA (see table 5.1). With trade liberalization, the continent deindustrialized and changed from a net exporter of food into a net importer. Despite more rapid growth, slowing from 2014, this trend has continued, and the share of manufacturing in GDP declined further. Although Asian developing countries absorbed growing numbers of workers into booming manufacturing sectors, Africa has failed to do so. Consequently, unemployment and underemployment are widespread, and low-productivity informal sector, including agricultural activities are the primary income sources for much of the population in many SSA countries.

Africa's slow growth in the 1980s and 1990s, and the failure to industrialize its economies are due to economic liberalization and the structural adjustment programs adopted from the early 1980s (Jomo, Schwank, and von Arnim 2013). In the 1960s, per capita GDP and GDP growth were actually higher in Africa than in Asia. The expectations then were that African countries would grow faster because of their superior resource endowments (World Bank 2005, 274). Primary commodities dominated exports, but many countries also showed strong industrial growth, averaging above 6 percent for more than half the countries for which data were available. Governments invested heavily in infrastructure, sometimes supported by donors, and pursued import substitution industrialization strategies. Growth was fueled by high investment rates, but this growth was not matched by domestic savings, which suggested a dependence on foreign capital, whether through aid or investment (Lawrence 2010). As a result, debt levels increased and made the continent more vulnerable to macrofinancial shocks.

In the last two decades of the twentieth century, SSA income growth barely kept pace with population growth. After a moderate increase in per capita income during the 1970s, SSA growth averaged 2.1 percent per year in the 1980s and 2.4 percent in the 1990s. Despite a short-lived recovery after the mid-1990s, SSA per capita income at the turn of the century was 10 percent below the level two decades earlier. Slow and erratic SSA growth was accompanied by more regressive income distribution. The drop in average per capita income for the poorest 20 percent in SSA was twice the average for everyone between 1980 and 1995 (United Nations Conference on Trade and Development [UNCTAD] 2001, 53).

The collapse of the Bretton Woods system, the two oil shocks of the 1970s, the interest rate hike of the early 1980s, slower world growth, and lower primary commodity prices all significantly affected Africa, triggering vicious downward spirals in many countries (figure 5.1). The neoliberal policy response—imposed by the Bretton Woods institutions on indebted governments, and subsequently dubbed the Washington Consensus—included prioritizing fiscal balance, reducing public expenditure in general and subsidies in particular, liberalizing interest rates and imports, pursuing privatization, and seeking economic deregulation (Williamson 1990). The Washington Consensus[1] is generally seen as the basis for the global trend toward greater economic liberalization and enhanced property rights since the 1980s. In Africa, liberalization and privatization measures sought to integrate countries into global markets and to attract private investment, replacing state interventions, notably support for infant industries and food production.

The outcomes of this policy shift were ambiguous, however, to say the least. Generally, they have increased, rather than reduced, Africa's vulnerability to global economic shocks. Negative average per capita income growth from the late 1970s into the early twenty-first century

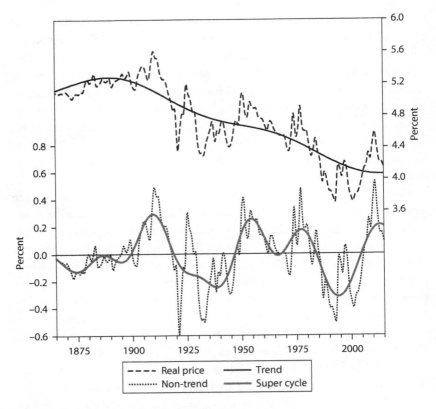

Figure 5.1   Real tropical agricultural price components

Source: Erten and Ocampo (2013).

also suggests that the reforms failed, but there is limited consensus over the reasons why. The link between the structural adjustments required by the Bretton Woods institutions and subsequent economic growth is tenuous: of the fifteen countries identified as core adjusters by the World Bank in 1993, only three were subsequently classified by the International Monetary Fund (IMF) as strong economic performers. Mkandawire (2005) has argued that IMF-led "adjustment" in Africa put the continent on a slow growth path—a view broadly supported by econometric studies of the broader impact of such programs (Barro and Lee 2002).

For SSA, the new generation of policies espoused by the Washington Consensus—first involving "getting prices right," and then, "getting

Table 5.1   Per Capita GDP Growth in Developing Countries, 1960–2014

Annual Average Compound Growth Rates	1960–1969 (%)	1970–1979 (%)	1980–1989 (%)	1990–1999 (%)	2000–2009 (%)	2010–2014 (%)
World	3.1	1.8	1.3	1.0	1.0	0.5
East Asia and Pacific	5.9	2.7	3.2	1.8	2.7	1.3
Europe and Central Asia	3.5	2.4	1.7	1.2	1.2	0.3
Latin America and Caribbean	2.5	3.1	−0.4	1.3	1.4	0.7
Middle East and North Africa		4.2	−2.1	1.3	2.4	0.5
Sub-Saharan Africa	1.8	0.7	−1.2	−0.7	2.0	0.6
South Asia	1.7	0.2	2.8	3.0	4.5	1.9

Sources: World Bank, *World Development Indicators*, and author's calculations (GDP per capita in constant 2005 U.S. dollars).

Note: GDP = gross domestic product.

institutions right" and "good governance"—are still offered as advice, if not imposed as conditionalities. Income levels in much of SSA are still too low to generate the domestic resources needed for rapid growth.

LESSONS FROM EAST ASIA?

SSA's development experiences contrast sharply with East Asia's. This study seeks to draw some lessons from the latter experiences, which seem crucial for developmental policy in SSA. To do so, it is necessary to understand the bases for the unprecedented development performance of economies in East Asia as well as some key differences within the region. At the heart of its overall growth and transformation has been rapid industrialization, and the productivity growth, learning, and adaptation of technologies associated with it. The underlying reasons for East Asia's successful catch-up have been much debated. Most important, there have been different interpretations of the role of the state and the specific nature of the region's integration into the global economy.

From the 1980s, and especially in the early and mid-1990s, there was growing international recognition of the rapid economic growth, structural change, and industrialization of the East Asian region, including the four economies of Southeast Asia, namely Singapore, Malaysia, Thailand, and Indonesia. Until the Japanese stagnation from the 1990s and the

1997–1998 Asian financial crises, nine East Asian economies experienced rapid growth and structural transformation over several decades (see table 5.1). The region achieved greater integration into the world economy, but it did so in radically different ways than have been sought by SSA in recent decades, as it simultaneously increased its shares of both exports and manufactures compared with GDP (Palma 2009).

The tendency has also been to see East Asia as much more economically homogenous than it actually was, and is, and a corresponding inclination to see economic progress in the region as similar in origin and nature. Terms such as the "Far East," "Asia-Pacific," "Pacific Asia," "East Asia," "Asian miracle," "yen bloc," "flying geese," "tigers," and "mini-dragons" have encouraged this perception of the region as far more economically integrated and similar than it actually was and is.

Although the World Bank study enhanced international recognition of the rapid economic growth, structural change, industrialization, and consequent poverty reduction, in the East Asian region, it also promoted a tendency to see East Asia as a much more economically coherent region than it actually was, and a corresponding tendency to see economic progress in the region as similar in origin and nature. Before the region's currency and financial crises of 1997–1998, the World Bank and others celebrated Malaysia, Thailand, and Indonesia as new models for emulation by other developing countries, especially in SSA. Similar claims have resurfaced more recently as East Asia seemed to have fared better than much of the rest of the world during the global economic slowdown following the 2008–2009 financial crises. Once again, it has been claimed that East Asian economies generally achieved sustained and equitable export-led high growth and rapid industrialization.

Implicit in the World Bank study was the claim that the achievements of these three Southeast Asian economies were similar to, and comparable with, the other East Asian economies in terms of growth, structural change and industrialization. The industrialization records of Malaysia, Thailand, and Indonesia, however, have significantly differed from, and been inferior to, those of Japan, South Korea, Taiwan, and Singapore (Jomo et al. 1997; Jomo 2001, 2003).

SOUTHEAST ASIAN DEVELOPMENT

The most important and influential document recognizing the rapid growth, structural change, and industrialization of much of East Asia has been the World Bank's (1993) *The East Asian Miracle*. At the behest of the Japanese executive director at the World Bank, the study was commissioned with Japanese government funding in recognition of the region's rapid growth and structural change. Sustained East Asian growth, transformation and industrialization sharply contrasted with the dismal experiences with structural adjustment programs (SAPs) in Latin America, Africa, and other parts of the world, resulting in recession and stagnation in several of these economies as well as in slow and unimpressive growth elsewhere. This stagnation resulted in the "lost decade" of the 1980s in Latin America and the "lost quarter-century" in SSA.

The study identified eight high-performing Asian economies: Japan; the four first-generation newly industrializing economies (NIEs) or countries (NICs), dragons or tigers, namely, South Korea, Taiwan, Hong Kong, and Singapore; and the three second-generation Southeast Asian NICs, namely, Malaysia, Thailand, and Indonesia. Importantly, China was deliberately left out. The study recognized that the likelihood of eight relatively contiguous economies growing so rapidly for such sustained periods of time was less than one in sixty thousand. Unlike the later 1997 *Emerging Asia* study, by the now-defunct Harvard Institute of International Development (HIID) for the Asian Development Bank (ADB 1997), also dominated by the Japanese government with U.S. government acquiescence, it did not have anything to say about geography.

The Miracle study helped shift the World Bank from its Washington Consensus market fundamentalism of the 1980s to acknowledge an important developmental role for the state in the 1990s. This impression has been reinforced by other World Bank publications, especially the 1997 *World Development Report*, which advocated effective—rather than minimalist—states (World Bank 1997), its *Economic Growth in the 1990s: Learning from a Decade of Reform* report (World Bank 2005), and the work of the Growth Commission it sponsored, chaired by Michael Spence. The study identified at least seven types of state interventions as having been important in East Asia, but it endorsed only four functional interventions for emulation by others:

- ensuring *macroeconomic* discipline and macroeconomic balances
- providing physical and social *infrastructure*
- providing good *governance* more generally
- raising *savings* and investment rates

These four functional interventions were deemed less distortive of markets or desirable to compensate for alleged market failures. However, the study was more critical of three identified "strategic" interventions—that is, directed, subsidized credit; international trade; and industrial policy interventions—all considered to be more distortive of markets.

It is useful to compare and contrast what actually happened in East Asia with the World Bank's version. There is little disagreement that maintaining macroeconomic balances was important in the region. But the Bank's recommended parameters of macroeconomic discipline were moot. For instance, inflation was generally kept under 20 percent in the high-performing Asian economies (HPAEs; the World Bank study's preferred term), but it was certainly not always below 10 percent, as urged by the World Bank. Single-digit inflation was neither a policy priority nor always ensured in some HPAEs during their high-growth periods.

Similarly, neither the fiscal balance nor the current account of the balance of payments were always maintained in balance, let alone in surplus. Malaysia and Thailand had relatively high current account surpluses throughout the 1990s, while countries with small budgetary deficits or even surpluses were not spared the 1997 currency attacks and massive depreciations of the Asian financial crisis.

The high level of East Asian savings mainly includes corporate or firm savings, rather than household savings. Household savings in Southeast Asia are not much higher than in the rest of the world, except in Malaysia. The difference in Malaysia is probably the result of mandatory or forced savings schemes introduced in Malaysia and Singapore during the late colonial period and the relatively high share of wage earners in the labor force. This contrasts with the widespread presumption that savings and investment rates are high in the region because East Asians are culturally inclined to be thriftier—unlike Africans and Latin Americans.

In pursuing the supposedly functional interventions, East Asian governments were not just market conforming; rather, they were playing important roles, which have been more than merely market augmenting. Clearly, such interventions were not in line with the Washington Consensus. As for the more controversial, so-called strategic interventions, the World Bank grudgingly claimed that only financial interventions were successful in East Asia, particularly in Northeast Asia—that is, in Japan, South Korea and Taiwan. The World Bank, however, also implied that nobody else was capable of successfully pursuing policies that the

Northeast Asians successfully implemented because state capabilities there were unique and could be not replicated.

Creating the conditions for attracting foreign direct investment (FDI)—rather than liberalizing financial markets—has had much more to do with reforming incentives and governance more generally to attract such investments. Southeast Asian governments, notably in Singapore and Malaysia, have especially sought to attract FDI. The rationale offered has been that domestic industrial capabilities are not capable of becoming internationally competitive.

Attracting FDI, however, should be distinguished from capital account liberalization, which came under renewed consideration after the 1997–1998 East Asian financial crises. Those crises were precipitated by an eventually successful currency attack on the overvalued Thai baht, with contagion greatly exacerbated by herd-like panicky withdrawals from the entire Southeast Asian region, inducing currency and stock market collapses (Jomo 1998). Because those who control financial assets had come to enjoy disproportionate political influence in Southeast Asian economies, liberalizing financial markets, ostensibly to induce net inflows of portfolio investments, enabled easier significant movements in and out of the market, especially at moments of crisis when such inflows were most needed.

The Miracle study claimed that government interventions were trade-distortionary and generally unsuccessful in East Asia, with minor exceptions. Contrary to the impression given, the Japanese, South Korean, and Taiwanese governments successfully pursued import-substituting industrialization from the 1950s, but they also promoted export orientation from the 1960s while ensuring that their industries quickly became internationally competitive by using conditional incentives and performance criteria to accelerate industrialization.

For example, infant industries were given *effective protection conditional on export promotion*, which had the effect of forcing firms and industries to quickly become internationally competitive. Firms were protected for certain periods, depending on the complexity of the products being made and assessments of reasonable learning time requirements. Strict discipline was imposed, requiring that firms begin exporting certain output shares within specified periods in return for temporary import protection and other incentives enjoyed. Such policies forced firms to reduce their production costs as quickly as possible, for example, by trying to achieve greater economies of scale and to accelerate learning. Requiring exports also meant that producers sought to achieve international quality standards quickly, imposing pressures to progress technologically in terms of both products as well as processes.

The Miracle study claimed that Southeast Asia began to take off only after economic liberalization in the mid-1980s, arguing that economic recovery, rapid growth, and industrialization were the consequences. This sweeping claim ignores the role of the region's undervalued exchange rates and other incentives during that period to relocate manufacturing output from Japan and the first-generation East Asian NIEs into the rest of Southeast Asia as well as China. Although exports may rise with greater external market access, imports also tend to rise strongly with trade liberalization, especially if the domestic currency appreciates as a consequence of greater exports. The possibility of increased agricultural exports, however, does not necessarily ensure stronger domestic economic growth, as the collapse of Sub-Saharan African manufacturing and the stagnation of Sub-Saharan African food agriculture from the late 1970s make clear. Thus, trade liberalization condemned SSA to economic regression by undermining, and not supporting, its nascent industries.

Although the World Bank did not really tout an East Asian model as such, the Miracle study often has been seen as recommending this. More generally, East Asia has been treated as a single entity constituting a flock of flying geese or even a yen bloc. Many commentators have discussed generic East Asian models, approaches, and ways of doing things. After the end of the Japanese boom in the early 1990s, in particular following the 1997–1998 regional financial crisis, sentiment on East Asia soured. Miracle talk was replaced with similarly broad-brushed generalizations about the East Asian debacle, crony capitalism, and other regional liabilities and afflictions.

Many lessons can be drawn from East Asian experiences, but they are certainly far from constituting variants of a single model. In addition, Southeast Asian countries were quite distinct from the rest of East Asia in some important respects (e.g., the role of FDI). Some deregulation in the mid-1980s was accompanied by some new private sector–oriented regulation, more appropriate to the new industrial policy priorities of the governments of Singapore, Malaysia, Thailand, and Indonesia (Jomo et al. 1997). In contrast, those most successful in developing indigenous industrial capacities and capabilities in East Asia then—namely, Japan, South Korea, and Taiwan—hardly depended on FDI, which played relatively small roles in the catch-up stage of their industrialization. There has also been considerable diversity in the role and performance of public investments, including state-owned enterprises, in Southeast Asia. For instance, the single largest Singapore firm investing abroad has been the Government Investment Corporation.

The World Bank's Miracle study urged other developing countries to emulate Southeast Asia, not Northeast Asia, even though the achievements of the first-tier East Asian NIEs (including Singapore) were clearly superior in economic performance compared with the second-tier Southeast Asian NICs. Thus, until the 1997–1998 financial crises, Singapore, Malaysia, Thailand, and Indonesia were presented as having achieved rapid, sustained, and equitable export-led growth and industrialization.

Despite Southeast Asia's much greater resource wealth-based growth, per capita income and economic welfare in Northeast Asia have been superior over the long term. From the 1960s until the early 1990s, growth rates in Northeast Asia averaged about 8 percent, compared with about 6 percent for Southeast Asia. This 2 percent difference, compounded over more than a quarter century, and lower population growth—except in Hong Kong because of immigration from China and, perhaps, Singapore—accounts for the growing gap between Northeast Asia and Southeast Asia. Immigration into Hong Kong, Malaysia, Singapore, and Thailand accounts for significant proportions of the labor forces while it also lowers wage costs, although Singapore has increasingly attracted more highly skilled professionals.

Southeast Asia's achievements have been less impressive in some critical ways, causing some to argue that resource wealth is not a blessing, but a curse, in so far as it postpones the imperative to develop in a more balanced way. Northeast Asia has long had more sophisticated and effective industrial policies compared with Southeast Asia, accounting for their important differences in industrial and technological capacities and capabilities. Industrialization in Southeast Asia, especially in Singapore and Malaysia, was primarily driven by FDI, in contrast with Northeast Asian industrialization.

Clearly, important lessons can be drawn from Southeast Asia, but there is no single Southeast Asian model either. For many reasons, it does not make much sense for any other country to try to emulate any particular economy in the region, let alone Southeast Asia more generally. Most other developing countries will find it impossible to emulate the Southeast Asian region, even if they want to, as the circumstances they face are quite different. Lessons to be drawn from Southeast Asian experiences are best drawn from carefully nuanced analysis, rather than by making generalizations about a rather diverse region.

The much greater Southeast Asian dependence on FDI raises questions about the actual nature of industrial and technological capacities and capabilities in these economies—in particular, about the region's supposedly most dynamic and export-oriented sectors. This, in turn, raises concerns about the sustainability of their growth and industrialization processes, especially if they are later deemed less attractive for further FDI—for example, as other more attractive locations become available. Dominance by foreign transnationals has often subordinated and marginalized domestic industrial capital in the region, allowing finance capital, both domestic and foreign, to become more influential in the region. Thus, transnational dominance of Southeast Asian industrialization has facilitated the ascendance and consolidation of financial interests and politically influential rentiers.

The 1997–1998 Southeast Asian debacle can be traced to poorly conceived and sequenced financial liberalization that resulted in attracting massive, but easily reversible, capital inflows into the region. Capital inflows tended to raise foreign reserves, domestic credit availability, and exchange rates. The combination of increased capital inflows, credit expansion, and exchange rate appreciation raised aggregate demand more rapidly than GDP, further increasing the current account deficit. There is no evidence that capital inflows into the region contributed significantly to accelerating economic growth, even in the tradable sectors of the economy. Instead, these inflows contributed greatly to asset price bubbles, whose inevitable collapses were accelerated by currency crises with devastating consequences. Other likely consequences included consumption binges as well as poor and excessive investments.

Thus, the Southeast Asian miracle—as represented by Malaysia, Thailand, and Indonesia—was inferior to the rest of the region's economic achievements in terms of growth, inequality, industrialization, policy formulation and implementation, human resource development, and industrial and technological development. Although the 1997–1998 financial crises were not direct outcomes of these factors, or even of cronyism or poor corporate governance, as was widely alleged, the fragility and vulnerability of the region's national financial systems were not unrelated (Jomo 1998, 2001, 2004). The region's weaknesses were beginning to adversely affect growth and industrialization in the region even before the crisis, with some failings continuing to limit growth and structural transformation since.

GOVERNMENT ROLE

The most moot aspect of East Asian growth has been the role of government. At the risk of caricature, there have been three—sometimes distinct, sometimes overlapping—characterizations of the role of the state in the East Asian economic miracle: a minimal state, a market-friendly state, or a developmental state.

The first, essentially laissez-faire view argues for a minimal role for the state, asserting that it has been largely irrelevant or actually obstructive of the essentially private market forces which have contributed to rapid growth and structural transformation, including industrialization. Little, Scitovsky, and Scott (1970) first articulated this view, but others have as well. Such a view became especially influential from the early 1980s in the Anglophone world with the election of Mrs. Thatcher and Mr. Reagan, inspiring what John Toye (1987) called the "counter-revolution" against development economics led by Peter Bauer and Deepak Lal, and reflected, for example, in the World Bank's *World Development Reports* of the early and mid-1980s.

The second market-friendly state perspective was greatly enhanced by the World Bank's (1993) *East Asian Miracle* study. Drawing from neoclassical welfare economics, this view made the case for government intervention on the basis of externalities and market failures. The World Bank (1993) approved of these "functional" interventions—as opposed to "market-unfriendly," "strategic" interventions, which it did not approve of.

Although largely accepting arguments for state interventions to address market failures, advocates of the developmental state perspective argued that government interventions in East Asia generally went well beyond the market-friendly functional interventions approved of by the World Bank study (1993). Although the Miracle study disapproved of so-called strategic interventions, proponents of the developmental state perspective claim that selective industrial policies—involving trade, financial, and other interventions—accounted for the "late industrialization" in East Asia (Amsden 1989; Chang 1994; Wade 1990).

The key argument is that such interventions have been crucial for developing new industrial capabilities that did not previously exist, and that would not have spontaneously emerged because of market forces alone. Governments used trade protection, subsidized credit, and export support to induce desired investments while also monitoring and evaluating performance with the credible threat of withdrawal of support or even sanctions to ensure compliance. Especially in Northeast Asia, countries thus created new capacities and capabilities in industries with prospects of "long-term growth in output, profits, and wages" (Wade 1990, 355), rather than simply expanding existing export activities.

TRADE OPENNESS?

Laissez-faire versions of East Asian experiences claim that market competition, openness, and export orientation were key ingredients of East Asia's impressive economic performance. But such an interpretation requires stretching the meaning of laissez faire. For example, East Asian governments have not been insistent on market competition at all times. This approach was justified as necessary to avoid wasteful, excessive competition and to enable firms to achieve economies of scale. Instead "contests," or "managed competition," as well as incremental exposure to foreign markets forced firms to become internationally competitive as quickly as possible "within reason." Specific policies have included licensing entry or conditional entry as well as regulation of capacity expansion.

In terms of economic openness and trade liberalization, there is a critical difference between free trade, à la Little, Scitovsky and Scott, and the juxtaposition of export promotion with import protection, as found in Northeast Asia. As many have noted, East Asian governments have not been as open to free trade as claimed, for example, by the ADB's (1997) *Emerging Asia: Changes and Challenges* study. Instead, Bhagwati (1988) and others have argued that free trade has only been simulated, with the consequences of import protection in East Asia partly offset by export subsidies. But this is certainly not free trade as generally understood.

The *Emerging Asia* study claimed that consistently open economies grew by an average of 2 percentage points more than considerably closed economies during 1965–1990. This finding relied on the categorization of countries as open or closed by Sachs and Warner (1995). They asserted that Thailand had been consistently open, that Indonesia had been open since 1970, and that the Philippines had been open only since 1988. Such an interpretation is based on a "selective reading" of the evidence and "creative classification of countries."[2]

In summary, East Asian economies did not simply build on their existing primary export activities, but instead, proactively promoted dynamic new industrial and even agricultural capacities and capabilities, thus transforming their engagement with the world economy—and did so quite differently from Latin America or SSA (Palma 2009). The economic histories of Japan, South Korea, and Taiwan suggest that most early industries began by producing for protected domestic markets—as is typical of import-substituting industrialization. The East Asian difference has been in effectively requiring and facilitating rapid transitions to production for export, often through the creative deployment of trade policy, which may be summed up as "effective protection conditional on export promotion."

Requiring exports also meant that producers had to achieve international quality standards quickly, which imposed pressures to progress technologically in terms of both products as well as processes.

Targeted trade, industrial investment and technology policies have been important in achieving structural transformation based on industrialization. Although Northeast Asia developed primarily with domestic capital, Southeast Asia has been more externally oriented, in terms of reliance on both foreign capital as well as markets. Hence, Southeast Asia has been more directly involved in the regionalization of production led by Japan, which often is referred to as involving a flying-geese pattern. The major Southeast Asian achievement in terms of industrial policy has involved the promotion of primary commodity raw material processing, for example, food and cut gem exports from Thailand, palm oil refining in Malaysia, and Indonesian plywood milling.

All this is not to imply that industrial policy has always been well motivated and successfully deployed. Nevertheless, the World Bank's claim of trade policy failure is both erroneous and methodologically problematic, and does not distinguish government interventions motivated by different considerations, such as the desire to enrich a politically influential, or otherwise favored, concessionaire. The *Emerging Asia* study (ADB 1997) cites problems with South Korea's heavy and chemical industrialization drive, but as with the undeniable policy failures attributed to the Japanese Ministry of International Trade and Industry, such selective evidence is not conclusive proof of the inevitable failure of all industrial policy.

SAD TROPICS?

The *Emerging Asia* study (ADB 1997) suggests that temperate countries grew, on average, by 1.3 percentage points more than tropical countries during the 1965–1990 period, after controlling for other factors. The study explains this significant shortfall in terms of the greater prevalence of disease, poorer soils, more frequent typhoons, and other natural calamities in the tropics. Surprisingly, the study seems oblivious of W. A. Lewis's pioneering work on economic conditions in the tropics. As Lewis (1978) has shown, tropical exports grew faster than temperate-zone exports during the last period of global liberalization from the end of the nineteenth century. For the period 1883–1913, for example, French Indochina, Thailand, British Ceylon, West Africa, and Madagascar all had average annual export growth rates of 5 percent or more, whereas Brazil experienced a 4.5 percent growth rate. The comparable rates for temperate settlements, the United States and Northwest Europe, ranged between 4.3 and 3.5 percent.

Although the tropics generally had more modest export bases than the temperate zone, they were able to respond to export demand despite the disadvantages they faced. Lewis emphasized that not all tropical countries were able to seize opportunities from increased export demand. He suggested that the exports in greater demand were largely water intensive; hence, they favored water-abundant countries, whereas more arid tropical grassland areas could not benefit from the increased demand for tropical agricultural products.

As the Southeast Asian newly industrializing countries and some other tropical countries have also grown rapidly since the 1960s, it is necessary to explain why most tropical countries have fared so poorly in the past two centuries. It is not enough to attribute the tropical growth shortfall simply to "pests, diseases, typhoons, and other natural calamities," although such factors may not have been unimportant.

Lewis observed that the terms of trade for tropical agricultural exports deteriorated badly against temperate exports. In the half century between 1916 and 1966, the price index for natural rubber fell from 100 to 16. This suggests that productivity gains in the tropics were largely lost to worsening terms of trade, and the situation has been even worse in cases in which few productivity gains were made. This Lewis thesis holds for the subsequent period as well, including during the commodity "super-cycle" (Erten and Ocampo 2012).

The Green Revolution of the 1960s and 1970s involved three cereal crops, namely rice, wheat, and maize, although subsequent research has also focused on other lucrative commercial or cash crops. With agricultural research and development (R&D) largely taken over by agribusiness corporations in recent decades, access to the means to raise productivity is increasingly determined by farmers' ability to pay the rising costs of these commercially controlled means for enhancing productivity. Intal (1997) argued that higher temperate agricultural productivity has partly been due to long, sustained, and larger investments in agricultural R&D, which temperate developing countries (e.g., Chile and South Korea) have been better able to take advantage of. The tropical Green Revolution in rice farming since the 1960s has mainly benefited irrigated farms in Southeast and South Asia, whereas dry-crop agricultural practices involving most food crops in Africa have generally been neglected. The Malaysian, Indonesian, and Thai successes with tree crop agriculture do offer some hope. In Malaysia, significant investments in tree crop agricultural R&D (e.g., rubber, oil palm, and cocoa), as well as rural infrastructure expedited significant productivity gains.

Government spending in rural areas and on agriculture in Southeast Asia has been motivated by political considerations, especially to secure rural political support. Also, except for land settlement schemes for the rural poor, most government spending on agriculture has not favored the poor. Instead, such public expenditure has tended to benefit the relatively better off, including those who have better access to land, credit, and markets. This is also true of improved rural infrastructure or social services, including health and schooling, and of agricultural subsidies in the form of subsidized fertilizer or other agricultural inputs usually distributed according to the amount of land owned or cultivated. Likewise, those with more land are more likely to increase their output with irrigation, improved seeds, and other factors of production. Nevertheless, the poor have benefited in so far as the rising tide of greater output lifts all boats.

In Malaysia and Indonesia, agricultural and infrastructure spending has benefited plantation, more than peasant or smallholder agriculture. As agricultural taxation has been generally proportional to land cultivated or to output, government rural and agricultural spending has benefited plantations as well as larger smallholders more than smaller smallholders, let alone tenants or sharecroppers. In the case of the rubber replanting and research funds in Malaysia, for example, total land cultivated was a major determinant of ease, and hence, frequency of replanting. Thus, larger farmers benefited more from replanting support payments and higher productivity from the latest rubber plant clones (Khoo 1980).

The geographic specificities of agriculture imply that for imported agricultural varieties and technologies to be successfully adopted, effective adaptive investments in R&D and extension are needed. Unfortunately, with the more modest growth of agriculture in recent decades, compared with industry and services, many governments have neglected agriculture, or worse, have become biased against it. This has exacerbated the condition of small farm agriculture, in turn worsening prospects for rural poverty eradication, typically heavily dependent on agricultural productivity gains.

RESOURCE CURSE?

In recent decades, many argue that being a natural resource-rich country is bad for growth, structural transformation, and development. Curiously, the *Emerging Asia* study (ADB 1997) defines natural resource abundance in terms of the ratio of net primary exports to GDP in 1971, without distinguishing between extractive natural resources (especially minerals) and agricultural products. So-called Dutch Disease mainly involves the former, which tends to be capital intensive and involves only a small share of the population in resource extraction. Consequently, the added income accrues to a few, whereas appreciation of the country's currency affects the entire population.

Agricultural exports generally involve much more of the population, and increased income usually accrues to all producers, diffusing the adverse consequences of currency appreciation. The Southeast Asian high-performing economies have been major agricultural exporters, successfully offsetting problems associated with the mineral exports of Malaysia and Indonesia—in sharp contrast to, say, Nigeria. Good macroeconomic management has also helped, especially to offset the tendency to indulge in expenditure on nontradable goods.

PERSPIRATION, NOT INSPIRATION?

Growth accounting exercises—suggesting little total factor productivity (TFP) growth in most of the region—have also been invoked by Paul Krugman (1994) and others to suggest that East Asian economic growth has not involved much technical progress. The claim is that rapid growth in the region has largely been due to massive factor (capital and labor) inputs resulting from high savings and investment rates, growth of the formal sector labor force, and human resource investments.[3] Further factor inputs were bound to run up against diminishing returns, and rapid East Asian growth could not be sustained, at least not at breakneck pace.

Comparing wage rates to labor productivity in manufacturing for 1992, Intal (1997, table 4) showed the high proportion of wages and salaries to value addition per worker in economies such as Hong Kong (0.51), India (0.39), and Singapore (0.34) compared with Malaysia (0.28), South Korea (0.26), Philippines (0.23), Sri Lanka (0.19), Thailand (0.15 in 1990), and Indonesia (0.14). This comparison suggests that the low wages received by Indian workers did not ensure their labor cost competitiveness. The situation in much of Africa suggests that not unlike Indian labor, African labor may also not be competitive in such wage and productivity comparisons.

Intal (1997) has argued that the marginal labor productivity, and hence the opportunity cost of farm labor moving to manufacturing, is higher in African economies compared with land-scarce Asian economies, even though average labor productivity is usually higher in the latter. Hence, he suggested, it is unlikely that the former will be able to compete with the latter in labor-intensive manufactures. The Malaysian experience suggests that such labor-scarce, land-abundant economies can only be competitive in skill-intensive, rather than in unskilled, labor-intensive manufactures, requiring considerable prior investments in human development.

SUBREGIONAL CONTRASTS

Although many lessons can be drawn from the East Asian experience, they certainly are far from constituting a single model. Southeast Asia is quite distinct from the rest of the region in many respects. Additionally, income inequalities are much lower in South Korea and Taiwan compared with Malaysia and Thailand, and most observers believe that inequality is much higher in Indonesia than what the published data have suggested. Both South Korea and Taiwan achieved this through land reforms in the early phase of their development. Conversely, most Southeast Asian countries have not addressed such initial asset distribution perpetuating inequality. Northeast Asia also ranks higher in terms of human development.

In sum, what Southeast Asia has achieved has been less impressive in some critical ways. Improvements in per capita income and economic welfare have been much more significant in Northeast Asia compared with Southeast Asia (with the exception of Singapore), despite the relatively far greater resource wealth of Southeast Asia. Consequently, some now argue that resource wealth is not a blessing, but rather, a curse, insofar as it postpones the imperative to develop in a more balanced way. The major policy differences between Northeast and Southeast Asia have had major consequences for late industrialization. Industrial policy has been far more extensively deployed in Japan, South Korea, and Taiwan than in the second-tier Southeast Asian NICs. The success of such industrial policy is reflected in the greater industrial and technological capabilities of the former compared with the latter.

For a number of other reasons too, it does not make much sense for any country to try to emulate any particular economy in the region or East Asia more generally. Most developing countries will find it impossible to emulate Southeast Asia, even if they want to. Nevertheless, some important lessons can be drawn from East Asian experiences.

IS THE EAST ASIAN EXPERIENCE STILL RELEVANT FOR AFRICAN DEVELOPMENT?

It remains useful to recall East Asian experiences when considering contemporary challenges facing African economic policy makers, especially following recent global trends, especially technological developments, international trade arrangements, and the changing roles of states. African countries had been largely "structurally adjusted" by the late 1990s, with major changes in African economic policies and institutions. Africa has thus been "liberalized" and opened to globalization. Most African countries have experienced currency devaluations, trade liberalization, and privatization besides implementing various foreign investor-friendly policies.

Mkandawire (2005) argued that structural adjustment in Africa and the deflationary bias of the macroeconomic policies favored by the Washington Consensus have put the continent on a "low growth path."[4] After all, the often-invoked determinants of growth, are themselves endogenously determined by growth (McPherson and Goldsmith 2001), including the global slowdown of the last two decades of the twentieth century (Easterly 2000). Growth was slower in the 1980s and 1990s following liberalization and globalization in most of the developing world, especially SSA, compared with the previous two decades (Weisbrot, Baker, Naiman, and Neta 2000; Weisbrot, Naiman, and Kim 2000; Weisbrot, Baker, Kraev, and Chen 2001). Slower growth can be partly attributed to the deflationary bias inherent in the Bretton Woods institutions' stabilization and structural adjustment programs. From early in the new century, investment and growth rates rose in much of the continent for more than a decade, although the consequences for human welfare varied quite significantly because of the minerals origins of much of the recent expansion.

Economic liberalization has seriously constrained the scope for government policy interventions, especially selective industrial promotion efforts. This is especially apparent in international economic relations, but it is also true of the domestic policy environment, where policy advice and conditionalities as well as World Trade Organization (WTO) and other obligations have radically transformed and constrained the scope for national economic policy initiatives. The question then becomes whether lessons from Asia are still relevant for Africa today, especially in the current context. Invariably, the circumstances of such policy changes as well as the limited policy capabilities of the governments concerned have meant that little preparation—in terms of a proactive strategy or transitional policies to anticipate and cope with the implications of sudden exposure to new international competition—has been undertaken.

Only some of the investment policy instruments of the past are viable or feasible today, including many used successfully under different circumstances of Cold War East Asia. Some of the main industrial policy tools still available have been used by many advanced industrial economies, including those that currently reject selective industrial promotion. Indeed, most advanced economies have a plethora of policies and institutions involved in R&D, skills training, investment promotion, and infrastructure provision, including, for example, for the new information and communication technologies (ICT).

Such policies are probably necessary, but they certainly are not sufficient for stimulating and sustaining economic growth and structural change for developing countries to try to catch up. Additional policies are urgently needed to prevent such economies—already at a historical disadvantage in various regards—from falling further behind the industrially more developed economies of the North as well as the other newly industrializing economies that have emerged in recent decades.

GLOBALIZATION

Recent globalization has gone well beyond the mere expansion of trade and investment flows. Global production patterns have changed in recent decades, particularly since the turn of the millennium, largely driven by transnational corporations' (TNCs) changing global value chains. As deepening globalization has been facilitated by changes in trade and investment rules, concern is growing that WTO and other trade regulations are limiting the policy space for developing countries, generally, and Africa, in particular.

Several specific measures adopted by East Asian governments in their industrialization strategies are no longer permitted under WTO rules, requiring reconsideration of development strategies. Most important, under the WTO's Agreement on Subsidies and Countervailing Measures, subsidies conditional on export performance and local content subsidies are prohibited, except for the least developed countries (LDCs). Similarly, local content, employment, and technology transfer requirements for FDI also have been limited (United Nations 2010). Stricter intellectual property protection further constrains developing countries from replicating and adapting technologies from abroad, which was a key aspect of East Asian development strategies. With nonagricultural market access regulations among the requirements set by powerful developed economies before considering conclusion of the WTO Doha Development Round trade negotiations, non-LDC African countries risk further loss of flexibility in using tariffs to pursue import-substitution industrialization strategies (UNCTAD 2011).

Meanwhile, globalization has deepened, as TNCs increasingly produce goods and services involving cross-border value-adding activities. Thus, the growth of export-oriented production in East Asia has involved greater geographical fragmentation of production. Instead of shallow integration characterized by trade in goods and services among corporations, recent decades have seen deeper integration, which often occurs within large firms or among affiliated business entities. Hence, development strategies involving industrialization and structural transformation following the East Asian experience are said to have become less relevant as global value chains have changed, and prices for manufacturing goods typically exported by low-income countries fell more rapidly with the entry of China into global markets (Kaplinsky 2006); more recently, this argument has been extended to include Vietnam, Bangladesh and more recent manufacturing economies. With the ability to industrially upgrade within value chains controlled by foreign firms much more difficult, the new international trade specialization risks consigning SSA countries to primary production of minerals and agriculture for export (Kaplinsky and Farooki 2010). Even exemptions and other privileges for LDCs have been eroded, exacerbated by the plethora of new trade, investment, and intellectual property rights treaties, rules, and regulations, including plurilateral and bilateral arrangements that increasingly challenge and undermine multilateralism.

TNCs are now believed to account for about two-thirds of international trade. About 40 percent of such trade takes place within—rather than between—companies. Since the 1980s, manufacturing value chains have grown faster than other contributions to international trade expansion. Thus, new and often-changing specialization or divisions of labor have emerged internationally, based on differences in wages, skills, technology, and logistics. With the early growth and spread of TNCs, greenfield FDI rose rapidly. With financial globalization accelerating in the 1990s, however, mergers and acquisitions (M&As)—rather than greenfield investments—came to account for most FDI. Although M&As do not add anything to productive capacity in and of themselves, they have contributed to growing international relocation and integration of production.

Domestic economic and technological capabilities have increasingly become important determinants for attracting FDI. Such capabilities may be reflected in the form of internationally competitive industrial firms or clusters. As Sanjaya Lall (2003) put it, successful globalization for host economies requires efficient localization. For investment, growth, and structural change to be sustained, it is necessary for the domestic investment environment to be attractive, requiring coordinated proactive efforts by national and local authorities. There is strong evidence of heavy concentration of FDI, particularly in more sophisticated activities involving greater value addition and worker incomes. With few exceptions, for example, mining, there is little reason to believe that such FDI has any particular interest in investing in most of Africa in current circumstances.

TECHNOLOGICAL CHANGE

Advances in transportation as well as ICT have been major drivers of globalization. The latter, in particular, is widely seen as the key general-purpose technology of globalization, driving technical progress in a wide range of sectors (Jovanovic and Rousseau 2005). ICT has enabled corporations to manage complex global supply chains, and thus, it has been a precondition for outsourcing and off-shoring production tasks, initially in manufacturing, such as apparel and electronics, and gradually, in more sectors, including services and knowledge work.

ICTs have eased the diffusion of information and facilitated better access to global knowledge for all, including developing countries. Because of science and technology's critical role in addressing the social, economic, or environmental challenges that countries face, this wider diffusion of information is contributing to progress in a wide range of areas. At the same time, innovative activity and technology development continue to be concentrated in a small number of advanced economies, with only a few developing countries, such as China, India, and Brazil, participating more significantly in recent decades. As core R&D activities are rarely outsourced, they tend to be controlled by corporate headquarters in developed countries (Castaldi, Cimoli, Correa, and Dosi 2009).

Given the pervasive and rapid nature of technological change, coordinated proactive efforts are needed. Private agents are not able to respond adequately to new situations and challenges, and cannot do so in the coordinated fashion needed to address the diverse needs of selective investment promotion efforts in the new circumstances. For Lall, some of the new circumstances to be considered include the following:

- *Compression of space*, with declining communications and transport costs, as well as faster services.
- *Greater information availability*, which is likely to grow, rather than recede, with more information on a greater range of issues more easily available.
- As *markets* become *more integrated*, new threats posed by greater competition tend to outweigh the new opportunities offered by greater access to larger markets.
- Economic activities have become *more technology intensive*, offering potential new benefits (e.g., more options, technology learning, productivity gains, spillover benefits, management flexibility) for those adequately prepared, but often placing others at greater disadvantage. The new technologies require new skills, management, institutions, and infrastructure. Using the new technologies effectively and efficiently also requires greater domestic technological capabilities as well as new forms of specialization and organization.

In Lall's (2003) survey of the developing world, East Asia led in terms of economic performance, with fastest growth, more exports, and greater technology intensity. He also noted significant differences in selective investment policy among East Asian countries, and found those in Southeast Asia to be poorer and far more vulnerable. In contrast, although some of the more industrialized Latin American countries had developed strong industrial capabilities and skills as well as ICT infrastructure, their technology and R&D institutions remained weak. FDI has been high in some Latin American countries in recent years, but much of this investment has involved M&As. Even greenfield FDI has generally not been as dynamic in transforming technological structures and capabilities as in Singapore or China. There is little evidence suggesting better prospects for FDI in Africa. Development prospects for Africa are generally quite poor because of inadequate and inappropriate investment-inducing policies and institutions, due to the influence of the Washington Consensus.

Clearly, industrial development in the new circumstances requires international competitiveness. Such competitiveness is increasingly determined by factors other than wage cost or exchange rate competitiveness, as important as these may be. The inability to compete effectively implies being by-passed, and ultimately, results in stagnation at the lower end of the technology and income ladder. In light of existing African industrial capacities and technological capabilities, it is difficult to imagine how trade liberalization can enhance African industrial development.

To date, globalization and liberalization have increased industrial and technological divergences, which often reflect differences in industrial competitiveness. Industrial rationalization at the global level may well lead to concentration in a few major production locations, particularly for successful first movers with strong technological capabilities and industrial agglomerations. But market forces augmented by economic liberalization cannot be relied on to check—let alone reverse—such differences in international competitiveness. For the few countries that successfully participate in such globalized production, sustaining growth will increasingly depend on the ability to upgrade industrial skills and indigenous technological capabilities, which cannot be ensured by previous achievements alone.

CONCLUSION: A NEW ROLE FOR THE STATE?

For SSA, the past few generations of policies espoused by the Washington Consensus—first involving "getting prices right" and then, "getting institutions right" and "good governance"—are still offered as advice, if not imposed as conditionalities. Meanwhile, income levels in much of SSA are still considered too low to generate the domestic resources needed for rapid growth. Historically, however, the record is clear that raising investment rates, in turn, raises savings rates, rather than the converse. Thus, creating enabling investment conditions will do much more for sustainable investments than the current emphasis on attracting FDI, which has met with modest and uneven success. The Northeast Asian experience also underscores the notion that ownership matters and that domestic investments are far more likely than foreign investments to lead to sustainable industrialization. The earlier emphasis on trying to raise savings rates without facilitating investment opportunities was also clearly unsuccessful.

The transformations of recent decades have had significant implications. Although economic liberalization at international and national levels undoubtedly constrain and limit investment policy options, current circumstances pose new challenges that can be adequately and successfully met and overcome only with appropriate proactive investment and technology policy measures. These are especially needed to enhance competitiveness in the face of pervasive market and institutional failures. Although market mechanisms may be efficient for static allocation, the main challenge for development remains the dynamic transformation of a country's comparative and competitive advantages.

Thus, economic liberalization, freer markets, and more mobile economic resources do not render industrial or investment policy obsolete, but they do require new feasible and viable investment policy options. The development of better indigenous technological capabilities cannot be left to markets, which are not capable of being developmentally proactive. The new investment policy must focus on building technological capabilities—in existing activities as well as in more sophisticated activities characterized by high growth and greater technological and other spillover benefits. Although policy space has been reduced, room exists to use some policies, which can be combined with remaining industrial policy instruments that are still permitted (UNCTAD 2011).

All this is not to suggest that one investment policy formula applies to all economies regardless of time and conditions. Instead, precisely the contrary is true—that is, context is all-important. For example, the degree of reliance on FDI must necessarily vary with circumstances, including perceived inadequacies and the likelihood of such weaknesses being addressed by FDI. There is no room for dogma, but instead, strategic pragmatism should prevail. Lall argued that appropriate investment policy will require selective interventions as well as effective coordination among firms, clusters, and factor markets, which should be consistent with a clear and coherent vision of the future besides providing a road map for achieving policy goals. For this purpose, many useful lessons can be drawn from the varied experiences of the East Asian economies, including the more modest and flawed achievements of the Southeast Asian NICs.

NOTES

1. The new intellectual and policy environment that emerged during the 1980s—under U.S. President Reagan and UK Prime Minister Thatcher—culminated in the so-called Washington Consensus, which has promoted market liberalizing and property rights strengthening policy reform. In recent decades, there has been widespread, sweeping, and rapid opening up of trade, investment, finance, and other flows. Very often, such liberalization has been externally imposed by the Bretton Woods institutions as part of conditions imposed to secure access to emergency credit during the debt crises of the 1980s, and since, in the wake of subsequent currency and financial crises. Various policy packages for (price) stabilization in the short term or for structural adjustment in the medium term have involved such conditionalities.

This has been especially true of much of Latin America and Africa, which experienced a lost decade of economic growth in the 1980s, following (sovereign) debt crises and ensuing stabilization and structural adjustment reforms, usually imposed by the international financial institutions. The 1990s were only slightly better, with a few spurts of high growth here and there, which have been touted as proof of the success of the Washington Consensus, when precisely the opposite has been true. Although the Washington Consensus has been challenged, if not discredited by serious researchers, it continues to provide the ideological basis for economic analysis and policy making in developing countries, especially in Africa, Latin America, and other economies.

2. Instead, citing Naya (1989, tables 2.8–2.9), Intal (1997, tables 1–3) showed the following:

- average import duties in the Philippines in 1982 were slightly lower than for Indonesia in 1980 and Thailand in 1983;
- for intermediate and capital goods, import duties for the Philippines in 1982 were lower, on average, than for Thailand in 1983; and
- quantitative import restrictions and other nontariff barriers in the Philippines in 1983 were lower than in Indonesia in 1980 for crude materials, chemicals, basic manufactures, and transport machinery. Seiji Naya et al., *ASEAN-US Initiative: Assessment and Recommendations for Improved Economic Relations: Joint Final Report* (Singapore: Institute of Southeast Asian Studies, 1989); and Ponciano S. Intal, "Comments on Chapter 2 of the Emerging Asia Study: Economic Growth and Transformation' " (Emerging Asia Seminar, Asian Development Bank, Manila, September 1–2, 1997).

Citing trade-weighted trade control measures from UNCTAD for the mid-1980s, he showed that total tariff and quasi-tariff measures were higher in Thailand than in the Philippines for all manufactures, as well as for both chemicals and machinery and equipment. Meanwhile, all nontariff measures were greater in Indonesia than in the Philippines for all manufactures and for chemicals, and only slightly less for machinery and equipment. Then, citing Ariff and Hill (1985, tables 3.3, 3.5, and 3.7), who offer comparable figures for Indonesia and the Philippines, Intal showed that the effective rates of protection for intermediate goods in Indonesia in 1975 and 1980 were much higher than for the Philippines in both 1974 and 1980; the data suggest that the converse was true for capital goods. The usual indices of trade openness did not allow Sachs and Warner to categorize the Philippines differently from Indonesia and Thailand. Claiming that the former was closed and the latter two were open most certainly would have affected findings about the alleged relationship between trade openness and economic growth because the latter two have performed so much better than the former in the past half century. Intal comes close to suggesting that their adverse view of the government's role in agricultural development—as reflected by their claim of a "state monopoly of major exports" as a measure of the "closedness" of an economy—affected Sachs and Warner's categorization and subsequent claims. Mohamed Ariff and Hal Hill, *Export-Oriented Industrialization: The ASEAN Experience* (Sydney: Allen and Unwin, 1985); and Jeffrey Sachs and Andrew Warner, "Natural Resource Abundance and Economic Growth" (HIID Discussion Paper No. 517A, Harvard Institute for International Development, Cambridge, MA, 1995).

3. This is not the place to go into an extended discussion of the theoretical as well as methodological issues involved. Note, however, Rodrik's observation (in Collins and Bosworth 1996, 192) that while "the evidence on investment rates is direct and speaks for itself, the evidence on TFP is indirect and has to be interpreted with care." Also, Collins and Bosworth (1996) found that, contrary to growth pessimists, East Asian economies had greater TFP gains since the 1980s with further development. Thus, future growth in the region could be sustained as the educational and skill profiles of their labor forces continue to improve. Susan M. Collins and Barry P. Bosworth, "Economic Growth in East Asia: Accumulation Versus Assimilation," *Brookings Papers on Economic Activity* 2 (1996): 135–203.

Many were deeply offended by Krugman's (1994) comparison of East Asian growth with that of the Soviet Union in earlier times, and his insistence that East Asian economic performance had not been impressive while slower growth was unavoidable and imminent. However, there has been less critical attention to the bases of his analysis, namely, the conventional growth accounting exercises by Alwyn Young (1995), on one hand, and the slightly more heterodox work by Kim and Lau (1994). Paul Krugman, "The Myth of Asia's Miracle," *Foreign Affairs* 73, no. 6 (1994): 62–78; Alwyn Young in "The Tyranny of Numbers: Confronting the Statistical Realities of the East Asian Growth Experience," *Quarterly Journal of Economics* 110, no. 3 (1995): 641–680; and Kim Jong-Il and Lawrence Lau, "The Sources of Economic Growth of the East Asian Newly Industrialized Countries," *Journal of the Japanese and International Economies* 8, no. 3 (1994): 235–271.Krugman is probably right in claiming that the new endogenous growth theory cannot be invoked against his arguments, as even higher TFP residuals would then be expected. If, however, technological learning becomes important only beyond a certain stage of development, or when technological progress requires changes in labor processes more conducive to such learning and shopfloor innovation, one would have different expectations of TFP growth in East Asia outside of Japan.

But even if we accept the theoretical and methodological bases for Krugman's (not unproblematic) claims, his insistence on lack of technological progress—when considering how differences in price determination in different product markets affect growth-accounting exercises—is moot. The important distinction is between more technologically sophisticated products, enjoying legally protected monopolistic rents from intellectual property, and other more mass-produced agricultural and manufactured commodities in far more competitive markets. Differences in exchange rate policies and the nature of labor markets have also had some bearing on product price determination. Most East Asian workers outside of Japan have been under-remunerated because of international labor immobility, among other factors, resulting in the relative "underpricing" of East Asian exports.

4. Keynesians argue that the causal chain is from growth to investment, and not the other way around. Elbadawi and Mwega (2000) and Mlambo and Oshikoya (2001) have found that causality runs from growth to investment in Africa as well. Capital needs are essentially determined by expected output, that is, investment demand is driven by expected growth. Meanwhile, endogenous growth theories suggest that some of these determinants of growth may themselves be dependent on growth. Ibrahim Elbadawi and Francis M. Mwega, "Can Africa's Saving Collapse Be Reversed?" *World Bank Economic Review* 14, no. 3 (2000): 415–443; and Kupukile Mlambo and Temitope Oshikoya, "Macroeconomic Factors and Investment in Africa," *Journal of African Economies* 10, no. 2 (2001): 12–47.

REFERENCES

Ariff, Mohamed, and Hal Hill. 1985. *Export-Oriented Industrialization: The ASEAN Experience.* Sydney, Australia: Allen and Unwin.

Asian Development Bank. 1997. *Emerging Asia: Changes and Challenges.* Manila, Phillipines: Asian Development Bank.

Amsden, Alice. 1989. *Asia's Next Giant.* New York: Oxford University Press.

Baer, Werner, William R. Miles, and Allen B. Moran. 1999. "The End of the Asian Myth: Why Were the Experts Fooled?" *World Development* 27 (10): 1735–1747.

Barro, Robert, and Jong-Wha Lee. 2002. "IMF Programs: Who Is Chosen and What Are the Effects?" NBER Working Paper 8951. National Bureau of Economic Research, Cambridge, MA.

Bhagwati, Jagdish. 1988. "Export-Promoting Trade Strategy: Issues and Evidence." *World Bank Research Observer* 3, no. 1 (January): 27–57.

Castaldi, Carolina, Mario Cimoli, Nelson Correa, and Giovanni Dosi. 2009. "Technological Learning, Policy Regimes, and Growth: The Long-Term Patterns and Some Specificities of a 'Globalized' Economy." In *Industrial Policy and Development. The Political Economy of Capabilities Accumulation,* ed. Mario Cimoli, Giovanni Dosi, and Joseph Stiglitz. New York: Oxford University Press.

Chang, Ha-Joon. 1994. *The Political Economy of Industrial Policy.* Basingstoke: Macmillan.

Collins, Susan M., and Barry P. Bosworth. 1996. "Economic Growth in East Asia: Accumulation Versus Assimilation." *Brookings Papers on Economic Activity* 2: 135–203.

Easterly, William. 2000. "The Lost Decades: Developing Countries Stagnation in Spite of Policy Reform, 1980–1998." *Journal of Economic Growth* 6: 135–157.

Elbadawi, Ibrahim, and Francis M. Mwega. 2000. "Can Africa's Saving Collapse Be Reversed?" *World Bank Economic Review* 14 (3): 415–443.

Erten, Bilge, and José Antonio Ocampo. 2013. "Super-Cycles of Commodity Prices since the Mid-Nineteenth Century." DESA Working Paper No. 110. UN Department of Economic and Social Affairs, United Nations, New York.

Intal, Ponciano S., Jr. 1997. "Comments on Chapter 2 of the Emerging Asia Study: 'Economic Growth and Transformation' ". Emerging Asia Seminar, Asian Development Bank, Manila, September 1–2.

Islam, Iyanatul, and Anis Chowdhury. 2001. *The Political Economy of East Asia: Post-Crisis Debates.* Oxford: Oxford University Press.

Jomo, Kwame Sundaram, ed. 1998. *Tigers in Trouble: Financial Governance, Liberalization and Crises in East Asia.* London: Zed Books.

——, ed. 2001. *South East Asia's Industrialization: Industrial Policy, Capabilities and Sustainability.* Houndmills, UK: Palgrave.

——, ed. 2003. *South East Asia's Paper Tigers: From Miracle to Debacle and Beyond.* London: Routledge.

——, ed. 2004. *After The Storm: Crisis, Recovery and Sustaining Development in East Asia.* Singapore: Singapore University Press.

Jomo, Kwame Sundaram, and Rudiger von Arnim. 2012. "Economic liberalization and constraints to development in Sub-Saharan Africa." In *Good Growth and Governance in Africa: Rethinking Development Strategies*, ed. Akbar Noman, Kwesi Botchwey, Howard Stein, and Joseph E. Stiglitz, 499–535. New York: Oxford University Press.

Jomo, Kwame Sundaram, with Chen Yun Chung, Brian C. Folk, Irfan ul-Haque, Pasuk Phongpaichit, Batara Simatupang, and Mayuri Tateishi. 1997. *South East Asia's Misunderstood Miracle: Industrial Policy and Economic Development in Thailand, Malaysia and Indonesia.* Boulder, CO: Westview Press.

Jomo, Kwame Sundaram, with Oliver Schwank and Rudiger von Arnim. 2013. *Globalization and Development in Sub-Saharan Africa.* New York: United Nations Press.

Jovanovic, Boyan, and Peter Rousseau. 2005. "General Purpose Technologies." In *Handbook of Economic Growth*, ed. Philippe Aghion and Steven Durlauf, 1181–1224. Amsterdam: Elsevier.

Kaplinsky, Raphael. 2006. "Revisiting the Revisited Terms of Trade: Will China Make a Difference?" *World Development* 34 (6): 981–995.

Kaplinsky, Raphael, and Masuma Farooki. 2010. "Global Value Chains, the Crisis, and the Shift of Markets from North to South." In *Global Value Chains in a Post-crisis World*, ed. Olivier Cattaneo, Gary Gereffi, and Cornelia Staritz. Washington, DC: World Bank.

Khoo Khay-Jin. 1980. "The Marketing of Smallholder Rubber." In *Rural-Urban Transformation and Regional Underdevelopment: The Case of Malaysia*, ed. Kamal Salih et al. *Rural-Urban Relations, Special Studies in the Malaysian Case.* UNCRD Project 50R, Study No. 6, School of Comparative Social Studies, Universiti Sains Malaysia, Penang. Nagoya, Japan: UN Center for Regional Development.

Kim Jong-Il, and Lawrence Lau. 1994. "The Sources of Economic Growth of the East Asian Newly Industrialized Countries." *Journal of the Japanese and International Economies* 8 (3): 235–271.

Krugman, Paul. 1994. "The Myth of Asia's Miracle." *Foreign Affairs* 73 (6): 62–78.

Lall, Sanjaya. 2003. "Reinventing Industrial Strategy: The Role of Government Policy in Building Industrial Competitiveness." Paper presented to the G-24 Intergovernmental Group on Monetary Affairs and Development, Geneva, September.

Lall, Sanjaya. 2004. "Industrializing Success and Failure in a Globalizing World." QEH Working Paper 102, Queen Elizabeth House, University of Oxford, Oxford.

Lall, Sanjaya, and Carlo Pietrobelli. 2002. *Failing to Compete: Technology Development and Technology Systems in Africa.* Cheltenham: Edward Elgar.

Lawrence, Peter. 2010. "The African Tragedy: International and National Roots." Chap. 2 in *The Political Economy of Africa*, ed. Vishnu Padayachee. New York: Routledge.

Lewis, W. A. 1978. *Growth and Fluctuations, 1870–1913.* London: Allen & Unwin.

Little, Ian. 1981. "The Experience and Causes of Rapid Labour-Intensive Development in Korea, Taiwan Province, Hong Kong and Singapore, and the Possibilities of Emulation." In *Export-Led Industrialization and Development*, ed. Eddy Lee. Asian Employment Program. Geneva: International Labour Organization.

Little, Ian, Tibor Scitovsky, and Maurice Scott. 1970. *Industry and Trade in Some Developing Countries: A Comparative Study.* New York: Basic Books.

McPherson, M. F., and A. A. Goldsmith. 2001. "Is Africa on the Move?" Cambridge, MA: Belfer Center for Science and International Affairs, John F. Kennedy School of Government, Harvard University.

Mkandawire, Thandika. 2005. "Maladjusted African Economies and Globalization." *Africa Development* 30 (1–2): 1–33.

Mlambo, Kupukile, and Temitope Oshikoya. 2001. "Macroeconomic Factors and Investment in Africa." *Journal of African Economies* 10 (2): 12–47.

Naya Seiji, Michael Plummer, Kernial Sandhu, and Narongchai Akrasanee. 1989. *ASEAN-US Initiative: Assessment and Recommendations For Improved Economic Relations: Joint Final Report.* Singapore: Institute of Southeast Asian Studies.

Noman, Akbar, and Joseph E. Stiglitz. 2012. "Strategies for African Development." In *Good Growth and Governance in Africa: Rethinking Development Strategies*, ed. Akbar Noman, Kwesi Botchwey, Howard Stein, and Joseph E. Stiglitz, 3–47. New York: Oxford University Press.

Palma, Gabriel. 2009. "Flying Geese and Waddling Ducks: The Different Capabilities of East Asia and Latin America to 'Demand-Adapt' and 'Supply-Upgrade' their Export Productive Capacity." Chap. 8 in *Industrial Policy and Development*, ed. Mario Cimoli, Giovanni Dosi, and Joseph Stiglitz. New York: Oxford University Press.

Sachs, Jeffrey, and Andrew Warner. 1995. "Natural Resource Abundance and Economic Growth." HIID Discussion Paper No. 517A. Harvard Institute for International Development, Cambridge, MA.

Toye, John. 1987. *The Dilemma of Development.* Oxford: Blackwell.

United Nations. 2010. *World Economic and Social Survey, 2010: Retooling Global Development.* New York: United Nations.

UNCTAD. 2001. *Economic Development in Africa: Performance, Prospects and Policy Issues.* Geneva: United Nations Conference on Trade and Development.

———. 2011. *Economic Development in Africa: Fostering Industrial Development in Africa in the New Global Environment.* Geneva: United Nations Conference on Trade and Development.

Wade, Robert. 1990. *Governing the Market.* Princeton, NJ: Princeton University Press.

Weisbrot, Mark, Dean Baker, Egor Kraev, and Judy Chen. 2001. "The Scoreboard on Globalization, 1980–2000: Twenty Years of Diminished Progress." Center for Economic and Policy Research, Washington, DC.

Weisbrot, Mark, Dean Baker, Robert Naiman, and Gila Neta. 2000. "Growth May Be Good for the Poor—But are IMF and World Bank Policies Good for Growth?" Center for Economic and Policy Research, Washington, DC.

Weisbrot, Mark, Robert Naiman, and Joyce Kim. 2000. "The Emperor Has No Growth: Declining Economic Growth rates in the Era of Globalization." Center for Economic and Policy Research, Washington, DC.

Williamson, John. 1990. "What Washington Means by Policy Reform." Chap. 2 in *Latin American Adjustment: How Much Has Happened?* ed. John Williamson. Washington, DC: Institute for International Economics.

World Bank. 1981. *Accelerated Development in Sub-Saharan Africa: An Agenda for Action.* Washington, DC: World Bank.

———. 1993. *The East Asian Miracle: Economic Growth and Public Policy.* New York: Oxford University Press for World Bank, Washington, DC.

———. 1997. *World Development Report.* New York: Oxford University Press for World Bank.

———. 2005. *Economic Growth in the 1990s: Learning from a Decade of Reform.* Washington, DC: World Bank.

Young, Alwyn. 1995. "The Tyranny of Numbers: Confronting the Statistical Realities of the East Asian Growth Experience." *Quarterly Journal of Economics* 110 (3): 641–680.

CHAPTER 6

Economic Transformation for High-Quality Growth

INSIGHTS FROM INTERNATIONAL COOPERATION

Akio Hosono

The United Nations plan of action, *Transforming Our World: The 2030 Agenda for Sustainable Development*,[1] states at its beginning: "We envisage a world in which every country enjoys sustained, inclusive and sustainable economic growth and decent work for all" (United Nations 2015, 4). The emphasis on the desired attributes of economic growth expressed in this vision of the Sustainable Development Goals (SDGs) coincides with the recent growth in attention toward the concept of quality growth. In the Asia-Pacific region, Asia Pacific Economic Cooperation (APEC) leaders agreed on an "APEC Growth Strategy" in 2010, which stressed that the quality of growth needs to be improved to ensure that it will be more balanced, inclusive, sustainable, innovative, and secure (APEC 2010).[2] APEC leaders further agreed on the "APEC Strategy for Strengthening Quality Growth" in 2015, which "will bring more synergy between the APEC Growth Strategy and the Sustainable Development Goals" (APEC 2015, 1). The "Development Cooperation Charter of Japan," also released in 2015, states that one of the most important challenges for development is "quality growth" and "poverty reduction through such growth," in which inclusiveness, sustainability, and resilience are stressed (Cabinet Office 2015, 5–6).

Along with this emphasis on quality, increasing attention is being paid to the importance of transformation, considered essential for development. As the Asian Development Bank (ADB) asserted: development is distinct from aggregate growth, which can occur without significant transformation, as in some oil rich economies (ADB 2013).

In this chapter, I provide insights on strategies to attain transformation with quality growth, along with effective approaches for implementing them. First, I present an overview of recent policy debates related to transformation and quality growth. On the basis of this discussion, I provide an analytical perspective and discuss key issues, identifying seven main strategies: three to address endowments and four to catalyze transformation. In subsequent sections, I discuss each specific strategy, drawing insights from relevant effective approaches. In the final section, I offer concluding remarks.

KEY ISSUES FROM AN ANALYTICAL PERSPECTIVE

OVERVIEW OF TRANSFORMATION AND QUALITY OF GROWTH IN EAST ASIA, LATIN AMERICA, AND AFRICA

The Report of the High-Level Panel of Eminent Persons on the Post-2015 Development Agenda, "A Global Partnership: Eradicate Poverty and Transform Economies through Sustainable Development" (2013), concluded that the post-2015 agenda needs to be driven by five transformational shifts, including a call for the transformation of economies for jobs and inclusive growth. The United Nations 2030 Agenda declares that "we are determined to take the bold and transformative steps which are urgently needed to shift the world on to a sustainable and resilient path" (UNGA 2015:2).

Thus, these governing bodies seem to have reached more of a consensus on the importance of quality of growth, on one hand, and transformation, on the other. This consensus is reflected in the recent publications of regional institutions pertaining to their region, including the Asian Development Bank (ADB), UN Economic and Social Commission for Asia and the Pacific (UNESCAP), Inter-American Development Bank, UN Economic Commission for Latin America and the Caribbean (UNECLAC), African Development Bank (AfDB), African Union, UN Economic Commission for Africa (UNECA), and the African Centre for Economic Transformation (ACET).[3] After elaborating on this trend in Africa, I will discuss this relationship between "quality of growth" and "transformation."

In the African region, heads of state and governments endorsed the African Union's transformation vision for 2063. The AfDB's long-term strategy, "At the Center of Africa's Transformation," has the goal of establishing Africa as the next global emerging market. Moreover, UNECA's Economic Report on Africa 2013 details what will be required to promote competitiveness, reduce dependence on primary commodity exports, and enable Africa to emerge as a new global growth pole (ACET 2014). Therefore, as ACET states, economic transformation is now the consensus paradigm for Africa's development. ACET's flagship report, *2014 African Transformation Report: Growth with Depth*, is considered to be the pioneering comprehensive study on transformation of the African economy.[4]

Behind the recent tendency in each of these three regions to emphasize transformation and quality of growth are concerns that growth does not necessarily enable development when it is not accompanied by transformation or by the attributes of the quality of growth. ACET's *2014 African Transformation Report* agrees that to "ensure that growth is sustainable and continues to improve the lives of many, countries need to vigorously promote economic transformation" (ACET 2014, 1).

In short, quality growth needs to be discussed in the context of transformation because it is both a driver of growth[5] and affects different attributes of growth.

TRANSFORMATION AND CHANGING ENDOWMENTS

This section summarizes the basic aspects of economic, industrial, and structural transformation on which there has been growing consensus in recent years. First, regarding the definition of transformation, a well-established body of literature affirms that development is about transforming the productive structure of the economy and accumulating the capabilities necessary to undertake this process (ADB 2013). This process can be best described by ACET's concept of growth with depth. On the basis of various studies, I identify four strategies for transformation.

Second, regarding how transformation can be achieved, consensus seems to be growing that structural transformation is closely related to changes of endowments or assets and changes in comparative advantage as well as to innovation and technological progress (e.g., see Noman and Stiglitz 2012; also see Lin 2012a).

Accordingly, endowments are extremely important for transformation based on changing or dynamic comparative advantage. In this regard, recent studies identified critical endowments for transformation. Along with the growing recognition of the importance of inclusiveness and innovation in quality growth, discussions on the importance of learning, as well as the accumulation of knowledge and capabilities, have deepened.

Stiglitz and Greenwald (2014) present a systematic and holistic analysis of what constitutes a learning society, arguing that "the most important 'endowment' from our perspective, is a society's learning capacities" (26). They further state that a country's policies have to be shaped to take advantage of its comparative advantage in knowledge and learning abilities in relation to its competitors, including its ability to learn and to learn to learn, and to support those capacities and capabilities further. Noman and Stiglitz (2017) reaffirm the importance of learning capacity, together with that of institutions: "Perhaps the most important 'endowment' of a country was assets that were not mobile—institutions and learning capacities that were embedded in local institutions. It was these that countries needed to take into account as they struggled to shape their long-term (dynamic) comparative advantage" (13).

Another important endowment could be infrastructure, both hard and soft. Lin (2012b) states that "economic development is a dynamic process that requires industrial upgrading and diversification along with corresponding improvements in 'hard' and 'soft' infrastructure at each new level." He further argues: "Such upgrading entails large externalities to firm transaction costs and the returns to capital investment. Therefore, in addition to an effective market mechanism, the government should coordinate or provide the improvements in infrastructure and compensate for the externalities to facilitate industrial upgrading and diversification" (10). Hard infrastructure consists of highways, telecommunications networks, port facilities, and power supplies, while soft infrastructure is made up of institutions, regulations, social capital, value systems, and other social and economic arrangements.

These endowments—namely, learning capacities (as defined by Stiglitz and Greenwald), infrastructure, and institutions (including other soft infrastructure as discussed by Lin)—are not mobile. These three essential endowments, along with factor endowments, such as labor, land, and capital,[6] are critical for the dynamic comparative advantage of a country.

These three essential endowments bear a close relation to the elements Japan's Development Cooperation Charter considers important: "Japan will attach importance to building the foundations of self-help efforts and self-reliant development such as human resources, socio-economic infrastructure, regulations and institutions" (Cabinet Office 2015, 5).[7] This view has been incorporated into Japan's Official Development Assistance policies for decades (Ministry of Foreign Affairs [MOFA] 2005).[8]

Thus, from the lens of quality growth through transformation, these essential endowments need to be enhanced, taking into account inclusiveness, sustainability, and resilience. From this, we can derive three strategies to enhance each of the essential endowments necessary for transformation for quality of growth. The other challenge lies in finding ways to catalyze transformation for quality growth. To address this challenge, we identify four additional strategies.

Transformation agendas differ among countries, such as countries with a very high proportion of the population living in rural areas, early industrializing countries, urbanizing countries, and countries that need to transform from a labor-intensive to a knowledge-intensive economy to overcome the middle-income trap. There is no one-size-fits-all model for transformation. Each country has its own transformation agenda and needs to identify the most appropriate strategies to achieve its goals.

VIRTUOUS CIRCLE OF ENDOWMENTS, TRANSFORMATION, AND QUALITY GROWTH

Transformation normally generates growth, as it did in East Asia, but growth is not always accompanied by transformation. Transformation-led growth is distinct from, for example, commodity boom-led growth. Transformation-led growth could be high-quality growth and could generate further transformation. This implies that a virtuous circle of transformation and high-quality growth could take place.

Generally speaking, given its attributes, quality growth enhances endowments, enabling further transformation. Inclusive growth, for example, could take the form of the participation of workers in the process of learning. Workers not only contribute to production but at the same time learn on the job, improving their learning capacity. Enterprises increase production, contribute to growth, and simultaneously achieve organizational learning and, often, innovation. Thus, if growth is genuinely inclusive and innovative, learning capacity should be strengthened through such growth. In this way, the quality of growth enhances the most important endowment, learning capacity, for further transformation and higher quality growth.

Furthermore, high growth is more likely to be sustained when it is inclusive because the strategy for such growth has wide social and political support. The report of the Growth Commission emphasizes this: "The Commission strongly believes that growth strategies cannot succeed without a commitment to equality of opportunity, giving everyone a fair chance to enjoy the fruits of growth" (Commission on Growth and Development 2008, 7). On the basis of an analysis of thirteen successful countries of long-term high growth (of which nine are East Asian economies), the report states that policy makers "must be trusted as stewards of the economy and their promise of future rewards must be believed. . . . Their promise must also be inclusive. . . . Governments forged an implicit or explicit social contract in support of growth, offering health, education, and sometimes redistribution. . . . Absent this kind of political foundation, sustaining policies that promote growth is very difficult if not impossible" (26–27).

Similarly, sustainability—especially in terms of environment (another attribute of quality growth)—is indispensable (Hosono 2013a). Outcomes of high-quality growth, with all its attributes, could enhance essential endowments and enable further transformation and quality growth, generating a virtuous circle. Therefore, a growth strategy and industrial strategy with policies pertaining to endowments and transformation are vital for high-quality growth.

STRATEGIES FOR ENHANCEMENT OF ESSENTIAL ENDOWMENTS FOR TRANSFORMATION FOR QUALITY GROWTH

This section identifies three strategies to enhance each of the essential endowments.

STRATEGY FOR THE ENHANCEMENT OF LEARNING CAPACITY

Quality growth depends on learning capacity in several ways. Low learning capacity impedes the creation of new industries that take advantage of opportunities for transformation, even if other endowments, such as hard infrastructure, exist. If learning capacity is limited to a small part of the population of a country, inclusive growth is unlikely to be attained. More important, from a learning society perspective, inclusive growth has an intrinsic relationship with innovative growth. Growth can be really inclusive and, at the same time, innovative, when it takes full advantage of the talents of its entire population. Stiglitz and Greenwald (2014) point out that "our argument for why inclusive growth is so important goes beyond the standard one that it is a waste of a country's most valuable resource, human talent, to fail to ensure that everyone lives up to his or her abilities" (468).

Learning contributes to growth through increases in productivity as well as innovation. Learning enables the development of innovative, and specific, ways to make more efficient use of existing endowments. At the same time, learning enhances learning capacity—especially learning to learn as the most important endowment. This contributes to dynamic comparative advantage, thereby enabling industrial transformation and high-quality growth.

Learning and learning to learn are also essential for the green economy, which results in improved human well-being and social equity, while significantly reducing ecological risks and scarcity. Widespread learning capacity facilitates sustainable growth because active participation is necessary for the success of many initiatives in areas such as preserving the environment and conservation of ecodiversity. Waste treatment, energy saving and efficient use of energy and resources, agroforestry, and management of water resources are also helped by inclusive learning. To enhance resilience to cope with disaster risks, innovative and inclusive approaches are indispensable. Disaster risk management is possible only with the participation of all residents and other stakeholders who, through mutual learning, have to find locally specific innovative solutions.

To enhance capacity for learning, both quality education and learning by doing are key. As Stiglitz and Greenwald note, "One should see formal education and on-the-job training as complements, with the former designed to enhance the productivity of the latter" (2014, 57).

To ensure complementarity between quality formal education, on one hand, and initiatives to strengthen learning by doing, on the other, is one of the crucial challenges to create a learning society.

CASE 1: EFFECTIVE APPROACHES TO STRENGTHENING CAPACITY TO LEARN TO LEARN BY LEARNING BY DOING

Hosono (2017a) reviewed several capacity development (CD)–related programs of international cooperation from the perspective of the enhancement of capacity for learning to learn. In all these programs, individuals and organizations learned to learn by learning by doing and by learning from others (i.e., mutual learning), and they cocreated innovative solutions to the issues they needed to address.

The aim of the life improvement program is primarily to enable rural women to become aware of the numerous problems that exist in daily life and to address them as problems to be solved. As such, the objective of this program is learning to learn through learning by doing and making efforts to improve quality of life in its multiple dimensions. Rural women were encouraged to actively identify problems in their living conditions, set the issues, and formulate living improvement plans. As such, this initiative was not just about life improvement but also was a learning process, particularly designed to enhance the capacity for learning to learn.

In the One Village One Product (OVOP) program, participants and their groups, taking part in multiple stages along a value chain, including production of raw materials, processing, marketing, and servicing, can maximize learning opportunities. Such comprehensive knowledge, based on these experiences of learning by doing and mutual learning, has helped them generate new ideas and innovative products. By enhancing learning opportunities in their activities and sharing ideas among members of the OVOP group, they work constantly toward reaching a better marketing mix (Hosono 2017a).

Through *kaizen* and related initiatives,[9] quality control circles are an effective approach for frontline workers to contribute to and receive the benefit of mutual learning and to enhance capacity for learning to learn. Total quality management also is an effective approach to organizational learning. These approaches ensure that everyone lives up to her or his abilities and enables genuine inclusive and innovative growth (Hosono 2017a).

These programs have several common features: (1) easy entry points are available to initiate the learning process; (2) the costs and risks are low; (3) the focus is on learning by doing and mutual learning to cocreate innovative solutions; and (4) learning makes an intrinsic contribution to the particular objective being pursued—that is, life improvement, inclusive business, quality and productivity improvement, and incremental innovation (Hosono 2017a).

STRATEGY FOR INVESTING IN QUALITY INFRASTRUCTURE

Regarding the relationship between infrastructure and growth, as Égert and Sutherland (2009) emphasize, infrastructure investments can have a positive effect on growth that goes beyond the effect of the capital stock because of economies of scale, the existence of network externalities, and competition-enhancing effects. They conclude that the evidence from cross-section regressions suggests that greater provision of infrastructure is associated with higher subsequent growth rates and that the link is nonlinear, with a potentially higher impact of additional infrastructure in countries with initially lower levels of provision. Infrastructure may not only have a positive impact on growth but also on some attributes of quality growth. Seneviratne and Sun (2013) found that better infrastructure, both in quantity and quality, improves income distribution. This result, along with the proven role of infrastructure in enhancing productivity and growth, suggests that infrastructure development can double the effects on poverty reduction and inclusive growth. According to Seneviratne and Sun, for the five original member countries of the Association of Southeast Asian Nations (the ASEAN-5), removing infrastructure gaps would not only raise potential growth but also spread the benefits of growth more evenly.

As such, from the quality growth perspective, quality infrastructure becomes one of the most featured aspects of the recent policy debate. First, the SDGs refer to "quality, reliable, sustainable and resilient infrastructure to support economic development and human well-being, with a focus on affordable and equitable access for all" (SDG9). In keeping with this goal, the declaration of APEC leaders meeting in Lima in 2016 under the theme of Quality of Growth and Human Development states: "We affirm our commitment to promote investment with a focus on infrastructure in terms of both quantity and quality. We reiterate the importance of quality infrastructure for sustainable economic growth. . . . , [and] We are committed to translate this concept into actions including in ICT, energy and transport" (APEC 2016a, 8).[10]

In this regard, two APEC reports have identified the basic aspects of quality infrastructure (APEC 2014b, 2016b) coinciding with the *G7 Ise-Shima Principles for Promoting Quality Infrastructure Investment.* These G7 principles are closely related to attributes of quality growth—especially inclusiveness, sustainability, and resilience:

Principle 1: Ensuring effective governance, reliable operations and economic efficiency in view of life-cycle cost as well as safety and resilience against natural disaster, terrorism and cyber-attack risks; Principle 2: Ensuring job creation, capacity building and transfer of expertise and know-how for local communities; Principle 3: Addressing social and environmental impacts; Principle 4: Ensuring alignment with economic and development strategies including aspects of climate change and environment at the national and regional levels; and Principle 5: Enhancing effective resource mobilization including through PPP. (G7 Summit 2016, 1–2)

On the basis of these five principles, many effective approaches to constructing a quality infrastructure can be envisaged. Many of the "corridors" programs discussed later (see Case 2) are examples of quality infrastructure. Numerous outstanding cases of quality infrastructure in diverse sectors, including railways, roads and bridges, airports and ports, energy, traffic systems, and disaster management, have been incorporated into the "Quality Infrastructure Investment Casebook" (MOFA 2015).

STRATEGY FOR STRENGTHENING INSTITUTIONS

Institutions are considered the basic determinants for long-term sustained economic growth (e.g., North 1990). From this perspective, Johnson, Ostry, and Subramanian (2007) define good economic institutions as those that create effective property rights for most people, including both protection against expropriation by the state (or powerful elites), and enforceable contracts between private parties.[11] They also state that good economic institutions are essential in creating markets and sustaining efficient market transactions. This definition of institutions appears to be a narrow interpretation of the quality of growth perspective. They recognize that "although this definition is far from requiring full equality of opportunity in society, it implies that societies where only a small fraction of the population have well-enforced property rights do not have good economic institutions" (2007, 7–8). De Soto (1989, 2000) asserts that a formal legal system is essential for poverty reduction to protect the property rights of the poor effectively and to enhance opportunities for them to engage in economic activities.

From a broader perspective, institutions matter for the most basic aspects of quality growth. For instance, progressive tax regimes as well as inclusive education and universal health-care institutions are crucial for inclusive growth. Acemoglu and Robinson (2012) made an important distinction between inclusive and extractive institutions. This distinction is useful for analyzing how types of institutions can determine the long-term prosperity of a locality, region, or nation. They claim that inclusive institutions can cause a virtuous circle of economic activities over a long period of time (Iizuka, Hosono, and Katz 2016). In this virtuous circle, learning and innovation under inclusive institutions could be critical. Needless to say, institutions also matter for sustainability and resilience.

STRATEGIES TO CATALYZE TRANSFORMATION
AND QUALITY GROWTH

Given the enhancement of essential endowments, and because of other factors, transformation takes place, but it does so along different paths.[12] The strategies of transformation could be different depending on these paths. Among others, some of the main paths of transformation could be (1) catching-up transformation, (2) transformation through integration into regional or global value chains (GVCs), (3) transformation led by innovation, and (4) transformation with development of inclusive business. The following sections discuss one possible strategy for each of these types of transformation.

STRATEGY FOR CATALYZING SEQUENTIAL
OR CATCHING-UP TRANSFORMATION

In East Asia, a sequential or catching-up transformation well known in the region as the flying-geese pattern (FGP) has taken place for decades. The process was enabled by dynamically changing endowments and comparative advantage. The three essential endowments for transformation for quality of growth played crucial roles.

Asia has grown faster than any other developing region, and a few of its economies have undergone a rapid and remarkable transformation. East Asian countries are most outstanding in this aspect. "In the four decades from 1956 to 1996, East Asian living standards, as measured by real (inflation-adjusted) output per person, rose at a rate faster than has ever been sustained anywhere" (ADB 2008, 27). Of the ten economies around the world that recorded average increases of 4.5 percent a year or more during that period, eight were in East Asia[13] (ADB 2008). This long-term high growth trend was not limited to East Asia, however. Other Asian economies rank in the upper tiers of world growth distribution: over those four decades, living standards in the sixteen "integrating Asian economies"[14] analyzed in the ADB study (2008) grew at an average of 5 percent a year, whereas the world as a whole averaged only 1.9 percent growth.

The ADB study states that "East Asian economies specialized in simple, labor-intensive manufactures. As the more advanced among them graduated to more sophisticated products, less developed economies filled the gap that they left behind. The Japanese economist Akamatsu (1962) famously compared this pattern of development to flying geese" (ADB 2008, 26). The study elaborates these aspects: "As Japan's exports shifted to more advanced products, East Asia's newly industrializing economies—Hong Kong, China; Republic of Korea; Singapore; and Taipei, China—filled the gap for labor-intensive products. In time, South East Asia and the People's Republic of China (hereafter, PRC) followed the similar trajectory" (ADB 2008, 29). These waves produced dramatic spurts of growth. Thus, "by the time the East Asian model had become widely celebrated (World Bank 1993, hereafter *East Asian Miracle* study), it had been at work for four decades" (ADB 2008, 29).

In the same year that the ADB study was published, the Commission on Growth and Development published its report. It identified some of the distinctive characteristics of thirteen high-growth economies that have been able to grow at more than 7 percent for periods of more than twenty-five years since World War II. Of the thirteen economies, nine are East Asian economies (high performing Asian economies [HPAEs] and China).[15] Referring to these economies of the "Growth Report," Lin argues that in East Asia there has been a sequential process of catching-up. He states that "the newly industrializing East Asian economies, for instance, exploited endowment structures similar to Japan's to follow that country's development in a flying-geese pattern" (Lin 2012b, 94). Aoki (2013, 2014) argues that the dynamics of the FGP are accompanied by a change of institutions. He proposes that the complex dynamics of demography, economy, and institutions—which are taking place in East Asia—could be conceptualized as FGP version 2.0, compared with FGP version 1.0 (based on Aoki's definition) originally proposed by Akamatsu (1962).

Although there has been an accumulation of literature on the FGP [16] in Asia, the most remarkable fact is that FGP demonstrates the sequence of transformation among the economies of East Asia and is intrinsically related to the long-term high economic growth of these economies as a whole. In terms of public policy, this fact indicates the relevance of the strategy and policies of industrial transformation adopted by East Asian countries. After almost four decades of high rates of growth, and improvement of welfare with inclusive development (to be discussed later) in most of the East Asian economies, which account for more than 30 percent of the world's population, this growth was not just a coincidence. The *East Asian Miracle* study confirms this: "If growth were randomly distributed, there is roughly one chance in ten thousand that success would have been so regionally concentrated" (World Bank 1993, 2).[17]

Asian tigers started to pursue industrial development strategies as early as the 1960s, with other Asian countries following. As a Japan International Cooperation Agency/Japan Bank for International Cooperation (JICA/JBIC) study (2008) summarizes,

> from the 1960s through to the 80s, the Asian countries promoted industrialization in a strategic manner by adopting import substitution policy (ISP) and export oriented policy (EOP)[18] for light and heavy industry at different times and sometimes in a cyclical manner, thus fostering domestic productive capacity while promoting export. During the second ISP period (for heavy and chemical industry), many countries pursued EOP simultaneously. After this period, most Asian countries shifted to EOP in the 1990s. (JICA/JBIC 2008, 33)

In the mid-1980s, ASEAN countries were desperately attempting to transform their primary goods-based export structure to one oriented toward labor-intensive light manufacturing goods and further to technology-intensive manufacturing (Shimomura 2013).

Since the 1980s, this FGP transformation has been reinforced by the development of electronics, automobiles, and other related industries, based on continuous innovation with consecutive expansion and deepening of regional and global value chains as well as supply chains. This process could be called "FGP + GVC-type transformation." I will elaborate later on this type of transformation.

The major driving force of East Asia's long-term remarkable growth has been industrial transformation from agriculture to labor-intensive light industries, and later, to knowledge-intensive industries led by FGP and the FGP + GVC process. This growth is affirmed by the fact that the reallocation of labor across sectors has been an important driver of productivity growth in several fast-growing East Asian economies. In China, it contributed 4.1 percent of 7.3 percent annual growth in aggregate labor productivity over the past decade (1999–2008); in Vietnam, it accounted for 2.6 percent out of 4.2 percent (World Bank 2012).

This sequential and catching-up transformation-led growth is closely related to the attributes of quality of growth in East Asia. Asian countries first promoted agricultural and rural development with the Green Revolution of the 1960s and 1970s and then started the intensive process of industrialization. From the end of the 1960s, in just a single decade, the introduction of high-yield rice and other primary crops, subsidies for fertilizers and other agricultural inputs, and the expansion of investment in irrigation improved agricultural productivity (JICA/JBIC 2008). From 1965 to 1988, growth in both agricultural output and agricultural productivity was higher in East Asia than in other regions. The *East Asian Miracle* study highlights that East Asian governments have actively supported agricultural research and extension services to speed the diffusion of agricultural revolution technologies (World Bank 1993). This transformation has had substantial effects both on inclusive and pro-poor growth and on further transformation in these countries.

Increased agricultural output and productivity have direct effects on the welfare of rural populations. At the same time, increased production normally results in a fall in the real price of food, contributing to improvements for both urban and rural populations. Furthermore, higher agricultural productivity allows excess rural workers to migrate to urban areas, which enables the expansion of labor-intensive industries, generating further transformation.

The essence of the East Asian miracle was "rapid growth with equity" (World Bank 1993, 8) for at least the first three decades of sequential and catching-up transformation-led growth.[19] Thus, we could say that "transformation with equity," considered the goal of development by UNECLAC (1990) was achieved in East Asia at least in the period between 1960 and 1990. The *East Asian Miracle* study emphasizes that "the HPEAs are unique in that they combine this rapid, sustained growth with highly equal income distributions" (World Bank 1993, 8).

In contrast, the Growth Commission's 2008 report highlights the reasons why long-term high growth was achieved: the strategy for such growth was inclusive and was supported by a wide range of people in East Asia.

In spite of transformation-led long-term high growth, challenges remain in Asia. Regarding some of its attributes, such as inclusiveness and sustainability, certain setbacks can be observed in some economies of East Asia. This is why the quality of growth in Asia has been hotly debated, according to Haddad, Kato, and Meisel (2015), who explain this is understandable because Asia is a region that has achieved remarkable economic development. The "APEC Strategy for Strengthening Quality Growth," agreed on in 2015 by APEC leaders, in which most East Asian economies participate, articulates that "while APEC as a region has made progress in achieving growth in all its attributes, much still remains to be done, particularly in making sure that the gains already achieved are further expanded and sustained" (APEC 2015, 1).

CASE 2: EFFECTIVE APPROACHES TO FACILITATE REGIONAL NETWORKS AND INTEGRATION THROUGH DEVELOPMENT CORRIDORS

According to JICA, "Urban unipolar concentrations of economic activities and populations lead to an expansion of regional disparities and a reduction of national growth" (2016b, 1–2). The "corridors" approach considers a trunk corridor as the key development axis that will stimulate and increase economic activity in countries and regions. By combining the development potential of a region with corridor infrastructure improvement, a strategic regional development plan can enable the revitalization of an entire region and create a virtuous spiral of investment promotion and market expansion.

In Asia, the ADB launched the "Greater Mekong Sub-region (GMS) Development Program" in 1992.[20] Six countries in the Mekong region—Thailand, Vietnam, Laos, Cambodia, China, and Myanmar—participated. The ADB secretariat functioned as an intermediary between the member countries and donors, while also coordinating eleven programs, including economic development corridors in the region's North-South, East-West, and Southern areas. These programs covered nine priority areas: traffic and transportation, energy, communication, tourism, environment, human resource development, trade, investment, and agriculture. These development corridors promoted poverty reduction and economic growth by creating a belt that would link impoverished inland areas to port cities that had access to world markets. Moreover, electricity and communication infrastructure was developed in parallel with roads, bridges, and other transport infrastructure. Linkages to agriculture, mining resources, and tourism also were created based on this infrastructure. Free trade zones were established in the border areas and industrial parks were constructed. Because the success or the failure of the GMS corridor depended on collaboration between governments and the private sector, the GMS Forum took a number of steps to facilitate this collaboration. It sponsored workshops for the private sector, nurtured the development of regional resources and processing industries in all countries along the corridor, and proposed private investment to form industrial clusters at locations along the corridor.

JICA/JBIC (2008) emphasizes that the GMS program was not originally launched by drafting and finalizing multilateral cooperative agreements, but rather it was based on a results-oriented approach. It focused on the cooperation already established by bilateral agreements in areas where something could realistically be achieved. The agencies further stress that "as both parties benefited, the framework was gradually expanded to other countries and built upon the principle of comparative advantages. Such flexible pragmatism was a principle factor behind the comprehensive and synthetic GMS framework in the Mekong area development" (JICA/JBIC 2008, 55–56).

In Africa, in accordance with the framework of the Tokyo International Conference on African Development VI (2016–2018), as a part of the initiative "Quality Africa: Promoting Structural Economic Transformation through Economic Diversification and Industrialization," corridor developments are now being promoted. The three priority areas are the Northern Corridor of East Africa, the Nacala Corridor, and the West Africa Growth Ring. The initiative aims to accelerate trade expansion by promoting a corridor development approach to comprehensively integrate industrial development, social sector development, and economic infrastructure development, encouraging public-private partnership from master planning stage to project implementation stage (JICA 2016b).

STRATEGY FOR TRANSFORMATION THROUGH INTEGRATION INTO GLOBAL VALUE CHAINS

East Asian economies have been pioneers in transforming their industrial structure through participation in GVCs. East Asia was best able to take advantage of the expanding electronics industry. Although the share of electric and electronic products in world trade of manufactured goods increased from 13.0 percent to 29.7 percent between 1970 and 2000, in East Asia, this share increased from 14.3 percent to 48.4 percent over the same period. In developing East Asia (i.e., East Asia except Japan), the share increased from 14.4 percent to 52.7 percent (to 55.7 percent in 2007) (Kumakura 2010). Later, the automobile industry significantly deepened GVCs.

This FGP + GVC-type transformation has been facilitated by intraregional trade agreements in East Asia since the mid-1990s. Moreover, this type of transformation has been extended to other Asian countries. In "integrating Asian economies,"[21] the share of parts and components trade in manufacturing trade increased from 24.3 percent in 1996 to 29.4 percent in 2006. The ADB (2008) study considers this a remarkable rise, because worldwide its share scarcely increased, edging up from 19.6 percent to 20.2 percent over the same period. Participation in GVCs creates opportunities for industrial transformation. The integration of small and medium enterprises (SMEs) into global and regional value chains is critical to making this transformation inclusive and innovative. A recent study by the Organisation of Economic Co-operation and Development (OECD) and the World Bank (2015) focuses on inclusive GVCs, highlighting the policy options in trade and complementary areas for GVC integration by SMEs. The report states: "Enhancing the integration into global markets of goods, services, investment, and knowledge of small and medium enterprises . . . represents a challenge for growth and job creation in all countries, at all levels of economic development" (OECD and World Bank 2015, 14).

Regional aspects of inclusive value chains are emphasized in a study by UNECLAC (2014), which argues that the rise of value chains in the global economy has brought renewed attention to the centrality of the regional space. The main global production networks are structured around specific regions, largely because of the importance of geographic proximity when it comes to organizing production processes that are fragmented across a number of countries.

CASE 3: EFFECTIVE APPROACHES FOR SME PARTICIPATION IN GVC THROUGH EXPANSION OF SUPPORTING INDUSTRIES

The automobile industry provides a highly relevant case for exploring SME participation and regional aspects of GVCs. Opportunities will be increased by investments of automobile companies, which require high-quality and competitive automobile parts and services. Development of an automobile industry requires skilled labor and supporting industries to provide up to thirty thousand parts and components. Supporting industries and automobile assembly plants are closely related and provide mutual externality.

Development of supporting industries, composed mostly of SMEs, is essential for a competitive automobile industry. If the industry becomes more competitive, production and exports will increase, demanding more parts and services. This is a typical case of growth begetting more growth when it is accompanied by higher productivity or higher value added, which often is achieved through innovation. Supporting industries are structured with supply chains that normally incorporate three or more tiers of suppliers in the case of the automobile industry.

The ratio of exported cars to cars produced in Mexico was around 80 percent in 2014. The increase of production and export of cars from Mexico has been remarkable: from less than 2.0 million cars in 2005 to over 3.4 million cars in 2014, of which 2.6 million cars were exported. This growth was enabled by years of efforts by the Mexican government and the private sector in such areas as human resource development, infrastructure development for highly efficient transport and logistics, automobile industry development policies, free trade agreements (North American Free Trade Agreement, European Union–Mexico Free Trade Agreement, and Japan–Mexico Economic Partnership Agreement), and institution-building of public and private entities related to automobile industry.[22]

These factors have been extremely important for Mexico to receive foreign direct investment in support of its automobile industry and to enhance opportunities for SMEs to participate in the industry's development. SMEs had to improve their capacity to respond to opportunities for industries supporting car production so that they could develop and make the country's car industry competitive. To strengthen SMEs, laws on the development of competitiveness of micro, small, and medium enterprises were enacted in 2003.

In this context, several joint projects between Mexico and Japan for promoting industrial development, strengthening SMEs, and training workers have been implemented. This cooperation reflects the priorities of Mexico's industrial policy.[23] On the basis of several cooperation projects, more structured and innovative cooperation to strengthen local supporting industries (i.e., SMEs) of the automobile industry, while adhering to the supply chain structure, has been realized. The projects include "Support for Formation of Automobile Industry Cluster and Supply Chain," "Technical Support for Universities and Colleges of Engineering," "Automotive Supply Chain Development Project," and "Improvement of Quality and Productivity of Small and Medium Supporting Industries for Automobile Production."

STRATEGY FOR INNOVATION-LED TRANSFORMATION

Although these cases of transformation (sequential and catching-up transformation and participation in GVCs) are closely related to technological innovation in many ways, other cases of transformation have been led mainly by technological innovation. In these cases, technological innovation, along with other factors or endowments, was the key enabling factor of transformation. Although the former cases often are characterized by the adoption and adaptation of foreign technology, the latter cases often are characterized by breakthrough innovations or incremental innovations, which were normally not available elsewhere in the world. An example of this is evident in the tropical agriculture and agroindustry, as well as agroforestry in tropical rainforests, for which industrial countries cannot provide technological innovation. Because the private sector cannot fully take the risk of investment in innovation, they underinvest in innovation activities, especially in developing countries (UN Industrial Development Organization [UNIDO] 2016, 151). To address this situation, governments need to lead or support investment in innovation. UNIDO (2016) lists the objectives, source, and agents of such support.

Hosono, Magno, and Hongo (2016) have analyzed the case of Cerrado agriculture, in which technological innovation produced a profound transformation in the Central-West region of Brazil. In effect, agriculture, livestock, and agroindustry transformation in some Latin American countries has been outstanding. Brazil was a net importer of grain until the 1980s, when the country achieved a major breakthrough to become a net exporter of grain after converting its vast barren land into some of the most productive agricultural fields in the world. Further transformation was achieved by a deepening of the agroindustrial value chains, especially of meat and dairy products.

In the case of the Cerrado agriculture, from its inception through the early development phases, the public or semipublic sector took the initiative and made the necessary investments in research and development and in infrastructure. Later, public and private partnerships became essential for the formation of clusters and value chains as well as learning and innovation ecosystems around clusters. In the case of the Brazilian Cerrado, breakthrough innovations enabled the start-up of the Cerrado agriculture and continuous and incremental innovation followed, allowing agricultural production and agroindustry value chains to scale up.

The following case illustrates the transformation enabled by farmers and their community with mainly incremental innovations for years of learning by doing in the tropical rainforest of the Amazon.

CASE 4: EFFECTIVE APPROACHES TO ESTABLISH SUSTAINABLE
AND INCLUSIVE AGROFORESTRY IN TROPICAL RAINFOREST WITH
TECHNOLOGICAL INNOVATION AND BEST PRACTICES

As natural capital, tropical rainforests are extremely important for a green economy. They are rich in biodiversity and function as huge reservoirs of carbon dioxide, but they are increasingly becoming endangered. Indeed, significant losses have already occurred worldwide. Shifting agriculture was thought to account for about one-third of the deforestation in Amazonia, while cattle ranching was responsible for at least half of the forest retreat (Smith et al. 1998). It was common practice for illegally deforested land to be used for a number of years as pasture for cattle ranching and other purposes and for the land then to be abandoned when its fertility was almost lost. Therefore, the challenge in the Amazon rainforest was not only the establishment of sustainable and inclusive agroforestry for small farmers but also for the regeneration of abandoned land by agroforestry,

In this context, in Tomé-Açu, in the state of Pará in the Brazilian Amazon region, crop diversification and critical production experience led to the development of an innovative agroforestry model (hereafter referred to as the Tomé-Açu model) that is well suited to the Amazonian environment. In the Tomé-Açu model, key factors include a combination of crops and trees and the sequence for planting them. The model is inclusive and sustainable. Using this model, 25 hectares of agroforestry produces the same level of income as 1,000 hectares of cattle ranching. Therefore, the former's income from 25 hectares is forty times that of the latter from the same extension of land. Moreover, the agroforestry creates jobs for ten to twenty workers with 25 hectares, whereas the ranching needs 50–75 hectares to create a job for one worker (Yamada 2003).

In one of its recent research projects, the Brazilian Agricultural Research Corporation (Embrapa) Eastern Amazon Center found striking similarities between the characteristics of agroforest soils of this model and those of the natural forest soil of the Amazon rainforest. This may imply the resilience of the agroforest ecosystem in terms of not only flora but also fauna. In fact, as agroforests have grown over the years, the number of observed bird species has increased, showing how agroforestry supports both ecosystem recovery in the Amazon and farmers' livelihoods. In acknowledgment of the establishment of the successful model, on December 1, 2010, the Tomé-Açu Multipurpose Agricultural Cooperative was awarded the first Brazil Regional Development Contribution Prize by the federal government of Brazil (Hosono 2013b).

STRATEGY FOR INCLUSIVE BUSINESS–LED TRANSFORMATION

In addition to the strategies discussed thus far, people-centered transformation strategies deserve special attention. These strategies proactively support inclusive and sustainable activities in which the base of the pyramid (BOP) can participate. The use of an inclusive business models, as proposed by the United Nations Development Programme (UNDP/Growing Inclusive Markets 2008), could provide one such strategy. These models include the poor on the demand side as clients and customers (*first category*), and on the supply side as employees, producers, and business owners at various points in the value chains (*second category*) [emphasis added].

Inclusive business is an important pathway to realize industrial transformation and quality growth locally and also to focus on BOP. For the first category of inclusive business, it is critical to produce goods at scale to make their price affordable for the poor and to expedite delivery. BOP business is different from a normal commercial business for a variety of reasons, including the limited purchasing power of low-income customers, the required innovative technology for consumption needs, the normally high levels of upfront investments, awareness and acceptance by users, and the difficulty of delivery (Kato and Hosono 2013). A comprehensive approach to addressing constraints of inclusive businesses for BOP is needed because (1) an affordable price is normally enabled by production at scale, which requires finance for scale; (2) delivery at scale is essential to make available new products for BOP; and (3) partnership at scale with governments, NGOs, international organizations, and other stakeholders is needed as well.

For the second category of inclusive business, it is essential to create and commercialize competitive products and services based on local resources, to support self-reliance and creativity, and to develop human resources . By learning about improvements to their livelihood, communities and their member will become more conscious of their needs (and challenges) and of BOP products to satisfy them. This approach enables communities to become involved in "participatory platforms for inclusive products and service design" (Casado Caneque and Hart 2015, 8) on the demand side of inclusive business. At the same time, it enables and strengthens their capacity on the supply side to become employees, producers, and business owners at various points in the value chains by participating in inclusive business. OVOP programs have resulted in a promising model of inclusive business from the supply side (i.e., the second category) (Hosono 2017a).

CONCLUSION

The strategies and case studies discussed in this chapter show that quality growth needs to be discussed in the context of transformation, which is the key driver of growth and a determinant of the various attributes of growth. As transformation is closely related to changing endowments and dynamic comparative advantage, the central theme has to be the relationships among these essential endowments, transformation paths, and attributes of quality growth.

It is clear that the enhancement of endowments and the transformation do not take place automatically. These processes are normally endogenous, but they need to be catalyzed or facilitated by industrial strategies and policies. As a corollary, it might be realistic to design policies and measures to attain the desired attributes of quality growth alongside the development of specific industries and their value chains, as transformation is taking place, while remembering specific transformation paths and quality growth agendas.

Transformation and quality growth need to be considered in a holistic manner, as a comprehensive target to be achieved. The APEC Growth Strategy could be regarded as a pioneering initiative with a holistic framework for attaining such a target. In developing a distinct transformation agenda for each country, the nature of quality growth should be fully taken into account, bearing in mind the interrelationships, synergy, sequences, and trade-offs among them.

As the transformation agenda differs between countries with distinctive characteristics, policies and measures to transform these different economies and attain the desired attributes of quality growth also would be different. No standard model addresses the challenges of transformation and quality growth. Each country requires a distinct combination of strategies as well as effective approaches toward realizing such strategies. The approaches discussed in this chapter may provide some means of envisioning alternative strategies.

The interrelationships among endowments, transformation, and quality growth are highly complex, and this chapter has covered these aspects only in part. Therefore, they deserve further in-depth analysis.

NOTES

1. This UN plan of action on Sustainable Development Goals (SDGs) was adopted by the UN General Assembly in 2015; see United Nations, "Transforming Our World: The 2030 Agenda for Sustainable Development," 2015, https://sustainabledevelopment.un.org/content/documents/21252030%20Agenda%20for%20Sustainable%20Development%20web.pdf.

2. The APEC Growth Strategy's definition of quality of growth, which focused on five desired attributes, appears to be one of the most widely agreed-on and most comprehensive definitions. It draws on the outcome of discussions on these attributes over a decade, and is reviewed in the following sections.

3. See, for example, Asian Development Bank, *Key Indicators for Asia and the Pacific 2013: Asia's Economic Transformation: Where to, How, and How Fast?* (Manila, Philippines: ADB, 2013); UN Economic and Social Commission for Asia and Pacific, *Shifting from Quantity to Quality: Growth with Equality, Efficiency, Sustainability and Dynamism* (Bangkok, Thailand: UNESCAP, 2013); UN Economic Commission for Latin America and the Caribbean, *Structural Change for Equality: An Integrated Approach to Development* (Santiago, Chile: UNECLAC, 2012); Inter-American Development Bank, *Rethinking Productive Development: Sound Policies and Institutions for Economic Transformation* (Washington, DC: IDB, 2014); UN Economic Commission for Africa, *Making the Most of Africa's Commodities: Industrializing for Growth, Jobs and Economic Transformation* (Addis Ababa, Ethiopia: UNECA, 2013); African Center for Economic Transformation, "2014 African Transformation Report: Growth with Depth" (Accra, Ghana: ACET, 2014).

4. The report emphasizes that what African countries need is growth with depth: "More Diversification, more Export competitiveness, more Productivity increase, more Technological upgrading, and more improvements in Human well-being" (the title of the ACET report, "Growth with Depth" is itself an acronym drawn from the names of the five elements). It states: "Only by doing so can they ensure that growth improves human well-being by providing more productive jobs and higher incomes and thus has everyone share in the new prosperity" (ACET, "2014 African Transformation Report," 1).

5. Aggregate productivity increases when the most productive sectors expand. This effect, referred to as productivity-enhancing structural change, is well documented in the case of labor shifts from agriculture to industry and services. Reallocation of labor across sectors has been an important driver of productivity growth in several fast-growing East Asian countries; see World Bank, *World Development Report 2013: Jobs* (Washington, DC: World Bank, 2012), 100.

6. Regarding factor endowments, it is essential to take into account mobility of capital and highly skilled labor, rapid technological change, and evolving global value chains. For a discussion on this aspect, see Akbar Noman and Joseph E. Stiglitz, "Learning, Industrial, and Technology Policies: An Overview." In *Efficiency, Finance, and Varieties of Industrial Policy: Guiding Resources, Learning, and Technology for Sustained Growth*, edited by Akbar Noman and Joseph E. Stiglitz (New York: Columbia University Press 2017), 12–13. Demographic transition also matters for long-term comparative advantage.

7. This is based on Japan's view of economic development and its experiences (see Hosono 2016, 173). In a similar manner, JICA/JBIC (2008, 17) considers infrastructure, human resources, and credit markets as fundamental growth-driving functions. Akio Hosono, "Catalyzing Transformation for Inclusive Growth," in *Japan's Development Assistance: Foreign Aid and the Post-2015 Agenda*, ed. Hiroshi Kato, John Page, and Yasutami Shimomura (New York: Palgrave Macmillan, 2016), 169–187; and Japan International Cooperation Agency/Japan Bank for International Cooperation, *Report of the Stocktaking Work on the Economic Development in Africa and the Asian Growth Experience* (Tokyo: JICA/JBIC, 2008).

8. Japan's Official Development Assistance white paper states that achieving economic growth requires improving the investment environment, which involves policy and institution building, human resources development, strengthening basic infrastructure, attracting foreign direct investment, and expanding trade. Japan has long insisted that economic growth through infrastructure development, etc., is crucial to poverty reduction, and has incorporated this viewpoint in its ODA policies. Ministry of Foreign Affairs, *Japan's Official Development Assistance 2005* (Part I, Section 2) (Tokyo: MOFA, 2005).

9. *Kaizen* is a management philosophy and know-how system that brings about continuous improvement of productivity and quality. It is a philosophy that has contributed to the development of Japan, especially in manufacturing industries. More recently, it has proved to be valid for use in other countries, cultures, and sectors. *Kaizen* is a human-centered approach that fosters teamwork, self-reliance, creativity, and ingenuity; see JICA, *Kaizen: Japan's Approach Towards Improved Quality and Productivity: The Driving Force of Japan's Rapid Growth* (Tokyo: JICA, 2016a).

10. The concept of "quality infrastructure" was first used in the APEC Leaders Declaration in 2013. The APEC Connectivity Blueprint was adopted the following year; see APEC, "APEC Connectivity Blueprint for 2015–2025" (Beijing, China: APEC, 2014a).

11. They compared Africa today with countries that were similarly weak in the past in terms of their institutional development and yet managed to escape from poverty. Inherited institutional weaknesses persist in Africa, and internal conflict and societal fractionalization remain concerns. However, the East Asian experience demonstrates that some institutional weaknesses can be escaped; see Simon Johnson, Jonathan D. Ostry, and Arvind Subramanian, "The Prospect for Sustained Growth in Africa: Benchmarking the Constraints" (NBER Working Paper, National Bureau of Economic Research, Cambridge, MA 2007), 36–37.

12. The ADB report on transformation explains: (1) countries' structural transformation (ST) is driven by demand and supply factors; (2) demographic and geographic variables and country size shape the pattern of ST; (3) good organizational capabilities that encompass all of the tacit knowledge necessary to produce a good or deliver a service allow faster ST; and (4) specific policies and actions, institutions, and politics often work jointly to determine the direction and pace of ST. ADB, *Key Indicators for Asia and the Pacific 2013: Asia's Economic Transformation: Where to, How, and How Fast?* (Manila, Philippines, 2013), 5.

13. The eight economies are the People's Republic of China, Japan, Malaysia, Thailand, and so-called Asian tigers (Hong Kong, Republic of Korea, Singapore, and

Chinese Taipei). The eight high-performing Asian economies (HPAEs) of the World Bank's study on the East Asian Miracle (cited later) are the Asian tigers, and Indonesia, Japan, Malaysia, and Thailand.

14. The sixteen "integrating Asian economies" are, in addition to the eight economies, the other ASEAN countries (Brunei Darussalam, Cambodia, Indonesia, Lao People's Democratic Republic, Myanmar, Philippines, and Vietnam) and India.

15. Regarding HPAEs, see footnote 13.

16. FGP is also referred to as flying wild geese (FWG); see Ippei Yamazawa, "Flying Wild Geese Pattern in Pacific: Pattern of Industrial Development among Asian Countries" (Distinguished speakers program, Asian Development Bank, Manila, 1990). For literature on FGP, see Akio Hosono, *Asia Pacific and Latin America: Dynamics of Regional Integration and International Cooperation*, International Trade Series 132 (Santiago, Chile: UNECLAC, 2017b).

17. In addition, The *East Asian Miracle* study states that since 1960, the HPAEs have grown more than twice as fast as the rest of East Asia, roughly three times as fast as Latin America and South Asia, and five times faster than Sub-Sahara Africa. They also significantly outperformed the industrial economies and the oil-rich Middle East—North Africa region. Between 1960 and 1980, real income per capita increased more than four times in Japan and the Four Tigers and more than doubled in the Southeast Asian NIEs. World Bank, *East Asian Miracle: Economic Growth and Public Policy* (Washington, DC: World Bank, 1993), 2.

18. IS and EO were used instead of ISP and EOP in the cited document.

19. The *East Asian Miracle* study classified countries of the world by a combination of the levels of GDP growth rate per capita and income inequality between 1965 and 1989: "There are 7 high growth, low-inequality economies. All of them are in East Asia," namely HPAEs except Malaysia (World Bank, *East Asian Miracle*, 30). The HPAEs have also achieved "unusually low and declining levels of inequality, contrary to historical experience and contemporary evidence in other regions (Kuznets 1955)" (World Bank *East Asian Miracle*, 29–30). Simon Kuznets, "Economic Growth and Income Inequality," *American Economic Review* 45, no. 1 (1955): 1–28.

20. This paragraph draws heavily from JICA/JBIC, *Report of the Stocktaking Work on the Economic Development in Africa and the Asian Growth Experience*. (Tokyo: JICA, 2008)

21. See footnote 14 in regard to integrating Asian economies.

22. For further information on Japanese investments and cooperation with the Mexican car industry, see IDB, *Japan and Latin America and the Caribbean: Building a Sustainable Trans-Pacific Relationship* (Washington, DC: IDB, 2013), 33–35; and *A Virtuous Cycle of Integration: The Past, Present, and Future of Japan-Latin America and the Caribbean Relations* (Washington, DC: IDB, 2016), 25–27.

23. These projects of cooperation are "Study on Promotion and Development Plan of Supporting Industries" in 1996–1997, "Study on Technology Transfer" in 1997–1999, "Press Process Technology Improvement Project" in 2006–2009, "Study on SMEs' Human Resources Development" in 2008–2009, and "Plastic Molding Technology Human Resources Development Project" in 2010–2014.

REFERENCES

Acemoglu, Daron, and James Robinson. 2012. *Why Nations Fail: The Origins of Power, Prosperity and Poverty.* New York: Crown Business.

ACET (African Centre for Economic Transformation). 2014. *2014 African Transformation Report: Growth with Depth.* Accra, Ghana: ACET.

ADB (Asian Development Bank). 2008. *Emerging Asian Regionalism: A Partnership for Shared Prosperity.* Manila: ADB.

———. 2013. *Key Indicators for Asia and the Pacific 2013: Asia's Economic Transformation: Where to, How, and How Fast?* Manila: ADB.

Akamatsu, Kaname. 1962. "A Historical Pattern of Economic Growth in Developing Countries." *The Developing Economies* 1 (1): 3–25. Tokyo: IDE-JETRO

Aoki, Masahiko. 2013. *Comparative Institutional Analysis: Theory, Corporations and East Asia. Selected Papers of Masahiko Aoki.* Cheltenham: Edward Edgar.

———. 2014. *Keizaigaku Nyumon* [Introduction to Economics]. Tokyo: Chikuma Shobo.

APEC (Asia Pacific Economic Cooperation). 2010. *The APEC Leaders Growth Strategy.* Yokohama, Japan: APEC.

———. 2014a. *APEC Connectivity Blueprint for 2015–2025.* Beijing: APEC.

———. 2014b. *APEC Guidebook on Quality of Infrastructure Development and Investment.* Beijing: APEC.

———. 2015. *APEC Strategy for Strengthening Quality Growth.* Manila: APEC.

———. 2016a. *2016 Leaders' Declaration.* Lima, Peru: APEC.

———. 2016b. *Study on Infrastructure Investment in the APEC Region.* Lima, Peru: APEC.

Cabinet Office (Japan). 2015. "Development Cooperation Charter." Tokyo: Cabinet Office.

Casado Caneque, Fernando, and Stuart L. Hart. 2015. *Base of the Pyramid 3.0: Sustainable Development through Innovation and Entrepreneurship.* Sheffield, UK: Greenleaf Publishing.

Commission on Growth and Development. 2008. *The Growth Report: Strategies for Sustained Growth and Inclusive Development.* Washington DC: World Bank.

De Soto, Hernando. 1989. *The Other Path: The Invisible Revolution in the Third World.* New York: Harper Collins.

———. 2000. *Mystery of Capital: Why Capitalism Triumphs in the West and Fails Everywhere Else.* New York: Basic Books.

Égert, B., T. Koźluk, and D. Sutherland. 2009. "Infrastructure and Growth: Empirical Evidence." OECD Economics Department Working Paper No. 685. OECD, Paris.

G7 Summit (Group of Seven). 2016. *G7 Ise-Shima Principles for Promoting Quality Infrastructure Investment.* Ise-Shima, Japan: G7.

High-Level Panel of Eminent Persons on the Post-2015 Development Agenda. 2013. *A New Global Partnership: Eradicate Poverty and Transform Economies Through Sustainable Development.* New York: United Nations.

Haddad, Lawrence, Hiroshi Kato, and Nicolas Meisel. 2015. "Introduction." In *Growth Is Dead, Long Live Growth: The Quality of Economic Growth and Why It Matters*, ed. Lawrence Haddad, Hiroshi Kato, and Nicolas Meisel, 1–16. Tokyo: JICA

Hosono, Akio. 2013a. "Industrial Transformation and Quality of Growth." In *Growth Is Dead, Long Live Growth: The Quality of Economic Growth and Why It Matters*, ed. Lawrence Haddad, Hiroshi Kato, and Nicolas Meisel, 267–300. Tokyo: JICA.

——. 2013b. "Catalyzing an Inclusive Green Economy through South-South and Triangular Cooperation: Lessons Learned from Three Relevant Cases." In *Tackling Global Challenges Through Triangular Cooperation*, ed. Hiroshi Kato and Shunichiro Honda, 53–80. Tokyo: JICA.

——. 2016. "Catalyzing Transformation for Inclusive Growth." In *Japan's Development Assistance: Foreign Aid and the Post-2015 Agenda*, ed. Hiroshi Kato, John Page, and Yasutami Shimomura, 169–187. New York: Palgrave McMillan.

——. 2017a. "Industrial Strategies: Toward a Learning Society for Quality Growth." In *Efficiency, Finance, and Varieties of Industrial Policy: Guiding Resources, Learning, and Technology for Sustained Growth*, ed. Akbar Noman and Joseph Stiglitz, 306–352. New York: Columbia University Press.

——. 2017b. *Asia Pacific and Latin America: Dynamics of Regional Integration and International Cooperation*. International Trade Series 132. Santiago, Chile: UNECLAC.

Hosono, Akio, Carlos Magno, and Yutaka Hongo, eds. 2016. *Development for Sustainable Agriculture: The Brazilian Cerrado*. New York: Palgrave McMillan.

IDB (Inter-American Development Bank). 2013. *Japan and Latin America and the Caribbean: Building a Sustainable Trans-Pacific Relationship*. Washington, DC: IDB.

——. 2014. *Rethinking Productive Development: Sound Policies and Institutions for Economic Transformation*. Washington, DC: IDB.

——. 2016. *A Virtuous Cycle of Integration: The Past, Present, and Future of Japan-Latin America and the Caribbean Relations*. Washington, DC: IDB.

Iizuka, Michiko, Akio Hosono, and Jorge Katz. 2016. "Conclusions and Policy Implications." Chap. 8 in *Chile's Salmon Industry: Policy Challenges in Managing Public Goods*, ed. Akio Hosono, Michiko Iizuka, and Jorge Katz, 195–205. Tokyo: Springer.

JICA (Japan International Cooperation Agency). 2016a. *Kaizen: Japan's Approach Towards Improved Quality and Productivity: The Driving Force of Japan's Rapid Growth*. Tokyo: JICA.

——. 2016b. *Corridor Development Approach*. Tokyo: JICA.

JICA/JBIC (Japan International Cooperation Agency/Japan Bank for International Cooperation). 2008. *Report of the Stocktaking Work on the Economic Development in Africa and the Asian Growth Experience*. Tokyo: JICA/JBIC.

Johnson, Simon, Jonathan D. Ostry, and Arvind Subramanian. 2007. "The Prospect for Sustained Growth in Africa: Benchmarking the Constraints," NBER Working Paper. National Bureau of Economic Research, Cambridge, MA..

Kato, Hiroshi, and Akio Hosono. 2013. "Meeting the Demand of the Poor: Two Cases of Business-led Scaling Up at the Base of Pyramid." In *Getting to Scale: How to Bring Development Solutions to Millions of Poor People*, ed. Laurence Chandy, Akio Hosono, Homi Kharas, and Johannes Linn, 220–235. Washington, DC: Brookings Institution.

Kumakura, Masanaga. 2010. "Interdependent Relations and Electronics Industry in Asia Pacific Economies." In *Asia Pacific and Progress of New Regionalism*, ed. Watanabe Akio. Tokyo: Chikura Shobo.

Kuznets, Simon. 1955. "Economic Growth and Income Inequality." *American Economic Review* 45(1): 1–28.

Lin, Justin Yifu. 2012a. *New Structural Economics: A Framework for Rethinking Development and Policy.* Washington, DC: World Bank.

———. 2012b. *The Quest for Prosperity: How Developing Economies Can Take Off.* Princeton, NJ: Princeton University Press.

MOFA (Ministry of Foreign Affairs, Japan). 2005. *Japan's Official Development Assistance 2005.* Tokyo: MOFA.

———, ed. 2015. *Quality Infrastructure Investment Casebook.* Tokyo: MOFA.

Noman, Akbar, and Joseph E. Stiglitz. 2012. "Strategies for African Development." In *Good Growth and Governance in Africa: Rethinking Development Strategies*, ed. Akbar Noman, Kwesi Botchwey, Howard Stein, and Joseph E. Stiglitz, 3–47. Oxford: Oxford University Press.

———. 2017. "Learning, Industrial, and Technology Policies: An Overview." In *Efficiency, Finance, and Varieties of Industrial Policy: Guiding Resources, Learning, and Technology for Sustained Growth*, ed. Akbar Noman and Joseph E. Stiglitz, 1–20. New York: Columbia University Press.

North, Douglas. 1990. *Institutions, Institutional Change and Economic Performance.* Cambridge: Cambridge University Press.

OECD (Organisation for Economic Co-operation and Development) and World Bank Group. 2015. *Inclusive Global Value Chains: Policy Options in Trade and Complementary Areas for GVC Integration by Small and Medium Enterprises and Low-income Developing Countries.* Paris: OECD.

Seneviratne, Dulani, and Yan Sun. 2013. "Infrastructure and Income Distribution in ASEAN-5: What Are the Links." IMF Working Papers 13/41. International Monetary Fund, Washington, DC.

Shimomura, Yasutami. 2013. "The Japanese View: With Particular Reference to the Shared Cognition Model in Asia," In *A Study on China's Foreign Aid: An Asian Perspective*, ed. Yasutami Shimomura and Hideo Ohashi, 145–68. New York: Palgrave Macmillan.

Smith, Nigel, Jean Dubois, Dean Current, Ernst Lutz, and Charles Clement. 1998. "Agroforestry Experiences in the Brazilian Amazon: Constraints and Opportunities." Working Paper No. 18592. World Bank, Washington, DC.

Stiglitz, Joseph, and Bruce Greenwald, 2014. *Creating a Learning Society: A New Approach to Growth, Development, and Social Progress.* New York: Columbia University Press.

UNDP (UN Development Programme)/Growing Inclusive Markets. 2008. *Creating Value for All: Strategies for Doing Business with the Poor.* New York: UNDP.

UNECA (UN Economic Commission for Africa). 2013. *Making the Most of Africa's Commodities: Industrializing for Growth, Jobs and Economic Transformation.* Addis Ababa, Ethiopia: UNECA.

UNECLAC (UN Economic Commission for Latin America and the Caribbean). 1990. *Changing Production Patterns with Social Equity: The Prime Task of Latin American and the Caribbean Development in 1990s.* Santiago, Chile: UNECLAC.

———. 2012. *Structural Change for Equality: An Integrated Approach to Development.* Santiago, Chile: UNECLAC.

———. 2014. *Regional Integration: Towards an Inclusive Value Chain Strategy.* Santiago, Chile: UNECLAC.

UNESCAP (UN Economic and Social Commission for Asia and Pacific). 2013. *Shifting from Quantity to Quality: Growth with Equality, Efficiency, Sustainability and Dynamism.* Bangkok: UNESCAP.

UNIDO (United Nations Industrial Development Organization). 2016. *Industrial Development Report 2016: The Role of Technology and Innovation in Inclusive and Sustainable Industrial Development.* Vienna: UNIDO.

United Nations. 2015. *Transforming Our World: The 2030 Agenda for Sustainable Development.* https://sustainabledevelopment.un.org/content/documents /21252030%20Agenda%20for%20Sustainable%20Development%20web.pdf.

World Bank. 1993. *East Asian Miracle: Economic Growth and Public Policy.* Washington, DC: World Bank.

———. 2012. *World Development Report 2013: Jobs.* Washington, DC: World Bank.

Yamada, Masaaki. 2003. Amazon no Nettai Urin to Agroforestry [Amazon Tropical Rainforest and Agroforestry] (in Japanese). *Chiri* [Geography] 48, no. 6 (June 2003). Tokyo: Kokon Shoin.

Yamazawa, Ippei. 1990. "Flying Wild Geese Pattern in Pacific: Pattern of Industrial Development among Asian Countries." Distinguished Speakers Program, Asian Development Bank, Manila.

PART III

Economic Transformation

INDUSTRIALIZING AGRICULTURE, COMPLEXITY, AND GLOBAL VALUE CHAINS

CHAPTER 7

Oranges Are Not Only Fruit

THE INDUSTRIALIZATION OF FRESHNESS AND THE QUALITY OF GROWTH

Christopher Cramer and John Sender

Despite rapid growth in many African countries in recent years, doubts remain about the sustainability and quality of that growth. Its sustainability is questioned on grounds of enduring dependence on primary commodities (especially minerals, fuels, and metals) and of the lack of structural change. Its quality is questioned on grounds of persistently high levels of extreme poverty and rising inequality.

For example, the African Centre for Economic Transformation (ACET 2014) highlights the fragility of recent African growth by comparing a core group of African economies against trends in eight comparator countries whose economies had many features in common with those of many African economies thirty to forty years ago. Production in the comparator economies has since grown more diverse and manufactured exports as a share of gross domestic product (GDP) as well as technological upgrading relative to the ACET–15 economies have increased. Newman et al. (2016, loc 159 of 4644 Kindle), highlighting that "only about one in five African workers leaving agriculture has moved into the industrial sector," compare African economies and a benchmark middle-income country whose average performance on a number of indicators suggests what might be required for African economies to become middle income. The manufacturing value added (MVA) and labor share in industry for African economies are only about half the corresponding levels for the benchmark. Industry in Africa takes up about half the share of GDP accounted for on average across all developing countries, and that share has been shrinking.

Meanwhile, global comparisons on the share of the population living below the international poverty line show that the truly dramatic reductions in poverty globally in the past thirty years or so have taken place in East Asia. Clear reductions have occurred elsewhere, but a far smaller reduction has occurred in Sub-Saharan Africa and its share of global poverty has risen. One World Bank study (2016a) estimated that 50.7 percent of the "global poor" lived in Sub-Saharan Africa in 2013.

Available evidence suggests that poverty rates have declined rapidly in some Sub-Saharan African countries, and other indicators often show marked improvements, including, for example, in life expectancy, basic literacy, and infant mortality. Although Sub-Saharan Africa still has the highest under-five mortality rate in the world, the annual rate of reduction in this key mortality rate has been accelerating (from 1.6 percent in the 1990s to 4.1 percent between 2000 and 2015); over the past decade, Sub-Saharan Africa's annual rate of reduction in the under-five mortality rate has been faster than the rates achieved in many other developing regions, including Southern and Southeast Asia (You et al. 2015). Although many African economies have undergone several years of rapid growth, this has not been converted into the kinds of widespread dramatic poverty reduction anticipated by development economists and experienced in other parts of the developing world.

Development economists have not always linked the structure and patterns of production with poverty reduction concerns. For a while, many economists were content to assume that "good" macroeconomic policy could unleash faster growth and that the rising tide of growth would lift all boats. Confidence in that view has faded to some extent, allowing space for the revival in attention to the links between structure (and structural change) and poverty dynamics (Ocampo, Rada, and Taylor 2009). Newman et al. write, "Lack of employment-intensive growth, together with the absence of progress in transforming traditional agriculture, are largely at the root of the region's slow pace of poverty reduction" (2016, loc 255 of 4644, Kindle). Wuyts (2011) emphasizes how pro-poor growth depends on the extent to which that growth is driven by productivity gains, the extent to which rising productivity drives up real wages, and how increasing productivity and employment are related. He also revives Kalecki's (1955) emphasis on the significance for poverty reduction, accumulation, and political stability of keeping the rate of food price inflation under control.

Concerns about the lack of structural change and the slow pace of poverty reduction in Africa also lie behind the revival in recent years of interest in and support for industrial policy (Stiglitz, Lin, and Monga 2013; Oqubay 2015; United Nations Economic Commission for Africa 2016), although there is not necessarily a shared idea of what this actually means and entails.

At the same time, there are pessimistic arguments that premature industrialization is afflicting African and other relatively low-income economies,
undermining the scope for industrialization (and by extension industrial
policy) to act as a powerful engine of growth and especially employment.

This paper contributes to the discussion of the quality of growth by
showing the importance of disaggregating the category of industry or
manufacturing. We argue that categorical distinctions among manufacturing, agriculture, and services have broken down as these activities
have seeped across the boundaries of traditional classification systems
in economics. At the heart of this process are both "servicification" (of
manufacturing and agriculture) and what we call the industrialization of
freshness. This matters to low-income (and middle-income) developing
countries because of the huge scope for productivity growth, export revenue growth, and employment creation in industrial agriculture and also
because it should lead to a reassessment of the scope of and priorities for
industrial policy. We show by example how, in particular, export-oriented
agricultural production increasingly involves the insertion of an intricate nexus of inputs and steps between a crop and the final consumption
good. We draw on examples from Ethiopia, and to some extent South
Africa, based on recent and ongoing primary research. And to explore the
Ethiopian example, and to arrive at some comments on the policy implications of the analysis, we first discuss the quality of growth in Ethiopia.

EMPLOYMENT, POVERTY, FOOD INFLATION, AND THE QUALITY OF GROWTH IN ETHIOPIA

In some way, Ethiopia epitomizes all of the themes just raised. There are
serious questions about the quality of Ethiopia's recent growth, although
its policy makers have committed to what amounts to a more coherent
and determined strategy for structural change than has been adopted in
many other countries.[1] Its economy has grown rapidly in the past fifteen
years, and it has been one of the fastest growing economies in the world.
Agricultural growth has been dramatic, even if the official figures over-
state that growth (Gollin 2011). Public spending on infrastructure (e.g.,
a huge road building program, railway construction, and hydropower
dam building, as well as capital investment to expand primary health-care
coverage and an impressive lower-middle-income housing condominium program) has been at the heart of much of this growth (Moller and
Wacker 2017). The country's transformation, including the proliferation

of light manufacturing, private building, and services, is immediately clear to any observer. But Ethiopia remains desperately poor in many respects and the efforts of the Growth and Transformation Plan I and II are yet to show through in sharp sustained indicators of structural change (Ministry of Finance and Economic Development 2010, 2015).

Ethiopia ranks seventeenth out of twenty countries listed in ACET's African Transformation Index, scoring especially low in the subcomponents of productivity and human welfare. A World Bank study of urban labor markets (2016b) highlighted the desperately low levels of labor productivity in most of the economy. Not so long ago it was possible (see Devereux, Teshome, and Sabates-Wheeler 2005) to wonder whether Ethiopia's development was constrained by "too little inequality." Although official data suggest a modest Gini coefficient of a little more than 0.33, widening inequality has gathered momentum. The most striking evidence (World Bank 2015) suggests that the poorest 15 percent of the population suffered declines in living standards between 2005 and 2011. In particular, falling consumption in rural areas drove the national figure, with a smaller share of the poorest urban Ethiopians experiencing consumption decline (figure 7.1). From the mid-1990s until around 2003, expenditure

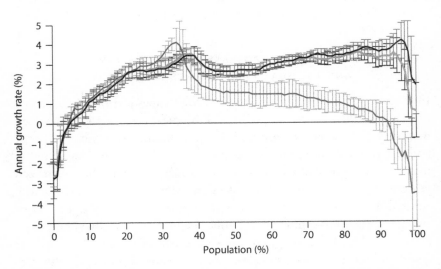

Figure 7.1   Growth incidence, Household Income Consumption and Expenditure Survey deflator, 2005–2011

Source: Authors' creation, adapted from World Bank (2015).

rose for lower-income Ethiopians, but after 2003, the growth of spending slowed for the bottom 60 percent, and by 2011, it had come to a standstill for the poorest 40 percent and was declining for the poorest 10 percent. At the same time, the official poverty headcount was falling sharply: poverty reduction was much faster in 2005–2011 than in 2000–2005, "while the well-being of most of the Ethiopian population improved significantly, extremely poor households were not as fortunate" (Stifel and Woldehanna 2016, 49).

One of the most likely reasons for this decline, and a fundamental dimension of the quality of growth, is the recent record of food price inflation in Ethiopia. Poorer households spend a larger proportion of their incomes on food, so how food prices behave relative to other prices (including wages) shapes distributional outcomes. This makes food price inflation, as Kalecki (1955) argued, a constraint on growth: if food prices are matched by nominal wage increases, investment and accumulation may be constrained; if nominal wages do not rise to absorb food price inflation, there may be a *political* constraint on accumulation. The evidence from Ethiopia is that food price inflation has been difficult to control. In 2008 and 2011, the country had the highest monthly food inflation in the developing world (Bachewe and Heady 2016). Between 2004 and 2011 food price inflation in Ethiopia was higher in all years bar one than in other relatively poor developing countries. More recently, aggregate food price inflation nationally was running at lower levels than overall inflation in 2013 and 2014; however, through 2015 and into 2016, food inflation was higher than general inflation, peaking at more than 16 percent in late 2015 (World Bank 2016). Disaggregating food inflation may be relevant to understanding the economic experience of the poorest Ethiopians, given that "luxury" goods like sugar, jam, honey, and chocolate brought the aggregate food price inflation down in 2013–2016 (World Bank 2016, figure 1.2.2).[2]

The evidence suggests that wages (both urban and rural) have not responded to absorb rising (and often volatile) food prices. The government has implemented a range of policies to try to protect welfare in this context, but these protection policies are imperfect. They have not been able to prevent profoundly political questions about the quality of growth from surfacing. Little direct analysis has been made of the role of relative prices in recent political instability, but these prices may well be part of the causal dynamics. Into 2018, there had been nearly three years of protests, clashes with security forces, and outbursts of violence (including against factories and commercial farms), triggered by complaints about the Addis Ababa expansion plan.[3] These clashes prompted the government to announce a state of emergency; in late 2017, plans were announced to release large numbers of people held prisoner after the protests; and in February 2018, the prime minister offered his resignation. Little reliable evidence is known about the scale of violence or the detailed dynamics of this political crisis. After years of basking in international praise and attention for rapid growth and poverty reduction, the quality of Ethiopia's development was once again very much in question.

The poorest Ethiopians, who are less likely to purchase jam and chocolate (or *teff*) and who are most likely to have been left behind by rapid growth, are net food buyers. This is so for both urban and rural poor households. In the latter, as Stifel and Woldehanna put it, "the detrimental effect of food price inflation tends to dominate the effect of rising producer prices given that the poor are generally net food buyers" (2016, 57). The poorest also are likely to depend on access to wage labor opportunities for their survival—ranging from poorly remunerated full-time employment as domestic servants to casual and seasonal work in agriculture.

Some evidence comes from recent research on coffee growing and floriculture production areas in southern Ethiopia. Cramer et al. (2016) found that households with at least one person recently engaged in manual (basic, low-skilled) agricultural wage labor were systematically poorer than households in their sample that did not depend on wage employment.[4] Whether measured by levels of education or by simple asset ownership, these poorest, wage-dependent households were also very poor by comparison with the poorest groups in other Ethiopian household surveys. The survey found that this experience of wage employment was prevalent, including in smallholder coffee-growing areas that often have been regarded as paragons of family self-employment and that labor market participation was far more significant than found in other surveys. For example, the Ethiopian Rural Socio-Economic Survey (Central Statistical Agency and World Bank, 2013) estimated that a mere 1 percent or less of Ethiopian women engage in wage employment. Our area census results show wage labor participation rates of 40 percent in one smallholder coffee-producing research site (Ferro, near Yirga Alem) and 55 percent in another (Kochere, farther to the south, and more distant from a sizeable town). In research sites, in the southwestern area of Jimma, where there are some larger coffee-growing businesses (with 100 hectares and more), more than 60 percent of those covered in the area census had worked for wages in the past year, and more than 95 percent had done so in the past three years. These figures underestimate how important wage work is to the lives of poor rural Ethiopians, because they exclusively detail wage work in coffee production, ignoring other forms of paid employment in such areas as construction, domestic service, retail, transport, and other crops. Estimates for the labor market participation rate in floriculture research sites, which tend to be peri-urban, not surprisingly, were higher on average.

Wages are key to the ability of net food-buying poor households to survive. The evidence suggests that Ethiopian wages have not adjusted to reflect food price inflation. Returning a year to a year and a half later to interview a sample of the respondents in the original Fairtrade, Employment and Poverty Reduction in Ethiopia and Uganda (FTEPR) survey, we found that wages were stuck. Using the official rural consumer price index (CPI) or a regional CPI does not allow for an accurate assessment of real wages. Trends in the prices of the basic foods consumed by the rural poor are difficult to measure because these prices often vary quite sharply not only between urban and rural areas or between agroclimatic regions of a country but also over short distances within rural areas. In addition to collecting information on nominal wage levels in the original and follow-up questionnaires, FTEPR researchers also asked respondents about the prices they had paid for food and gathered food price data from local stores. In coffee-growing research sites, for example, we found no evidence that rural wage workers have any ability to bargain in responses to the quite-frequent Ethiopian food price spikes.

Other research confirms this is true for urban and small-town Ethiopia. Headey et al. (2012, vi) find that "there is neither descriptive nor econometric evidence that wages substantially adjust to higher food prices, except in the long run." Over 2001–2014, urban wages, deflated by the overall CPI, rose; however, when deflated only by food prices, "then there is no upwards or downwards trend and the shortfalls brought about by the two food price hikes [2008 and 2011] are substantial" (Bachewe and Headey 2016, 6).

Addressing the quality of growth must surely involve a rapid rate of increase in many types of employment opportunities, ideally providing not only more jobs, which may generally tighten labor markets, but also providing high-productivity jobs, that is, good jobs (World Bank 2013) or decent work. Given that the majority of the poorest Ethiopians live in rural areas, and given the evidence that the poorest rural Ethiopians depend on access to wage employment, generating a rapid increase in rural wage employment must be a high policy priority. Creating wage employment will require rural structural transformation and industrialization, which implies the need for a more complex process than the conventional dualistic narrative of a linear shift from the countryside to urban factory employment.

PREMATURE DEINDUSTRIALIZATION AND THE INDUSTRIALIZATION OF FRESHNESS: CATEGORY OVERLAP

Officially enumerated employment has responded slowly to Ethiopia's phase of rapid growth (as it has in much of Africa). Ethiopia is said to have one of the lowest employment elasticities of growth: barely above 0.3, compared with around 0.7 and 0.85 in slower growing South Africa and Senegal, respectively (Page and Shimeles 2015). Less pessimistically, the same data also show that the total number of enumerated employees in Ethiopia increased dramatically in recent years—from 2.3 million in 2009 to 4.3 in 2013—although hardly any growth at all was found in the total number of enumerated employees in South Africa over the same period (ILOSTAT).[5]

Industrialization, and structural change that shifts people out of low productivity, pathetically unrewarding agricultural labor, may hold part of the key to a solution. Arguments suggest that industrialization, typically assumed to mean the growth of urban factory-based manufacturing, is the source of higher quality growth with rising productivity and employment. Newman et al. note that "industrial development offers a high employment, high productivity path for job creation, and evidence suggests it can accelerate the pace of poverty reduction" (2016, loc 256 of 4644, Kindle). Recent structural trends and sectoral shifts in employment in Ethiopia are regarded as disappointing: the officially enumerated share of total employment in industry remains small (about 7.5 percent in 2013). Although this share has risen slightly since 2005, the share of employment in agriculture has fallen over the same period (from about 79 percent to 72 percent). These shifts are underpinned by a more rapid decline in the share of total female employment in agriculture (from 75 percent to 65 percent).

This disappointment is often linked to an essentially pessimistic view that the Ethiopian and African governments generally cannot use the instruments of industrial policy to secure the radical transformations achieved in, notably, East Asia, and that "premature industrialization" (Rodrik 2016) is a kind of life sentence. The implications are particularly distressing for low-skilled labor: "deindustrialization shows up most clearly and in its strongest form in employment" (Rodrik 2016, 1), and most of the manufacturing employment loss in deindustrializing economies takes place in low-skilled jobs. Premature deindustrialization means that the gains from manufacturing as an engine of growth and catching up (from Kaldor's growth laws to Rodrik's automatic convergence effect) are effectively withdrawn from developing economies. Rodrik concludes that African economies will have to get what growth they can from the expansion of services, without strong employment generating effects, and that they will have to wait patiently for skill levels to rise, echoing earlier, factor endowment prognoses by others (e.g., Owens and Wood 1997).

Deindustrialization in other regions of the world has not proceeded at the same automatic rate; the pace and depth of deindustrialization in Organisation for Economic Co-operation and Development economies has varied depending on policy. For example, UK deindustrialization has been especially pronounced compared with that in Germany. By the same token, scope exists for a coherent policy to make a difference in lower income countries, to slow down or put off premature deindustrialization. Ethiopia, in fact, has seen a rise in its share of industry in GDP and in employment, albeit from an exceptionally low base. And evidence has pointed to a concerted policy effort to drive forward industrialization and manufactured exports. Policy makers have sought to overcome the disadvantages of landlockedness, of the lack of European settler colonialism and its institutional legacies, and of a so-called bad neighborhood through infrastructure expansion, institutional design, learning by doing, and pragmatic adaptation of international experiences. The wider evidence confirms that premature deindustrialization is not uniform or inevitable. Countries, especially in East Asia, that adopted deliberate strategies and succeeded in securing rapid growth through manufacturing have shown how important policy is to whether or not a country succumbs to premature deindustrialization.

This chapter, however, develops a different critique. To make claims about the pattern and prospects of industrialization or deindustrialization, especially across huge and diverse regions, involves a categorical fallacy that is growing increasingly problematic for economics. It presumes unit homogeneity for each of the main distinct sectors economists typically work with. But the economic activities within these sectors have become ever more closely intertwined, until the level of categorical imbrication has broken down the distinctions between categories.

All forms of classification involve the imposition of artificial discontinuities on a continuous reality. Therefore, it is always possible to quibble over the precision of categorical boundaries or coding rules. Classification or analytical taming of the "wild profusion of existing things" (Foucault 1971, 1), however, is necessary to make sense of the world. Questioning coding rules and classification systems becomes more than mere quibbling when these rules and systems obscure understanding and produce misleading policy arguments for resource allocation. We suggest that existing categories for primary commodities and manufactures risk doing just that; that they have become too crude to capture and facilitate analysis of the underlying reality. This is because of significant changes in global capitalism, including what we call the industrialization of freshness.

Herrendorf, Rogerson, and Valentinyi (2014, 929) agree that it would be "useful to refine the standard three-sector focus" of the literature on growth, production, and structural transformation. Their argument focuses on advances in services, such that some services like health care and education involve investments and high skill intensity and are characterized by high scope for productivity increases, whereas others, such as much of retail trade, are quite different. The three-sector classification of agriculture, manufacturing, and services is far too crude to capture this change in recent economic developments, especially in advanced economies.

It is not just that, for example, by exploring the World Input Output Database (Timmer et al. 2012), we find increasing interdependency between manufacturing and services. It is also, and more significant, that a process of "servicification" has emerged—that is, the increasing share of the value of final manufactured goods derived from services, including logistics, transport, embedded software, branding, and design (Koopman et al. 2010; Timmer et al. 2014). Baldwin, Forslid, and Ito (2015) argue that services have accounted for an increasing share of final goods value since the 1980s, and that in Asia, for example, the pattern of servicification is similar for relatively high-tech economies, like Japan and South Korea, as well as for lower wage economies like that of the Philippines. An important implication is that for development policy, the "classic focus on factories can be misleading" (Baldwin, Forslid, and Ito 2015, 26).

Meanwhile, the distinction between primary products, processed primary products, and manufactured goods has become fuzzier than it arguably already was. Some analytical confusion has always existed, because of the way that trade and production statistics internationally classify these sectors—that is, differences between definitions in the Standard International Trade Classification (SITC) and International Standard Industrial Classification (ISIC) systems. Wood and Mayer (1998) define three groups of product: manufactures, processed primary products, and unprocessed primary products. Their definition of manufactures is the narrow one of SITC categories 5–8 minus nonferrous metals. SITC classifies everything else as primary products, whether or not it is processed. Production and employment statisticians, though, as Wood and Mayer point out, use the broader ISIC category of manufactures that includes what they consider to be processed primary products—that is, goods that are "also produced in factories, but which use large inputs of local raw materials—for example, canned tuna, wine, cigarettes, paper and aluminium ingots" (1998, 6).

Wood and Mayer (1998, 11) also break down their initial grouping of products to account for high-skill and low-skill manufacturing, for agriculture and minerals and fuel, and for a division of agriculture into "static" and "dynamic" products. Dynamic products include those for which there is a high (greater than one) income elasticity of demand and whose expansion has been important to the growth of a number of developing countries. Their point is that there are unprocessed, but nevertheless dynamic, primary commodities.

Despite the different, overlapping, and at times conflicting ways of classifying primary, processed primary, and manufactured goods, they all share the idea that these types of good require different resource inputs. In Wood and Mayer, for example, "the basic difference between the resource inputs needed for manufacturing and for primary production is that the former requires a much higher ratio of skill to land" (1998, 4), with the implication that agricultural production requires little skill because it requires little by way of transformation and value addition to what nature and some tried-and-true practices provide. Their definition of processed primary products is that processing takes place in factories.

Beyond this definition, and alongside the servicification of manufacturing, we have seen an industrialization of agriculture. Agriculture, particularly globally traded agricultural production, is increasingly not merely "like" industry, it is industry. This industrialization of freshness is partly a function of the technological inputs into modern global agriculture, which have extended out of the factory and onto the farm, and it is partly a function of industrial process and organization.

Beneath the conventional coding rules that determine the allocation of value-producing activities to economic categories are long-running, at times shifting and unsteady, arguments about what defines these categories. A more fruitful way to understand processing and manufacturing than by taking a factory focus is to consider the historical evolution of manufacturing. Adam Smith (1776) refined the analysis of different types of division of labor, including the division of labor in the production of specific goods, such as a woolen coat:

> The shepherd, the sorter of the wool, the wool-comber or carder, the dyer, the scribbler, the spinner, the weaver, the fuller, the dresser, with many others, must all join their arts in order to complete . . . this . . . production. How many merchants and carriers, besides, must have been employed in transporting those materials from some of those workmen to others who often live in a very distant part of the country! . . . How many ship-builders, sailors, sail-makers, rope-makers, must have been employed in order to bring together the different drugs made use of by the dyer, which often come from the remotest corners of the world. (Smith [1776] 1979, 22–23)

Marx, later ([1867] 1977), was able to describe and analyze the transition to *large-scale industrial capitalism*, emphasizing the shift from tools to machinery and the implications for the role of human labor in the production process. Although Marx may have stressed the tendency toward economies of scale within specific firms and the integration of large-scale production, later still Young (1928) emphasized the counterbalancing tendency to industrial differentiation, the splitting of complex processes into sets or chains of simpler processes. This shift toward more "capitalistic" or "roundabout" production processes, sustained by the advance of the division of labor and of specialization, is the source of economies of scale. Over "a large part of the field of industry," wrote Young, "an increasingly intricate nexus has inserted itself between the producer of raw materials and the consumer of the final product" (1928, 538; quoted in Ho 2015). From this perspective, what matters less is whether or not production takes place in factories and instead what forms of industrial organization are at play and how roundabout is production.

Economists from Adam Smith to Albert Hirschman and beyond have suggested that there is less scope for the refined division of labor, for complex linkage dynamics, or for roundabout production processes in agriculture than in manufacturing. Hirschman argued in *The Strategy of Economic Development* (1958, 109), that "agriculture in general, and subsistence agriculture in particular, are . . . characterized by the scarcity of linkage effects." He later refined this view, accepting that more linkages, both backward and forward, are associated with agricultural production than he had initially supposed.

But neither Hirschman nor others anticipated the extent to which the sophistication of roundabout production processes and complex forms of industrial organization might move into agriculture. An "increasingly intricate nexus" is currently inserting itself between African (and other) rural producers, of a fresh orange, blueberry, avocado, or rose, for example, and the consumer of the final product. This makes for what we call the industrialization of freshness.

Moreover, the development of more processed products may depend on innovation in the agricultural sector. Brazil—a world leader in the paper and pulp industry—provides one example. The success of this sector is underpinned by state financing of one of the world's leading centers of agricultural research, Embrapa (the Brazilian Agricultural Research Corporation, Ministry of Agriculture, Livestock, and Food Supply), which coordinates a decentralized network of research institutes that have been central to the diversity of experimentation that innovation-based strategies in agriculture require. For example, the development of new seed varieties of eucalyptus trees by Embrapa researchers (more than two thousand doctoral graduates among them) has been central to the product innovation in Brazilian paper and pulp products (Figueiredo 2016).

Modern food systems are, to a large extent, distinct from agriculture; the industrialization of agricultural production means that consumer food prices are significantly decoupled from the domestic or international prices of agricultural commodities. The farm value share of consumer food expenditure in the United States (and elsewhere) has declined rapidly over the past fifty years, now amounting to about 15 percent (Gollin and Probst 2015). Food is now essentially an industrial product, based only loosely on agricultural commodities. Most of it is initially produced on large-scale units owned by a few farming corporations—the "landless farmers," as some interviewees for a recent study in South Africa conducted by Cramer and Sender (2015) described themselves—and distributed by a similarly concentrated group of supermarket retailers. Delivering these industrial products—processed and prepared foods—to consumers involves scale economies and an industrial mode of production. Although this requires continuous research and development (R&D) and inputs of highly skilled labor, it also generates a great deal of nonagricultural, low-skill wage employment in pack houses, postharvest fruit-management procedures, and retailing. The share of total wage employment generated by food and beverage processing, as well as by the retailing of processed agricultural products and by the food service sector (i.e., restaurants), is often significant in poor economies and is significantly higher in more developed than in developing countries.

Therefore, it is not clear how to define a processed agricultural commodity for policy purposes. Superficially, a carton of orange juice may appear more processed, or more like a manufactured good, than a fresh orange. But to export cans or cartons of orange juice requires much less technological sophistication; R&D; investment in packaging, temperature, and disease control; and computerized logistics than required to deliver a fresh orange (which has to be of much higher quality than an orange sent for juicing) to EU or U.S. supermarket shelves—and the returns are significantly lower.

This point was graphically illustrated when the managing director of Eurafruit, a South African blueberry producer, claimed to be working in the pharmaceutical industry (Cramer and Sender 2015). Picking out a single, chilled fresh blueberry from a plastic punnet, he described the complex industrial processes involved in acquiring the intellectual property rights to the planting material, producing, sorting, chilling, and air-freighting top-quality fresh berries to the European Union, saying that the berry should not be thought of as an agricultural product, but rather as a pill destined for a vitamin supplement market created through expensive branding and advertising campaigns. A blueberry, in other words, embodies industrial organization, manufacturing, and high-tech inputs and processes, and servicification. A similarly paradoxical contrast might be drawn between a low-value and technologically unsophisticated processed product like avocado oil and a fresh export quality avocado, specifically bred, precooled, chilled, packaged, and processed to ripen (in postharvest gaseous ripening facilities) exactly three days after shipment to EU supermarkets. "Just-in-time" industrial organization, famously developed in Japanese manufacturing, is now fundamental to the competitive success of international agriculture. International agreements, such as the Global Gap voluntary standards, widely used in international trade and in contracts with the major retail groups, have accelerated these trends, imposing requirements for barcoding, traceability, spraying, and residue detection—all part of the increasingly intricate nexus inserting itself between increasingly large-scale "farming" and the final product at the point of purchase.

EMPLOYMENT, THE "INTRICATE NEXUS," AND POLICY IN ETHIOPIA

There is a neglected policy case for concentrating state support in developing countries on products that have been exported successfully into the fastest-growing international markets, rather than on products bureaucratically and crudely defined as processed or manufactured. From this perspective, the promotion of fresh fruit and vegetables (plump blueberries from South Africa, ready-to-eat avocados, cut flowers, or herbs from Ethiopia) is at least as important as subsidizing the production of cars (in South Africa) or leather products or textiles and garments (in Ethiopia).

Servicification and the industrialization of freshness together have implications for policy efforts to improve the quality of growth in low-income countries. First, many low-income countries have significant scope to derive greater gains from agricultural production and trade. Along with the intricate nexus between farm and consumer comes huge scope for productivity gains and economies of scale: the benefits that structuralist development economists believed would stem from industrialization as an engine of growth may be generated now by high-productivity agriculture. Second, the linkages associated with combined industrialization and servicification of freshness mean that investment in these activities may raise productivity and yield spread effects outside of direct farm enterprise production. Third, where industrialization concentrated in urban factories appears to offer too slow a rate of absorption of low-skilled labor, agroindustrialization has enormous scope for employment creation.[6]

Selecting crops, irrigating, fertilizing, investing in on-farm pack houses, committing to the highest value output, cleaning bicarbonates from water with reverse osmosis machinery, erecting trellis frames for plants to grow on, investing in humidity control (€50,000 for fine misting in a greenhouse on one 12-hectare farm) and the manipulation of light (one Dutch farmer in Ethiopia agreed that his production process involved "torturing plants by sleep deprivation"), sorting and grading output, shifting crates into and out of cold storage rooms, and many other components of the intricate nexus all generate employment. Just as with urban industrial parks, there are both induced and indirect

employment effects with these farmland factories, too. Increasing numbers of pack houses and export-quality agricultural output potentially
makes viable a domestic supply of a new range of packaging materials.
At the same time, rising rural employment creates rising incomes and
demand for goods and services beyond just basic foods—construction
for wage workers sleeping in on-farm dormitories, bars and retail services, and transport employment.

One of the most obvious and dramatic examples of the employment
effects of the industrialization of freshness in Ethiopia is the dramatic
growth of towns like Ziway, with large inward migration of people from
quite distant rural areas, attracted by employment opportunities in and
linked to the town's floriculture concentration (and more recently wine
production). The expansion of export flower production has led to direct
employment in greenhouses and pack houses; in induced employment
in local supply of materials and services for the flower industry; and in
indirect employment in construction, hairdressing, bars and restaurants,
motorized rickshaw enterprises, and guard labor.

The industrialization of freshness may be relatively easy to see in the
production of blueberries, the manipulation of natural processes in the
propagation in Ethiopian greenhouses of poinsettia seedlings for Dutch
garden centers, and the intricate management of the rate of avocado ripening (together with the servicification involved in transport and storage
logistics, industrial design inputs to improved packaging, and the branding of "ripe and ready-to-eat" avocados). The employment implications of
these industrial processes, direct and indirect, are also starting to be clear.

But this intricate nexus of industry is also inserting itself into so-called
traditional agricultural commodities. One example is coffee. The global
assembly of a tin of Illy coffee, for example, echoes the assembly of smart-
phones or other more obviously high-tech manufactured goods, again
with employment implications. Most of the value is added in the innovation of product and process in Trieste, along with the branding and marketing investment. A single Illy "iperEspresso" capsule embodies seven
patents. Producing a consistent, high-quality espresso blend requires an
efficient sourcing of beans from a number of different countries. Coffee-
buying strategy is in part determined by technological investment: a spec-
trometer assesses the ratio of ripe to under-ripe, scorched, bruised, moldy,
or otherwise blemished beans in samples from different suppliers, guiding
sourcing decisions. Efficiency ultimately turns on direct links with suppliers in developing countries who are able to achieve a consistent supply of

high-quality beans. That, in turn, requires close and direct relationships between Illy and coffee farmers and washing stations.

Pursuit of reliably high-quality production involves changing patterns of coffee varieties, weeding, mulching, picking, and postharvest care, along with sifting, washing, demulcification, drying, and packing of coffee beans on washing stations. This commitment to quality—as interviewees both at Illy and with a number of specialty coffee roasters in the United Kingdom and with coffee farmers in Ethiopia confirmed—leads to higher levels of employment than the production of lower value coffee.[7]

In terms of the quality of growth concerns, other gains may be achieved. FTEPR research (Cramer et al. 2016) compared wages and working conditions on coffee farms in three different research sites in Ethiopia. One such site was a smallholder production area (albeit with high levels of heterogeneity among smallholders), defined around a Fairtrade-certified producer cooperative. Another site was a smallholder production area, but without any Fairtrade-certified producer organization locally. It was, however, near a very large private coffee-washing station (perhaps the largest in Africa), and until a recent policy change, it had a close link to a major international coffee firm committed to producing for a niche and very high-quality market. The third was an area dominated by several much larger coffee growers, each with roughly 100 hectares; these farms also were producing coffee generally regarded as high quality. FTEPR surveys found that wages were higher, and nonwage working conditions better, for coffee wage workers in the latter two research sites than on the Fairtrade-certified producer research site. The other farms also offered more days of work per year. Farm size was certainly correlated (and significantly) with higher wages, better conditions, and more days of work. But the comparison between the two smallholder sites was striking, not least because the non-Fairtrade research site was more remote and had fewer nonagricultural economic activities to tighten labor markets. The investment over time in producing higher quality coffee as an input to the washing station and with the support of the international buyer was the most plausible reason for these different labor market conditions.

This may support a hypothesis that the greater the intricacy of the nexus between producer and final consumption good in agriculture (or between plant and consumer good), the greater the scope for employment creation and better jobs. Certainly, other fieldwork in Ethiopia among large-scale horticulture and floriculture exporters, and corroborated by research in South Africa's commercial agriculture, confirms the significant contribution that these factors can make to employment. Crop choice, quality commitment, and technological sophistication (drip irrigation, cold storage, high-care pack houses, on-farm processing) all raise employment intensity per hectare.

If the industrialization of freshness offers significant scope for employment creation, "better" jobs, and other gains associated with structural transformation, then it becomes critical for policy makers to identify the constraints placed on reaping (more of) these gains and to develop interventions to relax those constraints. Drawing on some primary field research in Ethiopia (and South Africa), we can sketch briefly some of the kinds of constraints that hold back agroindustrialization. These include strategies, policies, and institutions poorly geared to the categorical blurring described earlier as well as underinvestment in (public) R&D and in relevant infrastructure and a failure adequately to resolve critical conflicts of interest over access to and use of land and water.

A classic example of the failure to appreciate how value is derived in the specialty coffee market is the Ethiopian Commodities Exchange (ECX), which took years to recover from its initial wiping out of traceability. Full traceability of coffee to specific farms is very much a form of servicification, because it lies behind the branding narratives that create higher prices and raise returns to producers as well as roasters and traders. Ethiopian coffee policies and institutional reforms also undermined value addition in coffee when disallowing commercial farmers from selling direct rather than through the ECX (only cooperatives could sell direct). This meant that sometimes long-established close relationships between an international "systems integrator" (Nolan, Zhang, and Liu 2008), a washing station, and producers, which sustained efficiencies in a production chain or an intricate nexus between the coffee plant and final consumer good, were erased instantly.

In other ways, too, the significance of industrial agriculture has escaped policy frameworks in Ethiopia. Thus, for example, horticulture firms (many employing eight hundred to one thousand two hundred workers) cannot benefit from the support for soil analysis and fertilizer mixes through the well-funded Agricultural Transformation Agency, because this is focused exclusively on smallholder farmers. Yet these large-scale horticultural firms are at the same time not within the domain of industrial policy focused on leather and garments. They have not received the same attention from government in, for example, setting up sector-specific institutes (as for leather and textiles) (Oqubay 2015).

Failure to appreciate the implications of the industrialization of freshness also lay behind South African decision making. An example is that sugar has been treated as industrial, and thus, it is eligible for substantial industrial policy support because of its closeness to sugar milling. Other agricultural producers, however, were not treated this way, despite evidence that producers of many export crops were capable of generating more competitive output, higher value output, and higher employment gains in what we have characterized as industrial agriculture. Indeed, the Manufacturing Competitiveness Enhancement Programme in South Africa excludes agricultural enterprises despite many of them being tightly integrated into a nexus of high-tech inputs, manufacturing processes, industrial organization, and complex servicification (Cramer and Sender 2015).

The politics of land and water often undermine the scope for productive expansion and efficiency in industrial agriculture. A number of vegetable producers in Ethiopia (particularly in Oromia state) cast envious eyes on Kenyan horticulture, partly because of the ability of Kenyan producers to move up the value chain by constructing high-care pack houses with special washing facilities and rigorous hygiene regimes, high-speed blast chillers, and packaging machines for ready-to-eat small packs of vegetables accredited by the British Retail Consortium. Several Ethiopian firms wanted to upgrade pack house facilities, but they could not primarily because this option would be viable only if they could acquire more land. This political tension between central government strategy and regional governments in Ethiopia's ethnic federal system frustrates output growth.[8] Again and again interviewees claimed that access to additional land was a more serious constraint than access to credit or the inconveniences of the foreign exchange and import regime. One technologically sophisticated producer of chrysanthemum and poinsettia cuttings wanted to expand, but *woreda* officials refused to allocate him the land, despite the fact that the land he had identified remained completely unused. This is a farm that employs one thousand two hundred people, 70 percent of them women, and 95 percent of them on permanent contracts. Several other employment-intensive horticultural exporters raised the same issue. Conflicts over water were also for some producers a constraint on yields, and for a passion fruit producer, this was one factor behind the juice-processing plant running seriously below capacity—"under capacity bites like a crocodile," as the farm manager put it.[9]

Land and water issues are compounded by infrastructure challenges: uncertain and uneven power supplies and poor roads, in particular. State infrastructure investments are not always focused on the needs of employment-intensive and export-orientated agribusiness. Both the Tibila africaJUICE passion fruit farm and the Maranque Plants chrysanthemum and poinsettia farm along the same road in the Upper Awash Valley have been frustrated by broken pledges to grade the road leading from their farms to the main road. Because of the poor state of the road, which leads to broken packaging and vacuum packs arriving in the Netherlands with leaks and fermentation, africaJUICE loses up to 12 percent of the value of every trucked container of passion fruit puree.

CONCLUSION

African economies appear to be caught in a bind. Pessimists argue that many have experienced rapid growth over a period of years, but with limited evidence of lasting structural change and without generating sustained increases in employment.

This chapter has argued that the concerns about the quality of recent growth, specifically in Ethiopia, are real enough, but that they may be overblown. First, although less the focus of this chapter, there is actually evidence of policy-driven industrialization, structural change, and improvement in children's mortality in Ethiopia (albeit from an extremely low base and, as yet, still limited). Second, there is scope for productivity gains, foreign exchange earnings, and rapid employment growth in the nexus of economic activities that we label the industrialization of freshness. The industrialization (and servicification) of agriculture globally is nothing new, but the extent to which this trend is reaching into globalized production of commodities, in which many developing countries have high levels of productive potential, has not been sufficiently acknowledged.

A focus on these activities, and on the ways that they confound traditional statistical and policy-making distinctions among agriculture, manufacturing industry, and services, illuminates the challenges for policy makers often trapped in outdated imaginary of a linear transition away from primary commodity production in rural areas to urban industrial factories. The evidence and analysis in this paper suggests a different set of criteria should be applied when policy makers decide on investments in infrastructure and R&D. Policy makers need to consider incentives in the light of the overall capacity of economic activities—whether in urban factories or on farms—to generate productive dynamism, technical learning and change, and employment.

This approach, in turn, requires the development of analytical capacity in policy-making institutions, with the ability and resources to identify potential gains from industrial agriculture and the constraints on further investment in "roundabout" production. Although this requirement may signal a limited scope for intervention where capabilities remain weak, arguably (and in the spirit of Albert Hirschman) the key is whether there is a sufficient compulsion at strategic levels to advance structural change. If there is, there is no reason to believe that states cannot acquire capabilities through a policy of learning by doing, even if this involves learning by failing.

NOTES

With apologies to Jeanette Winterson, *Oranges Are Not the Only Fruit* (New York: Grove Press, 1985). We would like to acknowledge and thank Agence Française du Développement (AFD) for financial support for research in Ethiopia ("High Value Agricultural Exports from Ethiopia") and the Ethiopian Development Research Institute (EDRI) for collaboration and research support.

1. Arguably, Ethiopia's government and its policies, labeled by the late–prime minister Meles Zenawi a "democratic developmental state" (de Waal 2013, 148), has resembled a developmental state more closely than any other in Africa; see Alex de Waal, "Review Article: The Theory and Practice of Meles Zenawi," *African Affairs* 112, no. 446 (2013): 148–155.

2. Stifel and Woldehanna (2016, 57) warn that poverty has probably declined by less than thought in Ethiopia, because Household Income, Consumption and Expenditure Survey (HICES) data could not fully deflate for food price inflation; see David Stifel and Tassew Woldehanna, "Poverty in Ethiopia, 2000–2011: Welfare Improvements in a Changing Economic Landscape," in *Growth and Poverty in Sub-Saharan Africa*, ed. Channing Ardnt, Andy McKay, and Finn Tarp, 57 (Oxford: Oxford University Press, 2016).

3. Clapham (2017) neatly summarizes the fundamental challenges of political cohesion in Ethiopia in terms of a long history of political power being concentrated in the highland core, while the source of economic reproduction has been in the lowland "periphery."

4. Data were collected for the Fairtrade, Employment and Poverty Reduction in Ethiopia and Uganda (FTEPR) project funded by the UK Department for International Development. The paper-based questionnaire survey included 1,700 respondents (928 of them in Ethiopia) and was carried out in Ethiopia in coffee-producing and floriculture sites. This survey collected information on a total population (determined for research sites by a Global Positioning System census) of a little more than 5,000 Ethiopians (and 3,200 Ugandans). It was supplemented by a short initial survey conducted with handheld personal assistant devices that gathered summary evidence from 4,700 respondents (2,470 in Ethiopia, 2,270 in Uganda). A separate,

follow-up survey of four hundred respondents was carried out a year and a half later. FTEPR researchers did around one hundred oral history interviews.

5. ILO data do not provide a reliable indicator of labor market trends in Sub-Saharan Africa (Sender, Cramer, and Oya 2005).

6. It also has high potential for addressing the balance-of-payments constraint on growth.

7. For a summary of the roundabout process involved in producing high-quality coffee, see Schäfer (2016). Schäfer also points out that the level of mechanization in Ethiopian coffee is not a good indicator of the degree of dynamism of a given producer, given high levels of heterogeneity among large-scale coffee producers.

8. Fieldwork carried out in mid-2016 revealed signs of the tensions that were to fuel the protests and clashes that led to a state of emergency later in the year. One farmer told us at the time about how much of his savings he had invested and how "if they put a light to it, it goes boom!" Another—the manager of a large passion fruit farm—was sure that local police were turning a blind eye when rival midsize water users sabotaged his irrigation equipment. And indeed this farm was burned down in October 2016.

9. These concerns echoed similar ones raised by South African producers of high-value, high-employment export crops, such as citrus producers in the Eastern Cape; see Christopher Cramer and John Sender, "Agro-Processing, Wage Employment and Export Revenue: Opportunities for Strategic Intervention" (Trade and Industrial Policy Strategies working paper, Department of Trade and Industry, Johannesburg, South Africa, 2015).

REFERENCES

African Centre for Economic Transformation. 2014. *2014 African Transformation Report: Growth with Depth*. Accra, Ghana: African Centre for Economic Transformation.

Baldwin, Richard, Rikard Forslid, and Tadashi Ito. 2015 "Unveiling the Evolving Sources of Value Added in Exports." Draft manuscript. Accessed April 4, 2017, http://www.ide.go.jp/English/Publish/Download/Jrp/pdf/161.pdf.

Bachewe, Fantu, and Derek Headey. 2016. "Urban Wage Behaviour and Food Price Inflation in Ethiopia." *Journal of Development Studies* 53 (8): 1207–1222. DOI: 10.1080/00220388.2016.1219343.

Central Statistical Agency (CSA) and World Bank. 2013. *Ethiopian Rural Socioeconomic Survey (ERSS)*. Addis Ababa, Ethiopia: CSA.

Clapham, Christopher. 2017. *The Horn of Africa: State Formation and Decay*. London: Hurst Publishers.

Cramer, Christopher, Deborah Johnston, Carlos Oya, and John Sender. 2014. "Fairtrade Cooperatives in Ethiopia and Uganda: Uncensored." *Review of African Political Economy* 41 (Suppl. 1): S115–S127.

Cramer, Christopher, and John Sender. 2015. "Agro-Processing, Wage Employment and Export Revenue: Opportunities for Strategic Intervention." Trade and Industrial Policy Strategies Working Paper. Department of Trade and Industry, Johannesburg, South Africa.

Cramer, Christopher, Deborah Johnston, Bernd Mueller, Carlos Oya, and John Sender. 2016. "Fairtrade and Labor Markets in Ethiopia and Uganda." *Journal of Development Studies* 53 (6): 841–856.

Devereux, Stephen, Amdissa Teshome, and Rachel Sabates-Wheeler. 2005. "Too Much Inequality or Too Little? Inequality and Stagnation in Ethiopian Agriculture." *IDS Bulletin* 36 (2): 121–126.

De Waal, Alex. 2013. "Review Article: The Theory and Practice of Meles Zenawi." *African Affairs* 112 (446): 148–155.

Figueiredo, P. 2016. "New challenges for public research organisations in agricultural innovation in developing economies: evidence from Embrapa in Brazil's soybean industry." *The Quarterly Review of Economics and Finance* 62: 21–32.

Foucault, Michel. 1971. *The Order of Things: An Archaeology of the Human Sciences.* New York: Pantheon.

Gollin, Douglas. 2011. "Crop Production in Ethiopia: Assessing the Evidence for a Green Revolution." Working Paper, May. Williams College, Williamstown, MA.

Gollin, Douglas, and L. T. Probst. 2015. "Food and Agriculture: Shifting Landscapes for Policy." *Oxford Review of Economic Policy* 31 (1): 8-25.

Headey, Derek, Fantu Bachewe Nisrane, Ibrahim Worku, Mekdim Dereje, and Alemaheyu Seyoum Tafesse. 2012. "Urban Wage Behavior and Food Price Inflation: The Case of Ethiopia." Ethiopia Strategy Support Program II (ESSP II), Working Paper 41. Addis Ababa: IFPRI.

Herrendorf, Berthold, Richard Rogerson, and Ákos Valentinyi. 2014. "Growth and Structural Transformation." In *Handbook of Economic Growth,* ed. P. Aghion and S. N. Durlauf, Vol. 2, 855–941. Amsterdam: Elsevier.

Hirschman, Albert O. 1958. *The Strategy of Economic Development.* New Haven, CT: Yale University Press.

Ho, P. Sai-wing. 2015. "Linking the Insights of Smith, Marx, Young and Hirschman on the Division of Labor: Implications for Economic Integration and Uneven Development." *Cambridge Journal of Economics* 40 (3): 913–939. doi: 10.1093/cje/bev012.

Kaldor, Nicholas. 1957. "A Model of Economic Growth." *The Economic Journal* 67 (268): 591–624. doi: 10.2307/2227704.

Kalecki, Michal. 1955. "The Problem of Financing Economic Development." *Indian Economic Review* 2 (3): 1–22.

Koopman, Robert, William Powers, Zhi Wang, and Shang-Jin Wei. 2010. "Give Credit Where Credit Is Due: Tracing Value Added in Global Production Chains." NBER Working Paper 16426. National Bureau of Economic Research, Cambridge, MA.

Marx, Karl. [1867] 1977. *Capital: A Critique of Political Economy, Vol.1.* Translated by B. Fowkes. New York: Vintage.

Ministry of Finance and Economic Development. 2010. *Growth and Transformation Plan, 2010/11–2014/15.* Addis Ababa, Ethiopia: MOFED.

———. 2015. *Growth and Transformation Plan II.* Addis Ababa, Ethiopia: MOFED.

Moller, Lars Christian, and Konstantin Wacker. 2017. "Explaining Ethiopia's Growth Acceleration: The Role of Infrastructure and Macroeconomic Policy." *World Development* 96 (Suppl. C): 198–215.

Newman, Carol, John Page, John Rand, Abebe Shimeles, Måns Söderbom, and Finn Tarp, eds. 2016. *Manufacturing Transformation: Comparative Studies of Industrial Development in Africa and Emerging Asia.* Oxford: Oxford University Press.

Nolan, Peter, Jin Zhang, and Chunhang Liu. 2008. "The Global Business Revolution, the Cascade Effect, and the Challenge for Firms from Developing Countries." *Cambridge Journal of Economics* 32 (1): 29–47.

Ocampo, José Antonio, Codrina Rada, and Lance Taylor. 2009. *Growth and Policy in Developing Countries: A Structuralist Approach.* New York: Columbia University Press.

Oqubay, Arkebe. 2015. *Made in Africa: Industrial Policy in Ethiopia.* Oxford: Oxford University Press.

Owens, Trudy, and Adrian Wood. 1997. "Export-Oriented Industrialization Through Primary Processing?" *World Development* 25 (9): 1453–1470.

Page, John, and Abebe Shimeles. 2015. "Aid, Employment and Poverty Reduction in Africa." *African Development Review* 27 (S1): 17–30.

Rodrik, Dani. 2016. "Premature Deindustrialization." *Journal of Economic Growth* 21 (1): 1–33.

Schäfer, Florian. 2016. *Revisiting the Agrarian Question: Coffee, Flowers and Ethiopia's New Capitalists.* PhD thesis. London: SOAS, University of London.

Sender, John, Christopher Cramer, and Carlos Oya. 2005. "Unequal Prospects: Disparities in the Quantity and Quality of Labour Supply in sub-Saharan Africa." Social Protection Unit, Human Development Network. Washington: World Bank.

Smith, Adam. [1776] 1979. *An Inquiry into the Nature and Causes of the Wealth of Nations.* Indianapolis: Liberty Classics.

Stifel, David, and Tassew Woldehanna. 2016. "Poverty in Ethiopia, 2000–2011: Welfare Improvements in a Changing Economic Landscape." Chap. 3 in *Growth and Poverty in Sub-Saharan Africa*, ed. Channing Ardnt, Andy McKay, and Finn Tarp. Oxford: Oxford University Press.

Stiglitz, Joseph, Justin Yifu Lin, and Célestin Monga. 2013. "The Rejuvenation of Industrial Policy." Policy Research Working Paper 6628. World Bank, Washington, DC.

Timmer, C. Peter, Margaret S. McMillan, Ousmane Badiane, Dani Rodrik, Hans Binswanger-Mkhize, and Fleur Wouterse. 2012. *Patterns of Growth and Structural Transformation in Africa.* WCAO Thematic Research Note. Dakar: IFPRI. Accessed December 2, 2015, http://cdm15738.contentdm.oclc.org/utils/getfile/collection/p15738coll2/id/126946/filename/127157.pdf.

Timmer, Marcel P., Abdul Azeez Erumban, Bart Los, Robert Stehrer, and Gaaitzen de Vries. 2014. "Slicing Up Global Value Chains." *Journal of Economic Perspectives* 28 (2): 99–118.

United Nations Economic Commission for Africa. 2016. *Transformative Industrial Policy for Africa.* Addis Ababa, Ethiopia: UNECA.

Wood, Adrian, and Jörg Mayer. 1998. "Africa's Export Structure in a Comparative Perspective." *SSRN Electronic Journal.* http://dx.doi.org/10.2139/ssrn.141202 .

World Bank. 2013. *World Development Report: Jobs.* Washington, DC: World Bank.

———. 2015. *Ethiopia Poverty Assessment 2014.* Washington, DC: World Bank.

———. 2016a. *Poverty and Shared Prosperity 2016: Taking on Inequality.* Washington, DC: World Bank.

———. 2016b. *Fifth Ethiopia Economic Update: Why So Idle? Wages and Employment in a Crowded Labor Market.* Washington, DC: World Bank.

Wuyts, Marc. 2011. "The Working Poor: A Macro Perspective." Valedictory lecture, Institute of Social Studies, The Hague, December 8.

You, Danzhen, Lucia Hug, Simon Ejdemyr, Priscila Idele, Daniel Hogan, Colin Mathers, Patrick Geerland, Jin Rou New, and Leontine Alkema. 2015. "Global, Regional, and National Levels and Trends in Under-5 Mortality Between 1990 and 2015, with Scenario-Based Projections to 2030: A Systematic Analysis by the UN Inter-agency Group for Child Mortality Estimation." *The Lancet* 386 (10010): 2275–2286.

Young, Allyn. 1928. "Increasing Returns and Economic Progress." *Economic Journal* 38 (152): 527–542.

CHAPTER 8

Sub-Saharan Africa's Manufacturing Sector

BUILDING COMPLEXITY

Haroon Bhorat, Ravi Kanbur, Christopher Rooney, and François Steenkamp

Before 2000, Africa's economic growth prospects were viewed with widespread pessimism. An over-reliance on mineral exports, civil war, and chronic corruption had ruined many of Africa's economies, culminating in *The Economist* labeling it the "hopeless continent" (*The Economist* 2000). Since the turn of the millennium, however, the narrative has changed. Pessimism has changed to optimism, buoyed by the growth of an African middle class (Shimeles and Ncube 2015) and increasing foreign direct investment, which reached $60 billion in 2013—five times its 2000 level (Diop et al. 2015).

This optimism, however, has been tempered by unemployment—especially among young people—that has accompanied high levels of economic growth. Between 2000 and 2008, the African working-age population (fifteen to sixty-four years old) increased from 443 million to 550 million, but only 73 million jobs were created over the same period (Organisation for Economic Co-operation and Development [OECD] 2012; Sparreboom and Albee 2011). The youth only obtained 16 million or 22 percent of those jobs (Sparreboom and Albee 2011). Indeed, the Sub-Saharan African (SSA) youth unemployment rate decreased by only 1 percent over the past twenty years—from 13.4 percent (1991–2000) to 12.3 percent (2001–2012) (International Labour Organization 2014). In effect, the high growth rates have not generated a sufficient quantum of jobs to match the expansion in the labor force. The challenge is further exacerbated by estimates that state that each year between 2015 and 2035, five hundred thousand people in SSA will turn fifteen years old (Filmer and Fox 2014).

In the context of a growing labor force, debate continues over the prospects of Africa following in the economic footsteps of East and South Asia and the pursuit of manufacturing-led structural transformation, thereby creating jobs for a young and growing labor force (McMillan, Rodrik, and Verduzco-Gallo 2014; Rodrik 2014; Page 2012). This chapter contributes to this debate, which typically views manufacturing at the aggregate level, by providing a more granular product-level analysis of SSA's evolving manufacturing sector, with the Asian experience serving as a counterpoint. The analysis is aided by the tools of complexity analysis, specifically those derived from *The Atlas of Economic Complexity* (see Hausmann et al. 2014).

SUB-SAHARAN AFRICA'S DEMOGRAPHIC DIVIDEND AND STRUCTURAL TRANSFORMATION

Over the next century, SSA is predicted to account for the majority share of world population growth. The world population is expected to grow by 3.9 billion by 2100, of which 2.9 billion or 75 percent will be from SSA (see table 8.1).[1] As a result, SSA's share of the world's population will increase from 14 percent to 35 percent. SSA's working-age population will increase by 2 billion, whereas in many other continents, that population will shrink as a result of aging. Nearly 40 percent of the world's working-age population is expected to reside in SSA by 2100—up from 10 percent in 2015.

The predicted growth of SSA's population on aggregate and, importantly, the growth in the working-age population, mask considerable country-level heterogeneity across the continent (Drummond, Thakoor, and Yu 2014; Bhorat et al. 2017). Considering the extent to which African countries have undergone their demographic transition, four groups have emerged. First, three countries have already hit the peak of their share of the working-age population: Mauritius, Seychelles, and Réunion. Second, five countries are relatively close to reaching their peak working-age population: Cabo Verde, South Africa, Botswana, Djibouti, and

Table 8.1   World and Sub-Saharan African Population Projections, 2015–2100

	Total Population (Billion)			Working-Age Population (Billion)		
	2015	2100	Change	2015	2100	Change
Sub-Saharan Africa	1.0	3.9	2.9	0.5	2.5	2
World	7.3	11.2	3.9	4.8	6.7	1.9
SSA proportion (%)	13.7	34.8	—	10.4	37.3	—

Source: Authors' calculations using the UN World Population Database.

Namibia). Third, approximately eighteen countries are expected to experience a 6 to 10 percentage point rise in the working-age share of their population. Fourth, twenty-four countries are expecting an 11 and 18 percentage point rise in the working-age share of their population. Notably, this group includes Nigeria, Ethiopia, the Democratic Republic of the Congo, and Tanzania—four of the top six most populous countries in Africa. Hence, the predicted working-age population growth for the continent is expected to be concentrated in a few countries—that is, just ten SSA countries will account for nearly 70 percent of the population growth in the region (Bhorat et al. 2017).

The rapid growth of Africa's working-age population presents both opportunities and risks. A growing labor force is an opportunity to increase the productive capacity of a country, thereby generating economic growth and increasing living standards—along with the promise of a large and growing consumer market. In contrast, a failure to utilize the economic potential of new jobseekers through absorption in the labor market will lead to rising unemployment and escalate the risk of social unrest. Ultimately, countries need to experience both economic growth and high levels of job creation to realize the dividends that come with an expansion of the labor force.

The region has experienced economic growth over the past one and a half decades. In the 1980s and 1990s, SSA's gross domestic product (GDP) per capita was falling by 1.1 percent per year, on average. When compared with other developing country blocs which experienced GDP per capita growth—such as those in East Asia (6.3 percent) and Latin America and the Caribbean (0.4 percent)—it was the worst-performing region by some distance. Since 2000, however, annual GDP per capita growth in SSA has averaged 2.3 percent, and it has outperformed not only Latin America and the Caribbean (1.6 percent) but also high-income countries (1.2 percent) as well. The global downturn caused by the 2007–2008 financial crisis, however, has raised questions about the sustainability of SSA's recent growth performance.

In particular, the OECD and others have raised concerns about the lack of structural transformation, defined as "the reallocation of economic activity away from the least productive sectors of the economy to more productive ones" (OECD 2013, 114), that is taking place across the region (McMillan and Rodrik 2011; United Nations Economic Commission for Africa 2014). Much of the growth has come from either large oil exporters (e.g., Nigeria) or from a large expansion of their services sector (e.g., Rwanda) (Rodrik 2013).

Figure 8.1 provides an overview of the degree of structural transformation in SSA between 1975 and 2010, depicting the shifts in employment across sectors in terms of productivity. We plotted the relative productivity across ten sectors in 2010 against the change in employment within these sectors, over the period from 1975 to 2010, for an SSA regional aggregate. In essence, the graph shows whether shifts in the structure of the economy, in terms of shifts in employment across sectors, have been toward productive or unproductive activities. A positively sloped fitted line indicates productivity-enhancing, and hence growth-inducing, structural change. Conversely, a negatively sloped fitted line indicates productivity-reducing, and hence growth-reducing, structural change.

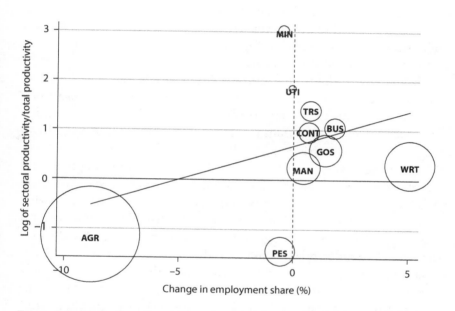

Figure 8.1   Sectoral productivity and employment changes in Africa, 1975–2010

Note: African countries include Botswana, Ethiopia, Ghana, Kenya, Malawi, Mauritius, Nigeria, Senegal, South Africa, Tanzania, and Zambia.

AGR = Agriculture; MIN = Mining; MAN = Manufacturing; UTI = Utilities; CONT = Construction; WRT = Trade Services; TRS = Transport Services; BUS = Business Services; GOS = Government Services; PES = Personal Services.

Size of circles represents employment shares in 2010.

Source: Authors' calculations using Groningen Growth and Development Centre ten-sector database (see Timmer, de Vries, and de Vries 2014).

Looking at figure 8.1, we see evidence of growth-inducing structural transformation in SSA over the period from 1975 to 2010.[2] Although the low-productivity agriculture sector remained the largest employer, it has incurred the highest employment losses over this thirty-five-year period.

Employment levels in the high-productivity manufacturing sector have remained stagnant. The biggest beneficiaries of SSA's growth have evidently been services, with government, transport, business, and trade services increasing their share of employment over the period. Unfortunately, the most productive sectors (mining and utilities) have not recorded employment growth. This is indicative of the high level of capital intensity associated with these industries. Ultimately, the African growth experience over the past thirty-five years, in general, can be characterized as having manifested in the growth of capital-intensive resource- and energy-based industries, which in turn have not generated a sufficient number of jobs. As a result, Africa's manufacturing sector has stagnated in terms of output and employment.

In contrast, the East and South Asian regional aggregate (now known as the Asian regional aggregate) illustrates the more typical manufacturing-led pattern of structural transformation (see figure 8.2). It is evident that employment has shifted from low-productivity agricultural activities to high-productivity activities, particularly in manufacturing.

In the aggregate, Asia has seen a dramatic decline in agricultural employment—approximately 30 percent. As in SSA, however, agriculture remains the dominant source of employment. Services, while showing employment growth, is minor compared with that of SSA, although it is off a bigger base. The most significant difference between SSA and Asia is driven by the differential outcomes in the manufacturing sector. Manufacturing is relatively more productive in Asia than in SSA; it not only has grown substantially between 1975 and 2010 but also accounts for the second largest share of employment (15.8 percent) after agriculture (40.1 percent).[3] This increase in employment is consistent with the view that manufacturing has been an engine of growth for the Asian region.

Comparing the SSA aggregate to the Asian aggregate, it is evident that both regions have experienced growth-inducing structural transformation over the period, but the nature of this transformation has been different. The Asian experience points to a shift from the low-productivity agricultural sector to the high-productivity manufacturing sector. The SSA experience points to a shift from the low-productivity agricultural sector (but to a lesser degree than in Asia) to the services sector. In particular,

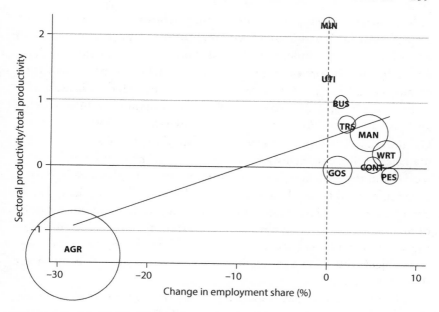

Figure 8.2   Sectoral productivity and employment changes in Asia, 1975–2010

Note: Asian markets include East Asia and South Asia, specifically China, Hong Kong, India, Indonesia, Japan, South Korea, Malaysia, Philippines, Singapore, Taiwan, and Thailand.

AGR = Agriculture; MIN = Mining; MAN = Manufacturing; UTI = Utilities; CONT = Construction; WRT = Trade Services; TRS = Transport Services; BUS = Business Services; GOS = Government Services; PES = Personal Services.

The estimated regression line, measuring the relationship between productivity and changes in employment share by sector, is not statistically significant.

Size of circles represents employment shares in 2010.

Source: Authors' calculations using Groningen Growth and Development Centre ten-sector database (see Timmer, de Vries, and de Vries 2014).

SSA has experienced a shift to wholesale and retail trade services, which typically has taken place within the informal sector. Therefore, in the context of a young and growing labor force in most countries in the SSA region, questions about which sectors are going to create jobs is front and center in the policy debate.

Stagnation in the manufacturing sector, however, is not solely due to Africa-specific factors. Recent evidence indicates that it is becoming increasingly difficult to industrialize. Considering cross-country patterns of industrialization, Rodrik (2016) shows that relative to early industrializers, developing countries are reaching peak manufacturing employment both earlier at a lower level of development and also at a lower level. For example, Nigeria and Zambia both experienced deindustrialization before manufacturing even reached 10 percent of total employment. Rodrik (2016) terms this "premature deindustrialization".

Rodrik (2014, 2016) attributes this phenomenon mainly to trade and globalization. As part of their membership of the World Trade Organization, developing countries were forced to liberalize many of their markets. At the time, many African countries had nascent manufacturing sectors and thus, when exposed to world markets, they became importers of manufactured goods. In addition, the relative decline in prices of manufactured goods in industrial countries threatened the economic viability of manufacturing sectors, especially in countries where the manufacturing sector was not well established. In contrast, Asian economies were not subject to the same trends because of their comparative advantage in manufacturing.

It is indisputable that it has become harder to industrialize. When developed countries and Asia industrialized, they did so under protectionist regimes, which allowed them to build a significant manufacturing base (Rodrik 2016). In contrast, SSA has had to compete in the world market with established manufacturing exporters. In addition, Asian exporters have successfully penetrated the domestic markets of SSA countries, making it even more challenging for these countries to build a productive manufacturing sector. Regardless of these hurdles, however, manufacturing remains the best hope for SSA to generate a large number of good jobs and reduce the prospects of political and social instability.

McMillan, Rodrik, and Verduzco-Gallo (2014), Rodrik (2016), and others provide insight into the extent to which African countries can industrialize and thereby create manufacturing jobs in the face of a growing labor force. These analyses, however, have sought to examine the evolution of the manufacturing sector across countries at the aggregate level, focusing on the manufacturing sector as a homogenous entity. The following analysis provides product-level insights into the evolution of the manufacturing sector in SSA, applying the Eastern and Southern Asian regions as counterpoints. The expansion of the manufacturing sector is not simply the expansion of a single aggregate entity but rather an evolution of heterogeneous productive activities within this aggregate. An evolving manufacturing sector is one that shifts production toward increasingly sophisticated forms of manufacturing activity. This shift requires a combination of embedded knowledge and capabilities, thereby ultimately building economic complexity. The aim is to provide nuance to the existing debate through a granular method of analysis.

EMPLOYMENT, MANUFACTURING, AND INCREASING COMPLEXITY

This section applies economic complexity analytics to provide product-level insights into SSA's development path in comparison with that of the Eastern and Southern Asian regions. Specific emphasis is placed on the evolution of the manufacturing sector within these regions. The Eastern and Southern Asian regions provide an example of a manufacturing success story, and thus act as useful counterpoints from which to compare the evolution of manufacturing in SSA. The section concludes by examining how the evolving manufacturing sectors across these regions act as a source of employment.

CONCEPTUALIZING COMPLEXITY AND CONNECTEDNESS

Hausmann et al. (2014) argue that the process of economic development involves the accumulation and mobilization of productive knowledge (i.e., capabilities). The amount of productive capabilities that a country is able to mobilize is reflected in its diversity of firms, the diversity of occupations that these firms require, and the level of interactions among these networks of firms. These productive capabilities are described as nontradable networks of collective know-how, such as logistics, finance, supply, and knowledge networks (Hidalgo, Hausmann, and Dasgupta 2009). The accumulation and mobilization of these productive capabilities is embodied in the measure of economic complexity, as developed by Hidalgo, Hausmann, and Dasgupta (2009).[4]

To measure the productive knowledge or capabilities embedded in a country, Hidalgo, Hausmann, and Dasgupta (2009) use international trade data to examine what products countries make, and from this, to infer their productive capabilities. Two components inform the construction of a measure of economic complexity for a country: First, countries with individuals and firms that possess more productive knowledge can produce a more diverse set of products. Second, products that require large amounts of productive knowledge are produced in only a few countries where this knowledge is available. Therefore, the more diverse a country's export portfolio and the less ubiquitous the products that make up its export portfolio, the more productive knowledge embedded in its economy.

Figure 8.3 illustrates how the dual measures of diversity and ubiquity can be used to measure economic and product complexity. One observes that Holland has the most diverse export basket (five products), whereas Ghana has the least diverse export basket (one product). This provides the first iteration of productive capabilities data, which suggest that Holland has more productive capabilities than Ghana. One also observes that Holland exports all five products, but interestingly, it exports the two least ubiquitous products (X-ray machines and pharmaceuticals), suggesting in part some form of specialized capability in the production and export of these goods. Holland also exports cream, cheese, and frozen fish, which are exported by Ghana and Argentina, and thus are relatively more ubiquitous. This second iteration of information reinforces the first, and the combination of diversity and ubiquity measures suggests that Holland has the most productive capabilities. The relative ubiquity of these products (cream, cheese, and frozen fish) suggests that the productive capabilities embedded in them are common across the three countries. This is even truer in the case of frozen fish, which is produced in all three countries. Only Holland, however, can produce X-ray machines and pharmaceuticals, which

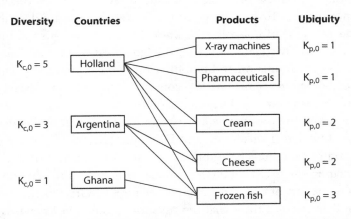

Figure 8.3   Example of country-product network used in method of reflections

Source: Authors' creation.

suggests that the productive capabilities embedded in these products are relatively more specialized and specific to Holland.

More formally, and informed by Hidalgo, Hausmann, and Dasgupta (2009), using bilateral trade data, diversity and ubiquity are defined as follows:

$$\text{Diversity} = k_{c,0} = \sum_p M_{cp}, \text{ and} \tag{8.1}$$

$$\text{Ubiquity} = k_{p,0} = \sum_c M_{cp}, \tag{8.2}$$

where M_{cp} is a matrix that is 1 if country c produces product p, and 0 otherwise. Diversity and ubiquity are measured by summing the rows and columns of the matrix, respectively. Hidalgo, Hausmann, and Dasgupta (2009) employ an iterative calculation, called the method of reflections, to generate measures of complexity. Each iteration of the calculation corrects information from the previous iteration, until the process converges. In the case of countries, one calculates the average ubiquity of the products that each country exports, the average diversity of the countries that make those products, and so forth. In the case of products, one calculates the average diversity of countries that export these products and the average ubiquity of the products that these countries make. Formally, this is expressed as follows:

$$k_{c,N} = \frac{1}{k_{c,0}} \sum_p M_{cp} . k_{p,N-1}, \text{ and} \tag{8.3}$$

$$k_{p,N} = \frac{1}{k_{p,0}} \sum_c M_{cp} . k_{c,N-1}. \tag{8.4}$$

Therefore, diversity is used to correct for information carried by ubiquity, and ubiquity is used to correct for information carried by diversity. Furthermore, ubiquity can be corrected by taking information from diversity that has already been corrected for by ubiquity, and so on. This mathematical process converges after a few iterations and generates measures of complexity for countries (i.e., economic complexity) and measures of complexity for products (i.e., *product complexity*).[5] The former measures the productive capabilities specific to each country, while the latter measures the productive capabilities needed to produce a product. Formally, this is presented by manipulating equations (8.3) and (8.4) to arrive at the following:

$$k_{c,N} = \sum_{c'} \tilde{M}_{cc'} k_{c',N-2},$$

(8.5)

where $\tilde{M}_{cc'}$ corresponds to the eigenvector capturing the largest eigenvalue in the system. Eigenvalues are a measure of economic complexity. More formally, this is represented as follows:

$$ECI = \frac{\vec{K} - [\vec{K}]}{stdev(\vec{K})},$$

(8.6)

where [] and *stdev* represent average and standard deviation, respectively; $\vec{K}$ represents the eigenvector of $\tilde{M}_{cc'}$ associated with the second largest eigenvalue.[6]

The connectedness of a country's productive structure, measured as the *opportunity value* index, using *The Atlas of Economic Complexity* measures (Hausmann et al. 2014), provides a value of "nearby" productive opportunities associated with a country's current export structure. Higher *opportunity value* indices indicate more connected productive structures, or productive structures that include a number of products that are relatively proximate (i.e., connected) to a large number of products that a country does not currently produce. In terms of capabilities, this means that the capabilities embedded in this connected productive structure are relatively proximate to those needed for products that are not currently produced. Conversely, the capabilities embedded in a less connected productive structure are relatively distant from those needed for products that are not currently produced.

Hausmann et al. (2014) show that increasingly complex products, which typically are manufactured products, are connected and proximate to more products than less complex primary products that are distant and less connected. Put differently, the capabilities needed to produce manufactured products are relatively similar to those needed to produce other manufactured products. Therefore, if a country already has an established manufacturing sector, it is better positioned to expand and diversify this sector than a country with a marginal manufacturing sector.

ECONOMIC COMPLEXITY AND MANUFACTURING

Hidalgo, Hausmann, and Dasgupta (2009) show that economic complexity is correlated with a country's current level of income and that deviations from this relationship predict future economic growth. As such, figure 8.4 shows the relationship between economic complexity and GDP per capita across a sample of countries varying in terms of level of development and region. The accumulation and mobilization of productive capabilities is associated with higher levels of economic development.

For this analysis, it is interesting to consider the position of SSA countries (black square markers) relative to developing economies in Eastern and Southern Asia (gray triangle markers) and to developed economies in East Asia (circle gray markers). It is evident that SSA countries are

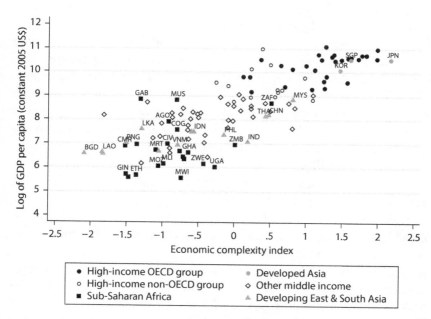

Figure 8.4   Economic complexity and the log of GDP per capita by analytical group, 2013

Note: The sample of countries is reduced to those for which complexity measures are estimated. OECD = Organisation for Economic Co-operation and Development.

Source: Authors' calculations using trade data from the BACI International Trade Database (HS six-digit revision 1992) and GDP per capita data from the *World Development Indicators.*

clustered in the southwest corner of the graph and thus are associated with lower levels of economic complexity and economic development. For the sample of SSA countries, South Africa (see acronym ZAF in figure 8.4) is an outlier with an economic complexity level in line with other middle-income countries.

As with their levels of economic development, economic complexity levels for the sample of Asian economies is distributed across countries. High-income Asian economies, including Japan (JPN), South Korea (KOR), and Singapore (SGP), have high levels of productive capabilities. A number of Asian economies have low levels of economic complexity, similar to or lower than the cluster of SSA countries, but with higher levels of economic development, including Sri Lanka (LKA), Papua New Guinea (PNG), and Indonesia (IDN). These Asian economies may be better able to exploit their productive capabilities than their SSA peers. A number of middle-income Asian economies, including China (CHN), India (IND), Malaysia (MYS), Philippines (PHL), and Thailand (THA), have relatively high levels of economic complexity.

Therefore, this sample of Asian economies, with some variation, tends to be characterized by higher levels of productive knowledge (or capabilities) than their SSA counterparts. This characterization may explain the relative differences in the manufacturing sectors across countries located within these two regions. Economic growth and development is about the accumulation of capabilities that allows firms within a country to produce increasingly complex products, which are typically manufactured products. This idea is taken further by considering the link between economic complexity and the number of manufacturing products a country produces.

Figure 8.5 shows the relationship between a country's productive capabilities, measured as economic complexity, and the number of manufacturing products that it produces. First, it is observed that countries with more productive capabilities produce a greater diversity of manufacturing products. In addition, figure 8.5 shows clearly that the SSA countries (excluding South Africa) are clustered at low levels of economic complexity and produce a relatively low number of manufactured products.

Second, the sample of Asian economies is spread across levels of economic complexity with varying numbers of manufacturing products. For example, Lao (LAO) and Papua New Guinea (PNG) have low levels of economic complexity and produce relatively few manufactured products.

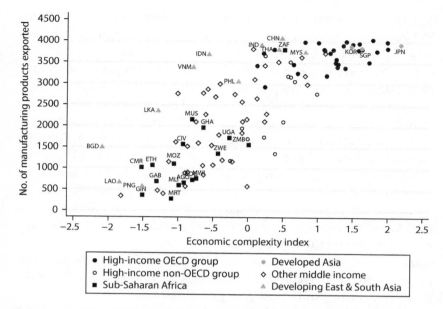

Figure 8.5 Economic complexity and number of manufactured products exported (HS6), 2013

Note: The sample of countries is reduced to those for which complexity measures are estimated. Determination of whether a manufactured product is exported by a country is not based on revealed comparative advantage. OECD = Organisation for Economic Co-operation and Development.

Source: Authors' calculations using trade data from BACI International Trade Database (HS six-digit, revision 1992).

Conversely, India (IND), Thailand (THA), China (CHN), Malaysia (MYS), South Korea (KOR), and Japan (JPN) are increasingly complex and produce a greater diversity of manufactured products. Developing countries in East and South Asia produce 2,545 different manufactured products at a standard deviation of 1,329 (at the six-digit level of the Harmonized System). In comparison, SSA countries produce, on average, 1,357 different manufactured products at a standard deviation of 803. Comparing SSA, this is consistent with the Asian region's composition of countries with a greater range of complexity. This translates into a greater range of manufacturing products being produced. Therefore, the Asian region, relative to SSA, is characterized by greater heterogeneity in economic complexity, which corresponds with a greater cross-country range of manufacturing exports.

Third, in several instances, for the same level of economic complexity, SSA countries produce relatively fewer manufactured products than their Asian peers, including Sri Lanka (LKA) versus Nigeria (NGA) and Vietnam (VNM) versus Mauritius (MUS). This might suggest that despite having similar levels of complexity, the capabilities embedded in the Asian economies, as revealed in their export baskets, are better aligned with manufacturing than the capabilities embedded in the SSA economies.

A final point worth considering is the extent to which there are regional spillovers of productive capabilities, and hence shifts in the production of manufactured products across the region (Bahar, Hausmann, and Hidalgo 2014). For example, surely it is easier for a country to develop manufacturing capabilities (e.g., Vietnam) if its neighbor (e.g., China) already has these productive capabilities (e.g., firms shifting production across the border to take advantage of lower input prices). Conversely, in SSA, fewer economies are clustered within a subregion that possess strong manufacturing capabilities, thus further constraining the potential to drive growth through regional spillovers.

Therefore, relative to their East and South Asian counterparts, SSA countries typically are characterized by lower amounts of productive capabilities, and this is reflected in less diverse and developed manufacturing sectors.

EVOLVING DEVELOPMENT PATHS AND MANUFACTURING

This section provides a comparative product-level analysis of the evolution of export structures for SSA and Eastern and Southern Asia for the period from 1995 to 2013.[7] This snapshot of these regions' respective development paths lends a specific focus on the transformation of their manufacturing sectors. These evolving export structures are examined along two product-level dimensions: the complexity of the product, and the capital-intensity associated with the production of the product. This allows us to (1) examine the notion that structural transformation is the process of shifting to increasingly complex products, and (2) consider the employment effects associated with such process.

With the use of scatterplots (see figures 8.6–8.10), the product-level evolution of the productive structures of these regional aggregates is shown within the product complexity and revealed physical capital intensity space.[8] This space is defined by a horizontal axis showing the level of product complexity for each manufacturing product and a vertical axis showing the revealed physical capital intensity for each manufacturing product.

The approach taken is as follows: manufacturing products are categorized according to whether they are entries into the regional export portfolio (i.e., products not exported in 1995 but exported in 2013) or whether they are existing exports (i.e., products exported in both 1995 and 2013). The former provides insight into the type of manufacturing products that countries within the regions are diversifying into, and the latter provides insight into the products that make up the existing manufacturing sector across countries within these regions. Separate graphs are provided for each product grouping in each regional grouping. The

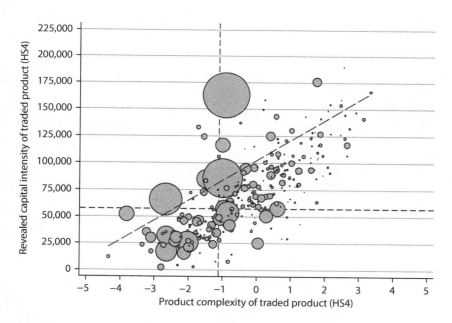

Figure 8.6   Evolution of Sub-Saharan Africa's export portfolio—existing products, 1995–2013

Note: Traded products are classified at the four-digit level of the Harmonised System, Revision 1992, with each bubble representing a four-digit product line. The size of each bubble represents the share of that product in total exports in the final period, 2013. Trade flows are restricted to products in which at least one country within a region has a revealed comparative advantage.

Source: Authors' calculations using trade data from BACI International Trade Database to create product complexity measure and revealed factor intensity data developed by Shirotori, Tumurchudur, and Cadot (2010).

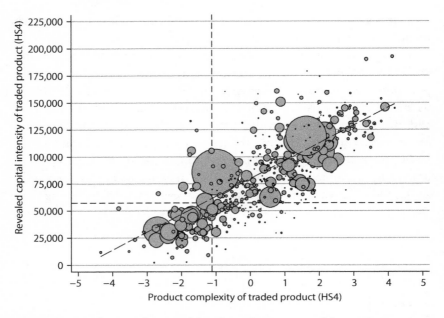

Figure 8.7   Evolution of East and South Asia's export portfolio—existing products, 1995–2013

Note: Traded products are classified at the four-digit level of the Harmonised System, Revision 1992, with each bubble representing a four-digit product line. The size of each bubble represents the share of that product in total exports in the final period, 2013. Trade flows are restricted to products in which at least one country within a region has a revealed comparative advantage.

Source: Authors' calculations using trade data from BACI International Trade Database to create product complexity measure and revealed factor intensity data developed by Shirotori, Tumurchudur, and Cadot (2010).

dashed horizontal and vertical lines in each scatterplot represent the mean revealed physical capital intensity and the mean product complexity for products classified as low-technology manufactures falling within the fashion cluster of the Lall (2000) classification—i.e. products falling within the relatively labor-intensive clothing and textiles industry. These lines provide a reference point for the capital intensity and product complexity associated with these labor-intensive products.

These scatterplots present the different stages of manufacturing export development over time, at the product level in the complexity-capital intensity space. An evolving export structure associated with both higher income levels and higher levels of employment would be expected to evolve and be

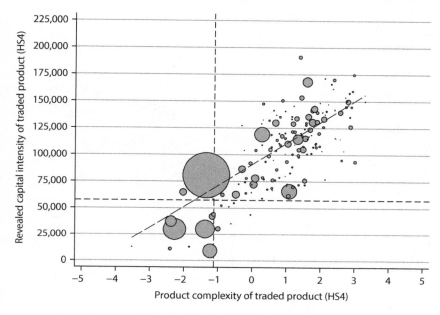

Figure 8.8   Evolution of Sub-Saharan Africa's export portfolio—entry into new products, 2013

Note: Traded products are classified at the four-digit level of the Harmonised System, Revision 1992, with each bubble representing a four-digit product line. The size of each bubble represents the share of that product in total exports in the final period, 2013. Trade flows are restricted to products in which at least one country within a region has a revealed comparative advantage.

Source: Authors' calculations using trade data from BACI International Trade Database to create product complexity measure and revealed factor intensity data developed by Shirotori, Tumurchudur, and Cadot (2010).

depicted as such: first, one would observe a large and dominant distribution of products in the southwest-west corner of the scatterplot, which are characterized by low complexity and high levels of labor intensity. Examples of clusters of products include clothing, textiles, and processed foods. Second, over time, one should observe a shift toward the northeast area of the scatterplot into more complex products—thereby generating an economic pathway to higher levels of income. Such complex products would include, for example, electronics, machinery, and chemicals.

Figures 8.6 and 8.7 present the export structure pertaining to existing products for the SSA and the Eastern and Southern Asian regions, respectively.[9]

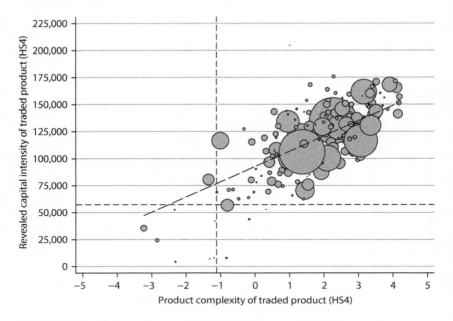

Figure 8.9   Evolution of East and South Asia's export portfolio—entry into new products, 2013

Note: Traded products are classified at the four-digit level of the Harmonised System, Revision 1992, with each bubble representing a four-digit product line. The size of each bubble represents the share of that product in total exports in the final period, 2013. Trade flows are restricted to products in which at least one country within a region has a revealed comparative advantage.

Source: Authors' calculations using trade data from BACI International Trade Database to create product complexity measure and revealed factor intensity data developed by Shirotori, Tumurchudur, and Cadot (2010).

The clustering of bubbles in the southwest corner of figure 8.6 suggests that exports from SSA countries typically possess low levels of product complexity. The cluster of products to the left of the dashed vertical line have complexity levels below the average complexity for clothing and textile products, showing that a large share of SSA manufacturing exports are characterized by low levels of complexity (i.e., products below the horizontal line, such as raw sugar, manganese ore, aluminum ore, precious metal ore, knit sweaters, palm oil, and knit t-shirts).[10] Existing manufacturing exports to the right of the dashed vertical line have complexity levels above the average for clothing and textiles and are not job generators. This is seen most predominantly for the two products, refined

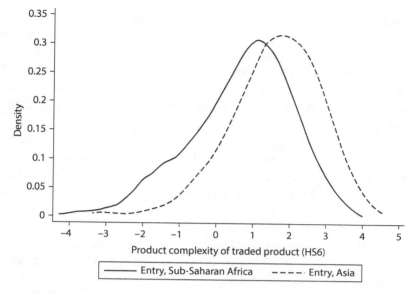

Figure 8.10   Distribution of entries by region

Note: Trade flows are restricted to products in which at least one country within a region has a revealed comparative advantage.

Source: Authors' calculations using trade data from BACI International Trade Database (HS six-digit, revision 1992) to create product complexity measure and revealed factor intensity data developed by Shirotori, Tumurchudur, and Cadot (2010).

petroleum and special purpose ships, depicted as the largest bubbles above the dashed horizontal line.

A number of existing exports clustered in the northeast corner of figure 8.6 are associated with higher levels of product complexity and capital intensity. The number of such products is limited, however, and their share of trade is small. The scatterplot points to a relatively underdeveloped manufacturing sector across the region.

Figure 8.6 also provides insight into the path dependency of the SSA export basket. Hausmann et al. (2014) show that a country's existing export basket influences its subsequent diversification. The more proximate the productive capabilities embodied in a country's existing export basket are to the productive capabilities associated with products that it does not currently produce, the more easily it can shift to these products. Hausmann et al. (2014) also show that more complex products, typically manufacturing products, are more proximate to other manufacturing products. Thus, it is easier to shift to these other complex manufactured products if you already produce a number of complex manufactured products. The implication of the SSA export basket being concentrated in products characterized by low levels of complexity and low levels of connectedness, is that it is harder for countries within the region to diversify into more complex manufacturing products.

In contrast, the East and South Asian export structure, observed in figure 8.7, points to an established and integrated manufacturing sector. The region's export structure is spread relatively evenly across this product complexity-revealed capital intensity space. The Asian export structure provides a number of insights. First, an integrated chain of products is evident in this product complexity-revealed capital intensity space, which suggests (much in the spirit of the product space approach) that Asian economies are taking advantage of proximate products and building capabilities in them fairly efficiently. Second, this is clearly not the case in SSA, where the product complexity-revealed capital intensity space is far more "lumpy" and disjointed.

Third, the thick cluster of low-complexity and low-capital-intensity products depicted in the southwest corner (typically textile and clothing products, such as nonknit women's suits, nonknit men's suits, knit sweaters, leather footwear, knit t-shirts, and nonretail pure cotton yarn) suggests consistent job creation in these established labor-intensive industries over time. This is in contrast with SSA where its cluster of products depicted in the southwest corner is relatively small in comparison, and it is concentrated in resource-based manufactures, such as raw sugar, manganese ore, aluminum ore, and precious metal ore.

Fourth, the cluster of products depicted in the northeast corner is relatively more complex and capital intensive (e.g., integrated circuits, computers, broadcasting equipment, telephones, office machine parts, semiconductor parts, rubber tires, video displays, air conditioners, and cyclic hydrocarbons). The magnitude and diversity of these complex machinery, electronic, and chemical products stand in contrast to the marginal nature of the types of complex products in the SSA export basket. This has implications on subsequent diversification, because complex products are associated with higher levels of connectedness. Thus, by already producing these types of products, Asian economies are better placed to diversify into increasingly complex products (observed in figure 8.9.)

Figure 8.8 depicts the manufacturing products to which SSA countries have shifted their focus, which illustrates the way in which export structures within these regions have evolved. Correspondingly, figure 8.9 depicts how the East and South Asian export portfolio has evolved over the period from 1995 to 2013.

The pattern of entry into new manufacturing products in the SSA region provides a number of insights. First, SSA appears to be stuck in some sort of low-complexity trap that is associated with both low (e.g., copper ore, nickel mattes, and titanium ore) and high (e.g., passenger and cargo ships) capital-intensity products.[11] Certainly, in terms of trade volumes, entry is concentrated in a handful of low-complexity products. These entries depicted in the southwest corner of the figure are concentrated in resource-based activities, which is unlike the light-manufacturing activities in clothing and textiles that drove employment growth in Asia.

Second, although entry into relatively more complex manufactured products is depicted in the northeast corner (e.g., broadcasting equipment, saturated acyclic monocarboxylic acids, and construction vehicles), the share of exports accounted for by these products, and hence the scale, is relatively small. In particular, the scale of these entries is too small to create a platform for global expansion. The marginal nature of the entries into more complex products stands in stark contrast to the East and South Asian experience over the same period.

SSA's existing export basket, as depicted in figure 8.8, which is associated with low levels of complexity and connectedness, has affected its subsequent pattern of diversification. The productive capabilities embodied in its existing export structure are distant from those needed to successfully shift into relatively more complex manufacturing products. As such, SSA countries have not accumulated the necessary capabilities needed for this shift, and hence, their manufacturing sectors have experienced relative stagnation.

The East and South Asian pattern of entry and hence diversification, depicted in figure 8.9, stands in stark contrast to that evident in SSA. This region's evolving export structure is biased toward increasingly complex and capital-intensive products (e.g., packaged medicaments, delivery trucks, vehicle parts, ethylene polymers, and industrial printers). Furthermore, the magnitude of these entries is relatively large, thus indicating that these manufacturing industries have experienced scale economies. Furthermore, a growth-inducing path dependency is associated with the pattern of development evident in the Asian picture.

The extent to which Asian firms have been able to shift into increasingly complex manufactured products, relative to the SSA region, is depicted in figure 8.10. The figure shows the distribution of product entries according to the level of complexity associated with the new product. On average, diversification in the Asian region is characterized by entries into more complex products relative to the SSA region. This is visible in the distribution of entries for Asia falling to the right of the distribution of entries for SSA.

A question worth considering is why Asian firms have been able to shift more easily into these increasingly complex manufactured products. Complexity analytics offers an explanation for this varying pattern of diversification across the two regions. In a recent working paper, Bhorat, Steenkamp, and Rooney (2016) use complexity analytics to explain manufacturing performance in Africa. Informed by Hidalgo et al. (2007), they argue that the process of structural transformation is a path-dependent process, whereby countries accumulate productive capabilities and thereby shift production toward increasingly complex and proximate manufacturing products. The ability to shift production is based on existing levels of capabilities. Hidalgo et al. (2007) find that the extent to which a country can diversify its export structure toward an increasing number of proximate manufactured products depends on the connectedness of its initial productive structure. If the capability set exists, these products can be expanded into. The dynamic process of growing a new productive structure, and hence export basket, revolves around the ability to upgrade a country's capability set over time.

This clarifies the observations from figures 8.6–8.9. Asian economies are better able to enter new manufacturing product markets because the required capabilities are similar or close to those they currently possess. For instance, if a firm in a country is able to assemble motor vehicles for the international market, a lot of the inputs needed to enter the international car parts market are already in place, including logistics networks, supply networks, port infrastructure, and the like. This supports the shift into new complex product markets depicted in the northeast corner of figure 8.9. Conversely, SSA's productive structure is concentrated in less complex resource-based products in which the embedded capabilities are relatively distant from those needed to produce complex manufactured products. This supports the SSA export structure remaining stagnant in the southwest corners of figure 8.7 and 8.9.

This analysis provides the following key points: First, the East and South Asian export structure and profile are more diverse and, consequently, more complex than its SSA counterpart. In Asia, a greater number of existing products and new products associated with higher levels of economic complexity are observed in the northeast corners of the scatterplots. In addition, the sheer scale of exports in these relatively complex products suggests established and integrated manufacturing sectors in Asia. In the SSA case, existing products as well as new products are typically located in the low-complexity southwest corners of the scatterplots. In addition, the share of exports is concentrated in a few of these products, thus suggesting a less diverse export basket. Second, and more important, during this period, East and South Asian firms not only found it easier to shift into increasingly complex manufactured products than their SSA counterparts, but also experienced substantial diversification. The integrated structure of the Asian export basket points to the productive capabilities embedded in its existing export basket being relatively proximate to those needed to shift into more complex manufactured products. The relatively disconnected and patchy export basket for SSA points to the productive capabilities embedded in its existing export basket being distant from those needed to successfully shift into more complex manufacturing products.

EMPLOYMENT AND MANUFACTURING

In light of the discussion on the development trajectories pertaining to each of these regions, we turn to a discussion about how these evolving productive structures relate to employment. The manufacturing sector in the Asian region, particularly the East Asian region, has been a major source of employment for the countries in this region. Hopefully, SSA countries will undergo similar manufacturing-led economic growth and thus will be able to employ a young and growing labor force.

The argument is that growing a manufacturing sector, and hence generating manufacturing jobs, is about shifting to a multitude of complex manufacturing activities and thereby building complexity within an economy. Therefore, we next consider the link between economic complexity and employment across the two regions over time. Table 8.2 shows the aggregate levels of employment in manufacturing and the mean economic complexity score for the two regions in 1995 and 2010. These data reveal trends in manufacturing employment growth in relation to economic

Table 8.2   Economic Complexity and Employment

Region	Total Employment in Manufacturing (Thousands)			Economic Complexity			Elasticity
	1995	2010	Δ	1995	2010	Δ	
Southeast Asia	61,059	78,291	17,232	−0.06	0.28	0.34	0.05
Sub-Saharan Africa	4,023	9,221	5,198	−1.05	−0.92	0.13	10.42

Source: Authors' calculations using Groningen Growth and Development Centre ten-sector database (see Timmer et al., 2014) and BACI International Trade Database data (Harmonized System six-digit, revision 1992) to create economic complexity measure.

Note: South and East Asian countries include India, Indonesia, Malaysia, Philippines, and Thailand. SSA countries include Ethiopia, Ghana, Kenya, Malawi, Mauritius, Nigeria, Senegal, Tanzania, and Zambia.

Elasticity is measured as follows: $\dfrac{\%\Delta\,Manufacturing\,Job}{\%\Delta\,ECI\,Score}$.

complexity growth. A simple elasticity measure is included, which shows the percentage change in manufacturing employment in response to a percentage change in economic complexity.

The employment data evident in table 8.2, in conjunction with the previous export data analysis, indicate the sheer scale of the manufacturing sector in the Eastern and Southern Asian regions, and thus identify it as a major source of employment. The manufacturing sector provided 61 million jobs in 1995 and this grew by 17 million to 78 million jobs in 2010. In comparison, the manufacturing sector in SSA is substantially smaller: the sector provided 4 million jobs in 1995, but notably, it more than doubled to 9 million in 2010. These data illustrate that the manufacturing sector in Asia is larger and more diverse than its SSA counterpart, and thus it is able to employ more workers. The Asian manufacturing sector is spread more evenly across products varying in complexity and capital intensity, and hence, it is able to offer more employment opportunities for a greater range of workers across the manufacturing spectrum. The SSA manufacturing sector, in contrast, is relatively small and concentrated, and thus, it offers substantially fewer employment opportunities to a smaller range of workers.

The export data analysis revealed that, relative to their SSA counterparts, Asian economies have been better able to shift production into increasingly complex manufactured products. Furthermore, the sheer scale of entry into these new product markets in Asia is again substantially greater than that achieved by its SSA counterpart. This is reflected in a greater increase in the Asian region's economic complexity index (0.34) relative to that experienced in SSA (0.13). Part of the explanation for the Asian region's ability to shift easily into relatively more complex manufactured products relates to the complexity of its existing export basket and the associated connectedness of this relatively more complex export basket. This is reflected in the economic complexity levels for the region, which have shifted from –0.06 to 0.28. Conversely, although shifting upward, the economic complexity levels in SSA are substantially lower (–1.05 to –0.92). The lower levels of connectedness associated with less complex export baskets provide insight into the region's inability to grow its productive capabilities and shift to more complex manufacturing products.

Finally, the elasticity of manufacturing employment in relation to a percentage change in economic complexity is substantially higher for SSA (10.42) than for Asia (0.05). This is perhaps unsurprising because employment growth in manufacturing in SSA is occurring off a relatively low base. This may suggest the potential for more rapid manufacturing-led employment growth within the SSA region, which offers hope to countries within the region that are faced, as noted previously, with young and growing labor forces.

CONCLUSION

The major challenge facing the countries that make up SSA is a young and growing labor force. This challenge can be viewed as an opportunity, because an expanded labor force, if employed, can increase output and thereby generate economic growth. The question of key importance concerns where these jobs will be generated. The Asian story is one in which industrialization and the growth of manufacturing activities acted as a source of growth and employment. As such, the question arises whether countries within SSA can experience a similar manufacturing-led growth path.

The analysis shows an SSA productive structure that is disconnected and that is characterized by products with low levels of economic complexity. Inherent in a productive structure characterized by lower levels of economic complexity is the notion of limited productive capabilities. Furthermore, as revealed in a previous study, these productive capabilities are distant from those needed to produce increasingly complex manufacture products (Bhorat et al. 2016). This stands in contrast to the productive structure in the East and South Asian region that is connected and complex. East and South Asian economies are able to shift into increasingly complex manufactured products because the productive capabilities imbedded in their existing productive structure are similar to those required to shift into these products.

This ability to shift has implications for the extent to which the manufacturing sector can generate employment. The sheer scale and diversity of the manufacturing sector in Asia allows for the generation of a large number and diversity of employment opportunities. Conversely, the marginal nature of the SSA manufacturing sector points to limited employment opportunities. The relatively high employment relative to the economic complexity elasticity for SSA offers hope. By growing complexity, countries within the region may be able to undergo relatively rapid employment growth if they grow their manufacturing sectors. Nevertheless, if SSA is to generate jobs through manufacturing-led industrialization, it needs to accumulate the productive capabilities that will allow it to do so.

NOTES

1. All projections beyond 2015 use the UN Population Division's medium variant projections.

2. Note that the estimated regression line, measuring the relationship between productivity and changes in employment share by sector, is not statistically significant.

3. In comparison, the employment shares in manufacturing and agriculture in 2010 in SSA were 6.6 and 58.9 percent, respectively.

4. Notably, a number of other researchers have developed alternative methods for measuring economic and product complexity; see Andrea Tacchella, Matthieu Cristelli, Guido Caldarelli, Andrea Gabrielli, and Luciano Pietronero, "A New Metrics for Countries' Fitness and Products' Complexity," *Scientific Reports* 2, no. 723 (2012): 1–4. We employ the methodology outlined in *The Atlas of Economic Complexity* (http://atlas.cid.harvard.edu), developed by a team of researchers at the Centre of International Development at Harvard University.

5. We generate measures of economic and product complexity using trade data from the BACI International Trade Database, made available by CEPII, and the Stata Programme—ecomplexity—developed by Sebastian Bustos and Muhammed Yildirim (Hidalgo, Hausmann & Dasgupta 2009; Hausmann et al. 2014).

6. A limitation of the complexity analytics described earlier is that the data set considers only products and not services. This is concerning in the face of the rising share of services in international trade. The inclusion of services into the complexity analytics is constrained by the relative scarcity of services trade data.

7. The proceeding analysis compares the evolving export structures of the SSA and Eastern and Southern Asian regions. For comparative purposes, export structures across countries within these regional groupings are aggregated into regional export structures. SSA includes a sample of countries within the region, excluding South Africa, and the Asian regional aggregate includes a sample of developing Eastern and

Southern Asian economies, excluding China. The sample across each region is determined by which economies are included in the complexity analytics.

8. Revealed physical capital intensity is a measure developed by Miho Shirotori, Bolormaa Tumurchudur, and Olivier Cadot, "Revealed Factor Intensity Indices," *Policy Issues in International Trade and Commodities Study Series No. 44* (New York: United Nations, 2010), https://unctad.org/en/Pages/DITC/Trade-Analysis/TAB-Data-and-Statistics.aspx.

9. South Africa and China are excluded from the SSA and East and South Asian aggregates, respectively. The figures do not change substantially.

10. Products with larger export shares (i.e., larger bubbles) are reported in brackets in the following discussion.

11. Resource-based manufacturing products are included; thus, products such as copper ore and titanium ore appear in the sample of manufacturing products. The same set of scatterplots for the sample of manufacturing products excluding resource-based manufactures provides qualitatively similar depictions of the SSA and Asian export structures.

REFERENCES

Bahar, Dany, Ricardo Hausmann, and César A. Hidalgo. 2014. "Neighbors and the Evolution of the Comparative Advantage of Nations: Evidence of International Knowledge diffusion?" *Journal of International Economics* 92 (1): 111–123.

Bhorat, Haroon, Francois Steenkamp, and Christopher. Rooney. 2016. "Africa's Manufacturing Malaise." UNDP-RBA Working Paper Series 3/2016, September 27. http://www.africa.undp.org/content/rba/en/home/library/working-papers/africa-s-manufacturing-malaise.html.

Bhorat, Haroon, Ravi Kanbur, Christopher Rooney, and Francois. Steenkamp. 2017. "Sub-Saharan Africa's Manufacturing Sector: Building Complexity." Working Paper Series No. 256. African Development Bank Group.

Diop, Makhtar, Yuan Li, Li Yong, and H.E. Ato Ahmed Shide. 2015. "Africa Still Poised to Become the Next Great Investment Destination." World Bank, June 30. Accessed March 1, 2017. http://www.worldbank.org/en/news/opinion/2015/06/30/africa-still-poised-to-become-the-next-great-investment-destination.

Drummond, Paulo, Vimal Thakoor, and Shu Yu. 2014. "Africa Rising: Harnessing the Demographic Dividend." IMF Working Paper WP/14/143. International Monetary Fund. Accessed January 29, 2019, http://dx.doi.org/10.5089/9781498379878.001.

Filmer, Deon, and Louise Fox. 2014. *Youth Employment in Sub-Saharan Africa.* Washington, DC: World Bank Group.

Hausmann, Ricardo, César A. Hidalgo, Sebastian Bustos, Michele Coscia, Alexander Simoes, and Muhammed Yildirim. 2014. *The Atlas of Economic Complexity: Mapping Paths to Prosperity.* Cambridge, MA: MIT Press.

Hidalgo, César. A., Bailey Klinger, Albert-László Barabási, and Ricardo Hausmann. 2007. "The Product Space Conditions the Development of Nations." *Science, New Series* 317 (5837): 482–487. http://www.jstor.org/stable/20037448.

Hidalgo, César A., Ricardo Hausmann, and Partha S. Dasgupta. 2009. "The Building Blocks of Economic Complexity." *Proceedings of the National Academy of Sciences of the United States of America* 106 (26): 10570–10575. Available at http://www.jstor.org/stable/40483593.

International Labour Organization. 2014. "Global Employment Trends 2014: Risk of a Jobless Recovery?" International Labour Organization, Geneva. http://www.ilo.org/wcmsp5/groups/public/---dgreports/---dcomm/---publ/documents/publication/wcms_233953.pdf.

Lall, Sanjaya. 2000. "The Technological Structure and Performance of Developing Country Manufactured Exports, 1985–98." *Oxford Development Studies* 28 (3): 337–369. http://dx.doi.org/10.1080/713688318.

McMillan, Margaret S., and Dani Rodrik. 2011. "Globalization, Structural Change and Productivity Growth." NBER Working Paper No. 1743. National Bureau of Economic Research, Cambridge, MA. http://www.nber.org/papers/w17143.pdf.

McMillan, Margaret S., Dani Rodrik, and Íñigo Verduzco-Gallo. 2014. "Globalization, Structural Change, and Productivity Growth, with an Update on Africa." *World Development* 63: pp.11–32. http://www.sciencedirect.com/science/article/pii/S0305750X13002246.

Organisation for Economic Co-operation and Development. 2012. "African Economic Outlook 2012: Promoting Youth Employment." Paris: Organisation for Economic Co-operation and Development.

——. 2013. "Africa Economic Outlook 2013: Structural Transformation and Natural Resources." Paris: Organisation for Economic Co-operation and Development.

Page, John. 2012. "Can Africa Industrialize?" *Journal of African Economies* 21 (2): ii86–ii125. http://jae.oxfordjournals.org/cgi/doi/10.1093/jae/ejr045.

Rodrik, Dani. 2013. "Africa's Structural Transformation Challenge." *Project Syndicate.* Accessed March 3, 2017, https://www.project-syndicate.org/commentary/dani-rodrik-shows-why-sub-saharan-africa-s-impressive-economic-performance-is-not-sustainable?barrier=accessreg.

——. 2014. "An African Growth Miracle?" NBER Working Paper No. 20188. National Bureau of Economic Research, Cambridge, MA. http://www.nber.org/papers/w20188%5Cnhttp://www.nber.org/papers/w20188.pdf.

——. 2016. "Premature Deindustrialization." *Journal of Economic Growth* 21 (1): 1–33.

Shimeles, Abebe, and Mthuli Ncube. 2015. "The Making of the Middle-Class in Africa: Evidence from DHS Data." *Journal of Development Studies* 51 (2): 178–193. http://www.tandfonline.com/doi/abs/10.1080/00220388.2014.968137.

Shirotori, Miho, Bolormaa Tumurchudur, and Olivier Cadot. 2010. "Revealed Factor Intensity Indices." *Policy Issues in International Trade and Commodities Study Series No. 44.* New York: United Nations.

Sparreboom, Theo, and Alana Albee, eds. 2011. *Towards Decent Work in Sub-Saharan Africa: Monitoring MDG Employment Indicators.* Geneva: International Labour Organization.

Tacchella, Andrea, Matthieu Cristelli, Guido Caldarelli, Andrea Gabrielli, and Luciano Pietronero. 2012. "A New Metrics for Countries' Fitness and Products' Complexity." *Scientific Reports* 2 (723): 1–4.

The Economist. 2000. "Hopeless Africa." May 11. http://www.economist.com /node/333429.

Timmer, Marcel P., Gaaitzen de Vries, and Klaas de Vries. 2014. "Patterns of Structural Change in Developing Countries." Groningen GGDC Research Memorandum 149, Growth and Development Centre, University of Groningen, Brussels.

United Nations. 2017. *World Population Prospects 2017.* https://population.un.org /wpp/Download/Standard/Population/.

United Nations Economic Commission for Africa. 2014. *Economic Report on Africa 2014.* Addis Ababa, Ethiopia: UN Economic Commission for Africa. https://www .uneca.org/sites/default/files/PublicationFiles/final_era2014_march25_en.pdf.

CHAPTER 9

A Generalized Linkage Approach to Local Production Systems Development in the Era of Global Value Chains, with Special Reference to Africa

Antonio Andreoni

Since the mid-1990s, the African continent has experienced an increasing integration into global value chains (GVCs), mainly led by the penetration (i.e., investment and value extraction) of transnational corporations (TNCs) in the continent. Within the new global production setting, particular attention has been given to the learning and industrialization opportunities offered by the integration of domestic companies into GVCs and their specialization in specific tasks (instead of sectoral development, both in the import substitution or export-oriented industrialization models).

In the majority of the African economies, this new industrialization model (i.e., integration into GVCs) has not led to increasing domestic value addition—in particular, it is lacking in manufacturing. It has also failed to create any significant transformation of the local production systems (LPS) whose structure remains quite dualistic in all African countries. In fact, a number of African economies have experienced premature deindustrialization and their dependence on primary commodity exports has even increased (Andreoni and Tregenna 2018).

This chapter refocuses the industrial policy debate in Africa from GVC integration to LPS development. It argues that the quality of growth in Africa critically depends on the cumulative processes of increasing value addition, collective learning, and linkage development in the LPSs. These processes must be coupled with strategic integration into regional value chains and GVCs.

Despite the increasing research on GVC functioning and typologies (e.g., buyer versus producer led or vertically specialized versus additive), we still have a limited understanding of the different types of LPSs in

African economies. This chapter addresses this gap by developing the generalized linkage approach of Albert Hirschman (1977) and, in particular, by disentangling the set of production, technology, consumption, and fiscal linkages constituting a LPS. The Hirschmanian linkage taxonomy is used to develop a new LPS framework for Africa. Within this framework, this chapter develops a stylized analysis of the different types of bottlenecks and specific factors, including political economic factors that affect technological learning, production diversification, and expansion of local or regional production networks.

The chapter concludes by focusing on industrial policy for LPS development in Africa. The development of LPSs requires focusing on the provision of production and technology services for improving firm-level organizational capabilities and technical skills; nurturing domestic mid-size companies, which are critical nodes between LPSs and GVCs; and governing learning rents and rent chains that exist both across LPSs and along GVCs.

GVCS INTEGRATION IN AFRICA: SOME EVIDENCE

The global business revolution and the emergence of global and regional value chains since the early 1990s have been made possible by a number of technological advances (e.g., falling transport costs, and more interconnectedness via information and communication technology), cost-reduction opportunities associated with offshoring labor-intensive manufacturing processes, and increasing openness in global markets for trade and investments (Nolan, Liu and Zhang 2001; Milberg and Winkler 2013; Neilson, Pritchard, and Wai-chung Yeung 2014; Gereffi 2014; Kaplinsky and Morris 2015).

From 1990 to 2013, foreign direct investment (FDI) inflows in developing countries upsurged from $35 billion to $778 billion (from 17 percent to 54 percent of world FDI inflows). In Africa, FDI inflows have increased nearly twenty-fold in the same period, from $3 billion to $57 billion (from 1.4 percent to 4 percent of world FDI inflows), although this increase has been concentrated mainly in a few sectors (e.g., services and mining) and countries (e.g., South Africa, Nigeria, and Egypt among the major economies; and Ethiopia, Tanzania, Mozambique, and Congo among the least developed countries). As shown in figure 9.1, between 2014 and 2016 developing economies registered a decline in FDI inflows (from $704 to $646 billion), with Africa moving from $71 to $59 billion,

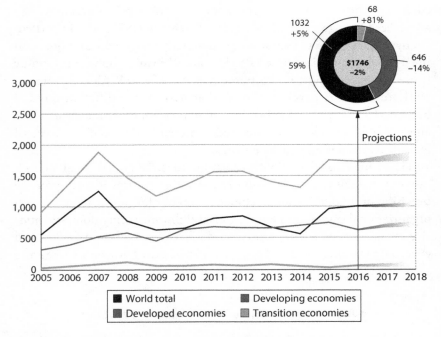

Figure 9.1   Foreign direct investment inflows—global and by group of economies (2005–2017, and projections)

Source: ©UNCTAD, FMI/MNE database (www.unctad.org/fdistatistics).

but projections suggest a recovery in the coming years (United Nations Conference on Trade and Development 2017).

During the trade boom from 1990 to 2013, the world trade dependence ratio increased from 19.5 to 30 percent, whereas in economies like the United States, firms that export and import accounted for almost 90 percent of known value (World Bank 2017). For a number of fast-catching-up economies, the internationalization of TNCs and the resulting global segmentation of production tasks have created opportunities to enter technology-based markets and capture value from advanced manufacturing technology.

Late industrializers, including China as well as South Korea and Taiwan (specifically between 1970 and 1980), began industrialization by linking (backward) to global supply chains and adding value (forward) in electronics and other sectors, starting from those characterized by short-technology cycles (Amsden 1985, 1989; Wade 1990; Chang 1993; Milberg and Winkler 2013; Lee 2013).

During the same period (1970–1980) and in the following two decades (1990–2010), in particular, African countries experienced another type of GVC integration. As shown by Foster-McGregor, Kaulich, and Stehrer (2015), although the value of world imports more than doubled during the 2000s, with intermediate goods accounting for 65 percent of world imports in 2011, African countries mainly have been experiencing "upstream integration." Specifically, much of Africa's participation in GVCs has developed in upstream production, with firms in Africa almost exclusively providing primary products to firms in countries further down the value chain where value addition is concentrated (figure 9.2). In addition, since 1995, Africa's downstream integration has weakened (figure 9.3).

For the majority of countries in Africa, as well as for some middle-income countries outside of Africa, such as the Philippines or Mexico, the

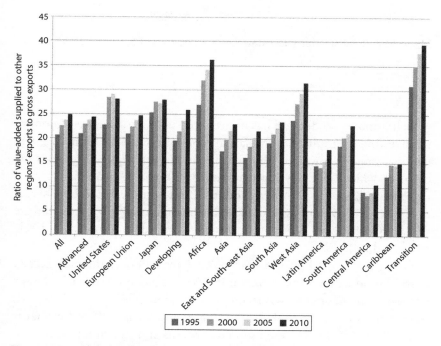

Figure 9.2   Global value chain upstream integration

Source: UNCOMTRADE Eora GVC Data.

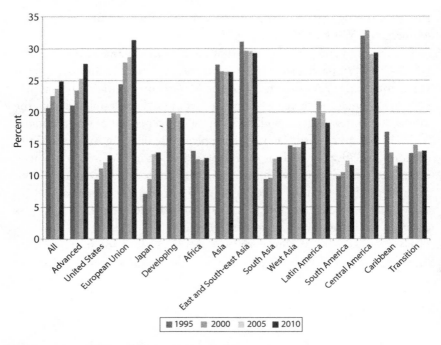

Figure 9.3   Global value chain downstream integration

Source: UNCOMTRADE Eora GVC Data.

globalization of production has not resulted in greater long-term domestic investments, capital accumulation, domestic value creation, or international value capture in manufacturing industries. Figure 9.4 shows the extent to which GVC development has contributed to changes in domestic value addition for all African countries and for different industrial sectors. Interestingly, mining and quarrying and financial intermediation are the sectors that have picked up the most alongside transport, wholesale trade, and utilities.

Given the limited impact that GVCs have had over the past decade or so in production transformation in Africa, we also wonder whether or not economic upgrading has resulted in social upgrading. In this regard, recent studies (Goger et al. 2014; Cramer and Chang 2015; Bernhardt and Pollack 2016) have raised several concerns and shown mixed results. At the global level, GVC integration has led to some form of economic upgrading in certain sectors (e.g., horticulture) in a limited number of

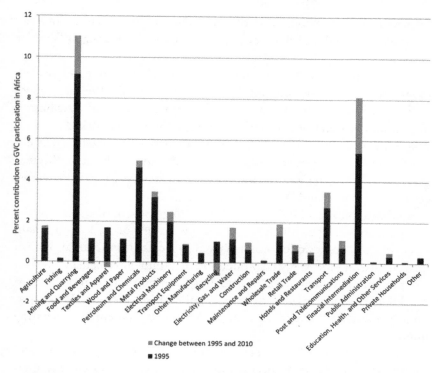

Figure 9.4   Global value chain–led increase in value addition in Africa between 1995 and 2010

Source: UNCOMTRADE Eora GVC Data.

countries in Africa. Even among successful country and sector cases, however, these economic upgrades have not necessarily translated into social upgrades.

A CRITICAL APPRAISAL OF THE GLOBAL VALUE CHAIN–LED INDUSTRIALIZATION MODEL

Today's global production system is made of complex and dynamic interdependencies spanning various industries and sectors as well as countries and regions. These interdependencies unfold in a wide range of technological, organizational, and institutional dimensions, and involve different actors. These include business organizations both competing and cooperating in multitiered and "glo-cal" production systems as well as various types of public and public-private technology intermediaries and multilevel public policy actors (Milberg and Winkler 2013; Andreoni 2018).

Over the past two decades, the GVC approach has gained increasing momentum in the business and development economics literature, especially with respect to (1) the analysis of the governance and distribution of production functions (or tasks) among different networked production units located in different countries (multitier organizational structure) and (2) the value creation and capture dynamics related to different governance structures and the impact of manufacturing relocation across countries (Milberg and Winkler 2013; Gereffi 2014).

Studies adopting a GVC approach tend to go beyond the sector as the main unit of analysis, which is replaced by the one of "task" and "chain or network." A production task is linked to a certain functional stage of the production process or the production of a finite intermediate product component. The network is multicountry (often more regionally confined than truly global) and is composed of multiple productive organizations involved in different stages of production and potentially operating in multiple sectors.

The GVC framework stresses the opportunities for companies (and countries) to specialize in specific production tasks or components, preferably high-value niches, while avoiding a build-up of vertically integrated industrial sectors or blocks of industries. In developed countries, the idea of a selective form of specialization in tasks, driven by capturing value opportunities, encourages companies to focus on activities such as research and development, design, and downstream post-sale services, while dismissing more traditional (at least perceived so) low-value manufacturing processes.

As for developing countries, the opportunities offered by a GVC-led industrialization model have been articulated in different ways. Among neoliberal scholars, under the mantra, "you need to import if you want to export," GVCs have been used to reemphasize the benefits of international trade and, thus, the need for more trade liberalization. Building on the same premise, although with more nuanced and articulated arguments, the opportunities that GVCs offer for economic growth also have been stressed increasingly in flagship reports and studies—for example, see the recent World Bank report by Farole and Winkler (2014) and the joint World Trade Organization, Organisation for Economic Co-operation and Development, and World Bank report on GVCs (2017).

Surprisingly, the majority of the developmentalist scholars have highlighted the opportunity offered to developing countries by the GVC-led industrialization model to overcome the highly uncertain and capital-demanding task of developing entirely new sectors. This model has been proposed as a way to move beyond more traditional import-substitution industrialization and as a new way to frame the successful export-led model of development of the Asian tigers and today's emerging economies. According to these scholars, GVC-led industrialization opens up opportunities to access regional and global markets and also to diversify and upgrade specific tasks and new products.

We need to carefully analyze the conditions required for countries and companies to benefit from GVC integration as well as the potential risks associated with this new GVC-led industrialization model. This is especially important when dealing with countries in Africa that have been experiencing deindustrialization, dramatic import penetration, and increasing competitiveness from emerging industrial giants like China and India.

Understanding the potential fallacies in the GVC-led model of industrialization is critical when assessing whether or not this model is going to be able to deliver quality of growth in Africa. The following six arguments provide a critical perspective on the GVC-led industrialization model from both an ontological (factual fallacies) and epistemological (theoretical premises) perspective. Following this critique, we propose a more systemic framework for industrialization in Africa, focusing on LPSs and different types of linkages.

TNC POWER AND ENDOGENOUS ASYMMETRY ARGUMENT

TNCs in command of regional and GVCs are extremely powerful organizations, whose internal economy can be comparable to the GDP of many developing countries. These TNCs exercise their power in global oligopolistic markets and command enormous global market shares. Nolan, Liu, and Zhang (2007) estimated that since 2000, in the majority of global industries, a handful of TNCs had controlled the market. This power is exercised in a systematic and strategic manner to capture value in the market by creating entry barriers in the forms of patents, quality standards, copyrights, and trademarks (what Kaldor [1960] understood as "institutional monopolies") and by squeezing supply chains. This is particularly true with commodity-based GVCs, in which big companies capture value by controlling the retail stage or production. It is also the case with low-tech manufacturing GVCs, in which TNCs squeeze value by inducing suppliers to increase scale and product quality, and then, when resources are committed, exercising downward pressures on prices (so-called hostage situations; see Williamson 1985).

The power of these TNCs is strictly related to the existence of endogenous asymmetries in multitiered international production networks. This industry concentration can be realized at different levels of the value chain (Milberg and Winkler 2013; see also chapter 4, in this volume). For example, we find strong lead firms (often operating as product system integrators) squeezing the entire value chain of the components they command. In other cases, we have powerful first-tier suppliers orchestrating (while squeezing) long supply chains for global lead firms. Finally, we have buyer-led supply chains in which players, such as supermarkets and retailers in the food industry, set up high markups while squeezing the supply chain.

DIFFERENCES IN SECTORAL VALUE CHAIN OPPORTUNITIES ARGUMENT

Although GVCs offer opportunities for production and trade integration, it still matters which sectoral value chains countries are integrating with and under what conditions they become part of them. Given the structural heterogeneity characterizing industries, in particular, manufacturing sectors (Andreoni and Chang 2017), we expect that the value creation and capture opportunities are distributed in different ways across value chains in different sectors. In the context of Africa, GVC integration has mainly involved upstream resource-based sectors. The ability to create and capture value in these types of sectoral value chains require domestic companies in developing countries to master production technologies whose application in beneficiation processes and industrial agriculture adds value. Unfortunately, African economies are not integrating in resource-based industries in this manner. Although there are some encouraging examples of successful integration in sectoral value chains (e.g., the flower and leather industry in Ethiopia, fruit industry in South Africa; see Cramer and Sander 2015; Andreoni and Tregenna 2018), without developing a number of key manufacturing industries delivering production technologies for the other sectoral value chains, these efforts will not be sufficient to transform these economies and trigger cumulative processes of intersectoral learning (Andreoni 2011, 2014).

From an analytical perspective, the fact that the GVC approach has increasingly become "a-sectoral"—that is, it has led to undermining a number of specificities of industrial sectors (or groups of industrial sectors)—is problematic. Although vertically integrated sectors are poor heuristics to understand the modern network–value chain mode of production, these networks and value chains are fundamentally heterogeneous. They present specific structural features in terms of their vertical disintegration and modularity potential, their length and value distribution, and the underpinning set of technological capabilities. In particular, the shape and length of different sectoral value chains will depend on multiple factors, including specific technological and organizational features, as well as a combination of complementary capabilities (i.e., technology platform) required to execute tasks in different stages of the chain. In addition, these tasks tend to be different across sectors (Andreoni 2014, 2018).

PRODUCTION LOCK-IN AND VALUE-CHAIN DELINKING ARGUMENT

From a learning perspective, the risk of committing scarce resources in specific assets to perform relatively unsophisticated activities (basic processing or assembling) can lead to a situation of "production lock-in" or "value-chain delinking" in the case of unmet technology and quality standard requirements or emerging competitors, respectively (Kaplinsky and Morris 2015). As a result of these processes, industrial systems in developing economies that are in the early stages of economic transformation are characterized by similar features. Foreign-owned companies create few backward and forward linkages to perform relatively unsophisticated activities because of limited supplier and processor capacities in the host economy. Existing small enterprises lack the scale and skills to provide reliable intermediate products, as well as the resources to invest in technological upgrading. Particularly problematic is the lack of midsize manufacturing firms that can do those things—the so-called missing-middle phenomenon. The few domestic companies engaged in large-scale production face the same constraints and rely on imports of semiprocessed raw materials and capital goods, as well as on the re-export of assembled products, rather than being successful in creating backward and forward linkages.

COMPLEMENTARITIES IN LEARNING ARGUMENT

Related to the previous argument, to capture high-value-niche opportunities along the value chain through task specialization, companies often have to develop multiple sets of complementary production capabilities cutting

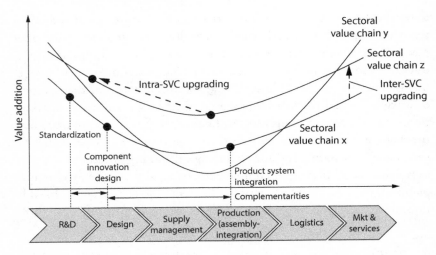

Figure 9.5   Capturing high-value niches and the need for multiple sets of complementary capabilities

Source: Author's creation.

across multiple stages of the value chain and different technology domains (figure 9.5). This is increasingly true in the case of complex high-tech, high-value products or components (Andreoni 2018). For example, the task specialization in design often requires direct access (often in the same location) to specific production capabilities for prototyping and manufacturing to scale up products and processes. Figure 9.5 presents close complementarities among the capabilities underpinning three sets of tasks—standardization, component innovation design, and product system integration. Task specialization requires the identification of complementary sets of capabilities, which constitute the technology platform underpinning the task or set of related tasks (Andreoni 2014). Countries whose companies specialize only on limited or isolated sets of tasks and capabilities will have reduced their learning and diversification opportunities.

In today's industrial economies, these sets of complementary capabilities were developed within vertically integrated firms (Penrose 1959), within so-called development blocks (Dahmen 1989), or to use a more recent theoretical framework, within industrial ecosystems (Andreoni 2018). According to Dahmen (1989), the development block "refers to a sequence of complementarities which by way of a series of structural tensions, i.e., disequilibria, may result in a balanced situation" (32).

In the process of structural change, the emergence of development blocks in an industrializing country may be the result of (1) ex post gap filling, whereby a structural tension or bottleneck is solved; or (2) ex ante creation of markets through coordinated entrepreneurial activities or economic planning by government institutions. In today's develop countries, successful industrial ecosystems, like the Boston route (Best 2018) and the Emilia Romagna region (Andreoni et al. 2017; Andreoni 2018), have developed complementary capabilities through different cycles of industrial transformation and renewal of vertically integrated firms. A dense network of local specialized suppliers and contractors have supported these efforts.

In sum, the possibility for firms in a certain location to develop a competitive advantage in a certain task or stage of a sectoral value chain, and thus capture a high-value niche, will depend on a set of different but complementary capabilities. More than one stage of development might require the involvement of the same or other sectoral value chains (both directly or indirectly with colocated firms).

THE INDUSTRY WITHOUT INDUSTRIALIZATION ARGUMENT

The industry without industrializing argument is strictly related to the previous argument and points to the excessive (in some cases almost exclusive) emphasis on the GVC-led industrialization model. This emphasis has been given to the creation of vertical linkages along value chain, while ignoring the important role of horizontal linkages among different firms positioned at each node along the value chain. Even more critically, many of these "horizontal linkages" cut across multiple sectoral value chains (see Andreoni 2018 in the context of the analysis of the architecture of industrial ecosystems). The narrow focus on building an industry through vertical supply chain relationships and international market access has been acknowledged by Gereffi and Lee (2016): "Global value chains and industrial clusters have been changing in significant ways in recent years. While the researchers who study these phenomena tend to focus on different levels of analysis—global and local, respectively—there is a need for more integrated frameworks that show how GVCs and clusters are connected through a variety of globalization processes" (35).[1]

From a policy perspective, the emphasis of the GVC-led industrialization model on the vertical supply chain relationship and international market access, instead of horizontal linkages development in the domestic economy, also reveals a fundamental misunderstanding of the relationship between import-substitution and export-led industrialization. As stressed by Chang (2010), "In East Asia, free trade, export promotion (which is, of course, not free trade), and infant industry protection were organically integrated, both in cross-section terms (so there always will be some industries subject to each category of policy, sometimes more than one at the same time) and over time (so, the same industry may be subject to more than one of the three over time)" (100). Export-led industrialization and GVC integration in East Asia developed hand in hand with the development of horizontal cross-sectoral linkages in the domestic economy and the resulting incremental domestic value addition in trade.

Along the same lines, Lee, Szapiro, and Mao (2017) suggest how successful catching-up economies followed an "in-out-in again" model of integration into GVC. They point out that

> at the initial stage of growth by a latecomer, increased participation in the GVC is necessary to learn foreign knowledge and production skills, functional upgrading at middle-income stage requires effort to seek separation and independence from existing foreign-dominated GVCs, and that latecomer firms and economies might have to seek reintegration back into the GVC after establishing their own local value chains. (Lee, Szapiro, and Mao 2017, abstract)

POLITICAL ECONOMY AND "RENTS CHAIN" ARGUMENT

The final argument in this critical appraisal of the GVC-led industrialization model is related to the fact that within this model, context-specific political economy dynamics are not addressed. Power dynamics in the GVC framework are very much acknowledged within the value chain and among the firms involved in the chain (i.e., GVC governance literature).[2]

At early and intermediate stages of industrialization, however, more fundamental context-specific political economy factors affect the competitiveness, upgrading, and value-added opportunities of firms. These factors are related to the conflicts and power struggles arising in the process of structural transformation of the economy (Andreoni and Chang 2019). These political economy factors set countries along different industrialization trajectories by shaping the sector-specific incentives structure and, thus, affecting industrial policy-rent allocations from the state. In addition, these factors create value-capture opportunities—what we call "rent chains"—beyond those opportunities strictly determined by the power distribution among firms along the value chains.

We define rent chains as the value that companies can capture as a result of political and regulatory arrangements favoring certain companies against others along the same chain. Thus, rent chains refer to value-capture opportunities that are politically or institutionally determined beyond the power distribution already linking companies along value chains. Examples of these rent chains might be related to a lack of enforcement of competition laws upstream in the value chain, or the political allocation of import or market licenses downstream the chain.

Despite historical and context specificities, across all countries in the African continent, these political economy forces and dynamics are intrinsically intertwined with the technological and organizational factors recognized in the GVC approach. Firms and farms in countries across Africa tend to be adversely affected by the existing distribution of organizational power in both the public and private sectors—thus, the countries' political settlement (Khan 2010; Whitfiled et al. 2015; Khan, Andreoni, and Roy 2016; Behuria, Buur, and Gray 2017; Khan 2018). This structure is typical of a nonindustrialized and nondiversified economy in which power remains highly concentrated in a few antagonistic factions. In particular, the concentration of power in upstream value chains and among traders through domestic manufacturers is a major political economy factor in Africa's industrialization—for example studies on Tanzania, see Andreoni (2017); South Africa, see Makhaya and Roberts (2013) and Andreoni and Tregenna (2018); and Ghana, Tanzania, Uganda, and Mozambique, see Whitfield et al. (2015).

In sum, while presenting a number of potential opportunities, the GVC-led industrialization model (especially in the way in which it has been articulated and implemented thus far with pro-GVC integration policies) might not be capable of delivering quality of growth in Africa for the following reasons: (1) the produced value might be concentrated and retained by TNCs (i.e., TNC power and endogenous asymmetry argument); (2) the sectoral value chains LDCs tend to be integrated with (or the GVC stages in which they are plugged in) are not those with high-value opportunities or margins for manufacturing development (i.e., differences in sectoral value chain opportunities argument); (3) production lock-in in low-value segments of the value chain (i.e., production lock-in and value chain delinking argument); (4) specialization in limited and isolated tasks and, thus underpinning capabilities might not be sufficient to trigger cross-segment and cross-sectoral learning dynamics (i.e., complementarities in learning argument); (5) developing vertical linkages in silos without horizontal linkages at each stage of the GVC does not allow for the transformation of the domestic production matrix(i.e., industry-without-industrialization argument); and (6) integration in GVCs given a certain political economy context might lead to entrenching power even more upstream and to consolidating an incentive structure biased toward importers more than producers (i.e., political economy and rents chain argument).

Building on these critical perspectives, and acknowledging the fact that regional value chains and GVCs are pervasive in today's manufacturing and trade landscapes, the question becomes how to make the GVC-led industrialization model more developmentalist. In addressing this question, the next section returns to the roots of the GVCs approach and its grounding in the classical economic development debate (Toner 1999; Andreoni and Chang 2017). In particular, contributions focusing on international trade, dependent development (Evans 1979; Gereffi 1984), linkages development (Hirschman 1954, 1958, 1977; Humphrey and Schmitz 2000), and microfirm and local-level research on learning and productive capabilities development (Richardson 1972; Lall 1992; Andreoni 2014). These streams of research—in particular Hirschman's contribution—offer important insights because they provide more systemic and learning-centered perspectives on industrialization, including, in some cases, an awareness of the political economy dynamics of development.

A GENERALIZED LINKAGE APPROACH TO LOCAL PRODUCTION SYSTEM DEVELOPMENT

In an article published in 1977, Hirschman reviewed the key analytical concept of "linkage"—that is, "how one thing leads to another"—introduced in his classical *Strategy of Economic Development* (1958, 98). In the 1977 contribution, he advanced a "generalized linkage approach to development, with special reference to staples." The original concept of linkage suggested that "development is accelerated through investment in projects and industries with strong forward and backward linkage effects" (Hirschman 1977, 159). Although this idea can be traced back to Quesnay's *Tableau Economique* and, later, to Leontief's input–output models and the debate on balanced and unbalanced growth animated by Rosestain-Rodan, Perroux, and Hirschman in the late 1940s and 1950s (for a review, see Toner 1999), the idea of an economy made up of linkages represented a powerful breakthrough in development thinking. Unlike the dominant macro-growth models (Harrod-Domar) and international trade theory (Samuelson), Hirschman focused on meso-level interdependencies in the production structure of a country and, specifically, how by acting on these structural interdependencies through targeted industrial policies, countries could be pushed toward different development pathways.

Hirschman defined the "linkage effect" of a given product line as "investment generating forces that are set in motion, through input–output relations, when productive facilities that supply inputs to that line or utilize its outputs are inadequate or not existent. Backward linkages lead to new investment in input-supplying facilities and forward linkages to investment in output-using facilities" (Hirschman 1977, 160). These backward and forward linkages in a country's input–output matrix are synchronic representations of structural interdependencies at a certain point in time. Changes over time are triggered by induced investments in domestic production—that is, the "production linkage effect." In considering the specific case of so-called staple economies, that is, countries that depend on resource extraction and primary industries, Hirschman introduced two additional concepts of linkages: "consumption linkage" and "fiscal linkage" (see also Andreoni 2015).

Building on Harold Innis's staple thesis, Hirschman advanced the idea of consumption linkages by focusing on the inducement mechanisms associated with staples. According to Hirschman, "the new incomes earned in the process of staple production and export may be spent originally on imports, but these imports, once grown to a sufficient volume, could eventually be substituted by domestic industries. The somewhat roundabout mechanism through which certain import-substituting industries are called into life by the staple in this manner has been aptly called consumption linkage" (1977, 161). The fact that this process is not automatic, and in fact that consumption linkages can be "outright negative rather than merely weak or non-existent" (Hirschman 1977) is also acknowledged as a distinctive feature of the first phases of export expansion in countries on the periphery. Imported goods can easily destroy existing handicraft and artisan activities and related capabilities, and in so doing, can leave the country worse off.

The concept of fiscal linkage is derived directly from a second-order effect of staples production in underdeveloped countries. Quoting Hirschman, if the state is "able to tap the income stream accruing from the staple to various parties, particularly to the owners of the mines and plantations" and if the state "levies taxes on these incomes and channels the proceeds into productive investment, it is possible to speak of fiscal linkages of the staple" (1977, 162). Like the problems associated with consumption linkages, Hirschman acknowledged how industries such as mining and petroleum tend to develop as enclaves and are controlled either by politically linked domestic private organizations or by foreign firms.

According to Hirschman, "fiscal linkage has a better chance to emerge if the enclave resource are owned by foreigners, for the same reason that an enclave is taxed more readily than an activity with a dense linkage network: taxing a foreign company comes more easily than assessing nationals who, besides owning the resources, are likely to run or 'own' the government as well" (1977, 163). This point recognized the fact that political economy forces and dynamics determine the incentives structure and the allocation of rents and rent-capture opportunities within and beyond sectoral value chains. Even if the state manages to allocate rents associated with fiscal linkages in the right direction (thus avoiding unproductive rent-seeking and capture), in many underdeveloped countries, the lack of the ability to invest productively might mean that these rents do not translate into productive investments.

Although Hirschman does not explicitly introduce a concept of technological linkages, technological interdependencies and their degree of strangeness (i.e., technology leap) are considered to be as potential factors opening up productive opportunities or slowing or closing down technology adoption, respectively. In particular, Hirschman stressed how

> some of the linkages, such as the backward and forward ones [production linkages], are directly tied to the technical conditions of production of the staple. Technological change will of course affect the number and kinds of such linkages, but they are invariant to social and political change. If attention is focused instead on, say, the fiscal linkages, the importance of the political context is immediately manifest. [However] it is after all possible to trace influences that go from the product and its technology—that is, from the "productive forces"—to a specific shape of economic development and to certain socio-political happenings, like nationalism and taxation, which define that shape. (1977, 180–81)

The expanded linkage taxonomy proposed by Hirschman suggests the need to understand production transformation from a multilinkages generalized perspective, with a focus on both the international value chain as well as—and more critically—the system of linkages in the domestic economy, that is, the LPS. More specifically, an LPS can be defined as the *structural configuration of multiple types of linkages in a given economy.*

A generalized linkage approach to LPS development must consider four key aspects: (1) the different *types of linkages*; (2) their different *hierarchical form*; (3) the different linkage effects, that is, the *inducement and constraining mechanisms* with a focus on those related to learning dynamics; (4) the relationship between political economy factors and linkage effects, that is, the way in which power distribution affect rents distribution and allocation as well as value creation dynamics.

TYPES OF LINKAGES

Building and expanding on Hirschman's taxonomy, we can distinguish four types of linkages (the political economy networks and thus power relationships are considered separately). Alongside production, consumption, and fiscal linkages (discussed above), technological linkages are another important set of interdependencies to consider in the LPS. Although input–output tables provide a good idea of the backward and forward linkages connecting different sectors in a production matrix, technological linkages capture the underlying direct and indirect transfer of technological capabilities from both within and across sectoral value chains. Technological linkages exist between firms operating at different tiers of the same sectoral value chains, say, from agriculture to agroprocessing, as well as firms operating at the same stage of the sectoral value chain, say, farmers supplying the same agroprocessors.

Technological linkages also exist between productive organizations operating across different sectoral value chains, for example, between farms and firms manufacturing production technologies and inputs such as fertilizers for agroprocessing (Andreoni 2011, 2014) or between extractive and mining equipment manufacturing (Andreoni 2015). These technological linkages are particularly important as they are the main channels through which intersectoral learning may occur. At times, technological linkages across sectoral value chains are so critical (e.g., the link between electronics components and mechanical equipment manufacturing) that even though the sectoral value chains may be separate (e.g., going from iron ore and metal/steel or going from chemical and electronics), they are, in fact, intrinsically connected by several technological linkages.

HIERARCHICAL FORM OF LINKAGES

In an LPS, different types of linkages may involve vertical linkages and horizontal linkages. Vertical linkages are those linking players hierarchically to each other along sectoral value chains (i.e., system integrator, multitier suppliers). Horizontal linkages are those connecting players operating at the same stage of the sectoral value chain or across different sectors in the LPS. Although the GVC literature emphasizes the governance and power relationships along the chain, from an LPS perspective, multiple horizontal linkages are determined, for example, by production relationships (i.e., intermediate and final goods demand and supply) and by technological linkages. Given the different length of the sectoral value chains as well as the overall production matrix in a certain country, we might have a dominance of either vertical or horizontal linkages.

Typically, staple economies or countries that have experienced upstream GVC integration are characterized by enclaves in which vertical linkages are dominant and by a limited number of players and sectors in which horizontal linkages are constrained. Industrialization opens up these enclaves by shifting the balance between vertical and horizontal linkages in favor of the latter. Industrialization changes the structural configuration of the LPS and is accompanied by local value creation and distribution. GVC-led industrialization has often left the structural configuration of the LPS unchanged, which affects the potential for domestic value addition and diversification.

Building on these first two considerations, figure 9.6 provides a stylized representation of an LPS that includes multiple types of linkages and involves players related by both horizontal and vertical linkages.

LINKAGE EFFECTS: INDUCEMENT AND CONSTRAINING MECHANISMS

The structural configuration of linkages—what we call LPS—is critical to understanding production transformation and how to achieve quality of growth. Alongside incentives and political economy forces, linkages

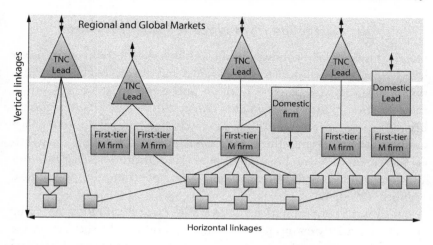

Figure 9.6   An analytical map of the local production system

Source: Author's creation.

and their country-specific structural configuration are responsible for a number of inducement and constraint mechanisms. A number of linkage effects noted by Hirschman have been discussed, including production, consumption, and fiscal linkages and their impact on investments (see the previous section).

As for technological linkages, at the micro (firms) and meso (sectoral value chain) levels, learning dynamics are structurally triggered by similarities, complementarities, and bottlenecks in production—that is, structural learning (Rosenberg 1969; Andreoni 2014, 2018; Andreoni et al. 2017). Not only technological linkages but also production and consumption linkages can induce learning and diversification dynamics, improvements in process efficiency, and scaling-up as well as improve product quality, standards, and functionalities. At the same time, the lack of these linkages—production and consumption, in particular— might make scale-efficient investment impossible and may result in production-related interlocking bottlenecks within and across value chains. For example, investment bottlenecks upstream might make it unprofitable to invest downstream in the sectoral value chain, whereas the lack of technological linkages might undermine technological upgrades in sectors that rely on manufacturing production technologies (e.g., agriculture and mining).

POLITICAL ECONOMY OF PRODUCTION TRANSFORMATION

Despite historical and context specificities, linkage effects are intrinsically intertwined with political economy forces and dynamics. The distribution of organizational power in both the public and private sectors—thus, the countries' "political settlement" (Khan 2010)—and the relationship between these powerful organizations (including elites and intermediate groups) affect rents and value-creation dynamics. Kahn defines the political settlement as "a combination of power and institutions that is mutually compatible and also sustainable in terms of economic and political viability" (2010, 4).

The reasons political settlement determines rent distribution and value creation are strictly connected. The allocation of rents by the state in the form of distribution of subsidies, licenses, and other forms of political income affects the extent to which productive organizations can respond (or not) to the inducement mechanisms arising from an LPS in transformation. Moreover, in setting up the institutional boundaries of the market through regulations, incentives, and rent allocation, the state will respond to multiple internal and external conflicting claims from different powerful organizations. With specific reference to sectoral value chains, these political economy forces and dynamics will result in rent chains, that is, opportunities for rentieristic behavior and value extraction in the LPS. For example, the concentration of power in upstream value chains as well as among traders by way of domestic manufacturers can hamper productive transformation in the LPS.

With changes in the political settlement, political economy forces and dynamics can also turn constraints into opportunities for productive investments. So, for example, the reduction in rent chains might reduce industrial and agricultural raw material costs, say, metals and sugar, and open the space to scale up downstream manufacturer producers of machine tools or agroprocessors in confectionary industries. Figure 9.7 stylizes the resulting changes in the LPS, in particular, the intensification of horizontal linkages. The reduction in rent capture might allow some firms to capture opportunities for diversification across sectoral value chains, too, for example, from production of metal pipes to plastic tubes and pipes. Industrial policies are thus critical in changing the political economy of production and unlocking the productive opportunities in the LPS in African countries (Mkandawire 2001; Andreoni and Chang 2019).

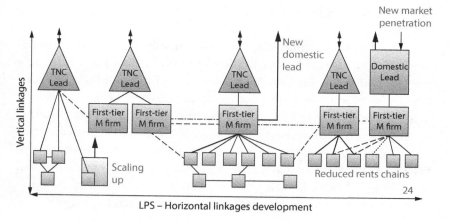

Figure 9.7   Linkage effects and political economy of production

Note: Production linkages are represented by continuous lines, technological linkages by dotted lines.

Source: Author's creation.

THE LPS IN AFRICA: STYLIZED FACTS

If we look at African countries through the lenses of the generalized linkages approach to LPS, a number of stylized facts emerge clearly.

First, with respect to production and consumption linkages, all countries, including the two major economies, Nigeria and South Africa, have been deindustrializing and are overdependent on imported final and intermediate goods, including agricultural and industrial raw materials. The importation of final and intermediate goods (in some cases, also available in the country) is driven by an incentive structure favoring traders as well as by a negative perception of domestically produced goods among consumers. Import dependence problems are exacerbated by the vast unrecorded trade that occurs within the continent and internationally, with smuggling and customs manipulation activities being fundamental threats to LPS development and the price competitiveness of its firms.

Second, limited improvements in agricultural productivity make downstream activities unfeasible or extremely uncompetitive given low quality standards and unreliable supply. The limited development of irrigation systems and low-quality seeds and fertilizers have affected production levels in countries with immense agricultural potential, like Tanzania, and have constrained the development of agroindustries (Andreoni 2017).

Third, LPSs are characterized by a structurally disarticulated configuration of linkages. The distribution of firms in the LPS is extremely skewed, with a few big players and myriads of micro- and small-scale companies producing mainly for the local market. The existence of so many micro-firms has been misinterpreted. In countries like Uganda, for example, where levels of youth unemployment are threatening the social sustainability of the current regime, the presence of many microenterprises has been read as a sign of great and diffused entrepreneurial capabilities, whereas, in fact, it is the manifestation of survival entrepreneurship and the lack of alternatives and occupational opportunities in industries.

Fourth, and connected to the third point, the lack of midsize companies is another key problematic feature—the so-called missing middle. This issue is particularly critical because midsize firms are in a better position to connect small-scale and large-scale firms, thus making the LPS more articulated and integrated. The missing-middle phenomenon has a direct impact on value creation and distribution. For example, as extensively documented by Andreoni (2017a, 2017b), in the case of Tanzania, 80 percent of manufacturing value addition is generated by two hundred establishments employing at least one hundred employees. If we look at manufacturing value added in export, the same group of companies contributes 87 percent of the total value exported (figures 9.8 and 9.9).

Fifth, firms' technological capabilities and linkages are limited, particularly given the chronic lack of investments in technology absorption, manufacturing extension services, engineering skills, and vocational training (Andreoni, 2018b). Many companies rely on the very old generation of domestic engineers, and they import specialized technicians from India and other major players in Southeast Asia. The upgrading of many vocational training institutions and polytechnics in universities has followed a detrimental tendency to produce non-STEM (science, technology, engineering, and math) graduates, leading to a workforce made of many generals aspiring to be managers (often with no relevant competencies) and a thin army of technicians. With some notable exceptions (e.g., see Ethiopia's industrial research center for leather), public technology intermediaries and extension services are largely underfunded and often have been replaced by ineffective incubators and other initiatives disconnected from potential production activities in the LPS. As a result, productivity

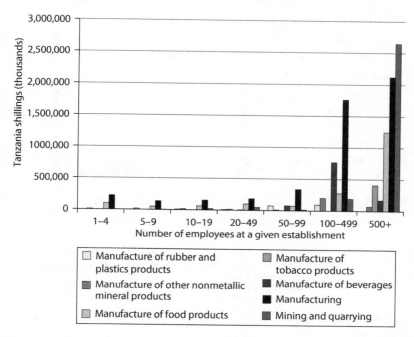

Figure 9.8   Manufacturing value added performances in Tanzania by establishment types and sectors, 2013

Source: Andreoni, 2017b.

has stagnated across the majority of sectors, undercapacity utilization is common, and process and quality standards are often not met.

Sixth, as for fiscal linkages, given the political settlement and the limited enforcement capabilities of the state, tax, royalties, and duty collections are limited. This means that the state has no resources to allocate for productive investments. Underreporting of extracted value and transfer pricing in the mining sectoral value chain, tax elusion in the tourism industry, and the overall dominance of the informal economy are critical dynamics diverting potential resources for LPS development.

Seventh, given the lack of industrial competitiveness, firms tend to rely on political connections to extract rents from the economy. This lack of competitiveness mixed with rent seeking in the private sector delineates a complex configuration of interests and power dynamics. Although conflicts between the traders (better to say importers) and local producers are widespread, it is often unclear who is who. Indeed, quite often,

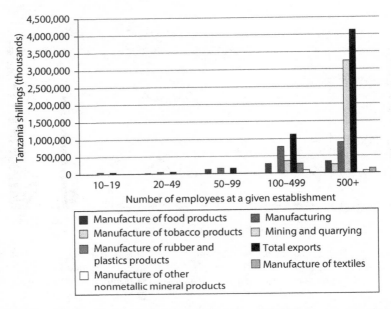

Figure 9.9   Export performances in Tanzania by establishment types and sectors, 2013

Source: Andreoni, 2017b.

the same powerful person is at the same time a trader and a producer, a businessman and a politician, and someone with domestic and foreign vested interests. This makes unpacking these conflicts and allocating rents through industrial policy particularly challenging.

Industrialization challenges and opportunities are structurally determined in a certain LPS and in the overall political economy of the country, in particular, in its political settlement. The last section sketches an industrial policy agenda to support LPS development in Africa.

IMPLICATIONS FOR INDUSTRIAL POLICY FOR AFRICA

The GVC-led industrialization model has gained significant support over the past few years, especially with reference to Africa. We have shown how GVC-integration has delivered, at best, limited quality of growth in Africa to date. We also proposed a critical appraisal of the theory behind this industrialization model and discussed some of its current shortcomings. Although GVC and regional value chains might offer some opportunities, it is the ways in which countries make strategic use of these GVCs that matter.

Therefore, in light of a more strategic and ultimately beneficial GVC integration in Africa, we proposed a move from a GVC-led industrialization model to a generalized linkage approach to LPS development. This approach stands on two fundamental ideas. First, the incremental and cumulative process of increasing value addition and linkage development in the LPS, coupled with strategic integration into regional and global value chains, can deliver the necessary quality of growth. Second, the LPS will never develop without shifting incentives from importers and rentiers to productive organizations, while also disciplining rents allocation and reducing rent chains and power concentration.

We have shown how this approach will allow us to get closer to the factual micro and institutional dynamics constraining industrialization in Africa, while pointing toward areas and opportunities for change through industrial policy. The effectiveness of industrial policy in Africa critically depends on targeting critical nodes and bottlenecks, organizations, and linkages in the LPS. First, this effort includes supporting midsize enterprises to make them cornerstone of LPS linkages development and supporting small enterprises to help them reach scale efficiency. Second, but related, increasing productivity not only is a function of investments and scale but also depends on how these scale-expanding investments are managed. Targeting organizational capabilities development to make more effective use of resources is a critical crosscutting area for intervention. Third, to trigger collective learning and technological linkages in the LPS, public technology intermediaries should be restructured and integrated with effective manufacturing and agriculture extension services. Fourth, the development of horizontal linkages across sectoral value chains in the LPS requires both reducing costs upstream and expanding market access downstream. Without productivity and surplus production in agriculture and other upstream primary industries, manufacturing development cannot pick up and, in turn, it cannot contribute to the transformation of the primary upstream sectors. To trigger a positive circular and cumulative causation dynamics across these sectors, strategic integration in regional value-chain and trade policies supporting trade complementarities are also critical. Finally, given the natural wealth in Africa, fiscal linkages should be targeted and linked to specific beneficiation activities in view of developing downstream industries.

Providing a detailed account of each of these policy areas goes far beyond the scope of this chapter, and would not be effective without considering country-specific aspects. Along the lines proposed by Hirschman, "the system laid out here makes it possible to translate technical information into a language that points directly toward development possibilities" (1977, 177). The generalized approach to LPS development identifies structurally feasible opportunities for production transformation and technological change, which would result in the necessary quality of growth. The structural feasibility of any policy intervention is the first benchmark against which policy proposals should be assessed. As suggested by the political settlement framework, political feasibility is the second test against which any industrial policy proposal should be considered. Thus, rather than simply look for unsustainable shortcuts, which might postpone production transformation and frustrate the current generations prospects across the continent, a new industrial policy for countries in Africa aiming at quality of growth should engage with the industrialization process—that is, the development of a LPS.

NOTES

1. An attempt in the same direction but with a focus on how actors in local clusters are linked to GVCs through manufacturing and innovation can be found in the recent volume by Valentina De Marchi, Eleonora Di Maria, and Gary Gereffi, *Local Clusters in Global Value Chains* (London: Routledge 2018).

2. For a recent discussion on the need to look at different forms of power in GVCs, see Mark Dallas, Stefano Ponte, and Timothy Sturgeon, "A Typology of Power in Global Value Chains" (Working Paper in Business and Politics No. 92, Copenhagen Business School, 2017).

REFERENCES

Amsden, Alice 1989. *Asia's Next Giant*. New York: Oxford University Press.
———. 1985. "The Division of Labour Is Limited by the Rate of Growth of the Market." Cambridge Journal of Economics 9 (3): 271–284.
Andreoni, Antonio. 2011. "Manufacturing Agrarian Change." *DRUID Working Paper Series* 11 (13): 1–36.
———. 2014. "Structural Learning: Embedding Discoveries and the Dynamics of Production." *Structural Change and Economic Dynamics* 29 (June): 58–74.
———. 2015. "On Manufacturing Development Under Resources Constraints." In *Resources, Production and Structural Dynamics*, ed. Mauro Baranzini, Claudia Rotondi, and Roberto Scazzieri, 407–423. Cambridge: Cambridge University Press.

———. 2016. "Varieties of Industrial Policy: Models, Packages and Transformation Cycles." In *Efficiency, Finance and Varieties of Industrial Policy*, ed. Akbar Noman and Joseph Stiglitz, 245–305. New York: Columbia University Press.

———. 2017. "Anti-Corruption in Tanzania: A Political Settlement Analysis." Working Paper 001: 1–58. ACE Research Consortium.

———. 2017b. "Mapping Industrial Production in Tanzania." Working Paper WP12: 1–75. United Nations Inclusive and Sustainable Industrial Development, New York.

———. 2018. "The Architecture and Dynamics of Industrial Ecosystems. Diversification and Innovative Industrial Renewal in the Emilia Romagna Region." *Cambridge Journal of Economics* 42 (6): 1613–1642.

———. 2018b. "Skilling Tanzania: Improving Financing, Governance and Outputs of the Skills Development Sector." Working Paper 6: 1–54. ACE Research Consortium.

Andreoni, Antonio, and Ha-Joon Chang. 2017. "Bringing Production and Employment Back into Development." *Cambridge Journal of Regions, Economy and Society* 10 (1): 173–187.

———. 2019. "The Political Economy of Industrial Policy: Structural Interdependencies, Policy Alignment and Conflict Management." *Structural Change and Economic Dynamics* 48 (March): 136–150, https://doi.org/10.1016/j.strueco.2018.10.007.

Andreoni Antonio, Ha-Joon Chang, and Isabella Estevez. 2019. "New Global Rules, Policy Space, and Quality of Growth in Africa." Chap. 4 in *The Quality of Growth in Africa*, ed. Ravi Kanbur, Akbar Noman, and Joseph E. Stiglitz (this volume). New York: Columbia University Press.

Andreoni, Antonio, Federico Frattini, and Giorgio Prodi. 2017. "Structural Cycles and Industrial Policy Alignment: The Private-Public Nexus in the Emilian Packaging Valley." *Cambridge Journal of Economics* 41 (3): 881–904.

Andreoni Antonio and Fiona Tregenna. 2018. "Stuck in the Middle: Premature Deindustrialization and Industrial Policy." University of Johannesburg CCRED Working Paper 4: 1–30.

Behuria Pritish, Lars Buur, and Hazel Gray. "Studying Political Settlements in Africa." *African Affairs* 116 (464): 508–525.

Bernhardt, Thomas, and Ruth Pollack. 2016. "Economic and Social Upgrading Dynamics in Global Manufacturing Value Chains." *Environment and Planning A: Economy and Space* 48 (7): 1220–1243.

Best, Michael. 2018. *How Growth Really Happens*. Princeton, NJ: Princeton University Press.

Chang, Ha-Joon. 1993. *The Political Economy of Industrial Policy*. Basingstoke: Palgrave Macmillan.

———. 2010. "Industrial Policy: Can We Go Beyond an Unproductive Debate?" In *Lessons from East Asia and the Global Financial Crisis*, ed. J. Y. Lin and B. Pleskovic. Annual World Bank Conference on Development Economics, Seoul.

Cramer, Chris, and Ha-Joon Chang. 2015. "Tigers or Tiger Prawns? The African "Growth" Tragedy and "Renaissance" in Perspective." In *The Oxford Handbook of Africa and Economics: Volume 1*, ed. Celestine Monga and Justin Yifu Lin. Oxford: Oxford University Press.

Cramer, Chris, and John Sander. 2015. "Agro-Processing, Wage Employment and Export Revenue: Opportunities for Strategic Intervention." Working Paper for the Department of Trade and Industrial Policy Strategies, Johannesburg, South Africa.

Dahmen, Erik. 1989. "Development Blocks in Industrial Economics." In *Development Blocks and Industrial Transformation*, ed. B. Carlsoon and R. Henriksson. Stockholm: The Industrial Institute for Economic and Social Research.

Dallas, Mark, Stefano Ponte, and Timothy Sturgeon. 2017. "A Typology of Power in Global Value Chains." Working Paper in Business and Politics No. 92. Copenhagen Business School.

De Marchi, Valentina, Eleonora Di Maria, and Gary Gereffi. 2018. *Local Clusters in Global Value Chains*. London: Routledge.

Evans, Peter. 1979. *Dependent Development. The Alliance of Multinational, State and Local Capital in Brazil*. Princeton, NJ: Princeton University Press.

Farole, Thomas, and Winkler, Deborah. 2014. *Making Foreign Direct Investment Work for Sub-Saharan Africa*. Washington, DC: World Bank.

Foster-McGregor, Neil, Florian Kaulich, and Robert Stehrer. 2015. "Global Value Chains in Africa." UNU-MERIT Working Paper 2015-024: 1–94. United Nations University–Maastricht Economic and Social Research Institute on Innovation and Technology.

Gereffi, Gary. 1984. "Power and Dependency in an Interdependent World: A Guide to Understanding the Contemporary Global Crisis." *International Journal of Comparative Sociology* 25 (1–2): 91–113.

——. 2014. "Global Value Chains in a Post–Washington Consensus World." *Review of International Political Economy* 21 (1): 9–37.

Gereffi, Gary, and Joonkoo Lee. 2016. "Economic and Social Upgrading in Global Value Chains and Industrial Clusters: Why Governance Matters." *Journal of Business Ethics* 133 (1): 25–38.

Goger, Annelies, Andy Hull, Stephanie Barrientos, Gary Gereffi, and Shane Godfrey. 2014. "Capturing the Gains in Africa: Making the Most of Global Value Chain Participation." Center on Globalization, Governance, and Competitiveness at the Social Science Research Institute, Duke University, Durham, NC.

Hirschman, Albert. 1954. "Economics and Investment Planning: Reflections Based on Experience in Colombia." In *A Bias for Hope*. New Haven, CT: Yale University Press.

——. 1958. *Strategy of Economic Development*. New Haven, CT: Yale University Press.

——. 1977. "A Generalised Linkage Approach to Development, with Special Reference to Staples." *Economic Development and Cultural Change* 25(Suppl.): 67–98.

Humphrey, John, and Hubert Schmitz. 2000. "Governance and Upgrading: Linking Industrial Cluster and Global Value Chain Research." Working Paper 120. Institute of Development Studies, Brighton, UK.

Kaldor, N. 1960. *Essays on Value and Distribution*. London: Duckworth.

Kaplinsky, Raphael, and Mike Morris. 2015. "Thinning and Thickening: Productive Sector Policies in the Era of Global Value Chains." *European Journal of Development Research* 28 (4): 1–21.

Khan, Mushtaq H. 2018. "Political Settlements and the Analysis of Institutions." *African Affairs* 117 (469): 636–655.

——. 2010. *Political Settlements and the Governance of Growth-Enhancing Institutions.* Mimeo. SOAS University of London.

Khan, Mushtaq H., Antonio Andreoni, and Pallavi Roy. 2016. "Anti-Corruption Evidence: A Strategic Approach." Mimeo. SOAS University of London.

Lall, Sanjaya. 1992. "Technological Capabilities and Industrialization." *World Development.* 20 (2): 165–186.

Lee, Keun. 2013. *Schumpeterian Analysis of Economic Catch-up.* Cambridge: Cambridge University Press.

Lee, Keun, Marina Szapiro, and Zhuqing Mao. 2017. "From Global Value Chains (GVC) to Innovation Systems for Local Value Chains and Knowledge Creation." *European Journal of Development Research* 30 (3): 424–441.

Milberg, William, and Deborah Winkler. 2013. *Outsourcing Economics.* Cambridge: Cambridge University Press.

Makhaya, Gertrude, and Simon Roberts. 2013. "Expectations and Outcomes: Considering Competition and Corporate Power in South Africa Under Democracy." *Review of African Political Economy* 40 (138): 556–571.

Mkandawire, Thandika. 2001. "Thinking About Developmental States in Africa." *Cambridge Journal of Economics* 25 (3): 289–313.

Neilson, Jeffrey, Bill Pritchard, and Henry Wai-chung Yeung. 2014. "Global Value Chains and Global Production Networks in the Changing International Political Economy: An Introduction." *Review of International Political Economy* 21 (1): 1–8.

Nolan, Peter. 2001. *China and the Global Economy.* New York: Palgrave.

Nolan, Peter, Chunhang Liu, and Jin Zhang. 2007. *Global Business Revolution and the Cascade Effect.* Basingstoke: Palgrave Macmillan.

Penrose, Edith. 1959. *The Theory of the Growth of the Firm.* Oxford: Oxford University Press.

Richardson, George. 1972. "The Organisation of Industry." *Economic Journal* 82 (327): 883–896.

Rosenberg, Nathan. 1969. "The Direction of Technological Change: Inducement Mechanisms and Focusing Devices." *Economic Development and Cultural Change* 18 (1): 1–24.

Toner, Philip. 1999. *Main Currents in Cumulative Causation Theory.* Basingstoke: Palgrave Macmillan.

United Nations Comtrade Database. Eora GVC Data. https://comtrade.un.org/.

United Nations Conference on Trade and Development (UNCTAD). 2017. *Beyond austerity. Towards a global new deal.* Trade and Development Report. Geneva: UNCTAD.

United Nations Conference on Trade and Development. FMI/MNE Database. www .unctad.org/fdistatistics.

United Nations Industrial Development Organization (UNIDO). 2017. *East African Community Industrial Competitiveness Report 2017.* Arusha, Tanzania: UNIDO.

Wade, Robert. 1990. *Governing the Market.* Princeton, NJ: Princeton University Press.

Whitfiled, Lindsay, Ole Therkildsen, Lars Burr, and Anne Mett. 2015. *The Politics of Industrial Policy in Africa*. Cambridge: Cambridge University Press.

Williamson, Oliver. 1985. *The Economic Institutions of Capitalism*. New York: Free Press.

World Bank. 2017. *World Development Indicators*. Washington, DC: World Bank.

World Trade Organization, Organisation for Economic Co-operation and Development, and World Bank. 2017. "Measuring and Analyzing the Impact of GVCs on Economic Development." Global Value Chain Development Report. International Bank for Reconstruction and Development, Washington, DC.

CHAPTER 10

(Re)Shaping Markets for Inclusive Economic Activity

COMPETITION AND INDUSTRIAL POLICIES RELATING TO FOOD
PRODUCTION IN SOUTHERN AFRICA

Simon Roberts

MARKETS AND CHANGES IN FOOD PRODUCTION IN SOUTHERN AFRICA

The workings of markets depend on who are the participants and the extent of their power. In other words, the nature and extent of competitive rivalry is central to market outcomes. This needs to be understood in dynamic terms, including whether competition relates to improving capabilities and allows opportunities for new local participants, or whether incumbents are able to evolve strategies to entrench their historical positions. A key challenge in economic development is to *generate* competition and competitors. This relates to a wider set of concerns about how markets are constructed and governed, in essence, what the rules are and how they are determined. Markets are shaped by regulations, previous industrial policies, and the dominant firms.

This chapter considers the shaping of markets and competition concerns through the example of food production in southern Africa. Food and agroprocessing, more broadly, also have been identified as critical for broader-based African industrialization (African Centre for Economic Transformation [ACET] 2017; Jayne, Chamberlin, and Benfica 2018). Agroprocessing is a substantial sector in manufacturing, and it brings together services in logistics, distribution, and retail, along with primary agricultural production. Developing the sector requires building linked industrial capabilities along with services and efficient testing and certification.

Rapid urbanization is leading to changes in consumption patterns across African countries to more processed and packaged foods (United Nations Economic Commission for Africa 2017). The growing demand from urban food markets means that these markets account for up to 70 percent of the food supply, even in countries with large rural populations. The value of urban food markets in Sub-Saharan African (SSA) is projected to treble from 2010 to 2030 (Food and Agriculture Organisation [FAO] 2018). This in turn is associated with changes in the ways in which food products are sold, with a rapid spread of supermarkets across the continent taking place. Meeting growing demand for food in African cities is one of the most critical industrial development challenges facing African countries. Imports of food have supported urbanization in the absence of a domestic agricultural surplus; however, food in African cities has been found to be around 35 percent more expensive than in comparator countries (Nakamura et al. 2016).

The fact that Africa is a net food importer and has low yields and poor agricultural productivity, while generally having good conditions for agricultural production, has been widely observed (ACET 2017; Suttie and Benfica 2016). A turning point in some countries, however, is apparent from 2005, with some improvements in agricultural productivity (Jayne and Ameyaw 2016). An important factor in low agricultural yields is the extremely low fertilizer usage. The supply and pricing of fertilizer is assessed below in the section on this product.

Although improved levels of agricultural production may be attained, there will be a rapidly growing trade deficit in Africa in processed food products without a substantially improved performance in the manufacturing of the food products (Jayne and Ameyaw 2016). Southern African Development Community (SADC) countries collectively recorded persistent trade deficits in many categories of processed food products from 2011 to 2016 (figure 10.1).

Given South Africa's more advanced industrial base as well as the spread of supermarkets, the changes in demand in southern Africa have further changed trade flows within the region, as South Africa's exports of food products to other SADC countries increased strongly from 2007 (Arndt and Roberts 2018).

There have been extensive policy reforms across African countries. Markets and international trade have been liberalized, although sensitive crops, such as maize, are still protected in many countries. Rapid integration into the global economy has included the expansion of major multinational traders, such as Cargill, Louis Dreyfus, and Bunge, across southern Africa, as well as ETG, which originated in Kenya. Cargill and Louis Dreyfus handle 70 percent of all the maize trading in South Africa

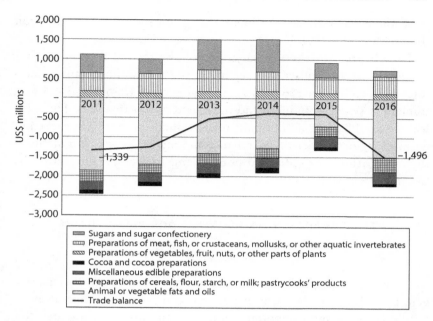

Figure 10.1   Southern African Development Community trade balance in processed food

Source: Adapted from data sourced in 2017 from ITC Trademap.

(Greenberg 2017). In South Africa, the two largest agroconglomerate groups, Afgri and Senwes, both of which evolved out of the former cooperatives supported under Apartheid, have been bought by or joint-ventured with international finance and trading companies (Makhaya and Roberts 2013). Afgri has been bought by Agrigroupe (with ownership in Mauritius and the Cayman Islands and a controlling shareholder based in Canada). Bunge and Senwes formed a joint venture in 2012. Louis Dreyfus is a joint shareholder in an operation of a smaller company, NWK.

To understand the issues raised, this chapter draws on a range of research on regional value chains and markets in southern Africa undertaken in recent years covering inputs, food processing, and retail.[1] A number of competition cases, especially in South Africa, also shed light on issues of market power and corporate conduct across southern Africa. The findings reflect a need to change the rules if markets are to support wider participation and long-term investment and hope to realize a different quality of growth. The need to make changes is even more critical given the evident effects of climate change on agricultural production (Brahmbhatt et al. 2016).

The chapter is structured as follows. The second section assesses developments in fertilizer, as a key input; sugar, as an important agricultural crop; animal feed to poultry, as a value chain from maize and soya through to poultry products; and the spread of supermarkets. The third section considers the implications for how markets have been shaped in terms of regional linkages, governance and market power, and discusses the implications for industrial policies and the role of the state. The fourth section concludes.

DEVELOPMENTS IN MAJOR INPUTS AND VALUE CHAINS

FERTILIZER[2]

There are three key plant nutrients provided by chemical fertilizers: nitrogen, potassium (in the form of potash), and phosphate. Nitrogenous fertilizers are the most important with the main product being urea, followed by ammonium nitrate–based fertilizers. Their production requires large, energy-intensive industrial plants, and these fertilizers normally are manufactured near sources of cheap natural gas. Phosphate and potash are mineral products with production depending on a country's natural resource endowment.

SSA countries rely on imports to meet local demand, even in the case of South Africa, which locally produces both ammonium nitrate and phosphate fertilizers.[3] Although sourcing fertilizer should be relatively easy, in practice, it appears that outcomes have been far from competitive. The scale required for economic shipping and the logistics and transport infrastructure for local distribution mean that, as a matter of fact, each country has only a few major suppliers. The prices of fertilizer in African countries have been significantly above benchmark world prices (see also World Bank 2016). Fertilizer prices directly affect its use by farmers and hence impact on food production (ACET 2017).

An assessment for Malawi, Tanzania, and Zambia reflects fertilizer prices that have become marked up over international prices by an even higher margin from 2012. Figure 10.2 compares the free-on-board (FOB) price of urea in the Arabian Gulf[4] with the average retail prices of urea sold to farmers across Malawi, Tanzania, and Zambia.[5] The direct costs of sea and land transport did not increase in this period. In 2012 through

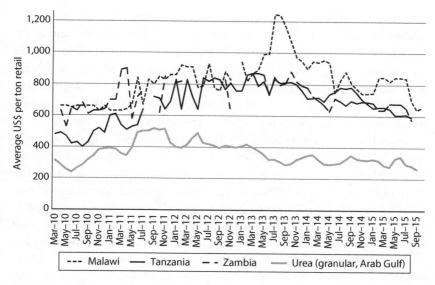

Figure 10.2   Urea prices across countries

Note: Prices in Malawi, Tanzania, and Zambia are average prices reported monthly to AMITSA by agrodealers.

Source: Adapted from data sourced from AMITSA in 2016.

to 2014, fertilizer retail prices in all three countries were around US$400 per ton higher than the FOB prices and, in the case of Malawi, for some of the time, prices were substantially higher.

The high prices of fertilizer are due to a number of international and local factors. First, it appears international prices were increased by collusion. Price increases from 2008 onward in all three main fertilizers were greater than explained by costs and, according to economic analysis were likely the result of collusion in nitrogenous fertilizers (Taylor and Moss 2013; Gnutzmann and Spiewanowski 2016). Higher levels of concentration have been found to be associated with higher prices for urea (Hernandez and Torero 2013). There are also government sanctioned export cartels in potash and phosphates (World Bank 2016). In potash, Canpotex is the marketing organization for the three largest North American potash producers, and BPC is a joint venture of the three largest Russian and Belarusian potash producers. Between them, Canada and Russia account for 80 percent of the global potash reserves. For the period from 2008 to 2012, price mark-ups from the collusion in potash have been estimated at around 50 percent to 63 percent (Jenny 2012; Gnutzmann and Spiewanowski 2016). In phosphates, PhosChem is a U.S. Webb-Pomerene export cartel whose members include PotashCorp and Mosaic, which are also members of Canpotex (World Bank 2016). The other major source of phosphate fertilizer is OCP of Morocco, which is a government-owned monopoly over phosphate mining in that country.

Second, suppliers have formed national and regional collusive arrangements (Vilakazi and Roberts 2018). These include arrangements in South Africa, likely extending to neighboring countries, which ran until the mid-2000s. Market participants used various arrangements to coordinate the sharing of information and implement collusive agreements, including a Nitrogen Balance Committee, Import Planning Committee, and Export Club (das Nair and Mncube 2012). An agreement on how list prices would be determined used agreed-on costs added to the international benchmark prices to get local prices in different regions. Cartel conduct was separately uncovered in Zambia in 2012 by the Competition and Consumer Protection Commission (CCPC 2013).

After the cartel enforcement in Zambia and alongside a new entrant, prices fell in Zambia relative to its neighbors in 2014 and 2015, such that Zambia, as a landlocked country, recorded prices in line with Tanzania (figure 10.2). Observed prices in Tanzania in 2013 and 2014 were some 20 percent higher than the prices calculated from cost and margin build-ups (including actual transport costs and reported trading margins), and in Malawi, by an even higher percentage (Ncube, Roberts, and Vilakazi 2016, tables 5.3 and 5.4).

Third, a combination of restrictions on transport, storage, and trading have supported incumbents and underpinned the higher prices in Malawi and Tanzania. A few large firms dominate bulk fertilizer supply in these countries, led by Yara. In this regard, Yara has been at the forefront of initiatives at the ports of Beira and Dar es Salaam (see also Vilakazi and Roberts 2018). In addition, when a smaller rival, Greenbelt, established a blending facility in Beira and became a major supplier in Mozambique, Malawi, and Zambia, Yara acquired it in 2016, removing a maverick regional competitor.[6] In addition, the fertilizer subsidy program in Malawi provided an effective floor price above the competitive price level.

The uncompetitive markets therefore are the result of a combination of factors. Although anticompetitive conduct is part of the picture, it is unclear how effective the enforcement by national authorities can be against regional and international arrangements. Identifying cartels of multinational suppliers is extremely difficult if not impossible for national authorities. The available margins and rents to be earned also mean that businesses have a strong incentive to lobby for rules and regulations that bolster their position and keep out rivals.

SUGAR AND CONFECTIONARY[7]

The sugar industry in SADC is highly concentrated with two multinationals, Illovo and Tongaat-Hulett, accounting for the majority of production. Illovo, controlled since 2006 by Associated British Foods, has its origins in Tate & Lyle. It has sugar mills in Malawi, Mozambique, South Africa, Swaziland, Tanzania, and Zambia. In 1996, it acquired Lonrho's sugar interests in South Africa, Mauritius, Swaziland, and Malawi and, in 1998, it acquired Kilombero Sugar in Tanzania (Chisanga et al. 2016). In 2013, it accounted for close to 100 percent of production in Malawi and Zambia and for between 30 percent and 40 percent in South Africa, Swaziland, and Tanzania. The second-largest producer, Tongaat Hulett is historically part of the Anglo-American group and has sugar mills in Mozambique, South Africa, Swaziland, and Zimbabwe. The third South African producer, TSB, is part of the Remgro group and also has operations in Mozambique.

The history of the sugar industry illustrates the intertwining of British and South African big business, from the colonial era onward. The main producers bring together Tate & Lyle, Lonrho, Anglo-American, and Remgro. Anglo and Remgro are historically the two largest South African family-controlled conglomerates (respectively, the Oppenheimer and Rupert families; see Chabane et al. 2006).

Countries such as Zambia and Malawi have excellent conditions for growing sugar and are among the lowest-cost producers in the world. This is reflected in a net trade surplus for SADC (das Nair et al. 2017). The prices charged in the domestic markets of many sugar-producing countries, however, are extremely high by international comparison, as also reflected in the margins of the leading producers in countries such as Zambia and Malawi (Chisanga et al. 2016). At the same time, the region has a net trade deficit in sugar confectionary and baked goods (in which sugar is an important input; das Nair et al. 2017).

Zambia and Malawi therefore have a single dominant firm, which effectively has unilateral pricing power. In addition, mergers have yielded greater regional concentration, such as through the acquisition of

Lonrho's interests in Malawi by Illovo. This means that the closest major rival across a border may be a related entity, which would not engage in head-to-head competition. Concerns also have been raised about tax avoidance (Lewis 2013).

The market power of producers over domestic markets is reinforced by regulation of international trade. For example, Zambia has required vitamin A fortification of household sugar, which effectively blocks imports from neighboring countries that do not have such a provision. In addition, importers, including of sugar for industrial use in food product manufacturing, require a license (Chisanga et al. 2016).

The SADC Sugar Cooperation Agreement is meant to facilitate trade within the region and to encourage development of the industry. The agreement provides for partial access to the Southern Africa Customs Union (SACU), which includes Botswana, Lesotho, Namibia, South Africa, and Swaziland, market for SADC surplus sugar producers in the form of import quotas. This process is managed by the Technical Committee on Sugar (TCS), which is made up of government and industry representatives. The sugar producers meet in their own forum, the Sugar Producers Consultative Forum, before the TCS (das Nair et al. 2017). Tanzania and Mozambique also have industry arrangements that are managed by business together with the government.

SACU has a system of regulation governing pricing and trade, with provisions under the Sugar Act of South Africa (das Nair et al. 2017). Under this system the South African Sugar Association has allocated each mill a quota for both the local and export markets and for managed exports through a special export corporation (das Nair et al. 2017). This has supported local prices above export prices, although prices in SACU have not been as high as in countries in which a quasi-monopoly producer has been able to exert its market power without oversight.

Although the high local sugar prices support cane farmers and profits of the millers, they undermine downstream manufacturers of food products, such as confectionary and baked goods. Some food-processing firms have relocated production from Zambia to South Africa, at least in part, because of the sugar price (das Nair et al. 2017).

POULTRY AND ANIMAL FEED

The animal feed to poultry value chain highlights the critical challenges that need to be met for local industrialization to satisfy the demand from growing urban populations, for whom poultry is the main source of protein. The competitiveness of the overall value chain depends on the pricing and supply of the feed components (of maize and soy, which depend in part on fertilizer), through the efficient production of poultry in breeding, broiler production, processing, and distribution arrangements. Linked investments at each level and overall coordination are essential (Ncube 2018).

Although almost all countries in southern African remain net importers, poultry production across the region has increased substantially (Bagopi et al. 2016). The growth in the poultry sector has been especially rapid in countries such as Zambia that have the potential to substantially expand production of maize and soy. This can lower the cost base of the region as a whole with the appropriate enabling framework and linked investments at different levels of production. Indeed, Zambia moved to being a net exporter in 2013–14, mainly to the Democratic Republic of Congo, Zimbabwe, and Malawi and, in 2017, Zambia exported animal feed and soy to South Africa (Paremoer 2018).

Animal feed and poultry production in the region is dominated by large vertically integrated firms, which hold the rights to breeding stock, typically on an exclusive basis, from European and North American multinational corporations (Ncube 2018). The regional producers are associated with three main companies, Rainbow (RCL Foods), Astral, and Country Bird Holdings. Their operations cover the two main inputs to poultry meat production—that is, feed and breeding stock which make up 58 percent and 13 percent, respectively, of the cost of a processed chicken.[8] Breeding operations produce parent stock and supply the day-old chicks for broiler production. Feed requires processing facilities, such as those for crushing soybeans and milling maize. The chickens have to be slaughtered, processed, and supplied to retail outlets and the fast food industry, which requires investments in abattoirs and the cold chain for distribution.

South Africa, by far the largest producer and consumer of poultry in SSA, is also a major net importer from Europe, North America, and South America, with imports having accounted for around 20 percent of local demand (Ncube et al. 2017). In addition to poultry, South Africa has been a large net importer of soybeans and oilcake (from Argentina and Brazil), much of which is destined for animal feed. Soy prices in South Africa are thus set at import prices.

By comparison, in years without drought conditions, maize supply in South Africa is in surplus, and the prices on the South African Futures

Exchange reflect this, being close to export parity prices. In drought years in South Africa, as in 2015 and 2016, the yellow maize price jumped by 40 to 50 percent, toward and even beyond import levels. Along with the import prices for soy, this placed further pressure on the poultry sector.

As a result of increased rainfall variability with climate change, and coupled with growing local demand, the poultry industry in South Africa will be affected by these shocks more frequently. By comparison, Zambia is not necessarily subject to the same rainfall variability as South Africa and, indeed, it had good harvests in 2015–16 when South Africa experienced a drought. As a result, maize prices in U.S. dollar declined in Zambia in 2015 and 2016, and Zambia allowed substantial exports in 2016 after ensuring that its local stocks were maintained. In Zambia, however, maize prices also have been sustained by a price floor decided by the government, at which the Food Reserve Agency will buy from small farmers.

Investments in expanding soy production in Zambia led to relative prices falling significantly from 2012, when supply exceeded demand and the country became a net exporter to its neighbors. For Zambia to be competitive in the largest regional source of demand, in the greater Johannesburg urban area in South Africa, it must be able to beat the price of Argentina oilcake in South Africa. As production in Zambia more than trebled in the five years to 2016, Zambia prices dipped below those in South Africa in 2016 (figure 10.3). Transport costs, at around US$100 per ton from Zambian producers to Johannesburg, placed Zambian farmers at a substantial disadvantage. In early 2017, however, transport costs from Zambia to South Africa for soy and animal feed fell to around US$40 per ton as Zambian exporters benefited from backhauls from the transport of consumer goods from South Africa to Zambia. This made Zambian soy and feed delivered in South Africa competitive.[9]

A more competitive regional value chain therefore requires cheaper animal feed, which in turn depends largely on the prices of soy and maize, combined with coordinated investments along the value chain to achieve economies of scale and throughput. The basis for the value chain lies in the ability to expand production from the best land for agriculture, such as in Zambia, to supply the major sources of consumption, such as in the big cities (led by Johannesburg). In Brazil, the distance from the center of the largest soy-production region of Mato Grosso state to Sao Paulo, the largest city, is around 1,800 kilometers. This is about the same as from the agricultural producers in Zambia to Johannesburg, South Africa. The United States transports grain across similar distances from Iowa and Illinois to the

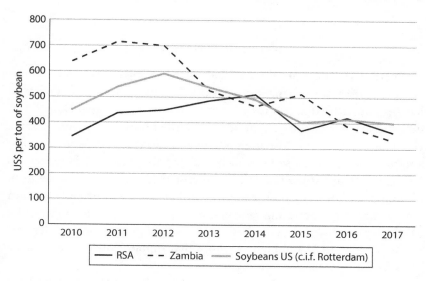

Figure 10.3   Soybean prices

Note: RSA: Republic of South Africa.

Sources: FAO, World Bank commodity prices, IAPRI (2017); Chapoto, Kabisa, and Chisanga (2018); Regional Network of Agricultural Policy Research Institutes (2018).

large East Coast urban conurbations. In southern Africa, coordination of investment and production along the value chain demands companies to work together across borders. This is the challenge of the colonial legacy and requires country cooperation as part of regional integration that is fostered by a joint industrial policy and not simply by liberalization.

The major companies in the region already have operations stretching across borders. Their vertical integration can support the large linked capital investments required at different levels of the value chain, but the concentration of these companies raises concerns about market power and anticompetitive conduct. This has been evident in the number of competition cases in South Africa and Zambia involving poultry producers. The effects of concentration were apparent in the pricing of day-old chicks in Zambia, which were more than twice that in South Africa in 2012. In subsequent years, increased investment in production and competition in breeding stock halved chick prices in Zambia, ensuring that this level of the value chain was competitive (Ncube, Roberts, and Zengeni 2016).

THE SPREAD OF SUPERMARKETS[10]

Southern African countries have experienced strong growth in the number and spread of supermarkets over the past two decades, part of what has been identified as a fourth international wave of expansion (Reardon and Hopkins 2006). Alongside rapid urbanization, supermarkets are changing food systems, driving trade flows in food and consumer goods, and promoting related services such as transport (Reardon, Timmer, and Berdegue 2004). At the same time, supermarkets have moved away from serving the traditional high-end affluent consumers in urban areas and are successfully penetrating new markets in lower-income communities (Tschirley et al. 2015). The diversity of offerings includes wholesalers extending into retail and buying groups that support independent supermarkets with purchasing and logistics.

The two main South African chains (Shoprite and Pick n Pay) have rapidly spread across southern Africa. In 2016, these groups had thirty-eight stores in Zambia up from just a handful ten years earlier (das Nair 2018). Zimbabwe has an established supermarket presence with the TM–Pick n Pay joint venture, Spar, and OK chains accounting for one hundred forty stores. Other chains are reaching across SSA countries, including Choppies of Botswana, Food Lovers Market, Game (Walmart), and Woolworths. The extension of stores in different countries remains small compared with the penetration of supermarkets in South Africa, and points to the continued expansion underway.

The routes to market of supermarkets are oriented toward processed and packaged food products, a large proportion of which are imported by SADC countries (other than South Africa). For example, it is estimated that more than 80 percent of the products sold in supermarkets in Zambia are imported, mostly from South Africa, even as local food processing has been growing in that country (das Nair, Chisoro, and Ziba 2018). The food, beverages, and tobacco sector accounts for more than 70 percent of manufacturing value added in Zambia.

Supplying supermarkets means meeting the private standards and requirements of supermarket chains in terms of costs, quality, packaging, delivery schedules, and quantities. These require significant investments in plant and capabilities. In some instances, obstacles also include charges for shelf space and long payment periods to suppliers. The results of a survey of supermarkets and suppliers in Zambia revealed that the perceptions of the capabilities of local suppliers deviated substantially from that of the supermarkets across a range of price and nonprice dimensions. The gap was most notable in terms of volume, lead times, and condition of the processing plant (das Nair et al. 2018).

The supermarkets have invested heavily in regional distribution centers and logistics to lower the costs of regional sourcing. Although this has led South African exports into other countries in the region, it also has opened the possibility of increased trade in the other direction, if the local producers can meet supermarket expectations.

For consumers, the growth of supermarkets in the region has improved competitive pricing and accessibility to a broader range of products and services in different countries. It also has imposed challenges on the ability of suppliers (specifically small farmers, food processing, and manufacturing firms) to enter the supermarkets' supply chains. These obstacles include meeting supermarkets' standards and packaging, investing in productive capabilities, cost-competitiveness in sourcing, and processing agricultural produce. The importance of investment in productive capabilities is highlighted by the association between investment in machinery and systems (such as barcoding) and supply to supermarkets. The supply by Zambian producers to the international supermarket chains in Zambia is also associated with exporting, as the spread of supermarkets across the region means they have effectively become key governors of routes to market (das Nair et al. 2018).

The largest supermarket groups are linked with property developers and secure space in shopping malls on an exclusive basis. This undermines the ability of local stores to access prime retail space and, given the concentration of supermarkets, raises competition issues. These issues can be addressed in different ways, including through urban planning.

Supermarkets are integrating the region through their investment in transport and logistics but are not necessarily doing this in ways that support local producers. This lack of support has exacerbated unbalanced trade and raised challenges for the adoption of regional strategies, especially when countries perceive that they are losing out from integration. The issue, therefore, is how supermarkets can be partners in regional industrial development for increased trade so that they may build capabilities across countries. This possibility holds the prospect of moving the southern African region as a whole from being a net processed food importer to being a net exporter of food products. A combination of supplier development initiatives with targets for local sourcing and agroprocessing policies are required to build the industrial capabilities of suppliers, with supermarkets serving as key routes to market.

Toward this effort, a code of conduct can ensure that the retail space is open, such that shelf space is available to smaller brands and anticompetitive arrangements are not employed to restrict rivalry. Such codes of conduct or similar quasi-regulatory measures have been used in European countries, including Ireland and Spain (das Nair et al. 2018). Supplier development initiatives combine advice by supermarkets on standards and supply requirements with commitments to stock products. These initiatives enable supermarkets to take on a critical role in fostering local supplier capabilities to meet concrete targets for local and regional sourcing. Without these expectations, individual supermarket chains do not have the incentive to develop suppliers who can also sell to their rivals. As such, there is a positive externality effect in supporting suppliers, which means the buyers underinvest in their upgrading. An alternative is for supermarkets to have exclusive arrangements with suppliers. Although this is a possible solution to a limited extent, suppliers need to achieve scale economies (and supply a wider range of customers). In addition, a buyer with market power can abuse these exclusive arrangements.

Initiatives to support local procurement by supermarkets can induce local production in food products (as well as other consumer goods) and regional trade. In the absence of such interventions, trade and production likely will be increasingly skewed to South Africa as well as toward deep-sea imports. In countries such as Zambia, soft interventions have induced supermarkets to increase local procurement of dairy, processed grains, edible oil, and household products over 2012 to 2017. For example, Shoprite committed to local procurement and has signed memoranda of understanding to work with the Zambian Development Agency and a private enterprise development program. Namibia has a formalized voluntary retail sector charter, which has led supermarkets to work to upgrade suppliers (das Nair 2019).

MARKETS AND INDUSTRIAL DEVELOPMENT IN AFRICA

The importance of developing more sophisticated and diversified capabilities in industrial production has been widely identified (see Cimoli, Dosi, and Stiglitz 2009). This diversification involves incremental learning processes, consistent with observations about the way capabilities can evolve across product space (Hidalgo et al. 2007). The ability to upgrade capabilities depends on (1) how firms are located in regional and international value chains in terms of the nature of the processes they undertake; (2) the differentiated product lines manufactured (in terms of quality and sophistication); (3) the functions, including design, research and development, and branding in which they are engaged; and (4) the ability to leverage capabilities to move to different sectors (Humphrey and Schmitz 2004).

The growth and increased trade in manufacturing across African countries from the mid-1990s onward has been from a very low base, and improvements in productivity have been relatively poor compared with other regions, raising concerns about development of manufacturing capabilities (Balchin et al. 2016; Diao, McMillan, and Rodrik 2017). The following discussion draws on the issues related to agriculture and food production to consider three main implications. First, what are the nature of regional and international linkages? Second, how do value chain governance and market power interact, and what is the role for competition policy? Third, what are the implications for industrial policy and the role of the state?

REGIONAL AND INTERNATIONAL LINKAGES

There has undoubtedly been greater international integration of food production in the economies of southern Africa. The question remains whether this integration has been accompanied by local investment and capabilities development. Inputs such as fertilizer and seed (not covered in this discussion) are supplied by a very few multinational corporations. African countries appear to be exposed to the market power of global companies, as discussed with reference to fertilizer, with no development of local production.

By comparison, in the production and retail of food, significant regional linkages have evolved to serve the main markets in the growing urban centers. The cases of sugar and poultry, however, are quite different. The sugar sector has seen production for export into deep-sea markets, while high prices are imposed on local buyers even as this undermines local industrialization through downstream processing.

In poultry, coordination and expanded production of animal feed, as part of the regional organization of production, is linked to the observed growth in trade. As highlighted in the studies drawn on in this chapter, international firms operate across the southern African region and make linked investments at different levels of processing, with trade in intermediate and final products to supply regional markets. A regional value chain approach recognizes the increasing organization of production within and between firms across borders and the potential for building strong regional production systems.

Supermarkets are making regional linkages through investments in distribution centers, logistics, and transport. The sector is highly concentrated, with a small number of mainly South African groups shaping routes to market for suppliers. The fact that the supermarkets are regionally rooted, however, means that there is scope to engage them to support local upgrading by suppliers to meet first regional and then international standards. In this way, the potential exists for firms to seek insertion into *regional* value chains to gain the capabilities required to then participate successfully in global value chains. This can be facilitated by supplier development programs.

Notwithstanding the somewhat-mixed picture, regional value chains in southern Africa remain relatively underdeveloped. Governments have not taken a coherent approach to support regional linkages associated with capabilities development and industrialization or to engage with regional business groups. The failure to develop coherent strategies is partly because of the regional spread of businesses and also because the importance of linkages across countries in developing competitive food value chains has largely been ignored.

GOVERNANCE AND MARKET POWER

Governance is at the heart of the value chain approach in describing the "process by which particular players in the chain exert control over other participants and how these lead firms appropriate or distribute the value that is created along the chain" (Bair 2009, 9). The lead firms are therefore critical in driving the coordination of activities across countries, generating and controlling the division of the returns. These economic forces at work are not new, nor, in many ways, are the challenges they pose to industrial policy in African countries. What is new is the much greater potential that coordination through value chains opensup for the functional integration of internationally dispersed activities and their control. This potential can be achieved through advances in logistics, design, branding, and marketing with the use of information and communication technology.

The nature of the coordination is a second important dimension to the role of the lead firm (Ponte and Sturgeon 2014). Possible coordination arrangements span a spectrum ranging from arm's-length market relations to modular, relational, captive, and hierarchical organization. These arrangements vary in terms of the balance of power between parties in the value chain, and with the specificity of assets, the ability to switch suppliers, the extent of collaboration on product development, and the tolerance of distance. In relational arrangements, a third level of governance can be identified in terms of setting the norms and conventions that establish the orders of worth or value (Ponte and Sturgeon 2014). For example, these may be values set by supermarkets as buyers, in terms of the uniformity of products, or they may be influenced by taste to impose standards related to the conditions under which production takes place, such as organic or free-range production.

These lead firms and complex governance structures influence the evolving nature of production and trade networks, including trajectories of upgrading and patterns of access or exclusion (Gereffi 2014). The value chain framework also enables identification of pressure points at which government interventions can influence the outcomes.

The studies of food production and retailing in southern Africa drawn on in this chapter emphasize the importance of understanding regional power relations in governing the location of economic activities and the returns to different parties. The spread of supermarkets is very much about regional investments and control across borders, where the major chains have bargaining power over suppliers and govern the supply chain. This has important implications for suppliers, for example, those in Zambia seeking to supply urban consumers in South Africa. Walmart, which has entered the market through an acquisition of a smaller South African chain, has failed to have the impact that was predicted by global value chain analysis. Instead, through the control over urban retail space (including exclusive arrangements with property developers), together with their investment in logistics and distribution, regional supermarket chains led by Shoprite have governed this activity (das Nair et al. 2018).

International studies have generally overlooked the importance of logistics (Coe 2014). For example, arrangements regarding port facilities, storage, warehousing, and transport are critical to the power exerted by suppliers of fertilizer as well as grain traders. Although notionally markets appear to be contestable, the mark-ups that are applied along the supply chain reflect the importance of control over these facilities. This also points to the rationale of large multinationals, such as Yara in fertilizer, promoting corridor initiatives alongside donors, to governments. For example, the Beira Agricultural Growth Corridor and the Southern Agricultural Growth Corridor of Tanzania, announced with much fanfare at the World Economic Forum, appear to be partly associated with control over the mundane activities of warehousing and bagging fertilizer at the ports of Beira and Dar es Salaam in the context of the very high fertilizer prices being earned.[11]

The ability of rivals such as ETG, which expanded operations from East Africa, and Greenbelt, from South Africa, to exert competitive pressure has depended partly on logistics. ETG's expansion was aided by being able to acquire Kynoch in 2014 with its blending and storage facilities (Greenberg 2017).[12] Greenbelt established a blending facility in Beira and became a major supplier in Mozambique, Malawi, and Zambia. Yara, however, neutralized the competitive threat it posed when it subsequently acquired Greenbelt.

In some markets, it is necessary to understand governance and market power in a global context. The influence of international cartels over prices and supplies has major effects on food production in Africa, most notably in the case of fertilizer. In sugar, the high levels of regional concentration and control over markets by subsidiaries of multinational companies have been reinforced by trade barriers and regulatory restrictions heavily influenced by the main industry participants. Although sugar production has grown, the high prices charged in many national markets have undermined downstream industrialization in food processing (das Nair et al. 2017), which has effectively reinforced southern Africa as an exporter of agricultural commodities and importer of manufactures.

These are examples of dominant firms and tight-knit oligopolies that have been able to entrench their positions and earn supracompetitive rents, creating long-term problems in the performance of the economic system. Global consolidation in agriculture and food production at different levels, from inputs through to retail, has been mirrored in southern Africa (Greenberg 2017).

These industries raise questions about the role for competition policy in setting rules for the market economy to encourage local investment and capabilities. It is evident that competition law cannot create local competitors or support linkages and collaboration as part of the ability to upgrade firms' capabilities. Competition *policy* must, therefore, extend beyond addressing cartels and be considered as part of a wider policy framework for markets (see Roberts 2010). For example, proactive intervention to lower transport costs and provide support services to poultry can promote a more integrated and competitive poultry industry. Similarly, regulatory provisions can mitigate supermarkets' buyer power over local suppliers and instead encourage supplier development.

INSTITUTIONS OF INDUSTRIAL POLICY, REGULATION, AND THE ROLE OF THE STATE

The analyses of value chain upgrading, the importance of developing more diverse and sophisticated export capabilities, and the need to recognize processes of learning and capabilities formation have not led to a consensus on the appropriate policies to be followed. At one extreme are recommendations that countries should lower labor and other costs and aggressively market themselves to foreign direct investors to compete to insert themselves into global value chains (e.g., see Morris, Kaplinsky, and Kaplan 2012). This may work well in attracting cut-flower exporters, but it is not evident how this suggestion would address the challenges of market power and ensure meaningful participation in value addition.

These challenges require effective regional institutions to regulate market power and support more competitive markets through value-chain upgrades with investments across borders, as has been seen to an extent in the poultry sector. These investments require productive rents as an incentive (Khan 2010). The credibility of government commitments in this regard is obviously important and does not need to be established through formal institutions (e.g., see Sen and te Velde 2012; Sen 2013). If the arrangements to which governments commit allow businesses simply to capture rents, however, then there will be little, if any, value from these deals for the host country. These arrangements will be at risk under a change of regime, no matter what formal backing they have. Instead institutional collaborations that support the provision of limited public goods, such as infrastructure and targeted skills, along with measures to address coordination failures, are important components to generate shared productive rents and facilitate learning (Khan 2010; Noman and Stiglitz 2012).

Institutional collaborations to support competitive food manufacturing, for example, could be set up on a regional basis, across countries in which the companies are located. A supermarket strategy for supplier development will be more effective if adopted by neighboring countries. Similarly, the development of the animal feed to poultry value chain requires regional arrangements to grow production in Zambia. It also requires efficient processing and supply across two borders to meet the largest demand in the region in the greater Johannesburg area.

Effective regional institutions are required for competition enforcement to discipline market power, including to identify regional cartels and adjudicate on mergers. Evidence of the regional nature of cartels in southern Africa was demonstrated by cartel cases uncovered by the South African authorities. Settlements revealed the regional extent of the conduct, including in fertilizer and cement (Kaira 2017).

If expectations are to be set for performance-based support, then the credibility of governments must relate not only to keeping commitments made to investors but also to disciplining abuses of market power. These are part of Amsden's (2001) reciprocal control mechanisms. In addition, industrial policies are important to foster competitive markets by supporting potentially efficient local participants. South Korea and Japan have used competition policy as part of a wider industrial policy to ensure effective rivalry (Amsden and Singh 1994). The Korean Fair Trade Commission also monitored subcontracting arrangements by the large *chaebols* to ensure that collaboration supported the development of subcontractor capabilities (Roberts 2010). Competition authorities can be understood as wider regulatory bodies for markets, generating competition, rather than simply as enforcers operating on the underlying mistaken premise that, in the absence of discrete conduct, competition will prevail (Budzinski and Beigi 2015).

It is essential to build regional industrial policy institutions across southern Africa. These include (1) development banks; (2) institutions supporting the adoption and adaptation of improved technologies; and (3) facilities for testing and certification of products to lower the costs of meeting standards as imposed, for example, by supermarkets as well as in export markets.

(RE)SHAPING MARKETS?

The agriculture and food-processing activities explored in this chapter illustrate the dimensions of regional and global integration, the ways in which power is entrenched and exerted, and the key challenges for the state. The regional spread of businesses, the linkages of production systems and value chains across borders, and the implications for industrialization require much greater attention in southern Africa. Businesses, including, notably, supermarkets, *are* integrating the region.

The analysis also has highlighted the impact of international and regional arrangements to exert market power in fertilizer and sugar. The high cost of fertilizer undermines agricultural production and is partially responsible for the high food prices in African cities. High sugar prices have undermined downstream processed food producers. The pricing and availability of agricultural products has affected the ability to expand the manufacturing of processed food products as part of industrialization.

By comparison, developments in the poultry sector demonstrate the potential to build regional value chains with linked investments across countries. The agricultural potential in Zambia has increased the supply of, and lowered prices for, animal feed. This effort has been supported by more efficient intraregional transport. Although growth in Zambia has been substantial, to achieve a significant regional impact on the competitiveness of poultry production in order to replace deep-sea imports, this growth needs to be sustained. In addition, coordinated actions along the value chain are necessary to ensure efficient processing of the required inputs for the supply of poultry products.

Ultimately, this analysis points to the challenge of moving the competition discourse from one of enforcement, which assumes that by addressing discrete anticompetitive conduct local competition will flourish, to the integration of competition policy with the development of local productive capabilities. It is important to address international cartels and this poses important challenges for the development of international regulatory regimes. We need to go further, however, to frame the agenda in terms of the ways in which industrial policy and economic regulation can reshape markets to generate competition within local and regional markets in southern Africa.

Three key areas are identified for this agenda. First, the regional scope of actual and potential linkages needs to be better understood. Big businesses are integrating their activities across the region, but they are not necessarily doing so to build productive capabilities for competitive production across borders. Second, we need to understand how the regional value chains are governed and the extent of market power and its exertion by large firms. The regional reach of businesses can reinforce cartels and the unilateral exertion of market power to earn rents and exclude local rivals, which in turn undermines industrialization. A competition policy agenda that links to industrial policy is essential to generate competitive markets and stimulate dynamic rivalry built on investments in improved capabilities. Third, effective regional institutions are required to simultaneously discipline market power and support industrialization.

NOTES

In addition to drawing on a wide range of research undertaken by researchers in CCRED and research partner organizations, as reflected in the specific sections, I am grateful to Tatenda Zengeni, Thando Vilakazi, and Tamara Paremoer for assistance with the data for the figures; to Thando Vilakazi and participants at the Initiative for Policy Dialogue Africa Task Force meeting on April 11–12, 2017, at Columbia University, New York, for helpful comments; and to the African Development Bank, which published an earlier version of this chapter as a working paper.

1. These papers include Ernest Bagopi et al., "Competition, Agro-Processing and Regional Development: The Case of the Poultry Sector in South Africa, Botswana, Namibia and Zambia," in *Competition in Africa*, ed. S. Roberts (Pretoria: HSRC Press, 2016); Brian Chisanga et al., "Agricultural Development, Competition and Investment: The Case of Sugar in Kenya, South Africa, Tanzania, and Zambia," in *Competition in Africa*, ed. S. Roberts. (Pretoria: HSRC Press, 2016); Reena das Nair, "The Internationalization of Supermarkets and the Nature of Competitive Rivalry in Retailing in Southern Africa," *Development Southern Africa* 35, no. 3 (2018): 315–333; Reena das Nair, Shingie Chisoro, and Francis Ziba, "The Implications for Suppliers of the Spread of Supermarkets in Southern Africa," *Development Southern Africa* 35, no. 3 (2018): 334–350; Reena das Nair et al., "Growth and Development in the Sugar to Confectionary Value Chain" (CCRED Working Paper 2017/16, Centre for Competition, Regulation and Economic Development, South Africa, 2017); Phumzile Ncube, Simon Roberts, and Tatenda Zengeni, "The Development of the Animal Feed to Poultry Value Chain Across Botswana, South Africa, Zambia and Zimbabwe" (WIDER Working Paper 2016/2, United Nations University World Institute for Development Economics Research, Helsinki, Finland, 2016); Phumzile Ncube, Simon Roberts, and Thando Selaelo Vilakazi, "Regulation and Rivalry in Transport and Supply of Fertilizer Industry in Malawi, Tanzania and Zambia," in *Competition in Africa—Insights from Key Industries*, ed. S. Roberts, 102–131 (Cape Town: HSRC Press, 2016); Phumzile Ncube et al. "Identifying Growth Opportunities in the Southern African Development Community Through Regional Value Chains—The Case of the Animal Feed to Poultry Value Chain" (WIDER Working Paper 2017/4, United Nations University World Institute for Development Economics Research, Helsinki, Finland, 2017); Thando Selaelo Vilakazi, "The Causes of High Intra-Regional Road Freight Rates for Food and Commodities in Southern Africa," *Development Southern Africa* 35, no. 3 (2018): 388–403; Francis Ziba and Mwanda Phiri, "The Expansion of Regional Supermarket Chains: Implications for Local Suppliers in Zambia" (WIDER Working Paper 2017/58, United Nations University World Institute for Development Economics Research, Helsinki, Finland, 2017).

2. Unless otherwise indicated, this section draws primarily from Ncube et al., "Regulation and Rivalry in Transport and Supply of Fertilizer."

3. In SADC, Minjingu in Tanzania is also a small producer of phosphate fertilizer.

4. The Arabian Gulf prices are most relevant for actual supplies to these countries through the ports of Dar es Salaam (in Tanzania) and Durban (in South Africa); however, the prices are similar to those quoted for shipments from the Black Sea and

from the United States, prices which are available to farmers, with overland transport costs added, in Eastern Europe and North America.

5. A similar picture is given by DAP and CAN prices. Urea and DAP are the two most important products in these countries. This is also consistent with the observations of Balu Bumb, "Improving Efficiency of the Fertilizer Supply Chain: A Comparative Analysis" (Third Annual Agricultural Policy Conference, Serena Hotel, Dar es Salaam, March 3, 2017), https://www.canr.msu.edu/fsp/uploads/files/News/3rd_Conf_TZ/AAPC__Supply_Chain_BL_Bumb_March2017.pdf.

6. Yara International, https://www.yara.com/news-and-media/news/archive/2016/yara_and_the_greenbelt_fertilizers_acquisition/ /. The merger was approved by the Comesa Competition Commission. Zambia and Malawi are members of Comesa; Mozambique and South Africa are not.

7. Unless otherwise indicated, this draws from Chisanga et al., "Agricultural Development, Competition and Investment" and das Nair et al., "Growth and Development in the Sugar to Confectionary Value Chain."

8. Calculated from costs for South African producer, including slaughtering costs (but not brining, freezing, and packaging); see Ncube et al., "Regulation and Rivalry in Transport and Supply of Fertilizer."

9. Interview with Heiko Koster, animal feed supplier, January 2017.

10. Unless otherwise indicated, this draws from das Nair, "The Internationalization of Supermarkets" and das Nair et al., "The Implications for Suppliers of the Spread of Supermarkets in Southern Africa."

11. See also Gertrude Makhaya and Simon Roberts, "Expectations and Outcomes—Considering Competition and Corporate Power in South Africa Under Democracy," *Review of African Political Economy* 138 (2013): 556–571.

12. See also Kynoch, "About Us," accessed April 4, 2017, http://www.kynoch.co.za/about-us/. In November 2012, ETG became co-owned by Carlyle, Standard Chartered Private Equity, and Pembani Remgro, although it appears Carlyle exited in August 2015.

REFERENCES

African Centre for Economic Transformation (ACET). 2017. *African Transformation Report 2017: Agriculture Powering Africa's Economic Transformation.* Accra, Ghana: CET.

Amsden, Alice. 2001. *The Rise of the "Rest": Challenges to the West Late-Industrialising Economies.* New York: Oxford University Press.

Amsden, Alice, and Ajit Singh. 1994. "The Optimal Degree of Competition and Dynamic Efficiency in Japan and Korea." *European Economic Review* 38: 940–951.

Arndt, Channing, and Simon Roberts. 2018. "Key Issues in Regional Growth and Integration in Southern Africa." *Development Southern Africa* 35 (3): 297–314.

Bagopi, Ernest, Emmanuel Chokwe, Pamela Halse, Josef Hausiku, Michael Humavindu, Wesley Kalapula, and Simon Roberts. 2016. "Competition, Agro-Processing and Regional Development: The Case of the Poultry Sector in South Africa, Botswana, Namibia and Zambia." In *Competition in Africa*, ed. S. Roberts, 66–101. Pretoria: HSRC Press.

Bair, Jennifer. 2009. "Global Commodity Chains." In *Frontiers of Commodity Research*, ed. J. Bair. Palo Alto, CA: Stanford University Press.

Balchin, Neil, Stephen Gelb, Jane Kennan, Hope Martin, Dirk Willem te Velde, and Carolin Williams. 2016. *Developing Export-Based Manufacturing in Sub-Saharan Africa Report*. Supporting Economic Transformation Programme. London: Overseas Development Institute.

Brahmbhatt, Milan, Russell Bishop, Xiao Zhao, Alberto Lemma, Ilmi Granoff, Nick Godfrey, and Dirk Willem te Velde. 2016. *Africa's New Climate Economy: Economic Transformation and Social and Environmental Change*. London: New Climate Economy and Overseas Development Institute.

Budzinski, Oliver, and Maryam Beigi. 2015. "Generating Instead of Protecting Competition." In *Economic Characteristics of Developing Jurisdictions: Their Implications for Competition Law*, ed. M. Gal, M. Bakhoum, J. Drexl, E. Fox, and D. Gerber. Cheltenham: Edward Elgar.

Bumb, B. L. .2017. "Improving Efficiency of the Fertilizer Supply Chain: A Comparative Analysis." Third Annual Agricultural Policy Conference, Serena Hotel, Dar es Salaam, March 3, 2017. Accessed October 10, 2017, http://foodsecuritypolicy.msu.edu.

Chabane, Neo, Simon Roberts, and Andrea Goldstein. 2006. "The Changing Face and Strategies of Big Business in South Africa: More Than a Decade of Political Democracy." *Industrial and Corporate Change* 15 (3): 549–578.

Chapoto, Antony, Mulajo Kabisa, and Brian Chisanga. 2018. "Zambia Agriculture Status Report 2017. https://www.researchgate.net/publication/322676437_Zambia_Agriculture_Status_Report_2017.

Chisanga, Brian, John Gathiaka, George Nguruse, Stellah Onyancha, and Thando Selaelo Vilakazi. 2016. "Agricultural Development, Competition and Investment: The Case of Sugar in Kenya, South Africa, Tanzania, and Zambia." In *Competition in Africa*, ed. S. Roberts, 41–65. Pretoria: HSRC Press.

Cimoli, Mario, Giovanni Dosi, and Joseph E. Stiglitz. 2009. *Industrial Policy and Development: The Political Economy of Capabilities Accumulation*. Oxford: Oxford University Press.

Coe, Neil M. 2014. "Missing Links: Logistics, Governance and Upgrading in a Shifting Global Economy." *Review of International Political Economy* 21 (1): 224–256.

Competition and Consumer Protection Commission of Zambia (CCPC). 2013. *Competition and Consumer Protection News* 6: 9.

das Nair, Reena. 2018. "The Internationalization of Supermarkets and the Nature of Competitive Rivalry in Retailing in Southern Africa." *Development Southern Africa* 35 (3): 315–333.

——. 2019. "The Spread and Internationalisation of South African Retail Chains and the Implications of Market Power." *International Review of Applied Economics* 33 (1): 30–50.

das Nair, Reena, Shingie Chisoro, and Francis Ziba 2018. "The Implications for Suppliers of the Spread of Supermarkets in Southern Africa." *Development Southern Africa* 35 (3): 334–350.

das Nair, Reena, M. Nkhonjera, Phumzile Ncube, and Francis Ziba. 2017. "Growth and Development in the Sugar to Confectionary Value Chain." CCRED Working Paper 2017/16. Centre for Competition, Regulation and Economic Development, South Africa.

das Nair, Reena, and Liberty Mncube. 2012. "The Role of Information Exchange in Facilitating Collusion: Insights from Selected Cases." In *The Development of Competition Law and Economics in South Africa*, ed. K. Moodaliyar and Simon Roberts. Pretoria: HSRC Press.

Diao, Xinshen, Margaret McMillan, and Dani Rodrik. 2017. "The Recent Growth Boom in Developing Economies: A Structural Change Perspective." NBER Working Paper 23132. National Bureau of Economic Research, Cambridge, MA.

Food and Agriculture Organisation (FAO). 2017. World Bank Commodity Prices, IAPRI. http://www.worldbank.org/en/research/commodity-markets

Food and Agriculture Organisation (FAO). 2018. *The State of Food and Agriculture: Migration Agriculture and Rural Development*. Rome: FAO.

Gereffi, Gary. 2014. "Global Value Chains in a Post–Washington Consensus World." *Review of International Political Economy* 21 (1): 9–37.

Gnutzmann, Hinnerk, and Piotr Spiewanowski. 2016. "Did the Fertilizer Cartel Cause the Food Crisis?" Beitrage zur Jahrestagung des Vereins fur Socialpolitik 2016: Demographischer Wandel, Session: International Trade and Development, No. A19-V2.

Greenberg, Stephen. 2017. "Corporate Power in the Agro-Food System and the Consumer Food Environment in South Africa." *Journal of Peasant Studies* 44 (2): 467–496.

Hernandez, Manuel, and Maximo Torero. 2013. "Market Concentration and Pricing Behavior in the Fertilizer Industry: A Global Approach." *Agricultural Economics* 44: 723–734.

Hidalgo, César., Bailey Klinger, Albert-László Barabási, and Ricardo Hausmann. 2007. "The Product Space Conditions the Development of Nations." *Science* 317: 482–487.

Humphrey, John, and Hubert Schmitz. 2004. "Governance in Global Value Chains." In *Local Enterprises in the Global Economy*, ed. H. Schmitz. Cheltenham: Edward Elgar.

Jayne, Thomas and David Sarfo Ameyaw. 2016. "Africa's Emerging Agricultural Transformation: evidence, Opportunities and Challenges." Chap. 1 in *Africa Agriculture Status Report 2016: Progress Towards Agriculture Transformation in Sub-Saharan Africa*. Nairobi Kenya: AGRA.

Jayne, Thomas, Jordan Chamberlin, and Rui Benfica. 2018. "Africa's Unfolding Economic Transformation." *Journal of Development Studies* 54 (5): 777–787.

Jenny, Frederic. 2012. "Export Cartels in Primary Products: The Potash Case in Perspective." In *Trade, Competition and the Pricing of Commodities*, ed. S. Evenett and F. Jenny. London: Centre for Economic Policy Research.

Kaira, Thula. 2017. "A Cartel in South Africa Is a Cartel in a Neighbouring Country." In *Competition Law and Economic Regulation: Addressing Market Power in Southern Africa*, ed. J. Klaaren, Simon Roberts, and I. Valodia. Johannesburg: Wits University Press.

Khan, Mushtaq 2010. *Political Settlements and the Governance of Growth-Enhancing Institutions*. London: SOAS University of London.

Kynoch. "About Us." Accessed April 4, 2017. http://www.kynoch.co.za/about-us/.

Lewis, Mike. 2013. *Sweet Nothings: The Human Cost of a British Sugar Giant Avoiding Taxes in Southern Africa*. Johannesburg: South Africa: ActionAid.

Makhaya, Gertrude, and Simon Roberts. 2013. "Expectations and Outcomes—Considering Competition and Corporate Power in South Africa Under Democracy." *Review of African Political Economy* 138: 556–571.

Morris, Mike, Raphael Kaplinsky, and David Kaplan. 2012. " 'One Thing Leads to Another'—Commodities, Linkages and Industrial Development." *Resources Policy* 37 (4): 405–484.

Nakamura, Shohei, Rawaa Harati, Somik V. Lall, Yuri M. Dikhanov, Nada Hamadeh, William Virgil Oliver, Marko Olavi Rissanen, and Mizuki Yamanaka. 2016. "Is Living in African Cities Expensive?" World Bank Policy Research Working Paper 7641. World Bank, Washington, DC.

Ncube, Phumzile. 2018. "The Southern African Poultry Value Chain: Corporate Strategies, Investments and Agro-Industrial Policies." *Development Southern Africa* 35 (3): 369–387.

Ncube, Phumzile, Simon Roberts, and Tatenda Zengeni. 2016. "The Development of the Animal Feed to Poultry Value Chain Across Botswana, South Africa, Zambia and Zimbabwe." WIDER Working Paper 2016/2. United Nations University World Institute for Development Economics Research, Helsinki, Finland.

Ncube, Phumzile, Simon Roberts, Paul C. Samboko, and Tatenda Zengeni. 2017. "Identifying Growth Opportunities in the Southern African Development Community Through Regional Value Chains—The Case of the Animal Feed to Poultry Value Chain." WIDER Working Paper 2017/4. United Nations University World Institute for Development Economics Research, Helsinki, Finland.

Ncube, Phumzile, Simon Roberts, and Thando Selaelo Vilakazi. 2016. "Regulation and Rivalry in Transport and Supply of Fertilizer Industry in Malawi, Tanzania and Zambia." In *Competition in Africa—Insights from Key Industries*, ed. Simon Roberts. Cape Town: HSRC Press.

Noman, Akbar, and Joseph E. Stiglitz. 2012. "Introduction." In *Good Growth and Governance in Africa: Rethinking Development Strategies*, ed. A. Noman, K. Botchwey, H. Stein, and J. E. Stiglitz. Oxford: Oxford University Press.

Paremoer, Tamara. 2018. "Regional Value Chains, Industrialization, and Climate Change: Exploring Linkages and Opportunities in the Agro-Processing Sector Across Five SADC Countries." CCRED Working Paper 2018/4. Centre for Competition, Regulation and Economic Development, South Africa.

Ponte, Stefano, and Timothy Sturgeon. 2014. "Explaining Governance in Global Value Chains: A Modular Theory-Building Effort." *Review of International Political Economy* 21 (1): 195–223.

Reardon, Thomas, and Rose Hopkins. 2006. "The Supermarket Revolution in Developing Countries: Policies to Address Emerging Tensions among Supermarkets, Suppliers, and Traditional Retailers." *European Journal of Development Research* 18 (4): 522–545.

Reardon, Thomas, Charles Timmer, and Julio Berdegue. 2004. "The Rapid Rise of Supermarkets in Developing Countries: Induced Organizational, Institutional, and Technological Change in Agrifood Systems." *e-Journal of Agricultural and Development Economics* 1 (2): 168–183.

Roberts, Simon. 2010. "Competition Policy, Competitive Rivalry and a Developmental State in South Africa." Chap. 11 in *Constructing a Democratic Developmental State in South Africa: Potentials and Challenges*, ed. O. Edigheji. Pretoria: HSRC Press.

Sen, Kunal. 2013. "The Political Dynamics of Economic Growth." World Development 47: 71–86.

Sen, Kunal, and Dirk Willem te Velde. 2012. "State–Business Relations, Investment Climate Reform and Economic Growth in Sub-Saharan Africa." Chap. 10 in *Good Growth and Governance in Africa: Rethinking Development Strategies*, ed. A. Noman, K. Botchwey, H. Stein and J.E. Stiglitz. Oxford: Oxford University Press.

Suttie, David, and Rui Benfica. 2016. "Fostering Inclusive Outcomes in Sub-Saharan African Agriculture: Improving Agricultural Productivity and Expanding Agribusiness Opportunities." IFAD Research Series 03. International Fund for Agricultural Development, Rome, Italy.

Taylor, C. Robert, and Diana L. Moss. 2013. *The Fertilizer Oligopoly: The Case for Global Antitrust Enforcement*. Washington DC: American Antitrust Institution.

Tschirley, David, Thomas Reardon, Michael Dolislager, and Jason Snyder. 2015. "The Rise of a Middle Class in East and Southern Africa: Implications for Food System Transformation." *Journal of International Development* 27 (5): 628–646.

United Nations Economic Commission for Africa. 2017. *Economic Report on Africa 2017: Urbanization and Industrialization for Africa's Transformation*. Addis Ababa, Ethiopia: United Nations Economic Commission for Africa.

Vilakazi, Thando Selaelo. 2018. "The Causes of High Intra-Regional Road Freight Rates for Food and Commodities in Southern Africa." *Development Southern Africa* 35 (3): 388–403.

Vilakazi, Thando Selaelo, and Simon Roberts. 2018. 'Cartels as fraud? Insights from collusion in southern and East Africa in the fertilizer and cement industries', *Review of African Political Economy* DOI: 10.1080/03056244.2018.1536974World Bank. 2016. *Breaking Down Barriers—Unlocking Africa's Potential Through Vigorous Competition Policy*. Washington, DC: World Bank.

Ziba, Francis, and Mwanda Phiri. 2017. "The Expansion of Regional Supermarket Chains: Implications for Local Suppliers in Zambia." WIDER Working Paper 2017/58. United Nations University World Institute for Development Economics Research, Helsinki, Finland.

PART IV

Environment

CHAPTER 11

Climate Change and the Quality of Growth in Africa

Ben Orlove

This chapter examines the effects of climate change on the quality of growth in Africa. It reviews the consequences observed since the last two decades of the previous century and examines the projections of future impacts.

The chapter opens with a review of the different assessments, which evaluate these effects. These assessments concur across broad outlines, agreeing that climate change threatens to limit growth and human well-being in a variety of ways; the assessments also disagree on the relative vulnerability of different nations. The second section of the chapter reviews the impacts of climate change on growth, emphasizing that it slows growth, exposes it to shocks, reduces the continent's stock of natural capital, and limits its ability to meet basic human needs, including physical security. This section also discusses the way climate change impacts create cascading risks that spill over from sectors that are directly affected (such as health) to others that are indirectly affected (such as education and employment).

The third section of the chapter reviews past, current, and projected adaptation efforts in Africa. Like the first section, it identifies some areas of consensus, noting agreement on the urgency of adaptation activity and on the obstacles to their planning, financing, and implementation, and it also identifies a number of differences, with a variety of disparate activities being presented under the rubric of adaptation. The final section provides a brief overview of a large subject, the place of energy in the future of economic growth in Africa; it reports on the potential of low-carbon and renewable energy resources to sustain growth.

OVERVIEW OF CLIMATE ASSESSMENTS IN AFRICA

Experts agree that Sub-Saharan Africa has already experienced significant climate change and is likely to experience additional impacts, many of them even more severe, during this century. These views are stated in a number of different reports dating back to the 1990s.

THE INTERGOVERNMENTAL PANEL ON CLIMATE CHANGE

The Intergovernmental Panel on Climate Change (IPCC) included a chapter on Africa in its most recent Fifth Assessment Report, known as AR5 (Niang et al. 2014). The report reflects significant input from the continent, as six of the seven lead authors are African. The AR5 notes a warming trend across the continent over the past fifty to one hundred years and that this trend will continue, with particularly strong rises in the more arid regions. The precise level of warming will depend on future global emissions, which are subject to policy decisions and other human actions, and that reflect physical as well as social uncertainties. There is very strong agreement, however, that temperature will increase by more than 2°C over much of Africa by the last decades of this century under medium-emissions scenarios. Under high-emissions scenarios, this warming could reach between 3°C and 6°C. The warming already has affected ecosystems and will exacerbate existing stresses on water availability, undermining sustainable economic growth (Nyantakyi-Frimpong and Bezner-Kerr 2015).

The AR5 traces a number of links of climate change to agriculture. The productivity of cereal crops is very likely to fall, and high-value perennial crops, such as cacao and coffee, could be adversely affected. Pests, weeds, and diseases will become more severe. Because African food systems are increasingly linked to regional and global supply chains, they are exposed to new vulnerabilities, as a result of fragilities in transportation networks, financial institutions, and other systems. Although some progress has been made in addressing short-term climate fluctuations, the long-term impacts of climate change on food supplies and export crops will be more severe, requiring new solutions.

In addition to food security, the AR5 discusses several other areas of human well-being. It notes that the impacts on health are harder to trace, because of the diversity of disease transmission systems and the lack of adequate health data, and that malnutrition could become more severe. It states that climate change could increase the frequency and spatial range of epidemics of several major diseases, including malaria, meningitis, and leishmaniasis. It also comments that food, health, and economic insecurity could lead to conflicts over the distribution of resources and could serve as drivers of urbanization and migration, in turn leading to political conflict.

The AR5 finds a few positive elements in the response to current and projected climate change. Governments are conducting planning processes, and autonomous adaptations, undertaken by local communities, have often been effective. Conservation agriculture (agroforestry, low-impact tillage, and the like) has generated positive results. Moreover, strong possibilities to develop adaptation pathways could incorporate other goals, such as economic growth and social inclusivity. Nonetheless, the report notes many challenges, above all the persistent nature of poverty and vulnerability. In addition, institutional frameworks are weak, underfinanced, and uncoordinated; technological support is inadequate; and financing is insufficient and often heavily constrained by donor requirements, which impede effective implementation of adaptation efforts. The report also identifies data and research gaps on climate and other environmental systems, and on key economic and social variables, which make planning more difficult.

This IPCC assessment is the most significant global assessment, but not the only one. To review these other assessments, which have generally adopted a sectoral focus, a simple code was developed to examine a set of prominent and widely cited assessments by the World Bank, the United Nations Development Programme (UNDP), the IPCC, and the Network of African Science Academies, as well as an international think-tank, the Centre for International Governance Innovation. The discussion of individual sectors in these reports was ranked on a three-point scale, with two for extensive discussion, one for some discussion, and zero for no discussion.

As table 11.1 shows, these assessments agree on areas of coverage, with all giving at least some treatment to a large number of sectors, with agriculture, including food security, being the topic most often discussed, followed closely by water, health, economic performance, and energy. Extreme events and conflict and migration receive a lower level of attention. There is no trend of increasing attention to sectors over this period, with the mean score per sector varying around 1.5 throughout the period of the reports. This high degree of agreement across the assessments could reflect shared concerns. It also might reflect the high degree of uncertainty

Table 11.1   Ranking of Sectors in Climate Change Assessments of Africa

	UNDP 2008	World Bank 2009	CIGI 2009	Schelln-huber 2013	IPCC 5AR 2014	NASAC 2015	World Bank 2016	Average
Water	2	2	1	2	1	2	2	1.71
Agriculture	1	2	2	2	2	2	2	1.86
Health	2	2	2	1	2	2	1	1.71
Economics	2	2	2	1	2	1	2	1.71
Extreme events	1	1	1	1	2	1	1	1.14
Conflict and migration	1	1	2	1	1	0	2	1.14
Energy	1	2	2	2	1	2	2	1.71
Forests	2	2	1	1	1	1	1	1.29
Mitigation	2	2	1	1	2	1	2	1.57
Average	1.50	1.75	1.63	1.33	1.50	1.33	1.67	1.54

Note: UNDP = United Nations Development Programme; CIGI = Center for International Governance Innovation; IPCC 5AR = Intergovernmental Panel on Climate Change Fifth Assessment Report; NASAC = Network of African Science Academies.

about impacts, which would create a reluctance to exclude any subject, or a recognition of the changing fashions of international funding. As a result, any topic that might provide the basis for a request for financing could be included. Finally, in this area, as in many others, there could be a tendency to base assessments on earlier assessments.

The issues in these assessments overlap with the priorities established by African countries, as reported in the Nationally Determined Contributions (NDCs) pursuant to the Paris Agreement of 2015. The primary goal is to bring concentrations of greenhouse gases to levels that will keep the increase in global average temperature to well below 2°C, and, ideally, to 1.5°C. Some NDCs also discuss steps to adapt to climate change, climate finance, and technology transfer. In this way, the NDCs are national assessments of climate change priorities, pointing toward nation-specific areas of vulnerability and preparedness. In total, forty-seven Sub-Saharan countries provided NDCs.

As with the sectoral assessments, there is a high degree of overlap. All forty-seven countries have promised concrete actions in mitigation, which is the key focus of the NDCs. They also indicated they have made at least some statements about reducing emissions in a large number of sectors. Six sectors appear regularly. Listed in order of frequency, they are energy, forestry, agriculture, waste, transportation, and industry, with the first four mentioned in forty or more plans, and the latter two mentioned in about twenty plans. The striking homogeneity of NDCs could reflect the newness of the instrument, with countries drawing on models and guidelines offered by nongovernmental organizations (NGOs) (Climate and Development Knowledge Network 2015; Holdaway et al. 2015). It might also reflect the wish to increase the possibility of external financing by increasing the number of areas that could be supported; all forty-seven countries refer to the need for external financing.

There is also agreement that African countries vary in their vulnerability and preparedness (Hulme et al. 2001). The AR5, for example, notes that agricultural impacts are more severe in semi-arid regions (Niang et al. 2014). Moreover, information on relative vulnerability and preparedness could be of great importance, as nations seek to determine the relation of climate change adaptation to other goals, and as international organizations and donors face decisions about the allocation of their resources. Several efforts to assess a number of African countries on these variables come up with somewhat-divergent rankings, indicating the challenges of gathering data and of judging the likelihood of suffering impacts and of responding to them—or perhaps the different goals of the different assessment efforts.

Since 1995, the Notre Dame Global Adaptation Initiative (ND-GAIN) has conducted the largest and most substantial of these annual rankings. The ND-GAIN Country Index uses annual country-level data to construct a number of indices for more than one hundred seventy countries around the world. It compiles these indices to establish metrics for two key dimensions of preparedness: vulnerability and readiness.

Vulnerability measures a country's exposure, sensitivity, and capacity to adapt to the negative effects of climate change. ND-GAIN measures overall vulnerability by considering six life-supporting sectors: food, water, health, ecosystem service, human habitat, and infrastructure. Readiness measures a country's ability to leverage investments and convert them to adaptation actions. ND-GAIN measures overall readiness by considering three components: economic readiness, governance readiness, and social readiness. Both of these dimensions range from 0 to 1. As their names suggest, countries are better off with lower vulnerability and higher readiness scores. The ND-GAIN score is computed through the following formula:

$$\text{ND-GAIN} = (\text{Readiness index} - \text{Vulnerability index} + 1) \times 50 \quad (11.1)$$

This formula generates scores ranging from 0 to 100.

The index provides data on 176 countries, 49 of which are in Sub-Saharan Africa. None of them are among the countries that score highest on preparedness. The country that scores as the most prepared in the region in 2016 is Mauritius, with a score of 55.7, ranked fifty. It ranks well below the top three countries—Norway, New Zealand, and Finland—with scores of 76.0, 73.8, and 72.3, respectively. The second-highest-ranked African country, the Seychelles, is also an island. It appears down the list, at ninety-one, followed by Botswana, at ninety-three. The bottom seven countries—Niger, Sudan, the Democratic Republic of the Congo, the Central African Republic, Eritrea, Chad, and Somalia—are all in Sub-Saharan Africa. Figure 11.1 shows trends in ND-GAIN scores across Sub-Saharan Africa for 1995 to 2005.

Two other major assessments of the preparedness of African countries have been produced by international organizations and draw on extensive sets of reports. In contrast to the data-driven work of ND-GAIN, these two assessments reflect a close familiarity with the countries and often have direct experience with them.

The first of these is the Climate Adaptation Country Profiles, produced by the World Bank. Written in a standardized format, these profiles are operational tools for practitioners in climate adaptation, disaster risk reduction, and economic development. They provide information to support the integration of climate resilience into planning and operations.

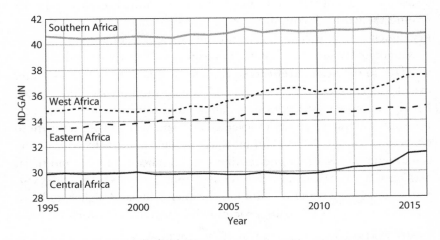

Figure 11.1   ND-GAIN of regions in Sub-Saharan Africa, 1995–2005

Source: World Bank, Notre Dame Global Adaptation Initiative.

Of the ninety-four countries for which the World Bank has prepared profiles, thirty-two are in Sub-Saharan Africa.

Of particular importance is the narrative section in each profile. These overviews summarize challenges and opportunities as well as efforts to address them.

The second set of country profiles comes from the UNDP. Some of these profiles are prepared in association with the Africa Adaptation Programme (AAP). The AAP ran from 2008 to 2012 and was launched with $92 million support from the government of Japan. This portal served two Sub-Saharan countries, providing narrative summaries of vulnerabilities and adaptation activities as well as quantitative data. The UNDP also prepared climate change country profiles for twenty-four other nations in Sub-Saharan Africa.

To establish quantitative scores from the qualitative verbal summaries in these profiles, a textual analysis was conducted. Each term or phrase that contained an evaluation was scored, with 1 for positive statements and –1 for negative statements. The mean score of these statements was calculated, and termed the sentiment score, which could range from 1 to –1. The negative correlation between the two (β = –0.033; R^2 = 0.19, $F_{(1,42)}$ = 9.274, p <0.005) is striking. In other words, ND-GAIN and the UNDP differed in their assessments (see figure 11.2). The results are

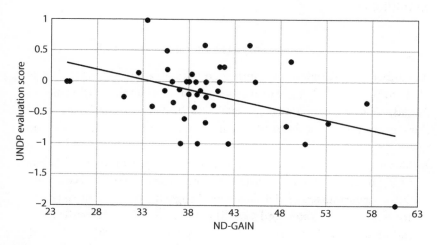

Figure 11.2   ND-GAIN scores and UNDP narrative assessment scores by country, 2015

Source: Notre Dame Global Adaptation Initiative, UNDP Climate Change Country Profiles.

similar for a comparison of the ND-GAIN and World Bank assessments. Several reasons could account for this difference between ND-GAIN scores and these qualitative assessments, beyond the matter of the latter's subjectivity. First, the values for the African countries in the ND-GAIN cluster in the lowest quartile, with relatively little spread; the small differences at this extreme end could have a disproportionate weight in the correlation, without reflecting the overall validity of the ND-GAIN index. Second, UNDP staff may have sugarcoated their negative assessments, providing a greater number of positive comments to offset the negative comments. Nonetheless, this discrepancy does suggest that it is difficult to reach agreement on the level of preparedness of different countries to address climate change. These difficulties, in turn, could stem from the relative newness of climate change as a policy area.

EFFECTS OF CLIMATE CHANGE ON THE QUALITY OF GROWTH IN AFRICA

A broad examination of the effects of climate change on the quality of growth in Africa reveals five areas of importance: reduced rates of growth, shocks, deterioration of natural capital, inadequate provision of basic needs, and cascading impacts. The effect of climate change on inequality is another area of importance, but little research has been done on this topic.

REDUCED RATES OF GROWTH

A number of researchers have indicated that advancing climate change is likely to present challenges to Africa's economic growth (Ford et al. 2015; Alagidede et al. 2016; Serdeczny et al. 2017). A representative example is this description of Southern Africa, applicable to the continent as a whole:

> Meaningful efforts to promote sustainable development in Sub-Saharan Africa in general and in Southern Africa in particular need to account for the probable impacts of global climate change. Its regional consequences are already observable and exacerbate the trends of desertification and biodiversity loss that are . . . diluting vital ecosystem services and thereby adverse to sustainable human development. . . . African states and societies will be severely affected by climate change, even if global warming is . . . stabilized at a global average of 2°C. . . . this implies

greater competition for scarce land and water resources, more humanitarian emergencies resulting from food insecurity, natural disasters and
local conflicts, and frequently recurring extreme weather events, notably
prolonged droughts and sudden flooding . . . Against this background,
opportunities to attract economic investment and improve production
in the crucial agricultural sector are also likely to diminish. . . . global
warming of 2°C is expected to lead to an increased risk of crop failure
and subsequent malnutrition and hunger. (Bauer and Scholz 2010, 87)

The IPCC's most recent overview of Africa concurs with this grim forecast, placing particular importance on agriculture and water resources
(Niang et al. 2014).

Figure 11.3 illustrates the associations between climate change and economic growth. It shows the relations between per capita gross domestic
product (GDP), GDP growth, and the ND-GAIN score for 2015. As is
often the case, the highest growth rates are found among relatively poorer
countries, and the rates of growth that are close to zero or negative are
found either in countries dependent on a single export commodity or in
countries that have faced political turmoil, epidemics, or both.

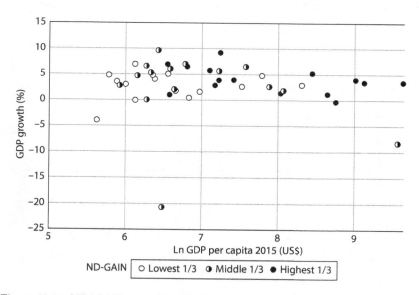

Figure 11.3   ND-GAIN scores, GDP growth rates, and per capita GDP of Sub-Saharan Africa, 2015

Source: World Bank, Notre Dame Global Adaptation Initiative.

An association also exists between per capita GDP and ND-GAIN scores, as was found in a study covering middle- and high-income countries worldwide (Lo and Chow 2015). The African countries in the lower tercile of ND-GAIN scores are concentrated among the poorest countries, whereas the richest countries primarily have high scores, with the exception of Angola. Although the ND-GAIN index was designed deliberately to exclude per capita GDP and other closely related measures from its set of components, it nonetheless does include some measures that are linked with per capita GDP, such as infrastructure elements like access to improved sanitation and paved roads. It includes other measures that are less correlated with per capita GDP, such as income inequality and percentage of land within protected areas (McKinney 2002). This association may indicate that higher levels of economic growth support adaptive capacity and reduce vulnerability; it also may indicate that climate preparedness favors economic growth (Kula et al. 2015).

Figure 11.4 displays information on economic growth that clarifies the relationship between climate and economic growth. It shows growth rates for different regions within Africa and indicates the timing of major El Niño and La Niña events, which tend to bring either unusually heavy or unusually scanty rains to certain areas. (These events often straddle two

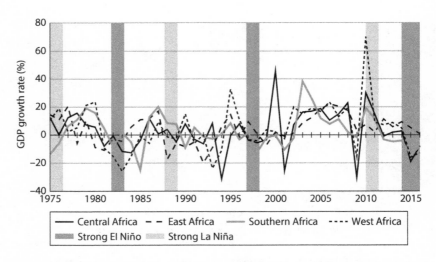

Figure 11.4   GDP growth rates by region of Sub-Saharan Africa, 1975–2016

Source: World Bank, NOAA Climate Prediction Center; NOAA Earth System Research Laboratory, Physical Sciences Division.

calendar years; for this figure, events were assigned to years if they were ranked high in strength for six or more months by the U.S. National Oceanic and Atmospheric Administration.) These events can serve as proxies for the shocks that are increasingly common with climate change. They have strong effects in East Africa and Southern Africa and have significant effects in the northern semi-arid Sahel of West Africa; they do not affect Central Africa (Mason and Goddard 2001; Lewis et al. 2016).

During the forty-year period from 1975–2015, there were strong El Niño events (1982–83, 1997–98, 2014–15) and La Niña events (1975, 1988–89, 2010–11). In years of such events, there would be a larger impact on economic growth—either immediately or with a short lag—in East and Southern Africa, a smaller one in West Africa, and none in Central Africa; the sensitivity of growth of economies, particularly in the developing world, to such shocks is well-established (Easterly et al. 1993). This climate signal would not be the only or main factor to influence economic growth in Africa, but its spatial and temporal specificity should allow it to be seen. Thus, one could recognize that the early 1980s was a period of economic crisis in Africa, when commodity prices were low and neoliberal policies were strongly enforced, whereas the late 1990s were a time of growth, with higher commodity prices and changes in some policy regimes. The climate shocks, if they are important, should appear differentially in different regions as short-term fluctuations against these trends.

Although a full analysis of the effects of these events on growth would require extensive econometric analysis beyond the scope of this paper (cf. Dell, Jones, and Olken 2008), this figure is suggestive. The spatially and temporally specific impacts of these events on growth do not appear to be present, even recognizing that the timing and level of decline and recovery might vary from one event or one region to another (Hsiang and Jina 2014). The trends do not show a consistent pattern of declines, either with all El Niño and La Niña events, or with the events associated most strongly with drought (i.e., El Niño in West Africa and Southern Africa; La Niña in East Africa). To be sure, there are some drops in GDP growth, as in Southern Africa in the year after the 1997–98 El Niño, but there are cases of increases as well (Funk et al. 2015).

This lack of association does not mean that climate change does not pose a significant threat to economic growth in Africa. The effects of climate on economic growth may have been swamped by other factors related to global economic conditions or policies. Moreover, there are signs that the most recent climate events have had particularly strong negative effects, as shown by the drought in South Africa, which severely affected agricultural exports, food security, and employment (Hlalele, Mokhatle, and Motlogeloa 2016) and created an unprecedented water crisis in Cape Town (Wolski, Hewitson, and Jack 2017). With this possibility in mind, we turn to the next two areas in which climate change has important impacts on the quality of growth in Africa.

SHOCKS

Extreme events associated with climate change can sharply reduce economic growth in particular years. Of particular importance are droughts and floods (Niang et al. 2014).

Cases of such shocks abound. Floods in western Uganda in 2016 were associated with unusually heavy rainfall, which is increasing in frequency with climate change. These flood led to the temporary displacement of one thousand eight hundred people, and the destruction of seventy buildings, five bridges, and two pipelines as well as water and electricity lines. These floods were exacerbated by recent deforestation in this area (Jacobs et al. 2016).

On a larger scale, Kenya's GDP declined 10–16 percent in the late 1990s as a result of El Niño flooding and La Niña drought from 1998 to 2000. Although agriculture was strongly affected, more than 80 percent of the economic losses in both events occurred in other sectors, with losses in transport resulting from floods that interrupted road travel and losses in hydropower and industrial production resulting from drought (World Bank 2004). A multicountry study, which included forty-two countries from Sub-Saharan Africa, constructed a country-level panel data set for the period 1975 to 2003 and showed that even moderate droughts had negative effects on growth (Brown et al. 2011).

Moreover, these effects of shocks can be long lasting. A study in Mali examined the recovery after a dry period that extended from 1970 through 2000. The rains returned, improving agriculture and incomes in some areas, but not all. Even after the rains returned, productivity and incomes remained low in drier areas in the northern portion of the country's agricultural zone (Giannini et al. 2017). The long drought led people in these areas to sell off their livestock, an important source of capital, leaving them less able to take advantage of the rains when they did come. They also lacked other income sources that are more available to farmers elsewhere in the country. Because variability in rainfall in this region is likely to increase with climate change, long-term declines such as this may well become a more serious problem (Giannini et al. 2013; Lewis and Buontempo 2016).

DETERIORATION OF NATURAL CAPITAL

Climate change threatens to weaken the natural environment, which is crucial for sustained economic growth and human well-being. Deforestation leads to the loss of soil capacity to retain water, exacerbating both flood and drought; it also contributes to erosion (Kadyampakeni 2014). A variety of adaptive measures are known to improve soil quality, such as low or zero tillage and incorporation of agricultural wastes (Kassam et al. 2012), water harvesting through the construction of bunds and other techniques (Larwanou and Saadou 2011), and incorporation of nitrogen-fixing trees into cropping systems (Garrity et al. 2010). Many of these techniques, however, require conditions that are often absent, particularly sustained support from governments and investment.

Infrastructure is highly vulnerable to climate change. Research has shown the impact of flooding on road networks and the effects of sea-level rise on buildings, seawalls, and other structures in coastal zones (Satterthwaite et al. 2009).

INADEQUATE PROVISION OF BASIC NEEDS

Climate change can threaten human well-being by affecting food security, health, and physical security. The discussion of agriculture has already shown the threats to food security (Connolly-Boutin and Smit 2016). A number of health impacts are also becoming apparent. A metastudy by Amegah, Rezza, and Jaakkola (2016) reviewed twenty-three studies that linked temperature variability—a correlate of climate change—with morbidity and mortality across Sub-Saharan Africa. It finds moderate evidence to link temperature variability with several health conditions, including cholera epidemics and increased rates of cardiovascular disease (Amegah, Rezza, and Jaakkola 2016).

Other health risks are likely to grow in coming years. Coastal West Africa is one of the regions of the world most threatened by the increasing risk of heat waves, in which rising temperatures in areas of high humidity cause not only discomfort but also mortality (Farrell 2014). Many people work outdoors and lack access to services (e.g., air conditioning, clean drinking water, medical facilities), which could moderate these risks. In addition, rapid urbanization in this region places an increasing proportion of the population in areas that experience an urban heat island effect, exacerbating the problem further (Coffel, Horton, and de Sherbinin 2018).

A number of studies have linked climate change to political conflict and violence in Sub-Saharan Africa. Hendrix and Salehyan (2012) draw on the Social Conflict in Africa Database, which contains six thousand instances of social conflict in forty-seven countries in the period from 1990 to 2008. By linking this data set with precipitation data, they find that both unusually wet and unusually dry years are associated with social conflict and violence. These results hold for both large-scale and small-scale events. Extreme deviations in rainfall—particularly dry and wet years—are associated with all types of social conflict (e.g., violent and nonviolent, government-targeted and non-government-targeted violence), although the relationship is strongest with respect to violent events, which are more responsive to abundant rather than scarce rainfall.

An analysis of a second database gives broadly similar results. The Uppsala Conflict Data Program reports communal conflict, excluding nonstate violence from rebel groups, civil wars, or groups with long-term military-like organizations. The database includes 286 instances of such conflict in Sub-Saharan Africa for the same period (1990–2008). The researchers find that communal conflict is more common in years of precipitation anomalies, particularly in dry years. Some governance variables, particularly political exclusion, are also associated with such conflict, but poverty is not (Fjelde and von Uexkull 2012).

This association of climate change, instability, and violence in Sub-Saharan Africa has been the subject of discussion in major international fora. In 2017, the United Nations Security Council issued Resolution 2349, which discussed "the situation in the Lake Chad Basin region." The resolution states that the Security Council "recognizes the adverse effects of climate change and ecological changes among other factors on the stability of the Region." A presidential statement in 2018 extends the area of concern. It states that "the Security Council recognizes the adverse effects of climate change and ecological changes among other factors on the stability of West Africa and the Sahel region"(United Nations Security Council 2018).

A recent study opens a new avenue of research into the relationship between climate change and physical security. It examines asylum applications into the European Union in the period from 2000 to 2014. These applications average about 351,000 per year, of which 94,000 are from Sub-Saharan Africa. The researchers find that temperatures deviations from a moderate optimum of around 20°C lead to an increase in asylum applications. This relationship is nonlinear, increasing sharply with larger deviations (Missirian and Schlenker 2017).

CASCADING IMPACTS

The impacts discussed thus far can compound one another. A recent review of the 1986 meningitis epidemic in Niger examines the effects of this climate-related health shock in Niger on gender differences in educational attainment, tracing its implications for inequality. Using data with fine-grained spatial resolution, the study shows that meningitis exposure is associated with reduced school attendance and reduced rates of completion of primary education years for girls of school age, but not for boys. This difference is likely due to parental investment; it is also likely to be associated with earlier ages of marriage and higher birth rates for the girls (Archibong and Annan 2017). Because meningitis in Niger is associated with climate variability (Garcia-Pando et al. 2014), it may well be exacerbated by climate change.

A study in Ethiopia, drawing on rural household surveys, also links climate variability with educational outcomes. Using fine-scaled temperature and precipitation data, it shows that children who grow up in years with normal temperatures and with above-average rainfall during the summer growing season are more likely to have completed at least one year of school. No gender effects were found in this case. In Ethiopia as in Niger, education is associated with higher incomes (Randell and Gray 2016). A recent study from Malawi finds similar patterns. Yields of plantain, a key staple in the region, underwent a decline of 43 percent in the period from 1991 to 2011, with yields tightly linked to temperature. There was also a decline of about half a year in the length of time for which students attended school. The study projects further declines in yields and decreases in education as warming continues (Fuller et al. 2018).

ADAPTATION ACTIVITIES

Although adaptation often has been promoted as a means of ameliorating the negative impacts of climate change, it face significant challenges in

Africa. The most recent IPCC assessment report offers a frank judgment on this topic:

> Since 2007, Africa has gained experience in conceptualizing, planning, and beginning to implement and support adaptation activities, from local to national levels and across a growing range of sectors. However, across the continent, most of the adaptation to climate variability and change is reactive in response to short-term motivations, is occurring autonomously at the individual/household level, and lacks support from government stakeholders and policies . . . A complex web of interacting barriers to local-level adaptation, manifesting from national to local scales, both constrains and highlights potential limits to adaptation. (Niang et al. 2014, 1225–1226)

The report mentions a few potential strengths, including abundance of some natural resources, strong social capital, and long traditions of crop and livelihood diversification, migration, and small-scale enterprises, although these may not be sufficient to overcome the obstacles to adaptation. These weaknesses point to the urgency of increasing support for adaptation, both from national governments and from international sources.

Some initial efforts have been limited. The much-discussed National Adaptation Plans of Action, which were launched in the mid-2000s, form one context in which adaptation measures have been discussed. Recent reviews find that they tend to focus narrowly on single sectors (agriculture, water, disaster risk reduction) and on short- and medium-term projects, rather than on more integrated planning, and that they address root causes of poverty that impede adaptation (Dinku 2010). Other studies point to a tendency to define adaptation so broadly that many activities of limited effectiveness or relevance to climate impacts are included. One review of thirteen countries in the Sahel and East Africa finds a number of adaptation activities, focusing largely on off-farm employment as a form of income diversification and on simple water-harnessing techniques, such as borehole drilling and the use of water pumps (Epule et al. 2017). Although these simple efforts may offset some of the impacts of drought and flooding, their consequences are small scale and often short term.

Other efforts are more substantial. In South Africa, a country that has both larger climate change impacts and greater scientific and organizational capacity than others, significant efforts have been completed: a National Climate Change Response White Paper in 2011 led to a set of Long-Term Adaptation Scenarios in 2013. These scenarios have resulted in a number of concrete activities in commercial agriculture (apple orchards, vineyards, rooibos farms, pasture production) and to the development of new organizational tools, such as insurance, to promote adaptation activities (Ziervogel et al. 2014).

For the Sahel, one of the poorest and most drought-prone areas, a recent study (Stith et al. 2016) traces the effects of adaptation projects on the recovery from the droughts of the late-twentieth century. The researchers examined 309 donor-funded interventions for the period from 1979 to 2001, many of which drew on sustainable land management practices (soil and water conservation, agroforestry, farmer-managed natural regeneration) in conjunction with precipitation records and sources on vegetation, which documented the "regreening" of the Sahel. They found that the combined effects of increased precipitation and of the adaptation projects could explain this revegetation.

A longitudinal panel study in Malawi traces the effects on 2,200 households of participation in an adaptation project. This project allowed farmers to experiment with a variety of techniques to manage crops, soil, and water, and to exchange information with other farmers. Participation in the project significantly increased household wealth and reduced food insecurity (Kangmennaang et al. 2017).

The International Red Cross/Red Crescent has developed forecast-based financing, a mechanism through which it provides funding, not once a disaster has occurred but rather well in advance. It uses forecasts to support planned efforts at risk reduction and preparedness. Pilot programs took place in Uganda and Togo, with distribution of relief supplies and construction of shelters in both countries. Activities included promoting the construction of trenches to manage floodwaters in the former and coordination with reservoir managers to facilitate releases in the latter. As climate change advances and extreme events increase in frequency and intensity, such preparatory efforts could constitute a significant adaptation (Red Cross/Red Crescent Climate Centre 2017).

ENERGY, CLIMATE MITIGATION, AND ADAPTATION-MITIGATION LINKS

This section offers a brief overview of an extensive subject: the role of energy in growth and sustainable development in Africa. It complements the previous section on adaptation, by focusing on mitigation, which addresses the root cause of climate change, principally by reducing emissions and secondarily by increasing uptake of carbon in terrestrial and marine ecosystems. The relation of adaptation and mitigation is expressed in the often-repeated phrase, which compares them, respectively, to "managing the unavoidable and avoiding the unmanageable."

Although many have expressed the view that mitigation is largely the responsibility of the developed and emerging countries that have been the major emitters, Africa has reasons to weigh mitigation seriously; the continent's emissions are growing and low-carbon energy sources represent major opportunities. Note as well that some agricultural adaptations reduce emissions, because traditional forms of agriculture, particularly those associated with burning savannahs, release significant amounts of greenhouse gases (Kim et al. 2016).

The scale of energy needs in Africa has sometimes led to hasty moves on opportunities to increase energy supply, without attending to potential climate impacts. Even though Africa lags the rest of the world in energy use, it has reasons to weigh its energy sources carefully, too (Baptista and Plananska 2017). Moreover, African governments are highly cognizant of the existence of a range of alternative energy pathways, as reflected by the inclusion of renewables in National Adaptation Programmes of Action and NDCs.

Given the deficits of grids and other energy infrastructure in Africa, large investments are needed for energy transmission as well as for generation. Official development assistance and other official flows for energy have more than tripled between 2005 and 2015, with the largest amounts coming from the World Bank, the European Union, and the African Development Bank (Tagliapietra and Bazilian 2017). China's contributions through its state-owned enterprises are rapidly growing, and represented 30 percent of the additions to Africa's energy capacity between 2010 and 2015 (International Energy Agency [IEA] 2016).

These sources of energy financing can promote attentiveness to renewable energy. The World Bank announced in 2017 that it would stop financing upstream oil and gas after 2019, making only occasional exceptions for upstream gas in the poorest countries, if such developments improve equity of energy access, and if they fit within the countries' NDCs. This move follows on its 2013 decision to limit financing of coal projects to highly exceptional cases. By contrast, the World Bank supports hydropower projects, although it includes a series of safeguards to protect local populations against displacement and to avoid harm to natural ecosystems. The World Bank (2017) notes that hydropower not only mitigates climate change because it displaces fossil fuels but also provides adaptation benefits by reducing disaster risks (both floods and droughts), improving water security, and supporting irrigation.

Hydropower has great potential in Africa, where more than 90 percent of the potential remains untapped (IEA 2014). Although environmental and social issues surround hydropower, particularly megaprojects, such as the Grand Inga Project in the Democratic Republic of the Congo, this source should not be neglected. Solar power also has great potential, particularly for the large rural populations living far from national grids.

Integrating energy planning with economic and social planning is critical in all areas. Significant opportunities exist in Africa's rapidly growing cities, where urban transport could involve electric vehicles, and the design of residences, workplaces, and institutions could aim to reduce energy needs for heating and cooling.

A variety of other opportunities exist for low-carbon energy sources. Chinese firms and agencies have supported solar power in Africa (Shen and Power 2017), in settings ranging from cities and economic development zones to remote rural areas. The performance in these recent projects has also varied, but some elements that contribute to success in rural minigrids are emerging. One study, based on expert interviews and visits to rural grids in Kenya, points to the value of participatory decision making and the establishment of property rights in overcoming obstacles that these systems have faced (Gollwitzer et al. 2018). These grids not only reduce the use of fossil fuels in generators, lanterns, and other uses but also contribute to improving equity, supporting education and healthcare delivery, and improving communications.

Other new forms of low-carbon energy sources are emerging as well. For example, China is investing in biomass and waste-generation capacity in Ethiopia, including projects that can handle more than two thousand metric tons per day (IEA 2016). These projects can address waste disposal issues and offer health benefits.

In sum, renewable energy sources, particularly hydropower and solar, merit close attention not only as means to reduce emissions but also as viable components of Africa's efforts to increase energy supply. The availability of international financing and the provision of adaptation cobenefits make renewables attractive.

CONCLUSION

Africa urgently needs to address climate change impacts. Assessments vary in their details, but they concur on the importance of this topic and on its broad outlines. The risks to the quality of growth are substantial, including lower rates of growth overall, vulnerability to shocks, loss of natural capital, and the decline of the ability of economies to address the basic needs of people. A number of adaptation programs are already underway, and others are being planned; the obstacles to such programs have been identified, and to varying degrees, are being addressed as well. In this way, addressing climate change links closely with other aspects of the quality of growth in Africa, including equity, basic needs, and sustainability. Growth that recognizes the urgency of addressing climate change is high-quality growth that will make progress on meeting the Sustainable Development Goals.

NOTE

This chapter benefited from the contributions of four thoughtful, hardworking research assistants. Adnan Hajizada conducted the data analysis for and developed figures 11.2 and 11.4. He also reviewed climate assessment reports for Africa and reviewed data on growth and ND-GAIN scores. Andrea Cristina Ruiz carried out the analysis of documents for and prepared table 11.1; she also conducted a literature review on energy. Natasha Ardiani reviewed and prepared the summary statistics for the NDCs, discussed in the second section. Kelsey Wooddell conducted the analysis for and prepared figure 11.1; she also prepared the bibliography and provided assistance with the final preparation of the manuscript. Their perspectives, drawing on their studies, experiences in developing countries, and other research greatly strengthened this chapter.

A number of colleagues provided helpful comments and suggestions as well, including Belina Archibong, Francesco Fiondella, Lorenzo Fioramonti, Kathleen Galvin, Alessandra Giannini, Amir Jina, Melissa Leach, Andy McKay, Akbar Noman, Jesse Ribot, and Madeleine Thomson.

REFERENCES

Alagidede, Paul, George Adu, and Prince Boakye Frimpong. 2016. "The Effect of Climate Change on Economic Growth: Evidence from Sub-Saharan Africa." *Environmental Economics and Policy Studies* 18 (3): 417–436. doi: 10.1007/s10018 -015-0116-3.

Amegah, A. Kofi, Giovanni Rezza, and Jouini J. K. Jaakkola. 2016. "Temperature-Related Morbidity and Mortality in Sub-Saharan Africa: A Systematic Review of the Empirical Evidence." *Environment International* 91: 133–149. doi: 10.1016/j .envint.2016.02.027.

Archibong, Belinda, and Francis Annan. 2017. "Disease and Gender Gaps in Human Capital Investment: Evidence from Niger's 1986 Meningitis Epidemic." *American Economic Review* 107 (5): 530–35. doi: doi: 10.1257/aer.p20171142.

Baptista, Idalina, and Jana Plananska. 2017. "The Landscape of Energy Initiatives in Sub-Saharan Africa: Going for Systemic Change or Reinforcing the Status Quo?" *Energy Policy* 110 (Suppl. C): 1–8. doi: https: //doi.org/10.1016/j.enpol.2017.08.006.

Bauer, Steffen, and Imme Scholz. 2010. "Adaptation to Climate Change in Southern Africa: New Boundaries for Sustainable Development." *Climate and Development* 2 (2): 83–93.

Besada, Hany, and Nelson K. Sewankambo, eds. 2009. Climate Change in Africa: Adaptation, Mitigation and Governance Challenges. CIGI Special Report. Ontario, Canada: Centre for International Governance Innovation.

Brown, Casey, Robyn Meeks, Kenneth Hunu, and Winston Yu. 2011. "Hydroclimate Risk to Economic Growth in sub-Saharan Africa." *Climatic Change* 106 (4): 621–647. doi: 10.1007/s10584-010-9956-9.

Climate and Development Knowledge Network. "Intended Nationally Determined Contributions (NDCS): Sharing Lessons and Resources." Climate and Development Knowledge Network. Accessed 31 January 2018. https: //cdkn.org/indc.

Coffel, Ethan D., Radley M. Horton, and Alex de Sherbinin. 2018. "Temperature and Humidity Based Projections of a Rapid Rise in Global Heat Stress Exposure During the 21st Century." *Environmental Research Letters* 13 (1): 9. doi: 10.1088/1748-9326 /aaa00e.

Connolly-Boutin, Liette, and Barry Smit. 2016. "Climate Change, Food Security, and Livelihoods in Sub-Saharan Africa." *Regional Environmental Change* 16 (2): 385–399. doi: 10.1007/s10113-015-0761-x.

Dell, Melissa, Benjamin F. Jones, and Benjamin A. Olken. 2008. "Climate Change and Economic Growth: Evidence from the Last Half Century." NBER Working Paper No. 14132. National Bureau of Economic Research, Cambridge, MA.

Dinku, Tufa. 2010. "The Need for National Centres for Climate and Development in Africa." *Climate and Development* 2 (1): 9–13. doi: 10.3763/cdev.2010.0029.

Easterly, William, Michael Kremer, Lant Pritchett, and Lawrence H. Summers. 1993. "Good Policy or Good Luck—Country Growth-Performance and Temporary Shocks." *Journal of Monetary Economics* 32 (3): 459–483. doi: 10.1016/0304 -3932(93)90026-c.

Epule, Terrence E., James D. Ford, Shuaib Lwasa, and Laurent Lepage. 2017. "Climate change adaptation in the Sahel." *Environmental Science & Policy* 75 : 121–137. doi: 10.1016/j.envsci.2017.05.018.

Farrell, Shannon L. 2014. "Turn Down the Heat: Climate Extremes, Regional Impacts, and the Case for Resilience." *Government Information Quarterly* 31 (2): 346–347. doi: 10.1016/j.giq.2014.02.002.

Filho, Walter Leal. 2011. *Experiences of Climate Change Adaptation in Africa.* Berlin: Springer Berlin.

Fjelde, Hanna, and Nina von Uexkull. 2012. "Climate Triggers: Rainfall Anomalies, Vulnerability and Communal Conflict in Sub-Saharan Africa." *Political Geography* 31 (7): 444–453. doi: 10.1016/j.polgeo.2012.08.004.

Ford, James D., Lea Berrang-Ford, Anna Bunce, Courtney McKay, Maya Irwin, and Tristan Pearce. 2015. "The Status of Climate Change Adaptation in Africa and Asia." *Regional Environmental Change* 15 (5): 801–814. doi: 10.1007/s10113-014-0648-2.

Fuller, Trevon L., Paul Sesink Clee, Kevin Y. Njabo, Anthony Trodchez, Katy Morgan, Demetrio Bocuma Mene, Nicky Anthony, Mary K. Gonder, Walter Allen, Rachid Hanna, and Thomas B. Smith. 2018. "Climate Warming Causes Declines in Crop Yields and Lowers School Attendance Rates in Central Africa." *Science of the Total Environment* 610: 503–510. doi: 10.1016/j.scitotenv.2017.08.041.

Funk, Chris, Frank Davenport, Laura Harrison, Tamuka Magadzire, Gideon. Galu, Guleid A. Artan, Shraddhanand Shukla, Diriba Korecha, Matayo Indeje, Catherine Pomposi, Denis Macharia, Gregory Husak, and Faka Dieudonne Nsadisa. 2017. "Anthropogenic Enhancement of Moderate-to-Strong El Niño Events Likely Contributed to Drought and Poor Harvests in Southern Africa During 2016." In *Explaining Extreme Events of 2016 from a Climate Perspective*. Boston, MA: American Meteorological Society.

Garcia-Pando, Carols P., Michelle C. Stanton, Peter J. Diggle, Sylwia Trzaska, Ron L. Miller, Jan P. Perlwitz, José. M. Baldasano, Emilio Cuevas, Pietro Ceccato, Pascal Yaka, and Madeleine C. Thomson. 2014. "Soil Dust Aerosols and Wind as Predictors of Seasonal Meningitis Incidence in Niger." *Environmental Health Perspectives* 122 (7): 679–686. doi: 10.1289/ehp.1306640.

Garrity, Dennis P., Festus K. Akinnifesi, Oluyede C. Ajayi, Sileshi G. Weldesemayat, Jeremias G. Mowo, Antoine Kalinganire, Mahamane Larwanou, and Jules Bayala. 2010. "Evergreen Agriculture: A Robust Approach to Sustainable Food Security in Africa." *Food Security* 2 (3): 197–214. doi: 10.1007/s12571-010-0070-7.

Giannini, Alessandra, P. Krishna Krishnamurthy, Rémi Cousin, Naouar Labidi, and Richard J. Choularton. 2017. "Climate Risk and Food Security in Mali: A Historical Perspective on Adaptation." *Earth's Future* 5 (2): 144–157. doi: 10.1002/2016EF000404.

Giannini, Alessandra, S. Salack, T. Lodoun, A. Ali, A. T. Gaye, and O. Ndiaye. 2013. "A Unifying View of Climate Change in the Sahel Linking Intra-Seasonal, Interannual and Longer Time Scales." *Environmental Research Letters* 8 (2): 8. doi: 10.1088/1748-9326/8/2/024010.

Gollwitzer, Lorenz, David Ockwell, Ben Muok, Adrian Ely, and Helene Ahlborg. 2018. "Rethinking the Sustainability and Institutional Governance of Electricity Access and Mini-Grids: Electricity as a Common Pool Resource." *Energy Research and Social Science* 39: 152–161. doi: https://doi.org/10.1016/j.erss.2017.10.033.

Grey, David, and Claudia W. Sadoff. 2007. "Sink or Swim? Water Security for Growth and Development." *Water Policy* 9 (6): 545–571. doi: 10.2166/wp.2007.021.

Haščič, I., J. Silva, and N. Johnstone 2012. *Climate Mitigation and Adaptation in Africa*. Paris: OECD Publishing.

Hendrix, Cullen S. 2017. "The Streetlight Effect in Climate Change Research on Africa." *Global Environmental Change-Human and Policy Dimensions* 43: 137–147. doi: 10.1016/j.gloenvcha.2017.01.009.

Hendrix, Cullen S., and Idean Salehyan. 2012. "Climate Change, Rainfall, and Social Conflict in Africa." *Journal of Peace Research* 49 (1): 35–50. doi: 10.1177/0022343311426165.

Hlalele, Bernard M., I. M. Mokhatle, and Rodney T. Motlogeloa. 2016. "Assessing Economic Impacts of Agricultural Drought: A Case of Thaba Nchu, South Africa." *Journal of Earth Science and Climate Change* 7 (1): 4. doi: 10.4172/2157-7617.1000327.

Holdaway, E., C. Dodwell, K. Sura, and H. Picot. 2015. *A Guide to NDCs: Intended Nationally Determined Contributions.* 2nd ed. London: Department for International Development.

Hsiang, Solomon M., and Amir S. Jina. 2014. "The Causal Effect of Environmental Catastrophe on Long-Run Economic Growth: Evidence from 6,700 Cyclones." *National Bureau of Economic Research Working Paper Series* No. 20352. doi: 10.3386/w20352.

Hulme, Mike, R. M. Doherty, T. N. M. Ngara, Mark George New, and David Lister. 2001. "African Climate Change: 1900–2100." *Climate Research* 17 (2): 145–168.

Ingram, D. S. 2014. "Book Review: *Climate Change and Agriculture in Sub-Saharan Africa.*" *Food Security* 6 (1): 147–149. doi: 10.1007/s12571-013-0316-2.

International Energy Agency. 2014. *Africa Energy Outlook: A Focus on Energy Prospects in Sub-Saharan Africa.* Paris: International Energy Agency.

——. 2016. *Boosting the Power Sector in Sub-Saharan Africa: China's Involvement.* Paris: International Energy Agency.

——. 2017. *World Energy Outlook 2017.* Paris: International Energy Agency.

Jacobs, Liesbet, Jan Maes, Kewan Mertens, John Sekajugo, Wim Thiery, Nicole van Lipzig, Jean Poesen, Matthieu. Kervyn, and Olivier Dewitte. 2016. "Reconstruction of a Flash Flood Event Through a Multi-Hazard Approach: Focus on the Rwenzori Mountains, Uganda." *Natural Hazards* 84 (2): 851–876. doi: 10.1007/s11069-016-2458-y.

Kadyampakeni, Davie M. 2014. "Soil, Water, and Nutrient Management Options for Climate Change Adaptation in Southern Africa." *Agronomy Journal* 106 (1): 100–110. doi: 10.2134/agronj2013.0307.

Kangmennaang, Joseph, Rachel B. Kerr, Esther Lupafya, Laifolo Dakishoni, Mangani Katundu, and Isaac Luginaah. 2017. "Impact of a Participatory Agroecological Development Project on Household Wealth and Food Security in Malawi." *Food Security* 9 (3): 561–576. doi: 10.1007/s12571-017-0669-z.

Kassam, Amir, Theodor Friedrich, Rolf Derpsch, Rabah Lahmar, Rachid Mrabet, Gottlieb Basch, Emilio J. González-Sánchez, and Rachid Serraj. 2012. "Conservation Agriculture in the Dry Mediterranean Climate." *Field Crops Research* 132: 7–17. doi: https://doi.org/10.1016/j.fcr.2012.02.023.

Kim, Dong-Gill, Andrew D. Thomas, David Pelster, Todd S. Rosenstock, and Alberto Sanz-Cobena. 2016. "Greenhouse Gas Emissions from Natural Ecosystems and Agricultural Lands in Sub-Saharan Africa: Synthesis of Available Data and Suggestions for Further Research." *Biogeosciences* 13 (16): 4789–4809. doi: 10.5194/bg-13-4789-2016.

Kula, Nothemba, Andy Haines, and Robert Fryatt. 2013. "Reducing Vulnerability to Climate Change in Sub-Saharan Africa: The Need for Better Evidence." *PLoS Medicine* 10 (1): 5. doi: 10.1371/journal.pmed.1001374.

Larwanou, Mahamane, and Mahamane Saadou. 2011. "The Role of Human Interventions in Tree Dynamics and Environmental Rehabilitation in the Sahel Zone of Niger." *Journal of Arid Environments* 75 (2): 194–200. doi: 10.1016/j.jaridenv .2010.09.016.

Lewis, Kirsty, and Carlo Buontempo. 2016. *Climate Impacts in the Sahel and West Africa.* Paris: OECD Publishing.

Lo, Alex Y., and Alex T. Chow. 2015. "The Relationship Between Climate Change Concern and National Wealth." *Climatic Change* 131 (2): 335–348. doi: 10.1007/s10584 -015-1378-2.

Mason, Simon J., and Lisa Goddard. 2001. "Probabilistic Precipitation Anomalies Associated with ENSO." *Bulletin of the American Meteorological Society* 82 (4): 619–638. doi: 10.1175/1520-0477(2001)082<0619: ppaawe>2.3.co;2.

McKinney, Michael L. 2002. "Effects of National Conservation Spending and Amount of Protected Area on Species Threat Rates." *Conservation Biology* 16 (2): 539–543. doi: 10.1046/j.1523-1739.2002.00442.x.

Missirian, Anouch, and Wolfram Schlenker. 2017. "Asylum Applications Respond to Temperature Fluctuations." *Science* 358 (6370): 1610–1613. doi: 10.1126/science. aao0432.

Network of African Science Academies. 2016. *Climate Change Adaptation and Resilience in Africa—Recommendations to Policymakers.* Nairobi: Network of African Science Academies.

Niang, Isabel, Olived. C. Ruppel, Muhammed A. Abdrabo, Ama, Essel, Christopher Lennard, Jonathan Padgham, and Penny Urquhart. 2014. "Africa." In *Climate Change 2014: Impacts, Adaptation, and Vulnerability. Part B: Regional Aspects. Contribution of Working Group II to the Fifth Assessment Report of the Intergovernmental Panel of Climate Change*, ed. V. R. Barros, C. B. Field, D. J. Dokken, M. D. Mastrandrea, K. J. Mach, T. E. Bilir, M. Chatterjee, K. L. Ebi, Y. O. Estrada, R. C. Genova, B. Girma, E. S. Kissel, A. N. Levy, S. MacCracken, P. R. Mastrandrea and L. L. White, 1199–1265. Cambridge: Cambridge University Press.

Nyantakyi-Frimpong, Hanson, and Rachel Bezner-Kerr. 2015. "The Relative Importance of Climate Change in the Context of Multiple Stressors in Semi-arid Ghana." *Global Environmental Change-Human and Policy Dimensions* 32: 40–56. doi: 10.1016/j.gloenvcha.2015.03.003.

Randell, Heather F., and Clark Gray. 2016. "Climate Variability and Educational Attainment: Evidence from Rural Ethiopia." *Global Environmental Change-Human and Policy Dimensions* 41: 111–123. doi: 10.1016/j.gloenvcha.2016.09.006.

Red Cross/Red Crescent Climate Centre. 2017. "Forecast-Based Financing: Case Studies from Togo and Uganda. 6." Accessed January 31, 2018, https: //www .preventionweb.net/publications/view/57131.

Satterthwaite, David, Saleemul Huq, Hannah Reid, Mark Pelling, and Patricia R. Lankao. 2009. "Adapting to Climate Change in Urban Areas: the Possibilities and Constraints in Low- and Middle-Income Nations." In *Adapting Cities to Climate*

Change. Understanding and Addressing the Development Challenges ed. J. Bicknell, D. Dodman and D. Satterthwaite, 3–50. Abingdon, UK: Earthscan.

Serdeczny, Olivia, Sophie Adams, Florent Baarsch, Dim Coumou, Alexander Robinson, William Hare, Michael Schaeffer, Mahé. Perrette, and Julia Reinhardt. 2017. "Climate Change Impacts in Sub-Saharan Africa: From Physical Changes to their Social Repercussions." *Regional Environmental Change* 17 (6): 1585–1600. doi: 10.1007/s10113-015-0910-2.

Shen, Wei, and Marcus Power. 2017. "Africa and the Export of China's Clean Energy Revolution." *Third World Quarterly* 38 (3): 678–697. doi: 10.1080/01436597.2016.1199262.

Stith, Mimi, Alessandra Giannini, John del Corral, Susana Adamo, and Alex de Sherbinin. 2016. "A Quantitative Evaluation of the Multiple Narratives of the Recent Sahelian Regreening." *Weather Climate and Society* 8 (1): 67–83. doi: 10.1175/wcas-d-15-0012.1.

Tagliapietra, Simone, and Morgan Bazilian. 2017. "The Role of International Institutions in Fostering Sub-Saharan Africa's Electrification." Columbia University Center on Global Energy Policy, New York.

United Nations. 2017. United Nations Security Council Resolution 2349, Peace and Security in Africa, S/RES/2349, March 31, 2017. http://www.un.org/en/ga/search/view_doc.asp?symbol=S/RES/2349(2017).

United Nations Security Council. 2018. Statement by the President of the Security Council, S/PRST/2018/3, January 13, 2018.

United Nations Development Programme. 2007. *Human Development Report 2007/2008*. New York: United Nations Development Programme.

United Nations Economic Commission for Africa. 2014. *Keeping Climate Impacts at Bay: A 6-Point Strategy for Climate-Resilient Economies in Africa*. Addis Ababa, Ethiopia: UN Economic Commission for Africa.

Wolski, Piotr, Bruce Hewitson, and Chris Jack. 2017. "Why Cape Town's Drought Was So Hard to Forecast." *The Conversation*, October 19. https://theconversation.com/why-cape-towns-drought-was-so-hard-to-forecast-84735.

World Bank. 2004. "Towards a Water-Secure Kenya: Water Resources Sector Memorandum.: Washington, DC: World Bank.

——. 2009. "Africa—Making Development Climate Resilient: A World Bank Strategy for Sub-Saharan Africa." Washington, DC: World Bank.

——. 2015. "Africa Climate Business Plan: Accelerating Climate-Resilient and Low-Carbon Development." Washington, DC: World Bank Group.

——. 2016. "Accelerating Climate-Resilient and Low-Carbon Development: Progress Report on the Implementation of the Africa Climate Business Plan." Washington, DC: World Bank Group.

——. 2017. "Understanding Poverty: Hydropower." Last Modified 10 April 2017, accessed 1 February. http://www.worldbank.org/en/topic/hydropower/overview.

Ziervogel, Gina, Mark New, Emma Archer van Garderen, Guy Midgley, Anna Taylor, Ralph Hamann, Sabine Stuart-Hill, Jonny Myers, and Michele Warburton. 2014. "Climate Change Impacts and Adaptation in South Africa." *Wiley Interdisciplinary Reviews-Climate Change* 5 (5): 605–620. doi: 10.1002/wcc.295.

CHAPTER 12

Does Environmental Policy Make African Industry
Less Competitive?

THE POSSIBILITIES IN GREEN INDUSTRIAL POLICY

Go Shimada

The consensus is that Africa needs structural transformation for economic development and to reduce extreme poverty. This situation presents challenges and opportunities. The challenge is that Africa also needs
to cope with environmental issues, such as climate change, which it is
not responsible for. Although Africa is a only minor emitter of green gas
pollution globally, it will be greatly affected by climate change because
of its dependence on agriculture for production and for employment.[1]
It is likely that environmental issues will affect Africa more severely than
other continents. Although the continent is still experiencing economic
growth, the adverse consequences of environmental degradation (e.g., air
pollution) are already apparent. Africa also has an opportunity, however,
to utilize technologies to their advantage as latecomers.

Therefore, the question for Africa today is not only how to make a
structural transformation in its economy but also how to make that transformation process sustainable. This transformation is in line with the
ninth Sustainable Development Goal (SDG), which states: "build resilient infrastructure, promote inclusive and sustainable industrialization
and foster innovation"(UN 2015, 20). As Africa needs to both achieve
economic growth and protect its environment, "sustainable industrialization" is a critical but daunting task.

The challenges and opportunities for Africa in this area lead to the
three questions that this chapter tackles.

First, is environmental conservation a new threat to the economic
growth of Africa? To answer this question, the chapter takes up two aspects
of the environment: climate change and pollution. Regarding climate
change, this chapter focuses on natural disasters, such as droughts and
floods, because these have huge impacts on people's lives in Africa.

Second, if environmental protection is needed, will the required environmental policy make the African economy less competitive? If environmental protection and economic growth are alternative choices, it may not be possible to achieve both goals at the same time. Porter (1991), however, argued that strict environmental regulations do not hinder competitiveness; rather, they enhance it because tougher standards promote innovation in a country (the Porter hypothesis). He argued this concept using data mainly from the United States and other developed economies. When considering Africa, tougher environment governance may stifle economic activities (the second section of this chapter discusses this concept).

Third, how does the international community need to support Africa to maximize its latecomer's advantage, utilizing available technologies? Considering this question, policy implications may be derived.

ARE NATURAL DISASTERS A NEW THREAT TO THE ECONOMIC GROWTH OF AFRICA?

Regarding the impact of climate change on Africa, another question comes to mind: is this an agenda for developed countries, and not for Africa? It may be too early to discuss environmental issues for Africa. Considering the continent's development stage, it has more important issues to deal with, such as poverty and unemployment. The quick answer to these doubts about the priority of environmental concerns is that despite Africa's early stage of development, environmental issue is important. The reasons are twofold: (1) as we see in the next section, natural disasters have been increasing in Africa, and they affect the lives of farmers and pastoralists because agriculture and livestock depend on climatic conditions; and (2) as economies develop, they often face increased air and water pollution, a situation that has a huge impact on human health conditions. The pollution level in Africa has already begun to increase, and it ultimately could have huge social impacts.

NATURAL DISASTERS

Environmental change is one issue that the Washington consensus has long neglected. The impact of climate change in Africa has already been enormous; and natural disasters have been one of its most important manifestations (The Intergovernmental Panel on Climate Change [IPCC] 2018). The number of natural disasters has increased rapidly since the 1990s. Figure 12.1 shows that a clear trend in Africa based on the EM-DAT

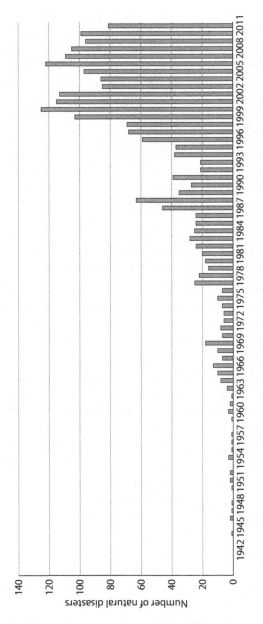

Figure 12.1 Frequency of natural disasters in Africa

Source: Author's creation based on the EM-DAT database, created by the Centre for Research on the Epidemiology of Disasters (CRED).

database, which contains data on the location and impact of more than twenty-two thousand mass-impact natural disasters that occurred across the world between 1900 and 2019.[2] Natural disasters in Africa gradually increased in the 1990s, becoming even more frequent from 2000. In the past, such natural disasters were rare, but this rising trend indicates that all plans to implement development and environmental policies should take into account the increased likelihood of natural disasters.

Among the types of natural disasters African communities typically endure, drought and flooding are the most common and severe (Shimada and Motomura 2017). In some parts of Africa, it rains too little; in others, it rains too much. Both are climate-related disasters, and a primary reason for this increase in natural disasters likely is climate change. Africa has already been severely affected, and a consequence of climate change is that the rapid increase in natural disasters has meant that scarce natural resources are even more difficult to find (e.g., drinking water and forest resources). It has affected land conditions as well: in Africa, usable land was never abundant, but previously scarce arable land has become increasingly less available because of climate-based natural disasters. The adverse impacts of this situation on agriculture and livestock rearing have huge implications for the lives of farmers as well as pastoralists.

As Figure 12.2 shows, the number of people displaced by natural disasters has been increasing. The absolute number is huge, but many others

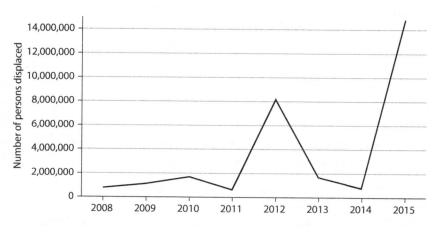

Figure 12.2   Number of displaced persons from natural disasters

Source: Author's creation based on the Internal Displacement Monitoring Centre data set (IDMC `2016).

remain in country as internally displaced persons (IDPs), while others are displaced across borders. This situation could become a destabilizing factor for Africa in the future, which will further hinder sound economic growth. The international community needs to extend humanitarian assistance to the people affected, but beyond this, the root cause of these natural disasters (i.e., climate change) needs to be effectively tackled.

POLLUTION

As we have seen, climate-based natural disasters are a new type of threat to the economic growth of Africa. This section discusses another aspect of the environmental issue: air and water pollution. Figure 12.3 shows the present situation relating to air quality in major African cities. The two vertical lines in the figures are the World Health Organization (WHO) guideline levels for particulate matter PM10 (upper line) and PM1.5 (bottom line), respectively. It is clear that the air quality in those cities is much worse than allowed by the WHO guidelines. Of course, as economies grow, the quality of air is usually worsened by economic activities, such as factory operations and car exhausts, but if this situation is not addressed, air pollution in African cities will further worsen and also will have huge repercussions on health, as was the case in Japan in the 1960s and in China more recently.

Water pollution also could cause additional illnesses. For instance in the process of Japan's economic growth, industrial mercury pollution caused *Minamata* disease, a type of poisoning. Comprehensive water pollution data, however, are not available for Africa (except for South Africa). Thus, given the impacts on water quality in past economic growth history globally, a monitoring mechanism should be built, and donor countries should support Africa in developing measures to tackle these environmental issues.

WILL ENVIRONMENTAL CONSERVATION POLICY MAKE THE AFRICAN ECONOMY LESS COMPETITIVE?

What are the implications of these environment issues for economic growth? First, agricultural production will be affected, because farmers will at least be required to switch to drought-resilient crops and to diversify crops to hedge the risk of further disasters. In the long run, this could change the comparative advantage of agriculture in Africa.

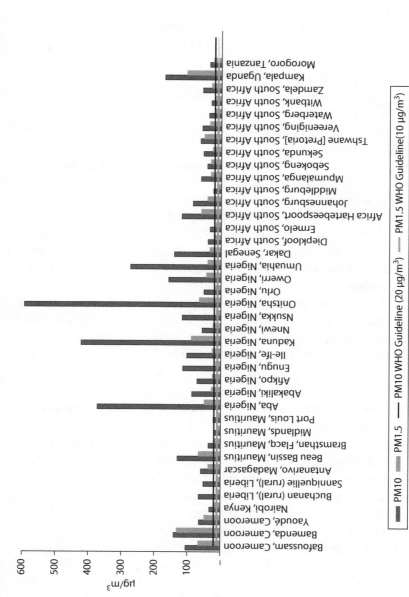

Figure 12.3   Air pollution in major African cities

Source: Author's creation based on World Bank (2016).

Higuchi and Shimada (2019) show how economic structures, using sectoral gross domestic product (GDP) per capita in log scale, changed in Asia and Africa (figure 12.4). Both regions were at a similar level in 1970, but they have since diverged. The difference is the industrial sector. In Asia, the industrial sector was the driver of economic growth, but the sector has been stagnant in Africa.[3]

Investment by private firms in Africa is less than optimal. This is because the return from their investment is often uncertain. This is a type of market failures due to asymmetry of information problem. It hinders desirable economic transformation, resulting in underdevelopment (Shimada 2015c; 2016).

The problem, however, does not just stop there; the adoption of new green technologies is also lower than the optimal level. If introduced, new technologies will generate positive spillovers, but it is difficult for private firms to see their benefits, particularly given the asymmetry of information. Another type of market failure is that the price of natural resources (e.g., water and air) is greatly distorted and difficult to measure. In particular, in the early stages of economic growth, the cost to the environment is often neglected by the government and by private firms.

To make economic growth green, "green industrial policy" is required (Rodrik 2014). Green industrial policy in developed economies promotes environmentally friendly technologies, which require technological innovation. Conversely, in developing economies, green industrial policy focuses on how to deploy existing technologies to prevent environmental damage. The international community has an important role to play in the promotion and introduction of such technologies in developing countries. As Stiglitz (2007) observes, it is the responsibility of past polluters to support efficient technologies that produce less pollution in developing countries. This point will be discussed in the last section of this chapter.

Are environmental regulations and standards useful as a tool of green industrial policy in developing countries? Considering the trade-off between economic growth and environmental protection, would such regulations and standards make African industry less competitive? Thus far, only a few studies have used regression analysis to analyze the trade-off between economic activities and environmental policies. For instance, contrary to the conventional view on the environment–economic activities trade-off, Esty and Porter (2005) find that strong environmental policy and governance has a positive correlation with competitiveness. Their paper mainly focused on developed economies, however, rather

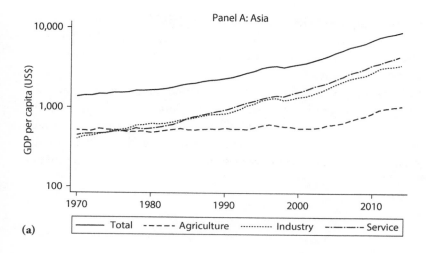

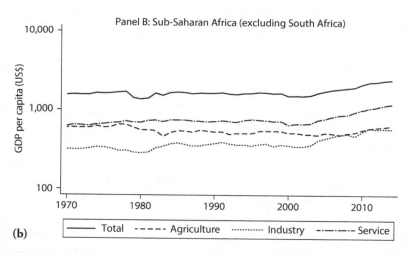

Figure 12.4   (a) Changes in sectoral GDP per capita in emerging Asia; (b) Changes in sectoral GDP per capital in Sub-Saharan Africa (excluding South Africa)

Note: GDP per capita is in U.S. dollars (in purchasing power parity–adjusted 2011 constant price) and is presented in log scale. Panel A presents weighted averages (weight by population) of BGD, CHN, IDN, IND, KOR, LKA, MYS, NPL, PAK, PHL, and THA. Japan is not included because Japan's economic development started much earlier than other Asian countries in the 1950s. Similarly, Panel B presents weighted averages of BDI, BEN, BFA, CAF, CIV, CMR, COG, GHA, GNB, KEN, LSO, MDG, MLI, MRT, MWI, NER, RWA, SDN, SLE, SWZ, TCD, TGO, UGA, ZMB, and ZWE. South Africa is not included because it is exceptional compared with other Sub-Saharan Africa countries.

Source: Higuchi and Shimada (2019, 200–201).

than developing countries, including Africa. This section aims to fill this knowledge gap with a view toward making green industrial policy more practical, by providing more evidence that green industrial policy can have a positive impact.

To investigate whether or not environmental policy makes a country's industry less competitive, this section will approach this issue from the following two perspectives: (1) how the environmental governance of each country affects the competitiveness of its industry; and (2) whether environmental policy makes a country less attractive to foreign direct investment (FDI).

DOES ENVIRONMENTAL GOVERNANCE AFFECT THE COMPETITIVENESS OF INDUSTRY?

If environmental policy and economic activities are not compatible, it will be difficult for developing countries to put greater emphasis on environmental protection over poverty reduction and job creation. If it is compatible, against the conventional belief surrounding the trade-off, then it is desirable to make industrial policy greener.

To examine whether environmental and economic activities are compatible, this study used the Environmental Governance Indicator from the 2005 Environmental Sustainability Index (ESI) developed by the World Economic Forum. The ESI is a measure of overall progress toward environmental sustainability, developed for 146 countries. It has twenty-one indicators, and the environmental governance indicator is one of these.[4] The governance indicator measures the performance of environmental policies and their implementation by each country. It consists of data on the structure of environmental regulations covering the following: air pollution regulations; chemical waste regulations; the clarity and stability of regulations; the flexibility of regulations; environmental regulatory innovation; leadership in environmental policy; consistency in regulation enforcement; environmental regulatory stringency; effective toxic waste disposal regulations; and effective water pollution regulations. For the measurement of competitiveness, this chapter used the total factor productivity (TFP) data produced by Penn World Figure (version 9.0).

Because the data used are cross-sectional, and not panel data, causal linkages cannot be definitively established. As shown in figures 12.5 and 12.6, however, even given this limitation, the simplified analysis produced

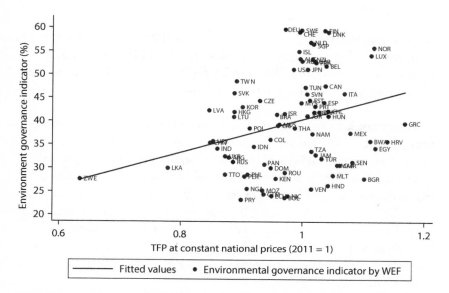

Figure 12.5 Environmental governance and total factor productivity (all countries)

Source: Author's creation based on the 2005 Environmental Sustainability Index (ESI) by the Yale Center for Environmental Law and Policy et al.; and Penn World Figure, version 9.0 by Feenstra et al. 2015.

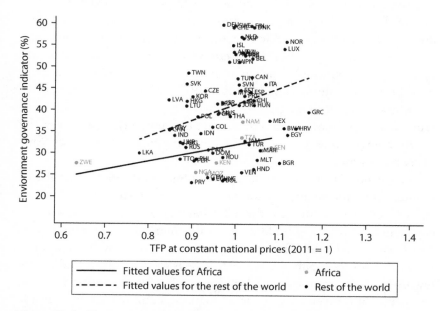

Figure 12.6 Environmental governance and total factor productivity

Source: Author's creation based on the 2005 Environmental Sustainability Index (ESI) by the Yale Center for Environmental Law and Policy et al.; and Penn World Figure, version 9.0 by Feenstra et al. 2015.

interesting results. Figure 12.5 illustrates the correlation between environmental governance (vertical axis) and TFP (horizontal axis). As the fitted line shows, the correlation is positive. This means that stronger environmental regulations and their enforcement make industry more competitive.

This result is in line with the experience of Japan's car manufacturing firms. In the 1970s, Japan's auto industry was not as competitive as it is today. The major market was the domestic market, and the producer's reputation was for "low-priced goods of poor quality." This situation changed after the introduction of the so-called Muskie Act (an extension of the U.S. Clean Air Act) in 1970, under which the automobile industry needed to reduce the emissions of carbon monoxide and hydrocarbons to 90 percent of 1970–1971 levels after 1975. The Muskie Act stated that if a company could not comply with the law, it would not be permitted to sell any cars in the American market.[5]

The U.S. and Japanese auto industries' reaction to this Act contrasted sharply. The big three U.S. car firms were against this Act, and requested that the U.S. government postpone its implementation. This request was initially rejected, but after long negotiations, the Act was watered down in 1974. The oil crisis of 1973 greatly changed the situation for U.S. producers, however, stimulating them to consider producing less gasoline-hungry vehicles. Conversely, in Japan, environmental issues were the biggest political item on the national agenda at that time (e.g., air pollution). The environment agency, established in 1971, introduced air pollution regulations in 1972, following the example of the Muskie Act. Immediately after their adoption, then-president of Honda Soichiro Honda announced that his company would meet the required environment standards by inventing new technologies (Shimada forthcoming).

Even if no plan to invent such technologies existed at the time of Honda's announcement, the compound vortex controlled combustion (CVCC) engine was invented the following year. The CVCC was the first engine in the world that could meet the requirements of the Muskie Act. The Civic model, which Honda sold with the CVCC engine, became a worldwide hit. Not only was the exhaust gas clean, it also could realize low fuel consumption through lean burn. After Honda, other Japanese companies also invented new technologies to comply with the Muskie Act. With these technologies, Japanese cars gained a worldwide reputation for fuel efficiency and good quality.

This technological breakthrough was achieved in a climate of strong criticisms against the air pollution regulations of 1972, inside and outside Japan. The United States and the European Union criticized these environmental standards as a form of nontariff barriers to trade. In Japan, the Industrial Bank of Japan criticized the regulations and published a report in 1975 analyzing their economic impact (Suwa 1975). This report stated that the regulations would raise automobile prices and that demand for domestic passenger cars would decline as a result. It concluded that employment would be lost because of the projected reduction in car sales compared with the previous year, which was estimated at six hundred thousand units.

Even if the air pollution regulations were condemned, however, public opinion was critical of the car industry over air pollution and its health impacts. The domestic car industry therefore had no choice but to abide by the regulations. Hirofumi Uzawa, an economics professor at the University of Tokyo, led this social movement. After returning to Tokyo from Chicago University, he wrote a book on the social cost of automobiles. The book quickly became a bestseller in Japan, launching a social movement against pollution (Uzawa 1974).

The case of the Japanese auto industry shows that environmental policy can make industry more competitive, as Japan's industry went on to dominate the world production of automobiles within a few years. Thus, this example demonstrates that stricter environmental policy and economic activities can be compatible, and no trade-off is needed.

It is still not clear, however, whether this situation applies only to developed countries. To test this theory, figure 12.6 disaggregates Africa from the rest of world. Although the sample size for African countries is limited, positive correlations can indeed be observed. In other words, even in Africa, stricter environmental policies and wider economic activities could be compatible. It is possible to say that environmental policy does not necessarily make industry less competitive. Instead, as these positive correlations and Japan's case show, stricter environmental policies can make industry more competitive.

Environmental policy, however, still may have a negative impact on economic activities, thus making the local economy less attractive to foreign investors. For African countries, FDI is important to the promotion of industrial development. If environmental policy has a negative impact in this area, it will be difficult for African countries to adopt stronger environmental regulations and standards. The next section discusses the correlation between environmental policy and FDI.

DOES ENVIRONMENTAL POLICY MAKE A COUNTRY LESS ATTRACTIVE TO FOREIGN DIRECT INVESTMENT?

To analyze the correlation between environmental policy and FDI, this section uses the World Bank's Policy and Institutions for Environmental Sustainability Rating of the Country Policy and Institutional Assessment (CPIA; see figure 12.7), and the Environment Performance Index (EPI; see figure 12.8). The FDI growth data comes from the Penn World Figure (version 9.0).

Figure 12.7 shows the correlation between the CPIA and FDI growth. The CPIA exercise of the World Bank was carried out to assess the quality of a country's policies and its institutional arrangements, mainly focusing on the elements under the country's control rather than the outcome, which can be affected by exogenous factors. The CPIA rating on policy and institutions for environmental sustainability measures the ability of the environmental policies of each government to foster the protection and sustainable use of natural resources and the management of pollution (World Bank 2017).[6] The horizontal axis shows the CPIA rating. The rating goes from 6 (high) to 1 (low) and is rated to the number of digits after the decimal point. As a dot moves from left to right, it means the rating improves. The gray circles mark Sub-Sahara African countries; the black

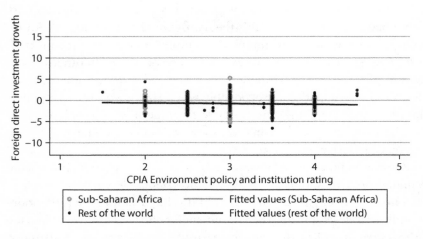

Figure 12.7   Country Policy and Institutional Assessment rating and foreign direct investment

Source: Author's creation based on CPIA by the World Bank (2017) and Penn World Figure, version 9.0 by Feenstra et al. 2015.

dots are for the rest of the world. The figure shows two almost identical fitted lines: one is for Sub-Saharan Africa, and the other is for the rest of the world. These are almost identical, which indicates that the correlation is similar between Africa and the rest of the world. Furthermore, the fitted line is horizontal, which means that CPIA ratings do not affect the growth of FDI. Thus, this analysis does not confirm that stronger environmental policies affect FDI flows.

To double-check this link, figure 12.8 shows the correlation between FDI growth and the EPI. The vertical axis shows FDI growth and the horizontal axis shows the EPI. The EPI measures how well countries perform on the protection of human health from environmental harm and on the protection of ecosystems.[7] The gray circles are for Africa and the black dots are for the rest of the world. As this figure shows, even if environmental performance improves (moving from left to right), the relationship remains almost flat, implying that there is almost no impact. The relationship is similar for Africa and for the rest of the world. Even if the data have limitations, this analysis shows that environmental policies do not have negative impacts on FDI growth. In other words, lower

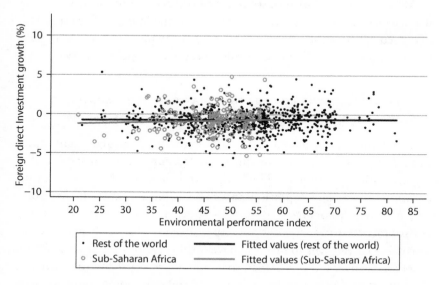

Figure 12.8   Environment performance index and foreign direct investment

Note: The Environmental Performance Index (EPI) is constructed through the calculation and aggregation of 20 indicators reflecting national-level environmental data. For technical details see http://archive.epi.yale.edu/our-methods.

Source: Author's creation based on the 2005 Environmental Sustainability Index (ESI) by the Yale Center for Environmental Law and Policy et al.; and Penn World Figure, version 9.0 by Feenstra et al. 2015.

environmental (or pollution) costs are not necessary the most important factor for foreign companies as they decide where to invest.

A possible reason for this is that environmental policies and regulations require strong institutional setups for their implementation and enforcement. For instance, governments need to inspect factories to enforce water pollution standards, which is not necessarily an easy task. Nevertheless, if a government has strong institutional capability over the environment, it also would be strong in other areas, such as promoting investment, providing business support, and establishing infrastructure and investment.

As noted, environmental policy does not necessarily undermine the competitiveness of African industry, and it does not have negative impacts on FDI. Rather, it has positive impacts in the long run, promoting innovation and continuous improvement within private firms. Above all, it will prevent negative health impacts through environmental pollution, which many Asian countries, including Japan (e.g., *Minamata* disease from methyl mercury; *Yokkaishi* asthma from sulfur dioxide; and *Itai-itai* disease from Cadmium poisoning), and China (air pollution), have suffered from.

Africa needs not just industrial policy but also green industrial policy that balances economic growth and environmental impact. Given this finding, what role can the international community play in support of green industrial policy? We next discuss this aspect to draw policy implications.

POLICY OPTIONS FOR THE INTERNATIONAL COMMUNITY TO MAXIMIZE THE LATECOMER'S ADVANTAGE OF AFRICA

The remaining question to tackle is how the international community should support Africa to maximize its latecomer's advantage, utilizing available technologies. The budget and capacity of African administrations to tackle adaptation and mitigation are limited; therefore, international donors have room to support these countries. Regarding environmental issues, Africa is not responsible for climate change, and the discussion often turns to blaming developed countries. As Stiglitz (2007) observes, we have but one planet, so blaming developed countries will not solve our shared problem. Both developed and developing countries need to take steps to tackle environment problems, because this is a global issue. Thus, the principles of action need to be fair and efficient—that is, common but differentiated responsibilities.

Three types of economic countermeasures can be used to mitigate environmental problems: (1) the price instrument; (2) the quantity instrument (e.g., carbon trading); and (3) adoption of existing technologies that may be found in developed countries.[8] So, which measures should donor countries support?

ENVIRONMENTAL TAX

The price instrument is an environmental tax (e.g., carbon tax, water tax). As Stiglitz (2016) discussed, if we can set an environmental protection price (e.g., carbon price) reflecting the social cost of carbon dioxide (CO_2) emissions, this would stimulate investment as part of green industrial policy, even if environmental pricing increases the prices of goods and services. Environmental taxes are expected to make the market work for both development and the environment by signaling appropriate prices for environmental protection, which would shift the economy toward a green economy. In the twenty-first century, many governments have incorporated carbon-pricing policies into their mitigation strategies. This environmental tax will ensure a level playing field with developed economies for Africa. Environmental taxes will also contribute to raising the funds necessary to finance public involvement.

From January 1, 2017, South Africa introduced a carbon tax, the first country in Africa to do so.[9] It is planned that the tax will be gradually raised and fully implemented by 2020 (Phase 1). The price will be R120 (US$11.20) per ton of CO_{2e} (Carbon dioxide equivalent) for 2017, which will be increased by 10 percent annually until December 31, 2019. This will cover approximately 80 percent of total emissions (World Bank 2015). After 2020, Phase 2 is planed from January 1, 2020, to December 31, 2024.[10]

QUANTITY INSTRUMENT

The quantity instrument is emission trading. Environmental taxes set a price for environmental impact (e.g., greenhouse gas [GHG] emissions), forcing polluters or emitters to face the full cost of their pollution and emissions. The emitters, therefore, need to consider the emission cost of their business activities. Conversely, emission trading establishes a cap on trade quantity, and emitters can trade their emission allowance (indirect price on GHG emissions). As Collier, Conway, and Venables (2008) argue, under an ideal cap-and-trade emission-trading scheme, each person would be endowed with the same emission rights. The financial results from sales of carbon rights would then be much larger than the current level of international aid. This could become attractive for both Africa and the donors of international aid.

So far, consensus has not been reached as to the preferred instrument because this depends on the situation, assumptions, and the time frame (long term or short term, where capital stock and technology are fixed) of each type. Some economists argue that a quantity-based instrument is better because we cannot know the true cost of climate change, and any other method might eventually lead to catastrophic consequences for the economy. Other economists, such as Nordhaus (2007), argue that a price instrument is better because the marginal cost of emissions depends on the flow of emissions, whereas the benefit depends on the stock of the emissions. When the U.S. Government Accountability Office (2008) examined policy options upon a request from the U.S. Congress, the opinions of the eighteen-member expert panel were divided.

In the case of developing countries, given the limited capacity of their administrative resources, an environmental tax is the easiest method to implement. This raises two issues: First, the efficiency of the tax instrument depends on the energy demand curve (and price elasticity). Under an environmental tax, the price is certain, but it is not clear by how much the tax can reduce emissions. Under emission trading, however, the quantity of the reduction is certain, but the price is not. This is the difference between the two schemes. Second, an environmental tax would be politically difficult to introduce. Any tax is difficult to introduce, but environmental taxes often are viewed as undermining economic activities. Making an environment tax a policy priority for African countries therefore would be difficult.

ADOPTION OF EXISTING TECHNOLOGIES

It would be better to start assisting African countries with this third option, and then move on to the others. An asymmetry of information exists not only for African private firms but also for African administrations. It is not clear how existing environmental technologies affect their economies, for example. As the traditional view of a trade-off between environment–economic activities persists, investment in green technologies will be likely much lower than optimal, resulting in the undermining of environmental policy.

One example of these existing technologies is desulfurization, which prevents the release of harmful sulfur oxides (SOx) from manufacturing factories into the atmosphere. SOx problems occur when fossil fuels containing sulfur, such as petroleum and coal, are burned, and cause air pollution leading to asthma and acid rain. In Japan, the development of flue gas desulfurization equipment began in the early 1960s, when environmental pollution problems started to emerge. So far, Japan International Cooperation Agency (JICA) has supported the introduction of desulfurization mainly in Asia, including in China and Thailand. Desulfurization is just one example of the existing technologies available in developed countries. African countries must be subsidized to introduce these technologies through official development assistance.

For example, the World Bank Country Survey of 2012 in Kenya showed that environmental protection is not the policy priority for Kenyan opinion leaders. A total of 373 opinion leaders participated in that survey.[11] The survey results showed instead that agricultural development was the first priority, with 19.7 percent of opinion leaders considering it the most important issue to tackle. This was followed by education (11.6 percent), poverty reduction (8.1 percent), transport (7.8 percent), governance (6.3 percent), and job creation (6.3 percent). Environment ranked 21st with 0.625 percent. This result is not surprising, but the environment should be more highly prioritized before it becomes too late, because one of the characteristics of environmental damage is irreversibility. Once impacts have begun, recovery ex post is difficult. The health impact is the most severe, and a typical example of this irreversibility. Japan suffered from pollution that caused diseases on a large scale during the 1950s and 1960s. Those people affected are still suffering some fifty to sixty years after the pollution was cleaned up.

CONCLUSION

As the African economy has been growing and transforming, environmental problems have begun to adversely affect its development. Natural disasters have been rising dramatically on the continent. Also, the air pollution in major cities in Africa is much worse than the recommended WHO standards, although we do not know its true cost. This chapter did not look at other types of pollution, such as water, because data are not available, but the water situation should be monitored as soon as possible. Sooner or later, as is the case in other regions of the world, Africa will face environmental problems. The environment and the economy in Africa, however, are not necessarily in conflict; protection of the environment and economic development can be compatible if handled competently. African countries need to implement green industrial policies and prioritize environmental protection. At the same time, donor countries have a responsibility to help African countries to introduce existing environmental technologies to maximize their latecomer's advantage.

NOTES

1. For other regions, the key concern is how to reduce carbon emissions, but for Africa, it is how to adapt its agricultural production system to the changing needs of the environment; see Paul Collier, Gordon Conway, and Tony Venables, "Climate Change and Africa," *Oxford Review of Economic Policy* 24, no. 2 (2008): 337–353. The impact of climate change on Africa's agriculture has already been discussed elsewhere; see W. R. Rachel Warren et al., "Understanding the Regional Impacts of Climate Change" (research report prepared for the Stern Review on the Economics of Climate Change, Tyndall Center for Climate Change Research, Working Paper 90, University of East Anglia, Norwich, UK, 2006); William R. Cline, "Global Warming and Agriculture," *Finance and Development* 45, no. 1 (Washington, DC: International Monetary Fund, 2008).

2. The EM-DAT was compiled by the Center for Research on the Epidemiology of Disasters, Université Catholique de Louvain in Belgium.

3. Other than the industrial sector, in Africa, sectors prematurely shifted to the service sector, bypassing the industrial sector; see John Page, "Structural Change and Africa's Poverty Puzzle," chap. 7 in *Last Mile in Ending Extreme Poverty*, ed. Laurence Chandy, Hiroshi Kato, and Homi Kharas, 219–248 (Washington, DC: Brookings Institution, 2015). This is against Petty-Clark's law, which says that the main driver of sector has changed over time from primary industry to secondary, and to the tertiary sector. The major reason for this premature shift was the Dutch disease effect; see Go Shimada, "The Economic Implications of Comprehensive Approach to Learning on Industrial Development (Policy and Managerial Capability Learning): A Case of Ethiopia," in *Industrial Policy and Economic Transformation in Africa*, ed. Akbar Noman and Joseph Stiglitz (New York: Columbia University Press, 2015) and "Inside the Black Box of Japan's Institution for Industrial Policy—An Institutional Analysis of Development Bank, Private Sector and Labor," in *Industrial Policy and Economic Transformation in Africa*, ed. Akbar Noman and Joseph Stiglitz (New York: Columbia University Press, 2016c). Because Africa is rich in natural resources, currencies tend to be overvalued, and this makes imports cheaper and exports more expensive.

4. The index was unveiled at the World Economic Forum's annual meeting, January 2005, Davos, Switzerland. The 2005 ESI is a joint product of the Yale Center for Environmental Law and Policy and the Columbia University Center for International Earth Science Information Network, in collaboration with the World Economic Forum and the Joint Research Centre of the European Commission.

5. The Muskie Act was named after Maine Senator Edmund Muskie who drafted the law.

6. For technical details, see World Bank, "CPIA Policy and Institutions for Environmental Sustainability Rating," accessed March 24, 2017, http://data.worldbank.org/indicator/IQ.CPA.ENVR.XQ.

7. The Environmental Performance Index (EPI) is constructed through the calculation and aggregation of twenty indicators reflecting national-level environmental data. These indicators are combined into nine issue categories, each of which fit under one of two overarching objectives. For technical details see https://epi.envirocenter.yale.edu/.

8. Since January 2017, a carbon tax has been implemented in countries such as Japan, Denmark, Finland, Ireland, the Netherland, Norway, Slovenia, Sweden, Switzerland, the United Kingdom, Canada, India, Costa Rica, China, and South Africa.

9. The administration of the carbon tax will be jointly undertaken by the South African Revenue Service and the Department of Environment Affairs, supported by the Department of Energy, and with the Designated National Authority responsible for the administration of the carbon offset mechanism.

10. The tax rate for Phase 2 has not yet been fixed.

11. Participants in the survey were drawn from among the offices of the president and prime minister; the office of a minister; the office of a parliamentarian; the employees of a ministry, ministerial department, or implementation agency; consultants and contractors working on World Bank–supported projects and programs; project management units overseeing implementation of a project; local government officials or staff; bilateral agencies; multilateral agencies; private sector organizations; private foundations; the financial sector/private banks; nongovernmental organizations; community-based organizations; the media; independent government institutions; trade unions; faith-based groups; academia and research institutes and think tanks; and the judiciary branch.

REFERENCES

Cline, William R. 2008. "Global Warming and Agriculture." *Finance and Development* 45(1). Washington, DC: International Monetary Fund.

Collier, Paul, Gordon Conway, and Tony Venables. 2008. "Climate Change and Africa." *Oxford Review of Economic Policy* 24 (2): 337–353.

Devarajan, Shantayanan, Delfin S. Go, Sherman Robinson, and Karen Thierfelder. 2009. "Tax Policy to Reduce Carbon Emissions in South Africa." World Bank Policy Research Working Paper Series 4933. World Bank, Washington, DC.

European Commission. 2008. *Taxation Trends in the European Union: Data for the EU Member States and Norway.* Brussels: Eurostat Statistical Books.

Environment Policy Index. 2014. *EPI2014.* Accessed March 24, 2017, http://archive.epi.yale.edu/our-methods.

Esty, Daniel C., and Michael R. Porter. 2005. "National Environmental Performance: An Empirical Analysis of Policy Results and Determinants." *Environment and Development Economics* 10: 391–434.

Feenstra, Robert C., Robert Inklaar, and Marcel P. Timmer. 2015. "The Next Generation of the Penn World Figure." *American Economic Review* 105 (10): 3150–3182.

Government Accountability Office. 2008. *Expert Opinion on the Economics of Policy Options to Address Climate Change.* Washington. DC: U.S. GAO Report to Congressional Requesters.

Glodblatt, Michael. 2010. "Comparison of Emissions of Trading and Carbon Taxation in South Africa." *Climate Policy* 10 (5): 511–526.

Higuchi, Yuki, and Go Shimada. 2019. "Industrial Policy, Industrial Development, and Structural Transformation in Asia and Africa." Chap. 9 in *Paths to the Emerging State in Asia and Africa,* ed. K. Otsuka and K. Sugihara, 195–218. Emerging-Economy State and International Policy Studies. Singapore: Springer.

Page, John. 2015. "Structural Change and Africa's Poverty Puzzle." Chap. 7 in *Last Mile in Ending Extreme Poverty,* ed. Laurence Chandy, Hiroshi Kato, and Homi Kharas, 219–248. Washington, DC: Brookings Institution.

Internal Displacement Monitoring Centre. 2016. Internal Displacement People Database. Geneva: Internal Displacement Monitoring Centre. Accessed December 16, 2016, http://www.internal-displacement.org/global-figures/#natural).

Intergovernmental Panel on Climate Change. 2018. *Global Warming of 1.5°C. An IPCC Special Report on the Impacts of Global Warming of 1.5°C Above Pre-industrial Levels and Related Global Greenhouse Gas Emission Pathways, in the Context of Strengthening the Global Response to the Threat of Climate Change, Sustainable Development, and Efforts to Eradicate Poverty,* ed. V. Masson-Delmotte, P. Zhai, H. O. Pörtner, D. Roberts, J. Skea, P. R. Shukla, A. Pirani, W. Moufouma-Okia, C. Péan, R. Pidcock, S. Connors, J. B. R. Matthews, Y. Chen, X. Zhou, M. I. Gomis, E. Lonnoy, T. Maycock, M. Tignor, and T. Waterfield. Geneva: World Meteorological Organization.

Kechichian, Etienne, Alexios Pantelias, Ari Reeves, Guy Henley, and Jiemei Liu. 2016. *A Greener Path to Competitiveness—Policies for Climate Action in Industries and Products.* Washington, DC: World Bank.

Nordhaus, William. 2007. "To Tax or Not to Tax: Alternative Approaches to Slowing Global Warming." *Review of Environmental Economics and Policy* 1 (1): 26–44.

Porter, Michael. 1996. "America's Green Strategy." *Scientific American* 264: 168–168.

Rodrik, Dani. 2014. "Green Industrial Policy." *Oxford Review of Economic Policy* 30 (3): 469–491.

Stern, Nicholas. 2007. *The Stern Review: The Economics of Climate Change.* Cambridge: Cambridge University Press.

Stiglitz, Joseph. 2016. An agenda for sustainable and inclusive growth for emerging markets. *Journal of Policy Modeling,* 38(4): 693-710.

Stiglitz, Joseph. 2007. "The Global Economics and Politics of Climate Change." Power Point Presentation at Jakarta on August 2007. Accessed April 4, 2017, https://www8.gsb.columbia.edu/faculty/jstiglitz/speeches.

Shimada, Go. Forthcoming. "Why is Kaizen Critical for Developing Countries? Kaizen as a Social Innovation in the Era of Global Inequality." In *Workers, Managers, Productivity: Kaizen in Developing Countries.* ed. Hosono Akio, John Page and Go Shimada. Singapore: Palgrave.

———. 2017. "A Quantitative Study of Social Capital in the Tertiary Sector of Kobe— Has social capital promoted economic reconstruction since the Great Hanshin Awaji Earthquake?" *International Journal of Disaster Risk Reduction* 22:494–502. doi: 10.1016/j.ijdrr.2016.10.002.

———. 2016. "Inside the Black Box of Japan's Institution for Industrial Policy— An Institutional Analysis of Development Bank, Private Sector and Labor." In *Industrial Policy and Economic Transformation in Africa*, ed. Akbar Noman and Joseph Stiglitz. New York: Columbia University Press.

———. 2015a. "Towards Community Resilience—The Role of Social Capital After Disasters." In *The Last Mile in Ending Extreme Poverty*, ed. Laurence Chandy, Hiroshi Kato, and Homi Kharas, 369–397. Washington, DC: Brookings Institute.

———. 2015b. "What Are the Macroeconomic Impacts of Natural Disasters? The Impacts of Natural Disasters on the Growth Rate of Gross Prefectural Domestic Product in Japan." In *Growth Is Dead, Long Live Growth: The Quality of Economic Growth and Why It Matters*, ed. Lawrence Haddad, Hiroshi Kato, and Nicolas Meisel, 243–264. Tokyo: JICA Research Institute.

———. 2015c. "The Economic Implications of Comprehensive Approach to Learning on Industrial Development (Policy and Managerial Capability Learning): A Case of Ethiopia." In *Industrial Policy and Economic Transformation in Africa*, ed. Akbar Noman and Joseph Stiglitz. New York: Columbia University Press.

———. 2015d. "The Role of Social Capital after Disasters: An Empirical Study of Japan based on Time-Series-Cross-Section (TSCS) Data from 1981 to 2012." *International Journal of Disaster Risk Reduction* 14: 388–394. doi:10.1016/j .ijdrr.2015.09.004

Shimada, Go, and Miki Motomura. 2017. "Building Resilience Through Social Capital as a Counter-Measure to Natural Disasters in Africa: A Case from a Project in Pastoralist and Agro-pastoralist communities in Borena, in the Oromia Region of Ethiopia." *Kyoto University Africa Study Monograph Supplementary Issue* 53: 35–51.

Suwa Keiichiro. 1975. "Economic Analysis of Automobile Exhaust Gas Regulations (in Japanese)." *Kogin Chosa* 180: 2–79. Tokyo: Industrial Bank of Japan.

United Nations. 2015. Resolution adopted by the General Assembly on 25 September 2015. *A/70/L.1.* New York: United Nations.

Uzawa, Hirofumi. 1974. *Social Cost of Automobile.* Tokyo: Iwanami.

Warren, Rachel, Nigel Arnell, Robert Nicholls, Peter Levy, and Jeff Price. 2006. "Understanding the Regional Impacts of Climate Change." Research report prepared for the Stern Review on the Economics of Climate Change. Tyndall Center for Climate Change Research, Working Paper 90. University of East Anglia, Norwich, UK.

World Bank. 2015. *Implementing a Carbon Tax in South Africa.* Washington, DC: World Bank. Accessed December 18, 2016, http://www.worldbank.org/en /results/2015/10/19/implementing-carbon-tax-south-africa.

———. 2016. *World Development Indicators.* Washington, DC: World Bank.

———. 2017. *CPIA Policy and Institutions for Environmental Sustainability Rating.* Washington, DC: World Bank. Accessed March 24, 2017, http://data.worldbank. org/indicator/IQ.CPA.ENVR.XQ). Accessed 24 March 2017.

World Bank and Institute for Health Metrics and Evaluation University of Washington. 2016. *The Cost of Air Pollution—Strengthening the Economic Case for Action*. Washington, DC: World Bank.

Yale Center for Environmental Law and Policy Yale University, Center for International Earth Science Information Network, Columbia University, World Economic Forum, and Joint Research Centre European Commission. 2005. *2005 Environmental Sustainability Index (ESI)*. Palisades, NY: NASA Socioeconomic Data and Applications Center. Accessed March 22, 2017, http://dx.doi.org/10.7927/H40V89R6.

PART V

Urbanization

CHAPTER 13

Urbanization and the Quality of Growth in Africa

Takyiwaa Manuh and Edlam Abera Yemeru

Africa's economies have been experiencing sustained growth in terms of gross domestic product (GDP). Doubts remain, however, as to the quality of growth given its limited impact on inclusive and sustainable development outcomes. Encapsulated in the continent's long-term development blue print, the African Union's *Agenda 2063*, the consensus now is on the need for structural transformation to translate Africa's economic growth into shared prosperity and well-being for its citizens (African Union 2015a). The aim is to improve the quality of economic growth through economic diversification and value addition in higher productivity sectors such as modern manufacturing and services.

As Africa pursues structural transformation to enhance the quality of growth, it does so in the midst of a major continental shift toward an urban future. Africa's urban population is projected to reach 50.9 percent by 2035, and at 3.58 percent, the continent's urban growth rate is the highest globally (United Nations Department of Economic and Social Affairs [UNDESA] 2018). By 2050, 1.48 billion Africans will be living in urban areas. Strong evidence, both theoretical and historical, associates urbanization and structural transformation (African Development Bank [AfDB] and Organisation for Economic Co-operation and Development [OECD] 2016; United Nations Economic Commission [UNECA] 2017). In addition, the significance of the urban shift for sustainable development at global and regional levels is widely recognized (see box). Africa must acknowledge the social, economic, and environmental implications of rapid urban growth, and its potential power to reshape the quality of growth. Only when economic growth is supported by well-planned and well-managed urbanization can structural transformation be achieved for inclusive and sustainable outcomes.

Recognition of Urbanization's Potential for Inclusive and Sustainable Development

"We are still far from adequately addressing these and other existing and emerging challenges, and there is a need to take advantage of the opportunities presented by urbanization as an engine of sustained and inclusive economic growth, social and cultural development, and environmental protection, and of its potential contributions to the achievement of transformative and sustainable development."—*New Urban Agenda* (United Nations 2017, 3)

"Africa must therefore, consolidate the positive turn around, using the opportunities of demographics, natural resources, urbanization, technology and trade as a springboard to ensure its transformation and renaissance to meet the people's aspirations."—*Agenda 2063* (African Union 2015a, 11)

"Rapid urbanization has brought enormous challenges, including growing numbers of slum dwellers, increased air pollution, inadequate basic services and infrastructure, and unplanned urban sprawl, which also make cities more vulnerable to disasters. Better urban planning and management are needed to make the world's urban spaces more inclusive, safe, resilient and sustainable."—*Sustainable Development Knowledge Platform Progress of Goal 11 in 2017* (United Nations 2017)

"Support positive economic, social and environmental links between urban, peri-urban and rural areas by strengthening national and regional development planning"—*SDGs Targets and Indicators of Goal 11* (United Nations 2015)

This chapter argues that the manner in which urbanization is planned and managed today will play a critical role in the quality of growth in Africa over the coming decades, and in particular the achievement of structural transformation through industrialization. In this respect, although Africa's urbanization offers possibilities to advance key economic, social, and environmental policy priorities, its current trajectory poses significant risks for the quality of growth.

The chapter is organized as follows: The first section considers the factors constraining the quality of growth in Africa, why Africa's economic growth has not been inclusive or sustainable thus far, and the need for structural transformation to address this. The second section outlines key trends, patterns, and conditions of Africa's urban transition, and the associated risks they pose if not deliberately linked to growth priorities. The third section critically examines why urbanization is important for the quality of growth in Africa, with a particular focus on the social, economic, and environmental opportunities that the urban transition presents, specifically for industrialization as a key vehicle for the desired structural change in the region. The fourth section suggests policy anchors for an integrated approach to urbanization at national, regional, and local levels, concluding that spatial and economic planning needs to be linked at various levels through a multisectoral approach.

STRUCTURAL TRANSFORMATION FOR QUALITY OF GROWTH IN AFRICA

In spite of the slowdown witnessed in 2016, in comparison with several other regions, Africa's economic growth has been steady since the beginning of this decade. The average rate of growth between 2010 and 2016 was estimated to be 4 percent (United Nations 2017). In 2018 and 2019, the GDP of African economies grew by a reported 3.2 percent (UNECA 2019). Naturally, significant variations exist within Africa, with some subregions—such as East Africa, which had a growth rate of 6.2 percent in 2018—outgrowing others (UNECA 2019). Despite this impressive economic performance, the continent has not seen a corresponding reduction in poverty and an improvement in its social indicators.

Africa continues to register low levels of human and social development. The number of poor people in Africa has stagnated to 2002 levels in absolute terms (around 390 million). This stagnation, coupled with impressive poverty reduction in Asia, has resulted in Africa being home to 50 percent of the world's total poor in 2013, up from 15 percent in 1990 (World Bank 2016). In terms of employment, in 2015, North Africa had the highest unemployment rates among all regions in the world at 12.1 percent. Although the unemployment rate in the rest of Africa was a lot lower at 7.1 percent, an estimated 70 percent of the total employed were in vulnerable employment, compared with the global average of 46.3 percent (International Labour Organization [ILO] 2016a). The situation is particularly dire for the continent's young people, with youth unemployment rates for North Africa and the rest of Africa registering at 29.3 percent and 10.9 percent, respectively, in 2016 (ILO 2016b).

Moreover, income inequality is highest in Africa (excluding North Africa) compared with all other world regions, with the exception of Latin America and the Caribbean (International Monetary Fund 2015). Similarly, Africa's gender inequality index is also the highest. This index is calculated according to the maternal mortality ratio, adolescent birth rate, female share of seats in parliament, the differential in male and female education attainment, and labor force participation (United Nations Development Programme [UNDP] 2016).

The limited impact of Africa's economic growth on welfare has been linked to the drivers of growth. The traditional path to economic development entails a transition from less productive to more productive economic activities, namely, agriculture to manufacturing and eventually to services, signifying an economy-wide transition to high productivity (e.g., Herrendorf, Rogerson, and Akos Valentinyi. 2014). Experience shows that it is rare for a country to move to high-income status without a sectoral transition that sees economic output and employment shift from agriculture to manufacturing and services.

In contrast, Africa's growth has been driven by its dependence on commodities and a transition to low-productivity informal sector services (UNECA 2015). Although the agricultural sector has diminished in its contribution to net value added from 23.4 percent of GDP in 1990 to 17.9 percent in 2016 (World Bank 2017), it still accounts for some 50 percent of employment (UNECA 2017). These trends mean that growth is not translating into inclusive and sustainable improvements for the lives of most of its inhabitants, and thus it is not of adequate quality.

High levels of inequality limit the ability of economic growth to alleviate poverty and disseminate positive social externalities, thus perpetuating the vicious circle generated by the inadequacy of the quality of growth in Africa. Economic growth results in weaker poverty reduction in countries suffering from high initial inequality because, for the bottom quintiles, the absolute increases in income associated with rising average incomes are less significant (Chandy 2015). In Africa, because the bottom quintiles start further down the poverty line than other regions of the world, the effects of high inequality and noninclusive growth are even more pronounced for poverty alleviation (UNECA 2017).

In addition, Africa is characterized by specific demographic realities that have critical implications in terms of both economic growth and social development. First, the continent has an age structure that is skewed toward youth. Africa has the youngest population in the world, with around two hundred million youth between the ages of fifteen and twenty-four years old. This figure is predicted to double by 2045 (AfDB, OECD, and UNDP 2012). Second, unlike other developing regions, which have been experiencing a declining population growth level over the past twenty-five years, the annual population growth rate in Africa has been fluctuating close to the rate of 2.5 percent (UNDESA 2013). In 2025–2030, Africa will account for fourteen of the fifteen countries[1] that have the highest fertility rates (Overseas Development Institute 2016). These demographic trends necessitate inclusive and robust economic growth to ensure that young people contribute to development and that the economic growth rate can offset the effects of population growth.

Through Agenda 2063, African countries have clearly prioritized structural transformation to foster inclusive, poverty-alleviating, and employment-centric economic growth (African Union 2015a). It becomes important to consider the implications of key megatrends in the region for the pursuit of this agenda. Africa's rapid urban transition is one such shift among many others that have profound consequences for the region's efforts to achieve quality growth. The growing concentration of people, resources, and economic activities in and around urban areas in Africa means that the quality of urbanization will without doubt affect the quality of growth in the coming decades.

THE URBAN TRANSITION IN AFRICA

Africa's future is unquestionably urban. Studies have suggested that no country has leaped to middle-income status without significant urban population growth (World Bank 2009), highlighting the economic potential that cities possess. The simultaneous progression of the urban and demographic transitions in Africa calls for deliberate policy responses to fully exploit the productive advantages these transitions offer and to do so before the economic and social implications are too advanced to reverse.

The current form of largely unplanned urban transition in Africa means that countries are not taking advantage of the potential socioeconomic benefits of urban growth. If this growth continues to be poorly planned and managed, the urban transition will pose significant risks for the quality of growth in Africa. This section examines the key trends, patterns, and conditions of the urban transition in Africa in light of this evaluation to consider the related implications.

DEMOGRAPHIC DIMENSIONS

Africa is the region with the highest rate of urban growth globally, with an average annual rate of 3.58 percent between 2010 and 2015 (UNDESA 2018). In less than twenty years (i.e., by 2035), the majority of the continent's population will be living in urban areas, and by 2050, an estimated 1.48 billion Africans will live in urban areas (UNDESA 2018).

This urbanization is driven increasingly less by rural-to-urban migration, which previously accounted for less than 30 percent of Africa's urban growth (UNDESA 2014). Natural population growth is now a major driver of urban growth, with the top-ten countries[2] having the highest urban fertility rates being in Africa (Mo Ibrahim Foundation 2015). Because of this high urban fertility rate, Africa has the youngest population in the world. In addition to these 1.48 billion urban dwellers by 2050, Africa also will have 1 billion rural dwellers (UNDESA 2018), as shown in figure 13.1. Thus, urban development in Africa must be considered in the context of rural transformation, especially in terms of establishing productive linkages between rural and urban economies.

Figure 13.2 shows the significant regional- and country-level variations in Africa's urban transition. For instance, the fastest-urbanizing countries are those countries that are the least urbanized, and the already urbanized countries have slower rates of urbanization. In countries that are more

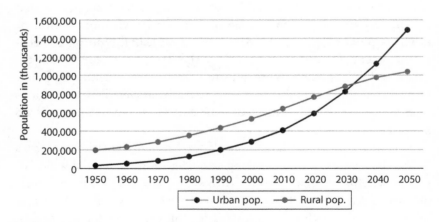

Figure 13.1   Urban and rural population, Africa, 1950–2050

Source: UNDESA (2018).

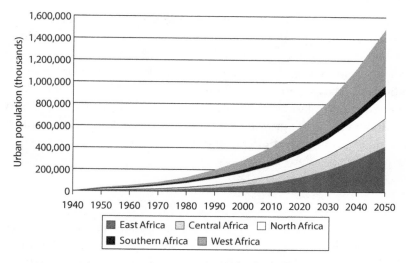

Figure 13.2   Urban populations, Africa by subregion, 1940–2050

Source: UNDESA (2018).

than 60 percent urbanized, the annual rate of growth in urban population is only 2.23 percent, which is less than half of the rate in countries with an urbanization level below 30 percent (UNDP 2015). The general trend is that the countries with the fastest rate of urban growth (and by extension also the lowest levels of urbanization) are situated in East Africa, whereas the opposite is true for Southern Africa. Rwanda, in East Africa, for example, has the second-fastest urban growth rate in the world, at 6.4 percent (Mo Ibrahim Foundation 2015).

A large number of African countries are still characterized by urban primacy, which invariably entails the concentration of population and economic activity in one large city, which is frequently the capital. Urban growth in Africa still follows the remnants of the colonial past—in forty-six countries, the urban primacy is manifested in the form of a dominant colonial capital, main port, or port capital. This is true for twenty-eight of the fifty largest cities in Africa (Mo Ibrahim Foundation 2015).

The fast growth of secondary cities provides potential for economic growth as these cities have complementary functions to support the primary cities. The potential these cities hold includes hosting smaller or input-based industries, such as agriculture or natural resources, and allowing for the division of functions. In addition, a diverse national system of cities is advantageous, allowing firms the flexibility to choose optimal locations according to their requirements (UNECA 2017). As the primary city becomes the center of knowledge and innovation, the secondary cities will accommodate specialized industrial clusters and labor-intensive industries. Malawi and Mozambique are two of the countries that are experiencing this fast growth of secondary cities. In the former, twenty-five urban centers are growing faster than the overall population growth, and in the latter, sixteen urban centers have exceeded the growth rate of the primary city (Potts 2014).

ECONOMIC DIMENSIONS

Africa is urbanizing under lower levels of income than the rest of the world, which has been described as "urbanization without growth" (World Bank 2001; Fay and Opal 2000). For instance, out of the fifteen African countries with income levels above US$6,000, only five countries (Angola, Egypt, Equatorial Guinea, Mauritius, and Namibia) reached this income level before becoming more than 50 percent urbanized (UNDP 2015). When urbanization is delinked from economic growth and countries urbanize at low levels of GDP per capita, it also becomes disconnected from the desired structural change from lower productivity sectors toward higher productivity urban-based sectors (such as manufacturing and modern services).

Delinked from high productivity and job-intensive activities, such as manufacturing, African cities face high unemployment, underemployment, and the prevalence of informal employment. For example, 66 percent of nonagricultural employment in Sub-Saharan Africa is informal (Vanek et al. 2014). The dominance of informal services in the economy has been widely recognized, with statistics demonstrating that these services have permeated to the principal sectors as a substantial part of core workers and enterprises in cities (Budlender 2011a, 2011b, 2011c). Despite the drawbacks of the informal sector dominance, a massive opportunity exists if informal sector firms are facilitated in their ability to increase productivity and advance and if links are established between formal and informal sector enterprises.

African cities are major drivers of national economies. In quantitative terms, cities account for an estimated 55 percent of Africa's GDP (AfDB 2012), which affirms that urbanization can play a fundamental role in unleashing the latent economic potential of regions and countries.

Table 13.1   Urban Contribution to GDP in Selected African Countries

Countries	GDP Contribution of Cities (%)
Ethiopia	57.6
Kenya	70
Madagascar	65
Malawi	50
Nigeria	70
Sudan	72.6
Tanzania	50
Tunisia	85
Uganda	70

Source: Extracted from national reports prepared for the Third United Nations Conference on Housing and Sustainable Urban Development (unpublished).

Note: GDP = gross domestic product.

Although the contribution of cities to GDP in Africa varies by country, in a number of cases, the urban contribution to GDP forms the lion's share of the total, despite the population of the continent still being predominantly rural (see Table 13.1).

SOCIAL DIMENSIONS

The trajectory of urbanization in Africa thus far has been accompanied by rising poverty, inequality, and informality, partly because of the disjuncture between urban and industrial development. Currently, more than half of Sub-Saharan Africa's urban population (55.9 percent) lives in slums (UN-Habitat 2016). It is further estimated that 26 percent of the urban population make up the urban poor, and inequality in African cities is the second highest in the world (Mo Ibrahim Foundation 2015). More than half of the African population lives in countries with high or very high levels of inequality (UNECA 2017). The average daily consumption of the poor in Africa (excluding North Africa) is $1.16 a day (2011 purchasing power parity), which is far below the international poverty line of $1.90 (Beegle et al. 2016).

In terms of basic services and infrastructure, the urban population with access to piped water connection declined from 40 percent in 2000 to 33 percent in 2015 (WHO and UNICEF 2015). Except for North Africa, all regions of Africa have below 50 percent access to electricity, and less than 60 percent of classified paved roads are recorded to be in "good condition" (UNECA 2017). Only around 4 percent of Africa's GDP is invested in infrastructure (Gutman, Sy, and Chattopadhyay 2015), which, although close to the global average of 3.8 percent (Woetzel et al. 2016), is far below the demands of growing urban populations in the continent.

ENVIRONMENTAL DIMENSIONS

Unmanaged urban growth is also putting a strain on the environment. Because of inadequate infrastructure, access to electricity in some African countries depends on private generators fueled by diesel or gasoline, or solid fuels like biomass, leading to increased mortality from pneumonia and other acute respiratory diseases among children, which cause six hundred thousand preventable deaths a year in Africa (Mo Ibrahim Foundation 2015). Some 90 percent of the poorest fifth in Africa use solid fuels for cooking, which is a major contributor to indoor air pollution (World Health Organization [WHO] 2016). In addition, the lack of solid waste management has left two options for waste disposal: unsanitary landfill or open dumping. Open dumping usually occurs adjacent to the informal settlements, resulting in serious health consequences. Evidence shows that less than half of the solid waste generated in Africa is collected, with most of that neither containerized nor recycled (Mo Ibrahim Foundation 2015). Gases generated from uncontained waste, such as methane and chlorofluorocarbons, damage the atmosphere and add to climate change.

Slums, lack of fresh water supply, and high-density settlements increase risks of infectious diseases spreading. In particular, noncommunicable diseases (NCDs), such as cardiovascular diseases, cancer, chronic respiratory conditions, and diabetes, have been the main health challenges of cities. The WHO has estimated that the prevalence of NCDs will increase by 27 percent in Africa in the coming decades. HIV/AIDS epidemic is also concentrated in urban settings, and nearly half of those with HIV live in urban areas of Sub-Saharan Africa, with those living in informal settlements facing greater exposure to infections. For example, almost 75 percent of adult deaths between 2003 and 2012 in slums in Nairobi have been attributed to HIV/AIDS, tuberculosis, injuries, and cardiovascular diseases (WHO 2016).

Despite the growing dangers of climate change and environmental issues in the urban setting, until recently, urban environmental issues in Africa generally have been neglected (United Nations 2017). Urban regions, despite their contribution and vulnerability to environmental issues, are better equipped to apply sustainable interventions, including the development and implementation of new technology, waste-management systems, power generation, and transportation. These efforts, however, have been lacking in urban planning in Africa because of insufficient political will or inadequate climate change knowledge. Cities are becoming more vulnerable to disasters as a result of a combination of factors, such as hazardous locations (usually port cities), poor local governance, environmental degradation, poor infrastructure, and overstretching of resources (UNDP 2010). Additionally, thirty-seven cities of Africa with populations exceeding one million are within low-elevation, coastal zones, which will expose them to ensuing sea-level rise, coastal erosion, storms, and floods (United Nations Office for Disaster Risk Reduction 2014).

QUALITY URBANIZATION FOR QUALITY GROWTH

The rapid urban transition that Africa is undergoing can propel the continent along the path of quality growth so that it can achieve sustained and inclusive outcomes, not only in the economic but also in the social and environmental realms (figure 13.3). Although considerable challenges are associated with urbanization in Africa, especially in terms of inequality, unplanned expansion, environmental degradation, slums, and pressure on infrastructure, with the right planning and foresight, urbanization can deliver profound dividends for all three dimensions of sustainable development.

URBANIZATION AND ECONOMIC GROWTH

Urbanization has a particularly important role to play in ensuring the quality of economic growth through structural transformation because of the productivity benefits that may be accrued as a result of the spatial concentration of labor, resources, and knowledge that cities permit. Urbanization offers opportunities for the shift to higher productivity sectors mainly by virtue of agglomeration economies, which can have strong positive social outcomes, in particular through the creation of decent jobs at scale. Agglomeration economies refer to the benefits accrued from the spatial concentration of a variety of firms in an area that possesses requisite the soft and hard infrastructure needed to support local economic

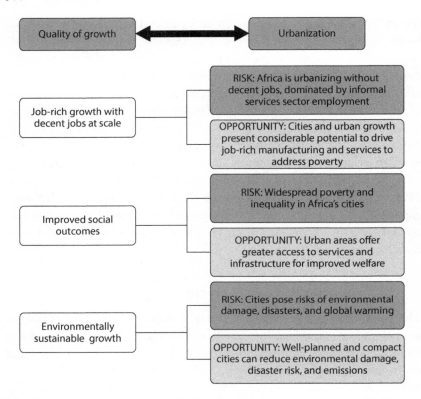

Figure 13.3   Urbanization and the quality of growth—opportunities and risks

Source: Author's creation.

activity. The benefits of agglomeration economies are encapsulated by three main functions: sharing, matching, and learning (Duranton and Puga 2004). First, the growth of cities enables firms to share infrastructure, institutions, and ancillary services required to support activities in a more efficient and economical manner than places with low population density. Second, because of larger markets, cities facilitate matching of labor, inputs, and space according to the specific requirements of firms. Last, proximity and face-to-face interactions permit learning through the exchange of immobile and tacit knowledge between firms and suppliers, which can be critical for spurring innovation and moving up the productivity ladder (Turok and McGranahan 2013). As cities grow and these three forces gain momentum, competitive advantage for firms increase, resulting in the acceleration of both the transition toward more productive sectors, as well as intrasectoral increases in productivity. These productivity advantages ultimately translate into the creation of decent employment opportunities at a magnitude sufficient to absorb the growing urban population in a city's economy. In doing so, these employment opportunities can result in a swift improvement in the lives of citizens and have positive multiplier effects that manifest in multiple dimensions. As more firms locate in a spatial entity because of the pull of agglomeration economies, the countervailing forces of urbanization also gain momentum. These negative externalities can be especially influential if the form and pattern of urbanization are far from optimal.

In addition, with changing patterns in consumption resulting from a growing middle class and urban populations, major opportunities for industrialization, especially in manufactured and processed goods, become available. It is estimated that the middle class (defined as those earning between US$4 and US$20 per day) in Africa will grow from 355 million in 2010 to 1.1 billion in 2060 (AfDB 2011). In addition, household consumption is expected to grow by 3.8 percent each year, reaching $2.1 trillion by 2025 (Bughin et al. 2016). One particular entry point, which to date has yet to be tapped sufficiently to meet consumer demand in Africa, is the processed food industry. The import of consumer-oriented food products in Sub-Saharan Africa has grown by almost 70 percent between 2010 and 2015 (USDA 2015). This growth points to the significant opportunities for promoting food value chains as well as rural-urban linkages to meet urban consumer demands by value addition to Africa's agriculture commodities. Africa's rapid urbanization can thus enable agricultural modernization, which is a top policy priority for the region. Rising demand for urban housing and infrastructure can also generate jobs in construction and services sectors and stimulate the industrialization process. For example, in Morocco the government has focused on several housing programs, which has resulted in fifty-one of its eighty-five townships and urban centers becoming slum free between 2004 and 2014 (UNECA 2017), has led to the creation of employment, and has supported the domestic construction industry.

Despite the potential for urban growth to accelerate job-rich economic growth and for poverty reduction and the alleviation of inequality, these benefits have not yet been realized in Africa. Industrialization in the continent has not corresponded to rapid urban growth as in other developing regions. Manufacturing productivity growth in Africa has been dropping since the 2000s, from an average of 7.4 percent between 2000 and 2008 to an average of 3.5 percent between 2009 and 2014. Growth in agricultural productivity has been decreasing from an average of 9.9 percent between 2000 and 2008 to 4.0 percent between 2009 and 2014. Productivity growth in the services sector was negative in the first three years of the twenty-first century, and after rising to approximate the growth rate of manufacturing during 2004–2008, it declined sharply to virtually no growth during 2012–2014 (UNECA 2017). It has thus been asserted that many African countries are seeing "premature urbanization," in which urbanization is being driven by consumption fueled by natural resource use, rather than by industrialization (Gollin, Jedwab, and Vollrath 2014). This is one of the key missing links for structural transformation and inclusive economic growth in the continent.

URBANIZATION AND IMPROVED SOCIAL OUTCOMES

In addition to enacting social development in the long run on account of structural transformation inducing economic growth, urbanization also has the potential to facilitate positive social outcomes by virtue of enhancing access to essential basic services and infrastructure. Cities offer economies of scale for local planning authorities in terms of providing access to education, health, vocational training, electricity, sanitation, and housing, which can be critical for improving social indicators. The potential of urban areas to enhance access to essential services is especially crucial in the context of Africa where governments are often constricted in terms of resources, but where large populations need to be served. The transition of populations to cities also has been correlated with lower fertility rates.

Although 74 percent of the rural population in Sub-Saharan Africa suffers multidimensional poverty, the rate for the same indicator in urban areas is only 31 percent (UNDP 2016). Rural–urban social disparities are manifested explicitly for specific social outcomes. For instance, in Nigeria, the under-five mortality rate in urban areas is one hundred per one thousand live births, but in rural areas, this mortality rate is significantly higher (167 per 1,000 live births) (National Population Commission 2014). With regards to education, Tanzania's 2012 census revealed that 29.73 percent of rural children five years old or older had never attended school, compared with only 8.84 percent of children five years or older in urban areas (United Republic of Tanzania 2014). In terms of child stunting in Africa, when countries are grouped by rates of urbanization, a clear difference emerges when comparing countries with low urbanization with highly urbanized countries. Indeed, the rate of child stunting for the fourteen countries in the continent with less than 30 percent urbanization is 41.9 percent, whereas in the ten countries that have an urbanization rate in excess of 60 percent, the rate of child stunting is almost half, at 26.3 percent (Sinha and Assefa 2017). Similarly, Gabon, which is a highly urbanized (87 percent urbanized) country according to African standards, also has social indicators that far exceed the averages on the continent. For example, the country has a youth literacy rate of approximately 98 percent and an estimated 88 percent of its population has access to improved sources of drinking water (United Nations Children's Fund 2015). These urban–rural disparities have many and varied causes and correlates, including the association between incomes per capita and rates of urbanization.

Nonetheless, urbanization offers significant opportunities to accelerate the alleviation of poverty and reduction of inequality, including gender inequalities. At present, however, basic services and infrastructure in many African cities cannot adequately meet the needs of populations in an equitable manner. Inequality in African cities is high, with the expansion of slums and informal housing becoming widespread. There is a clear and imminent risk that urbanization in Africa, instead of resulting in the amelioration of poverty and inequality, could lead to cities becoming centers of impoverishment, disparities, and social strife.

URBANIZATION AND ENVIRONMENTAL SUSTAINABILITY

Africa's rapid ongoing urbanization also has the potential to direct the continent on the course of environmental sustainability and green growth (UNECA 2016). Urban areas with adequate planning and a prescient approach to future expansion can be the engines of efficiency in terms of transportation, energy, infrastructure, construction, and consumption. This may be achieved not only because of the economies of scale that cities enable but also because of the knowledge spillovers and innovation that cities can generate. For Africa in particular, knowledge spillovers with regards to urban efficiency, coupled with local innovation and solutions for the continent's peculiar circumstances, can deliver powerful and lasting environmental dividends. In doing so, significant economic benefits can be accrued with the quality of growth contributing to inclusiveness and the amelioration of economic and social disparities.

Current pathways of urbanization in Africa, which are by and large characterized by continuous sprawl, lack of public transportation and dependence on cars, fossil fuel-based energy consumption, unsustainable construction methods, and inefficient infrastructure, are exacerbating environmental degradation and are undermining economic development and structural transformation. Instead of enabling sustainability and green growth, such unplanned urban growth can adversely affect the environment, compromise climate change mitigation, and place hundreds of millions of people at increased risk of natural disasters.

URBANIZATION FOR QUALITY GROWTH: POLICY ANCHORS

The immense potential that urbanization has to enact quality growth in Africa needs to be harnessed by prudent and prescient policy making that acknowledges the impacts of urbanization at all geographical scales. Specifically, economic and urban or spatial planning need to be linked at the national, regional, and local levels through an approach that combines subsector targeting and industrial policies with spatial targeting and urban and regional policies.

REGIONAL POLICIES

Because Africa is predominantly rural, urbanization can be used to harness regional development and uplift rural as well as peri-urban areas. This can happen only when a harmonized rural-urban perspective does not view urban and rural development as mutually exclusive. It is of paramount importance to have regional-level targets that promote forward and backward linkages among cities, towns, and villages to optimize synergies between urban and rural areas. Specific importance should be given to taking maximum benefit from Africa's natural resource endowments by using urbanization for agricultural transformation. Under the framework of the broader national development policy, regional policies that promote specialization and trade-based complementary functions within subregions based on the comparative advantages of cities as well as rural areas are also essential. This specialization can be critical in optimizing synergies among geographical entities at the regional level to drive quality growth for entire regions and subregions in an equitable, inclusive, and sustainable manner.

Another important consideration at the regional level is the promotion of regional integration. This integration can entail targeted and strategic investments in infrastructure to make trade and transportation at the regional and subregional levels fast, cheap, and convenient. This is particularly critical when granting access to regional markets for farmers. At present, African farmers are to a large degree cut off from markets and transportation channels because of poor infrastructure, thus severely limiting their ability to harvest and market economically advantageous crops. For example, the African Union's Programme for Infrastructure Development in Africa has immense potential for unlocking synergies in Africa and promoting equitable growth by enhancing trade links at all levels in the continent (African Union 2015b). Regional integration not only should not be limited to physical infrastructure but also should promote knowledge sharing and network connections.

NATIONAL POLICIES

Considering the fact that the impacts of urbanization transcend sectoral boundaries, it is imperative for African governments to incorporate urbanization in national development planning as a cross-sectoral issue in the overall development strategy, instead of taking a narrow, sectoral, and functional approach. For example, Ethiopia's Second Growth and Transformation Plan explicitly targets the harnessing of urbanization for economic growth and identifies specific coordination and strategic mechanisms to facilitate this growth (Federal Democratic Republic of Ethiopia 2015). To enhance the benefits of urbanization for structural transformation, it is fundamental to coordinate its various facets and outcomes from an integrated perspective. This coordination can only be achieved when cross-sectoral mechanisms are created, which enable comprehensive and multidimensional planning of urbanization that is synchronized with broader development objectives.

Also critical is ensuring a balanced and well-connected national urban system. Currently, urbanization in Africa is characterized by excessive primacy, with the concentration of economic activity and population in one large city, often the capital. Although large cities offer significant agglomeration benefits, to ensure that urbanization drives inclusive and quality growth for all citizens, states should seek to promote well-functioning systems of cities that also include efficient and viable secondary cities. The promotion of secondary cities can offer some firms competitive advantages, as a result of lower costs and a means to avoid diseconomies of scale that might affect primary cities. For example, Rwanda, through its Vision 2020, has focused Kigali as well as six secondary cities as key drivers of urbanization to achieve middle-income status.

It is also important to strengthen the planning capacity for urbanization with a particular focus on the compilation of data from a multidimensional perspective. At present, the focus on urban data is mainly on demographic and social indicators, which is useful for matters of urban functionality (UNECA 2017). To realize the potential of urbanization for structural transformation from a national perspective, however, the availability of multidimensional data is necessary. The particular paucity of data on the economic dimensions of urbanization in Africa has limited the extent to which national development planning can strategically integrate the related implications.

LOCAL POLICIES

At the local level, it is essential for city administrators to proactively maximize the agglomeration effects of cities and minimize the negative externalities and diseconomies of scale by nurturing well-functioning and efficient cities. Specific measures are needed to address barriers to the economic efficiency of cities, including facilitating regulatory frameworks for firms; ensuring adequate services and infrastructure; enhancing connectivity and compactness; and eliminating spatial, social, and gender segregation.

Economies of scale that urbanization enables should be harnessed for the efficient provision of public services, with a particular emphasis on health, education, and skills development. These services can result in multifaceted and sustained dividends for structural transformation in the long run. Uplifting human capital is directly linked to the transition of economies toward more productive sectors as well as in intrasectoral enhancements of productivity.

The urban transition that Africa is undergoing is also coinciding with a demographic transition that is resulting in a rapid increase in the population of young people in the continent. To ensure an adequate utilization of this youth bulge for structural transformation and quality growth, it is of paramount importance for young people to be given sufficient educational and employment opportunities. The role of cities in this regard can be crucial. Targeted and timely interventions to involve young people in urban economies through practical and employment-oriented skills development training can deliver profound dividends. The involvement of the private sector in such initiatives can be of critical importance and lead to tangible results. In addition, a dedicated effort needs to be made to enhance opportunities for girls and young women with a view to making use of their potential and offering them equal opportunities.

Revenue generation at the local level can be significantly important in enabling cities to finance essential development programs, infrastructure, and services. At present, most African cities are dependent on transfers from national governments. Local revenue generation through a variety of instruments, in a way that does not adversely affect citizens and businesses, can be significant in financing initiatives based on urgent requirements and local preferences. Harnessing the value of public land can be a major source of financing for a sustainable urban infrastructure if done in a transparent and prudent manner. For instance, in 2007, the public auction of land designated for a new city outside Cairo raised US$3.12 billion, which was the equivalent of one hundred times the annual property tax revenues of all local governments in Egypt (Peterson 2009).

CONCLUSION

Urbanization in Africa is an inevitable and irreversible process, and the future of the continent will largely be determined in its growing cities. Therefore, the way in which urbanization unfolds will have a profound impact on the quality of growth in Africa as well as on the future of its citizens. The swift urbanization that the continent is experiencing combined with the demographic dynamic of an immensely youthful population profile present the continent not only with a challenge but also with an unprecedented opportunity to usher in a period of rapid, inclusive, and sustained growth. This opportunity, to a large degree, remains unharnessed. The reasons for this are multiple and vary in the context of different countries. Overall, policy responses to urbanization and its associated dynamics remain weak, compartmentalized, and fragmented. Moreover, appreciation for the potential of urbanization is not proportionate to its wide-ranging implications for economic growth, social development, and environmental sustainability. Thus, it is imperative for African states to unleash the potential of their cities by fusing economic and urban policy in a holistic manner, thereby reaping synergies that can uplift their entire countries in a swift, equitable, and sustainable manner.

NOTES

The authors gratefully acknowledge the generous support and assistance of Mr. Arslan Chaudhary and Ms. Hyungbin Lim, both of the Social Development Policy Division, UN Economic Commission.

1. These fourteen countries in order of projected fertility by 2025–2030 are as follows: Niger, Somalia, Mali, Angola, Burundi, Gambia, Chad, Democratic Republic of Congo, Nigeria, Uganda, Zambia, Burkina Faso, Mozambique, and Tanzania.

2. The countries are Niger, Democratic Republic Congo, Mali, Burundi, Nigeria, Mozambique, Benin, Congo, Malawi, and Senegal.

REFERENCES

African Development Bank. 2011. 'The Middle of the Pyramid: Dynamics of the Middle Class in Africa.' Market Brief April 20, 2011. Abidjan: AFDB

——. 2012. *The Bank Group's Urban Development Strategy: Transforming Africa's Cities and Towns into Engines of Economic Growth and Social Development.* Abidjan: African Development Bank.

African Development Bank and Organisation for Economic Co-operation and Development. 2016. *African Economic Outlook 2016 Sustainable Cities and Structural Transformation.* Paris: Organisation for Economic Co-operation and Development.

African Development Bank, Organisation for Economic Co-operation and Development, and United Nations Development Programme. 2012. *African Economic Outlook: Promoting Youth Employment.* Paris: Organisation for Economic Co-operation and Development.

African Union. 2015a. *Agenda 2063: Popular Version.* https://au.int/en/Agenda2063/popular_version.

——. 2015b. *Programme for Infrastructure Development in Africa.* Addis Ababa, Ethiopia: African Union.

Beegle, Katherine, Luc Christiansen, Andrew Dablen, and Isis Gaddis. 2016. *Poverty in a Rising Africa.* Washington, DC: World Bank. Accessed March 31, 2019, https://openknowledge.worldbank.org/handle/10986/22575.

Budlender, Debbie. 2011a. "Statistics on Informal Employment in Ghana." WIEGO Statistical Brief No. 6. May 2011. Women in Informal Employment Globalizing and Organizing. Accessed March 31, 2019, http://www.wiego.org/sites/default/files/publications/files/Budlender_WIEGO_SB6.pdf.

——. 2011b. "Statistics on Informal Employment in Kenya." WIEGO Statistical Brief No. 5. May 2011. Women in Informal Employment Globalizing and Organizing. Accessed March 31, 2019, http://www.inclusivecities.org/wp-content/uploads/2012/07/Budlender_WIEGO_SB5.pdf.

——. 2011c. "Statistics on Informal Employment in South Africa." WIEGO Statistical Brief No. 3. May 2011. Women in Informal Employment Globalizing and Organizing. Accessed March 31, 2019, http://www.wiego.org/sites/default/files/publications/files/Budlender_WIEGO_SB3.pdf.

Bughin, Jacques, Mutsa Chironga, Georges Desvaux, Tenbite Ermias, Paul Jacobson, Omid Kassiri, Acha Leke, Susan Lund, Arend van Wamelen, and Yassir Zouaoui. 2016. "Lions on the Move II: Realizing the Potential of Africa's Economies." McKinsey Global Institute. Accessed April 4, 2019, https://www.mckinsey.com /global-themes/middle-east-and-africa/lions-on-the-move-realizing-the-potential -of-africas-economies.

Chandy, Laurence. 2015. "Why Is the Number of Poor People in Africa Increasing When Africa's Economies Are Growing?" *Africa in Focus*, May 4. Washington, DC: Brookings Institution. Accessed March 31, 2019, https://www.brookings.edu /blog/africa-in-focus/2015/05/04/why-is-the-number-of-poor-people-in-africa -increasing-when-africas-economies-are-growing/.

Duranton, Gilles, and Diego Puga. 2004. "Micro-Foundations of Urban Agglomeration Economies." In *Handbook of Regional and Urban Economics*, edited by J. V. Henderson and J. F. Thisse, 2063–2117. Amsterdam: Elsevier.

Fay, Marianne, and Charlotte Opal. 2000. "Urbanization Without Growth, A Not-So-Uncommon Phenomenon." Policy Research Working Paper 2412. World Bank, Washington, DC.

Federal Democratic Republic of Ethiopia. 2015. *Draft Second Growth and Transformation Plan 2015/6–2019/20*. Addis Ababa, Ethiopia: National Planning Commission.

Gollin, Douglas, Remi Jedwab, and Dietrich Vollrath. 2014. "Urbanization With and Without Industrialization." *Journal of Economic Growth* 21 (1): 35–70.

Gutman, Jeffrey, Amadou Sy, and Soumya Chattopadhyay. 2015. "Financing African Infrastructure: Can the World Deliver?" Report, March 20. Brookings Institution. https://www.brookings.edu/research/financing-african-infrastructure -can-the-world-deliver/

Herrendorf, Berthold, Richard Rogerson, and Akos Valentinyi. 2014. "Growth and Structural Transformation." In *Handbook of Economic Growth*, edited by Philippe Aghion and Steven N. Durlauf, 855–941. Amsterdam: Elsevier

International Labour Organization. 2015a. *World Employment and Social Outlook 2015*. Geneva: International Labour Organization.

——. 2015b. *ILO-KLM Database*. http://www. ilo.org/global/statistics-and-databases /research-and-databases/kilm/lang—en/index.htm.

——. 2016a. *World Employment and Social Outlook Trends 2016*. Geneva: International Labour Organization.

——. 2016b. *World Employment and Social Outlook: Trends for Youth 2016*. Geneva: International Labour Organization.

International Monetary Fund. 2015. *Regional Economic Outlook-Sub-Saharan Africa: Dealing with the Gathering Clouds*. Washington, DC: International Monetary Fund.

Mo Ibrahim Foundation. 2015. "Facts & Figures: African Urban Dynamics." Accessed April 4, 2019, http://static.moibrahimfoundation.org/u/2015/11/19115202/2015-Facts -Figures-African-Urban-Dynamics.pdf.

National Population Commission, NPC/Nigeria and ICF International. 2014. *Nigeria Demographic and Health Survey 2013*. Abuja, Nigeria: NPC/Nigeria and ICF International

Overseas Development Institute. 2016. "Child Poverty, Inequality and Demography: Why Sub-Saharan Africa Matters for Sustainable Development Goals." Available at: https://www.odi.org/sites/odi.org.uk/files/resource-documents/10794.pdf.

Peterson, George E. 2009. "Unlocking Land Values to Finance Urban Infrastructure: Land-Based Financing Options for Cities." *Gridlines* 40. Washington, DC: World Bank.

Potts, Deborah. 2014. *Whatever Happened to Africa's Rapid Urbanization?* London: Africa Research Institute.

Sinha, Saurabh, and Kalkidan Assefa. 2017. "Analysing Child Stunting in Africa: Does Urbanization Make a Difference?" Presentation delivered at the International Conference on Putting Children First: Identifying Solutions and Taking Action to Tackle Child Poverty and Inequality in Africa, Addis Ababa, October 23–25.

Turok, Ivan, and Gordon McGranahan. 2013. "Urbanization and Economic Growth: The Arguments and Evidence from Africa and Asia." *Environment and Urbanization* 25 (2): 465–482.

United Nations. 2015. *Transforming our World: The 2030 Agenda for Sustainable Development.* New York: United Nations

——. 2016. "Kigali Sparkles on the Hills." *Africa Renewal Online.* Available at: http://www.un.org/africarenewal/magazine/april-2016/kigali-sparkles-hills.

——. 2017. *World Economic Situation and Prospects.* New York: United Nations.

United Nations Children's Fund. 2015, *State of the World's Children: 2015.* New York: United Nations Children's Fund.

United Nations Department of Economic and Social Affairs. 2017. *Sustainable Development Knowledge Platform.* https://sustainabledevelopment.un.org.

United Nations Department of Economic and Social Affairs, Population Division. 2014. *World Urbanization Prospects.*

——. 2018. *World Urbanization Prospects.*

United National Development Programme. 2015. *Human Development Report 2015: Work for Human Development.* New York: United National Development Programme.

——. 2016. *Human Development Report 2017: Human Development for Everyone.* New York: United National Development Programme.

United National Development Programme, Bureau for Crisis Prevention and Recovery. 2010. *Urban Risk Management.* New York: United National Development Programme.

United Nations Economic Commission. 2014. "Industrialization and Structural Transformation." Issues paper presented at the Conference of ministers of Finance, Economic Development and Planning. Abuja, Nigeria, March 2014.

——. 2015. *Macroeconomic Policy for Structural Transformation of African Economies: Policy brief.* Addis Ababa, Ethiopia: Economic Commission for Africa.

——. 2017. *Economic Report on Africa 2017: Urbanization and Industrialization for Africa's Transformation.* Addis Ababa, Ethiopia: Economic Commission for Africa.

——. 2019. *Economic Report on Africa 2018.* Addis Ababa, Ethiopia: Economic Commission for Africa.

United Nations Human Settlements Programme (UN-Habitat). 2016 *World Cities Report*. Nairobi, Kenya: United Nations.

———. 2017. *New Urban Agenda*. Quito, Ecuador: United Nations Habitat III Secretariat.

United Nations Office for Disaster Risk Reduction. 2014. *Disaster Risk Reduction in Africa*. Geneva: United Nations Office for Disaster Risk Reduction.

United Republic of Tanzania. 2014. "Basic Demographic and Socio-economic Profile Statistical Table." Ministry of Finance and Office of Chief Government Statistician, President's Office, Dar es Salam.United States Department of Agriculture. 2015. "A Turning Point for Agricultural Exports to Sub-Saharan Africa." Foreign Agricultural Service. Washington D.C.: U.S. Department of Agriculture.

Vanek, Joann, Martha Alter Chen, Fracoise Carre, James Heintz, and Ralf Hussmans. 2014. "Statistics on the Informal Economy: Definition, Regional Estimates and Challenges." Working Paper (Statistics) No. 2, April 2014. Women in Informal Employment Globalizing and Organizing. Accessed March 31, 2019, http://www.wiego.org/sites/default/files/publications/files/Vanek-Statistics-WIEGO-WP2.pdf.

Woetzel, Jonathan, Nicklas Garemo, Jan Mischke, Martin Hjerpe, and Robert Palter. 2016. "Bridging Global Infrastructure Gaps." McKinsey Global Institute. Accessed April 4, 2019, https://www.mckinsey.com/industries/capital-projects-and-infrastructure/our-insights/bridging-global-infrastructure-gaps.

World Bank. 2001. *World Development Report 2000/2001: Attacking Poverty*. Washington, DC: World Bank.

———. 2009. *Systems of Cities: Harnessing Urbanization for Growth and Poverty Alleviation—World Bank Urban and Local Government Strategy*. Washington, DC: World Bank.

———. 2016. *Poverty and Shared Prosperity 2016: Taking on Inequality*. Washington, DC: World Bank.

———. 2017. *Africa's Cities: Opening Doors to the World*. Washington, DC: World Bank.

World Health Organization. 2016. *Global Report on Urban Health*. Geneva: World Health Organization.

Zhang, Dandan, Xin Li, and Jinjun Xue. 2015. "Education Inequality between Rural and Urban Areas of the People's Republic of China, Migrants' Children Education, and Some Implications." *Asian Development Review* 32 (1): 196–224.

CHAPTER 14

Migrants, Towns, Poverty, and Jobs

INSIGHTS FROM TANZANIA

Luc Christiaensen, Joachim De Weerdt, Bert Ingelaere, and Ravi Kanbur

LOOKING BEYOND URBAN AGGREGATES

By 2030, almost 60 percent of the world will live in urban areas, with urbanization concentrating in Asia and Africa (United Nations 2015) and occurring at an unprecedented pace. Although it took Industrial Europe one hundred ten years (1800–1910) to increase its rate of urbanization from 15 to 40 percent, Asia and Africa did so in just fifty (1960–2010) (Jedwab, Christiaensen, and Gindelsky 2017).

Not surprisingly, urbanization is widely studied. It also remains hotly debated, including the two-way causal relationship between urbanization and growth; the associations among unemployment, poverty reduction, and urbanization; and whether or not urbanization is delivering the benefits of agglomeration.

In these debates the national rate of urbanization is usually the variable to be explained or the variable doing the explaining.[1] And the opportunities and challenges posed by urbanization are often taken to be synonymous with those offered and experienced by the main urban centers (i.e., the political or commercial capitals, or the big cities).

Take the case of Tanzania. According to the 2012 census, around 10 percent of the population lived in Dar es Salaam, the political capital. At around 4.5 million, this was the largest urban agglomeration in Tanzania by a huge margin. The population of Dar grew dramatically over the past fifty years, and the bulk of this growth was accounted for by in-migration (Wenban-Smith 2015).

Facts such as these, seen in this way, have colored much of the urbanization discourse both in Tanzania and in the rest of the world. They lead to a focus on investment in large cities in response to in-migration. And

because these are migrants from poor rural areas, the argument goes, public investment in countries' metropoles is also of primordial importance
to address poverty.

Consider, however, the following perspective, also taken from Wenban-
Smith (2015). In 2012, Dar accounted for about one-third of the urban
population. But it also accounted for about one-third of the urban population in 2002, in 1988, in 1978, and so on back. Thus, non-Dar urban
areas have grown as fast as Dar in Tanzania's history. If we further divide
non-Dar urban areas into regional capitals (with an average population
of around two hundred thousand) and small towns (with an average
population of around twenty thousand), an even more interesting trend
appears—small towns are forming an ever-increasing proportion of the
urban population of Tanzania (figure 14.1).

Clearly, a lot of urbanization action is going on in small towns. The
movement out of rural areas, which is undeniable as a major trend, is
as much to small towns as to Dar. In fact, in Africa, the distribution of
urban agglomerations by population size is bimodal. Two-fifths of the
urban population are living in cities larger than one million people, but
two-fifths are also living in towns of less than a quarter million people
(Dorosh and Thurlow 2013).[2] Nonetheless, the literature and the policy
discourse seldom go beyond the dichotomous rural–urban distinction.

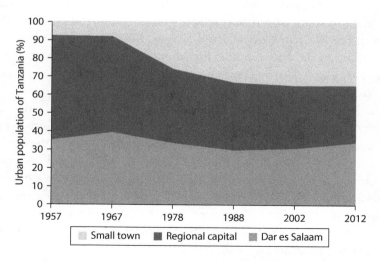

Figure 14.1 The evolution of urban composition in Tanzania

Source: Compiled from Wenban-Smith (2015).

Our central contention is that the *composition* of urbanization could be as important for employment generation and poverty reduction as the overall aggregate national rate. It is certainly an important policy question faced by any African government—at the margin, should the government of Tanzania tilt toward public investment in small towns rather than the capital city? To address this question, it is important to understand why the composition of urbanization matters for the speed of poverty reduction and thus for the creation of employment and poverty-reducing policies.

Three interdependent forces are at play: (1) intra-urban agglomeration effects and congestion costs, (2) economic linkages between urban and rural areas, and (3) rural–urban migration flows.[3] The new economic geography literature emphasizes the importance that urban size plays in fostering economies of scale and agglomeration, which are found to propel economic growth (Overman and Venables 2010). There is, however, a tipping point beyond which returns to size may start to decline and congestion may set in (Henderson 2003). And the positive effect of average city size on economic growth may not hold up to the same degree in developing countries as it did in developed countries. Indications are that it may even be negative (Frick and Rodriguez-Pose 2016).

Positive spillovers of urban centers on the rural hinterlands also accrue through consumption linkages, urban–rural remittances, upward pressure on agricultural wages, and the generation of rural nonfarm employment (Cali 2013). It is unclear whether, in the aggregate, spillovers are larger when the urban population is concentrated in few large urban centers, or when it is more spread out across a greater number of smaller urban centers. For Mexico, Berdegué and Soloaga (2018) find that cities with populations in the three hundred fifty thousand to five hundred thousand range have more positive effects on rural areas than smaller or larger cities. But more evidence is needed.

Finally, because of a series of migration barriers, rural people may find it easier to connect to growth and jobs in and around smaller urban centers nearby than when these jobs are created farther away in the limited number of large cities. A larger share of the rural population lives within the hinterlands of smaller towns than within the hinterlands of cities (Food and Agriculture Organization 2017) and most of the poor are rural (Beegle et al. 2016). From this perspective, the finding from India that the rural poor benefit more from growth of towns than from growth of cities does not surprise (Gibson et al. 2017).

Ultimately it is a matter for empirical investigation and resolution. The variety of forces can go in opposite way. But the investigation cannot begin if we stick with the conventional rural–urban dichotomy. The objective of this chapter is to provide such an empirical exploration, considering a range of issues and methods linking migration, small towns, poverty, and jobs for one country.

In particular, we review the different insights from our body of work of the past couple of years in the context of Tanzania addressing the question of whether the composition of urbanization matters for poverty reduction. This work has drawn heavily on the remarkable, two-decadal database from Kagera, northwestern Tanzania (De Weerdt et al. 2012) and looks at the question from different methodological angles (theoretical and empirical, quantitative and qualitative).[4]

To the extent that the findings from these different approaches point in the same direction, they can at least demonstrate the need for a more disaggregated perspective to the questions of urbanization and development, and raise recognition that secondary towns may well be particularly conducive to poverty reduction.

The chapter proceeds as follows. Through novel decomposition, drawing on the peculiar features of individual panel data, the second section documents the empirical contributions of towns and cities to growth and poverty reduction in Tanzania. This is followed in the third section by a basic theoretical framework, building on the Harris-Todaro framework (H-T; 1970), to identify some of the potential mechanisms behind the observed contributions.

Although the higher earning potential in cities has been considered a common feature of the urban landscape (Ferré, Ferreira, and Lanjouw 2012), greater proximity of the rural population to towns than to cities emerges as an important additional factor to understand why many more rural citizens (many of them poor) end up in (nearby) towns rather than in the city, thereby making towns in Tanzania even more important contributors to poverty reduction than its cities. To examine this more rigorously, the fourth section presents the findings of an econometric test, confirming the importance of distance in determining migrant destination choice. The econometric results are probed further in the fifth section through qualitative analysis (life histories), with a subset of migrants from the Kagera panel. The last section concludes.

MIGRATION, TOWNS, AND POVERTY REDUCTION IN TANZANIA

To get a handle on the effect of the composition of urbanization on growth and poverty reduction, consider the following: Suppose we had nationally representative panel data at time t and $t + 1$. This would give us a person's individual location as well as their income (or consumption) in each period. National poverty change can then be decomposed into the poverty effects of (1) income growth among those who stayed in rural areas, small towns, and cities; and (2) income changes as the result of (net) migration across these categories.[5]

Christiaensen et al. (2017) apply this approach using the National Panel Survey of Tanzania (2008–2012) (table 14.1).[6] Overall, the poverty rate did not decline much over this period (by 0.42 percentage points), consistent with the low annual growth in consumption (1.16 percent). Yet, these averages hide a lot of heterogeneity, especially between non-movers and movers and depending on the destination (rural, town, city).[7] The vast majority of the population (91 percent) did not move and experienced very little consumption growth[8] or poverty reduction. Among the non-movers, poverty reduction was largest among those who stayed in secondary towns. Among non-moving city dwellers, growth was even slightly negative, and the poverty headcount increased slightly.

These relatively small changes in (average) welfare contrast with the changes observed among the movers. Their poverty declined by 5.8 percentage points (and their average annual consumption growth amounted to 8.4 percent). More strikingly, income growth and poverty decline were especially substantial among rural–urban migrants, whereas moves back to the rural areas (from the town or the city) came along with a substantial increase in poverty incidence (from 4.5 to 14.8 percent and from 0 to 13.1 percent, respectively). Urban–rural migration did not necessarily result in a decline of average income growth though. Return migration does not signify failure for everyone (Hirvonen and Lilleor 2015).

Looking within the urban space, rural–town migration contributed most to overall poverty reduction (twice as much as rural–city migration), even though rural–city migration contributed more to overall income growth. The reason for the larger contribution to poverty reduction by rural–town migration follows from the fact that four years later about twice as many rural citizens were found in secondary towns than in cities (3.4 percent versus 1.7 percent), although the decline in poverty incidence (i.e., the average probability of exiting poverty when moving) among both groups was similar (13.1 and 12.4 percentage points, respectively). When it comes to income growth, however, rural–city movers saw their incomes grow much more than those moving to towns, overcompensating for the fact that only half as many ended up in the city.

Source: Christiaensen et al. (2017).

Table 14.1 Secondary Towns Contribute Substantially More Than Cities to Poverty Reduction in Tanzania, 2008–2012

Household Movement	Population Share^a (%)	Poverty Headcount (%)				Population Share^b (%)	Consumption/Adult Equivalent (Thousands of Tanzanian Shillings)			
		2008	2012	Total Reduction (% Point)	Share of National Poverty Reduction (%)		2008	2012	Annual Growth (%)	Share of Total National Consumption Growth (%)
Non-Movers	**91.14**	**19.42**	**19.53**	**0.11**	**-23.87**	**91.09**	**634.5**	**643.2**	**0.34**	**26.51**
Rural–Rural	69.83	23.39	24.04	0.65	-108.08	69.02	488.4	499.1	0.55	24.73
Secondary towns–Secondary town	10.61	12.04	8.78	-3.26	82.28	10.97	784.6	838.2	1.66	19.55
Cities–Cities	10.70	0.83	0.69	-0.14	3.57	10.95	1,392.5	1,344.7	-0.87	-17.40
Movers	**8.86**	**16.23**	**10.44**	**-5.79**	**122.12**	**8.91**	**654.4**	**902.0**	**8.35**	**73.51**
Rural–Rural	1.55	20.42	18.50	-1.92	7.07	1.45	506.5	571.2	3.05	3.13
Rural–Secondary towns	3.38	23.21	10.09	-13.13	105.64	3.42	555.6	667.0	4.68	12.69
Rural–Cities	1.67	16.19	3.77	-12.42	49.38	1.66	544.4	1,332.1	25.07	43.55
Secondary towns–Cities	0.50	1.74	0.00	-1.74	2.08	0.55	696.2	1,615.2	23.42	16.83
Secondary towns–Rural	1.31	4.53	14.83	10.30	-32.11	1.36	929.0	971.5	1.12	1.92
Cities–Secondary towns	0.14	0.00	0.00	0.00	0.00	0.15	1,688.1	1,290.4	-6.50	-1.99
Cities–Rural	0.31	0.00	13.16	13.16	-9.71	0.29	1,317.2	915.3	-8.70	-3.88
National	**100**	**19.14**	**18.72**	**-0.42**	**100**	**100**	**636.2**	**666.3**	**1.16**	**100**

Note: This table describes poverty and consumption changes of households that moved spatially between 2008 and 2012. A household is defined as a mover if their location of residence, such as cities, secondary town, or rural in 2012 differs from that in 2008 or if a rural household has changed region. A household that moved within cities or secondary towns is considered as a non-mover.

a Weighted by panel weight multiplied by household size.

b Weighted by panel weight multiplied by total adult equivalent.

These findings draw attention to the critical role secondary towns appear to have played in poverty reduction in Tanzania. This follows, at least in an accounting sense, from the fact that many more rural dwellers (including poor rural dwellers) ended up in towns, even though the average income gains among those who were found in the city were much larger. Application of the same decomposition to the long-running Kagera Health and Development Survey (KHDS) provides complementary insights. KHDS is a distinct and large data set of individuals who were tracked in time and across space over two decades, from the early 1990s to 2010. The database includes information on 4,339 individuals. These people were first interviewed in their baseline communities in the early 1990s in Kagera, a large, remote, and primarily rural region in the northwestern part of Tanzania and then interviewed again nearly two decades later in 2010, irrespective of whether they stayed or left for other rural areas, towns, and cities (De Weerdt et al. 2012).

Contrary to the 2008–2012 period at the national level, over its eighteen-year span, the KHDS sample experienced a considerable amount of growth and poverty reduction (table 14.2). Per capita incomes rose by 77 percent and the poverty headcount declined by 24 percentage points. As before, however, movers contributed more than non-movers in terms of poverty reduction (55 versus 45 percent) and notably in terms of growth (71 versus 29 percent). Further disaggregation of the contribution of the movers shows that rural–urban migration contributed more than migration within rural areas and, in particular, that rural–town migration contributed more to poverty reduction than migration of rural citizens to the cities, despite a much larger reduction in poverty from moves to the city.[9] As in the national panel, this follows from the substantially larger share of the migration population ending up in towns than in the city (just under twice as much). In the KHDS sample, migration to towns also contributed more to income growth—the difference in the per capita income gain between migrants to cities and towns was not large enough to offset the effect of the much larger number of rural–urban migrants that ended up in the towns.

In conclusion, the typical move from rural to big city increases income and reduces poverty by more than the typical move from rural to small town. But, because of the greater number of moves from rural to small towns, in aggregate, these moves (i.e., the rural–town part of urbanization) account for the greater share of poverty reduction. In turn, this raises a question: if the move to the big city is expected to raise income by far more,

Table 14.2 Secondary Towns Contribute Substantially More to Poverty Reduction Than Cities in Kagera, Early 1990s–2010

Household Movement	Population Share (%)	Poverty Headcount (%)		Total Reduction (% Point)	Share in Total Net Poverty Reduction (%)	Consumption/Capita (Thousands of Tanzanian Shillings)			Share of Total National Consumption Growth (%)
		1991–1994 Average	2010			1991–1994 Average	2010	Total Growth (TSH)	
Non-Movers	**52**	**57**	**36**	**-21**	**45**	**343**	**493**	**149**	**29**
Rural–Rural	49	59	38	-21	42	336	476	140	25
Town–Town	3	29	7	-22	3	451	747	296	4
Movers	**48**	**50**	**23**	**-27**	**55**	**370**	**776**	**407**	**71**
Rural–Rural	24	57	36	-21	22	344	573	229	20
Rural–Town	13	50	16	-34	18	373	871	497	24
Rural–Cities	7	47	3	-44	14	389	1,184	795	21
Town–Rural	1	34	25	-8	0	405	570	165	1
Town–Town	2	15	5	-10	1	489	969	481	3
Town–City	1	9	3	6	0	540	1,452	913	3
National	**100**	**54**	**30**	**24**	**100**	**356**	**629**	**273**	**100**

Source: Author's calculations based on KHDS data.

why would anyone move to the small town at all, especially given that the difference in poverty incidence at baseline (an indicator of credit constraint) between town and city migrants is relatively small in the national data, or even zero in the case of the KHDS sample?

One obvious explanation may relate to selectivity. This would hold that it is especially the more educated and the more entrepreneurial, who are smaller in number, who make it to and in the city, where the returns to skills are higher (Young 2013; Diamond 2016; Hicks et al. 2017). There are some signs that this is true. The KHDS data show a clear education gradient with respect to migration destination. Among migrants from rural origins, who are no longer in school, those moving to other rural areas have an average of six years of formal education, those who moved to secondary towns have seven years, and those who moved to cities have eight years. The city disproportionately attracts people with more years of formal schooling. This is also consistent with the larger gain in income among those moving to the city.

The fact that more of the better educated end up in the cities, however, does not necessarily imply that the less educated cannot realize extra income gains from moving to the city compared with moving to the towns. To get a systematic handle on the question why, in equilibrium, more rural people move to towns, even though the gains are larger when moving to the city, the next section builds on insights from Harris-Todaro (1970).

EXTENDING THE HARRIS-TODARO FRAMEWORK

The classic papers by Todaro (1969) and Harris and Todaro (1970) worked out the contours of a migration equilibrium when there is a single destination from the rural area. There have been many advances in the literature since then, but the power of the framework to address migration issues remains undiminished.[10] We will use this framework to answer the question posed in the last section: if the typical move from rural to big city leads to a larger gain than the typical move from rural to small town, why are there so many more moves to small towns?[11]

We begin the analysis with a single urban destination to introduce notation and establish benchmarks. In the simple Todaro (1969) model, agents are identical: there is a single rural wage w_r and a single urban modern sector wage w. There are E modern sector jobs, and those who do not get these jobs survive in the informal economy ("unemployment") at wage w_0. The probability of modern sector employment is e, the employment rate. We assume

$$w_0 < w_r < w \qquad (14.1)$$

as a stylized representation of the facts. With risk neutral agents, migration equilibrium occurs when the certain rural wage equals the expected urban wage:

$$w_r = ew + (1-e)w_0. \qquad (14.2)$$

The equilibrium value of the adjusting variable e (all other variables are assumed to be constant) is thus:

$$e = \frac{w_r - w_0}{w - w_0}. \qquad (14.3)$$

With total population given as the sum of the rural (N_r) and urban (N_u) population,

$$N = N_r + N_u \qquad (14.4)$$

the equilibrium distribution of population can be derived as

$$N_u = \frac{E}{e} = E \frac{w - w_0}{w_r - w_0}. \qquad (14.5)$$

As is now well known, an increase in the modern sector wage increases the unemployment rate and the size of the urban population, in other words, more migration.

A cost for migration (e.g., transport, settlement, and job search costs) also has not been included in the standard H-T models. Denote this cost as t. Introducing such a cost makes the model more realistic. Informal urban wages are in practice typically at least as high as rural wages, which, under the traditional H-T assumptions, would suggest an empty countryside. The equilibrium condition now becomes:

$$e = \frac{w_r + t - w_0}{w - w_0}. \qquad (14.6)$$

In this scenario, an increase in t comes along with an increase in the employment rate in equilibrium, to compensate, and there is less migration ($N_u = \frac{E}{e} = E \dfrac{w - w_0}{w_r + t - w_0}$ declines). These results are intuitive and have formed the basis for empirical exploration.

Let us now extend the basic model to one with two destinations, with subscripts c for city and s for small town. The equilibrium conditions are now given by the following:

$$w_r = e_s w_s + (1 - e_s)\, w_{os} - t_s = e_c w_c + (1 - e_c)\, w_{os} - t_c. \tag{14.7}$$

In equilibrium, the city and town populations are given by the following:

$$N_c = \frac{E_c}{e_c} = E_c\, \frac{w_c - w_{0c}}{w_r - w_{0c} + t_c}, \tag{14.8}$$

$$N_s = \frac{E_s}{e_s} = E_s\, \frac{w_s - w_{0s}}{w_r - w_{0s} + t_s}, \tag{14.9}$$

$$N_r = N - N_c - N_s. \tag{14.10}$$

It can now be shown that migration declines with t_i (with $i = c$ or s), but increases with w_i and w_{oi}.[12] Put differently, according to the model, in equilibrium, the size of the migration flow to a destination (city or town) depends on the number of formal (or high-paying jobs) (E_i), the wage gap between the formal and informal job at destination $(w_i\text{-}w_{oi})$, the wage gap between the job at origin and the informal job at destination $(w_r\text{-}w_{oi})$, and the cost of migration (t_i).

These equations give a handle on key factors that affect the number of people that end up in cities versus towns in equilibrium. Parameterization further allows us to explore the empirical relevance of its insights. If empirical resolution of the right-hand side of equations (14.8) and (14.9) yields migration patterns that correspond to those observed (N_c, N_s), then this would suggest that the model has explanatory power. It would support its use as an entry point in understanding why so many people end up in towns when more can be gained from moving to the city.

Information on the population size (N_i), the size of formal employment (E_i), and the formal and informal wage rates or income in the three locations (w_i, w_{oi}, w_r) can be obtained. Yet, empirical measures of the full migration cost (t_i) beyond transport (settlement and jobs search costs as well as psychosocial adjustment) are hard to come by. This makes it difficult to empirically verify equations (14.8) and (141.9) directly. Therefore, equations (14.8) and (14.9) are rewritten as a ratio:

$$\frac{N_s}{N_c} = \frac{E_s}{E_c}\, \frac{w_s - w_{os}}{w_c - w_{oc}}\, \frac{w_r - w_{oc} + t_c}{w_r - w_{os} + t_s}. \tag{14.11}$$

Given information on all parameters except t_c and t_s, and assuming $t_c > t_s$, the ratio of t_c/t_s needed to solve equation (14.11) can then be derived and its empirical plausibility assessed. This will give a sense of the empirical importance of the cost differences between migrating to cities and towns in understanding why many more people moved to towns than to the city.

The long-running KHDS panel provides an ideal opportunity to do so. The spatial and sectoral distribution of its population by 2010 could be seen as the long-run equilibrium outcome of the migration process, represented by the model. Furthermore, virtually everybody of the KHDS sample living in the rural areas in 2010 worked in the informal sector (only 3.5 percent relied on a formal wage job), which corresponds closely with the rural population reflected in the model—that is, employed in the informal sector at a lower income (w_r).

In 2010, there are 557 town migrants and 315 city migrants, or $N_s/N_c = 1.77$. We subsequently calculate $\left(\frac{E_s}{E_c}\right)$ and the observed wage gap between working in the formal and informal sector in the towns and the city $\left(\frac{w_s - w_{ot}}{w_c - w_{oc}}\right)$. This provides the necessary information to identify a range of t_c/t_s combinations that can solve equation (14.11). In the towns, 18.9 percent lives in a household that relies on formal wage employment; in the cities, this share rises to 22.2 percent.[13] The E_s/E_c ratio thus equals 1.5.[14]

Figure 14.2 overlays the cumulative density functions (cdf) of annual consumption per capita for each of the five income groups of interest (i.e., informal rural employment, informal and formal town employment, and informal and formal city employment).[15] For the largest part, the income distributions first order dominate each other in the expected manner: $w_r < w_{os} < w_{oc} < w_s < w_c$. Note that this is different from the assumptions in the traditional H-T model, whereby $w_o < w_r < w$, underscoring the importance to account for migration costs for the basic H-T assumption to hold empirically.

Taking median incomes (in thousand TSH) of each group yields: $w_r = 372 < w_{os} = 613 < w_{oc} = 871 < w_s = 1{,}088 < w_c = 1{,}475$.[16] The ratio of the town and city income gaps between formal and informal incomes, thus equals 0.79,[17] suggesting greater income polarization in cities than in towns, as expected (Ferré, Ferreira, and Lanjouw, 2012).

Returning to equation (14.11), it can be seen that $\dfrac{w_r - w_{oc} + t_c}{w_r - w_{os} + t_s} =$
$\dfrac{(-499) + t_c}{(-241) + t_s}$ needs to equal 1.5, and that $t_c > 499$ and $t_s > 241$ for equation (14.11) to hold.[18] Several (t_c, t_s) pairs can be found that meet these conditions. For

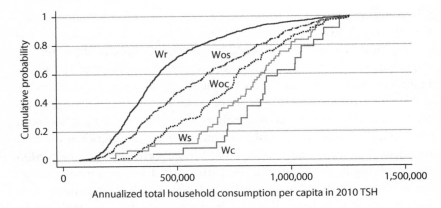

Figure 14.2   Cumulative density function of income by income groups, 2010

Note: TSH = Tanzanian shillings. The 10 percent highest consumption per capita values were dropped for a better rendition of the graph.

Source: Kanbur, Christaensen, and De Weerdt (Forthcoming)

example, setting t_c at 500, or 133 percent of annual rural income per capita, t_s must equal, 242, or 66 percent of annual rural income per capita, for the model to hold empirically. Under these assumptions, $t_c/t_s = 2$, or migration to the city is about twice as expensive as migration to towns.[19]

Circumstantial evidence supports the notion that migrating to the city is substantially more expensive in the KHDS sample than moving to towns. Reported one-way transport costs are on average two times higher to the city than to the towns (47,140 TSH versus 23,346 TSH, respectively) and migrants to towns are 8 percentage points more likely to have found work before moving than migrants to the city, illustrating differences in search costs. Reliance on friends and family for the first residence was also much more important for city migrants (56 percent) than for town migrants (30 percent) who were more likely to own a dwelling (32 percent versus 16 percent in cities) or have housing provided by the employer (8 percent, versus 2 percent in cities). In each case, about 30 percent rented a dwelling (Kanbur, Christiaensen, and De Weerdt (Forthcoming).

Overall, these simulations suggest substantially higher barriers for city migration, and a greater role of family and friends to overcome them, than for migration to the more proximate and familiar towns. Differences in migration costs may well play a much more important role in understanding why many migrants end up in towns rather than in the city, than is currently appreciated, despite higher earnings on average in the latter. One way to empirically test this is to explore how much distance to the destination affects its choice, the topic of the next section.

PROXIMITY RULES: ECONOMETRIC EVIDENCE

We began the chapter by showing how the contribution of small town moves to overall poverty reduction was greater because because there were many more of them. Given that the typical move to a big city is lucrative, we then wondered why there are not more of them. We attributed this lower number of big city moves to higher migration costs in the broad sense, encompassing actual physical costs of transportation over distance, as well as other costs associated with distance, including lack of information, uncertainty, and search and settlement costs. Indeed, distance has been a consistently significant factor in the literature on migration decisions.[20] The Kagera sample affords a distinct opportunity to test the impact of distance on migration and thus to circle back to our original assertion of the importance of migration to small towns in poverty reduction. Our augmented H-T model motivates an empirical specification to do so.

If we are to understand destination choice among migrants, then there is not only value in knowing where the migrant migrated to but also in knowing the potential destinations the migrant did not migrate to (Fafchamps and Shilpi 2013). Information about both the chosen and foregone destinations can be exploited to identify the effect of the characteristics of the destination, such as distance and earnings potential (while controlling for selectivity by controlling for the individual characteristics of the migrants). Because towns are typically closer, with lower earnings potential, the relative empirical importance of these different factors in determining why more migrants end up in towns can then be explored.

Internal KHDS migrants moved to fifty-seven different districts, within which further moves can be distinguished to rural or urban areas, to arrive at a total of seventy-eight locations. These are assumed to be the potential destinations for our sample of migrants.[21] Each of the migrants in our sample has chosen to move to one potential destination and therefore, has also chosen *not* to move to the seventy-seven other potential destinations. To understand the factors determining that choice better, we created a dyadic data set that contains seventy-eight observations for each migrant i; and one observation for each potential destination d.[22] The dependent variable Y_{id} is a dummy equal to one if i was found in location d during the last survey round and zero otherwise. The correlates of Y_{id} are then examined by estimating the following equation:

$$Y_{id} = W_d\beta_1 + R_{id}\beta_2 + \alpha_i + \varepsilon_{id}. \tag{14.12}$$

Motivated by the H-T model, we explain destination choice with W_d, the expected income at destination, and R_{id}, a set of relational variables that are specific to the i–d pair. We first explore the effect of distance between individual i and destination d. In further regression specifications, we add to R_{id} interaction effects between the characteristics of the destination and the individual as such interactions have been hypothesized to matter for destination choice (Young 2013; Bryan, Chowdhury, and Mobarak 2014; Diamond 2016). The coefficients are estimated using individual fixed effects regressions (α_i is the fixed effect), with standard errors clustered by origin village; and ε_{id} is an error term. We construct wealth indices W_d for each destination using the 2002 census and measure distance in natural logarithms of distance in kilometers between baseline location and destination.[23]

In the first column of table 14.3, we report the findings of the estimation of equation (14.12) on a dyadic data set that links all migrants to all destinations. Both wealth and distance are significantly correlated to destination choice, with opposite signs: the farther away the potential destination, the less likely that it will be chosen; the wealthier the potential destination, the more likely it will be chosen. The (absolute) magnitude of the distance coefficient is four times that of the wealth coefficient. Multiplying those coefficients by the standard deviations of the corresponding variables in the dyadic data set (0.97 for distance and 0.71 for wealth), we find that wealth would need to go up by 5.7 standard deviations to offset the negative effect of a one standard deviation increase in distance.

In the second and third columns of table 14.3, we interact distance and wealth with individual characteristics: baseline poverty status (1 = poor) and years of formal education. Coming from a poor baseline household exacerbates the negative effect of distance and reduces the attraction of high wealth at the destination. Proximity is even more important for poorer households and wealth at destination is substantially less powerful as incentive for the poor. Education, however, attenuates the friction related to distance and reinforces the pull of high-wealth areas.

Clearly, the econometric results suggest that at least in this sample, distance, a broad (and exogenous) proxy for the cost or barrier to migrate, is an important determinant of migrant destination choice.

Table 14.3   Distance Reduces the Attraction of a Destination

	(1)	(2)	(3)
Distance to Destination (ln km)	−0.025***	−0.023***	−0.039***
	(−21.176)	(−18.077)	(−31.178)
(-"-)*(poor HH)		−0.003*	
		(−1.825)	
(-"-)*(years of schooling)			0.002***
			(12.043)
Wealth index	0.006***	0.009***	−0.006***
	(6.062)	(8.244)	(−5.880)
(-"-)*(poor HH)		−0.006***	
		(−4.642)	
(-"-)*(years of schooling)			0.002***
			(12.496)
R²	0.0443	0.0449	0.0497
F	827	427	568
p-value of F	0.000	0.000	0.000
N	156,936	156,936	156,936

Source: Reproduced from De Weerdt, Christiaensen, and Kanbur (2019).

Note: Linear Probability Model estimates of equation (14.12) with standard errors clustered by the fifty-one origin enumeration areas. Regression coefficients with t-statistics in parentheses. *** statistically significant at the 1 percent level; ** statistically significant at the 5 percent level; * statistically significant at the 10 percent level. The dyads are formed by linking all 2,012 KHDS migrants to all possible seventy-eight destinations. Destination wealth is the average household wealth index at destination calculated from the census. The wealth index is the first principal component using the following variables: the number of bedrooms per person; whether the dwelling has an iron sheet roof (or better), walls from baked bricks (or better), a tile or cement floor, electric lighting, piped water, and a flush toilet; and whether the person owns a radio, a phone, and an iron. Distance is the natural logarithm of distance in kilometers between the baseline location and the potential destination, as the crow flies.

UNPACKING DISTANCE THROUGH QUALITATIVE INVESTIGATION

A selection of KHDS respondents were further approached to talk about their migration experience in their own words (Ingelaere et al. 2018). This life-history method provides a rich, contextual complement to the more conventional economic approaches presented earlier and enables us to probe into migrants' motivation in choosing their destination. Specifically, seventy-five migrants were interviewed from six selected KHDS villages. They were pairwise similar in their socioeconomic characteristics in the early 1990s, but they displayed quite different migration patterns.

The core insights from this qualitative investigation as to why more people may end up in towns than in cities are well illustrated through the account of R.[24] Born in 1978 in village F, R left the village in 1997 and returned in 2014. In that period, he changed residence eight times and engaged in seven different activities to make a living.

When he was nineteen years old, he moved to the small town of Bukoba. Here is how he describes his motives for moving: "What made me move from [my village] to Bukoba was the economic situation. Because at that time I had completed school. Also, once a car like this passed by me, I wondered the speed it moved. Following this I desired going to driving school. That was the reason: to move to Bukoba town and learn how to drive. Having arrived in Bukoba town, I did some work and got money, went to [. . .] the driving School. So, I liked driving very much."

While living in his village and, later, Bukoba, R was exposed to images from and stories about Tanzania's capital: "People say Arusha is a city, but Dar is something else. There used to be video shows in our village and all the famous football players, like Runyamila, seemed to live in Dar. We were childish at the time and we thought that if we went to Dar we'd see all these people." At the time, however, a lack of resources did not allow him to make the trip: "I would have gone to Dar es Salaam but when you know you have nobody in Dar es Salaam, someone to host you, [you can't undertake the trip]. But also [having] the fare sometimes is not enough, because going to a place like Dar es Salaam, you have to plan in advance to get there."

So, R's trajectory continued and included a return to the village as well as time spent in Mwanza (Tanzania's second-largest city), in small urban centers in the Kagera region, and in makeshift camps on Lake Victoria's Islands. But he did not give up his plan to live in Dar, and he eventually traveled to Dar despite having no connections: "Yes, as I told you that there must be a person to host or welcome you. You might get imprisoned and this person becomes your referee or else you must be having money. The good thing is God helped me; the time I was moving to Dar es Salaam I had money so for whatever case maybe I would hire a taxi and would rent a room, put a mattress."

Although he did not have a host in the capital, he did have some money, was more skilled, and knew better how to navigate urban environments. Between 2006 and 2014, while residing in Dar, he worked as a construction foreman, a laborer sorting scrap metal, a waiter, and a security guard.

So, what are the insights gained from R's story and the stories of the seventy-five respondents? First, two key features emerge to understand migration: a person's action space and cumulative causation. Action space defines the range of possible destinations a migrant can realistically move to and is determined by a complex of factors, such as aspirations, resources, and social norms. But migration is not a one-shot event, and a migrant's action space continuously evolves, expands, or contracts, through cumulative causation.

Second, urban centers are seen as having more "circulation" (*mzunguko wa pesa*), that is, the circulation of money, goods, people, and ideas. This makes them particularly attractive. With circulation also comes an anonymity that is valued, but the closeness of the village links, and the security this brings, in case things go wrong, are set against this. And city life is fully cash driven. The small town then emerges as the more accessible alternative, in between the village and the big city. It offers circulation and thus opportunities, and some degree of anonymity, while the distance to the village remains surmountable, which is important, in case things go awry. Although the capital city Dar is the preferred destination, the nearest small town is more accessible, especially for first-time migrants.

Third, the first move is different, in that it is mostly about getting away from the village and about breaking the cycle, and it is not so much about maximizing one's income. Having money to pay for the fare and a helpful connection in the destination are key to a move. This is more likely the case for secondary towns than in cities. But the migration process doesn't stop there. As time moves on and migrants settle in their occupations and advance in their life cycle, the window of opportunity for migration closes. Family obligations grow and aspirations subside.

Ingelaere et al. (2018) conclude that this complex of factors, all linked to proximity, explains why many rural migrants end up in secondary towns; they are much easier to access and navigate and thus that is where rural migrants often move and stay.

CONCLUSION

The tidal wave of urbanization that is underway in developing countries, and particularly in Africa, needs policy responses. As shown in this chapter, viewing urbanization as an aggregate is empirically inaccurate. The composition of urbanization also matters. In particular, the small town versus big city distinction should be made clearly and consistently. But it is not just a matter of empirical inaccuracy. The natural policy inclination is to equate urbanization with big city growth. Together with the natural metropolitan bias among national elites, this leads to disproportionate public investment in the capital city and other large urban agglomerations. This neglects small towns, however, where much of the urbanization is increasingly taking place and which contribute significantly to poverty reduction.

We report a line of research and policy analysis focused on Tanzania, which highlights the role of secondary towns in migration and in poverty reduction. Using the national panel data as well as the KHDS panel, we find that migration to secondary towns contributes more in aggregate to poverty reduction than migration to big cities, even though the typical move from a rural area to a town reduces poverty by less than the typical move from a rural area to a city. This is because there are many more people moving from rural areas to towns than to the city. But why does this happen, if the typical move to a city is so beneficial?

We answer this question by introducing distance and migration costs, not only in the physical sense (transport) but also in the sense of information, uncertainty, and contacts in a broader setting. We adapt the standard H-T framework to incorporate these costs and show that, in equilibrium, we can indeed have more migration to small towns.

Empirical simulation with the KHDS data illustrates how the higher migration costs of moving to a city than to a town can solve the observed migration equilibriums, given the going wage rates across the different locations and sectors. We further show econometrically the importance of physical distance in explaining migration choice, it being understood that physical distance could stand as a proxy for all kinds of economic and social distance. Finally, qualitative analysis of the experience of a selection of migrants in the KHDS panel corroborates the role played by small towns in expanding migrants' action space and as a crucial node in the cumulative causation that underlies many migration trajectories.

We hope that these insights from Tanzania will lead to further research on small towns and their role in migration and poverty reduction, and that this role will increasingly be factored into policy analysis and decision making.

NOTES

1. Exceptions include J. Vernon Henderson, "The Urbanization Process and Economic Growth: The So-What Question," *Journal of Economic Growth* 8, no. 1 (2003): 47–71; Ravi Kanbur and Anthony J. Venables, "Spatial Disparities and Economic Development," in *Global Inequality*, ed. D. Held and A. Kaya (with A. J. Venables), 204–215 (Cambridge: Polity Press, 2007); and Luc Christiaensen and Ravi Kanbur, "Secondary Towns and Poverty Reduction: Refocusing the Urbanization Agenda," *Annual Review of Resource Economics* 9 (2017): 405–419.

2. Of course, what exactly is a small town depends on the country context.

3. The theoretical and empirical literature on this is still in its infancy. For an overview of the incipient findings, see Christiaensen and Kanbur, "Secondary Towns and Poverty Reduction."

4. The different papers the chapter draws on are referenced throughout the chapter.

5. For an elaboration on the technical basis for these decompositions, see Luc Christiaensen, Joachim De Weerdt, and Ravi Kanbur, "Decomposing the Contribution of Migration to Poverty Reduction: Methodology and Application to Tanzania," *Applied Economics Letters* 26, no. 12 (2019): 978–982.

6. Among those who stay in rural areas, they further split off people who go to a rural area in another region.

7. In their decomposition, urban centers with more than five hundred thousand inhabitants are classified as cities. They include Dar es Salaam and Mwanza (the capital of the Mwanza region), with an estimated population of 4.36 million and 0.7 people, respectively, as of 2012.

8. Consumption and income will be used interchangeably.

9. As in the national panel, Dar es Salaam and Mwanza are the only two cities considered. Tightening the definition to count only Dar as a city or broadening it to include all cities administratively defined as cities, does not change the conclusions.

10. For a recent paper that incorporates many of these advances, see Arnab Basu, Nancy Chau, Gary Fields, and Ravi Kanbur, "Job Creation in a Multi-Sector Labor Market Model for Developing Economies," *Oxford Economic Papers* 71, no. 1 (2019): 119–144.

11. This section draws on the analysis presented in Ravi Kanbur, Luc Christiaensen, and Joachim De Weerdt, "Where to Create Jobs to Reduce Poverty: Cities or Towns?" *Journal of Economic Inequality* Forthcoming.

12. By holding the number of formal or high paying jobs (E_c, E_s) fixed in each location, and thus independent of city size (N_c, N_s), we abstract from the potential of agglomeration economies. Although the evidence for the developed world clearly indicates that larger urban centers (by population size) also enjoy faster economic growth, such a relationship has not been empirically established for urban centers in the developing world; see Gilles Duranton, "Growing Through Cities in Developing Countries," *World Bank Research Observer* 30 (2015): 40–73. It may even be negative; see Susanne Frick and Andrés Rodriguez-Pose "Average City Size and Economic Growth," *Cambridge Journal of Regions, Economy and Society* 9, no. 2 (2016): 301–318.

13. Contrary to expectations, after about two decades, the degree of formal employment among city migrants is not that much higher than among town migrants.

14. E_s, the total number of migrants formally employed in towns equals 105 (= 0.189 * 557); E_c, the total number of migrants formally employed in cities equals 70 (= 0.222 * 315), or $E_s/E_c = 105/70 = 1.5$.

15. Given the difficulties in obtaining reliable income data in African settings, consumption per capita, spatially deflated and expressed in 2010 Tanzanian shilling

(TSH), is taken as proxy for income. For a detailed description of the data and the consumption variable construction, see Joachim De Weerdt et al., "Kagera Health and Development Survey 2010: Basic Information Document" (Rockwool Foundation Working Paper Series No. 46, Rockwool Group, Hedehusene, Denmark, 2012).

16. A similar gradient is observed when taking average incomes, which are more sensitive to outliers: $w_r = 495 < w_{os} = 765 < w_{oc} = 1,063 < w_s = 1,325 < w_c = 1,605$.

17. $\dfrac{w_s - w_{os}}{w_c - w_{oc}} = \dfrac{1088 - 613}{1475 - 871} = \dfrac{475}{604} = 0.79$

18. Rearranging equation (14.11), we have $\dfrac{w_r - w_{oc} + t_c}{w_r - w_{os} + t_s} = \dfrac{\frac{N_s}{N_c}}{\frac{E_s}{E_c} \cdot \frac{w_s - w_{os}}{w_c - w_{oc}}} =$

$\dfrac{1.77}{1.5 \times 0.79} = 1.5$. Further note that for an interior solution (i.e. $N_r > 0$, $N_i > 0$), $w_r + t_c > w_{oc}$ and $w_r + t_s > w_{os}$.

19. Similar city–town migration costs ratios are found for higher values of the city migration cost.

20. The importance of distance in understanding migration patterns has been highlighted earlier, but it has disappeared to the background lately, in favor of a focus on issues of selection; see Larry A. Sjaastadt, "The Costs and Returns to Human Migration," *Journal of Political Economy* 70, no. 5 (1962): 80–93. 1962; and Aba Schwartz, "Interpreting the Effect of Distance on Migration," *Journal of Political Economy* 81, no. 5 (1973): 1153–1169.

21. For further details, see Joachim De Weerdt, Luc Christiaensen, and Ravi Kanbur, "When Distance Drives Destination, Towns Can Stimulate Development" (mimeographed, 2019) from which the analysis here is taken.

22. We analyze only those respondents who have migrated to avoid confounding the destination choice with the migration choice.

23. Further details on how the census is used to measure wealth at destination are provided in De Weerdt, Christiaensen, and Kanbur, "When Distance Drives Destination" and in the note under table 14.3.

24. Anonymized for confidentiality purposes. Interview rural village in Kagera, September 29, 2015.

REFERENCES

Basu, Arnab, Nancy Chau, Gary Fields, and Ravi Kanbur. 2019. "Job Creation in a Multi-Sector Labor Market Model for Developing Economies." *Oxford Economic Papers* 71 (1): 119–144.

Berdegué, Julio, and Isidro Soloaga. 2018. "Small and Medium Cities and Development of Mexican Rural Areas." *World Development* 107: 277–288.

Beegle, Kathleen, Luc Christiaensen, Andrew Dabalen, and Isis Gaddis, 2016. *Poverty in a Rising Africa.* Washington, DC: World Bank Group.

Bryan, Gharad, Shyamal, Chowdhury, and Ahmed Mushfiq, Mobarak, 2014. "Underinvestment in a Profitable Technology: The Case of Seasonal Migration in Bangladesh." *Econometrica*, 82–5: 1671–1748.

Cali, Massimiliano, 2013. "Does Urbanization Affect Rural Poverty? Evidence from Indian Districts." *World Bank Economic Review*, 27–2: 171–201.

Christiaensen, Luc, and Ravi Kanbur. 2017. "Secondary Towns and Poverty Reduction: Refocusing the Urbanization Agenda." *Annual Review of Resource Economics* 9: 405–419.

——. 2019. "Decomposing the Contribution of Migration to Poverty Reduction: Methodology and Application to Tanzania." *Applied Economics Letters* 26 (12): 978–982.

Christiaensen, Luc, Jonathan Kaminski, Armand Sim, and Yue Wang. 2017. "Poverty, Employment and Migration Patterns in Tanzania 2008–2012—The Role of Secondary Towns." Mimeographed.

De Weerdt, Joachim, Luc Christiaensen, and Ravi Kanbur. 2019. "When Distance Drives Destination, Towns Can Stimulate Development." Mimeographed.

De Weerdt, Joachim, Kathleen Beegle, Helene Bie Lilleør, Stefan Dercon, Kalle Hirvonen, Martina Kirchberger, and Sofya Krutikova. 2012. "Kagera Health and Development Survey 2010: Basic Information Document." Rockwool Foundation Working Paper Series No. 46. Rockwool Group, Hedehusene, Denmark.

Diamond, Rebecca. 2016. "The Determinants and Welfare Implications of US Workers' Diverging Location Choices by Skill: 1980–2000." *American Economic Review* 106–3: 479–524.

Dorosh, P., and J. Thurlow 2013. "Agriculture and small towns in Africa." *Agricultural Economics*. 44:449–59.

Duranton, Gilles. 2015. "Growing Through Cities in Developing Countries." *World Bank Research Observer* 30: 40–73.

Fafchamps, Marcel, and Forhad Shilpi. 2013. "Determinants of the Choice of Migration Destination." *Oxford Bulletin of Economics and Statistics* 75–3: 388–409.

Ferré, Céline, Francisco H. G. Ferreira, and Peter Lanjouw. 2012. "Is There a Metropolitan Bias? The Relationship Between Poverty and City Size in a Selection of Developing Countries." *World Bank Economic Review* 26 (3): 351–382.

Food and Agriculture Organization. 2017. "*State of Food and Agriculture 2017—Leveraging Food Systems for Inclusive Rural Transformation.*" Rome: Food and Agriculture Organization.

Frick, Susanne A., and Andrés Rodríguez-Pose. 2016. "Average City Size and Economic Growth." *Cambridge Journal of Regions, Economy and Society* 9 (2): 301–318.

Gibson, John, Gaurav Datt, Rinku Murgai, and Martin Ravallion. 2017. "For India's Rural Poor, Growing Towns Matter More than Growing Cities." *World Development* 98: 413–429.

Harris, John, and Michael Todaro. 1970. "Migration, Unemployment, and Development: A Two Sector Analysis," *American Economic Review* 40: 126–142.

Henderson, J. Vernon. 2003. "The Urbanization Process and Economic Growth: The So-What Question." *Journal of Economic Growth* 8 (1): 47–71.

Hicks, Joan, Marieke Kleemans, Nicholas Li, and Edward Miguel. 2017. "Re-evaluating Agricultural Productivity Gaps with Longitudinal Microdata." NBER Working Paper 23253. National Bureau of Economic Research, Cambridge, MA.

Hirvonen, Kalle, and Helene Bie Lilleor. 2015. "Going Back Home: Internal Return Migration in Rural Tanzania." *World Development* 70: 186–202.

Ingelaere, Bert, Luc Christiaensen, Joachim De Weerdt and Ravi Kanbur. 2018. "Why Secondary Towns Can Be Important for Poverty Reduction—A Migrant Perspective." *World Development* 105: 273–282.

Jedwab, Remi, Luc Christiaensen, and Marina Gindelsky. 2017. "Demography, Urbanization and Development: Rural Push, Urban Pull and . . . Urban Push?" *Journal of Urban Economics* 98: 6–16.

Kanbur, Ravi, and Anthony J. Venables. 2007. "Spatial Disparities and Economic Development." In *Global Inequality*, ed. D. Held and A. Kaya (with A. J. Venables), 204–215. Cambridge: Polity Press.

Kanbur, Ravi, Luc Christiaensen, and Joachim De Weerdt. Forthcoming. "Where to Create Jobs to Reduce Poverty: Cities or Towns?" Journal of Economic Inequality.

Overman, H. G., and Anthony J. Venables. 2010. "Evolving City Systems." In *Urbanization and Development: Multidisciplinary Perspectives*, ed. J. Beall, B. Guha-Khasnobis, and R. Kanbur, 103–123. Oxford: Oxford University Press.

Schwartz, Aba. 1973. "Interpreting the Effect of Distance on Migration." *Journal of Political Economy* 81 (5): 1153–1169.

Sjaastad, Larry A. 1962. "The Costs and Returns to Human Migration." *Journal of Political Economy* 70 (5): 80–93.

Todaro, Michael P. 1969. "A Model of Labor Migration and Urban Unemployment in Less Developed Countries." *American Economic Review* 59 (1): 138–148.

United Nations, Department of Economic and Social Affairs, Population Division. 2015. *World Urbanization Prospects: The 2014 Revision*. New York: United Nations.

Wenban-Smith, H. B. 2015. "Population Growth, Internal Migration and Urbanisation in TANZANIA, 1967–2012. Phase 2, Final Report." Working Paper C-40211-TZA-1. International Growth Centre, London.

Young, Alwyn. 2013. "Inequality, the Urban-Rural Gap and Migration." *Quarterly Journal of Economics* 128 (4): 1727–1785.

CHAPTER 15

Distributing Benefits from Africa's Urban Growth

Gabriella Y. Carolini

The urbanization–industrialization nexus has gained attention as a critical mechanism for strengthening economic growth strategies in African countries. The recent focus on urbanization and industrialization policies at the national level is welcome, as countries have suffered from the absence of substantial and informed national interventions on both fronts. Infrastructure development is recognized as a required input for both meeting the basic needs of a growing urban population and for facilitating industrial development.[1] Although infrastructure systems (e.g., in water and sanitation, transport, energy, and telecommunications) are inherent in the quality of life in cities, experiences around the world show how infrastructure development is no guarantee of prosperity. Indeed, urban infrastructure development implemented *without* an understanding of who benefits and who pays often leads to excessive debt, displacement, and growing inequities (Robinson 2003; de Wet 2006; Chakrabarti and Dhar 2009; Flyvbjerg 2014; Hannan and Sutherland 2015; Carolini 2017). The essential challenge for African cities then is not simply to develop infrastructure for its urban population growth and economic development but also to ensure that policies targeting urban infrastructure development equitably consider and address the impacts of policies and projects on the quality of life and standards of living of all urban residents.

Greater emphasis, however, must be placed on understanding what "all" urban residents actually refers to in practice. The critical mass— and unmet basic needs—of the urban poor (or slum dwellers[2]) cannot be overstated in the urban African context. Figure 15.1 shows that close to 60 percent of urban dwellers (i.e., the majority of urban residents) in Sub-Saharan Africa live in slums. This number has steadily grown over the past three decades (see figure 15.2). Indeed, as global population growth

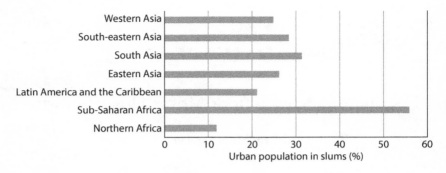

Figure 15.1   Percent of urban population living in slums

Source: Adapted from data in United Nations Human Settlement Programme's Global Urban Indicators Database (2015).

is expected to be greatest in African (and Asian) small and midsize cities, if no action is taken, the slum population in African cities is expected to continue on this growth trajectory (United Nations 2015b).

Given this context, I argue that urban infrastructure investments made in the name of modernization alone, without attention to the basic needs of the majority of the urban population (i.e., the income poor), risk delimiting the real potential for quality economic growth in African cities. The following sections present experiences with municipal finance, infrastructure development, and urban planning in Africa. Borrowing

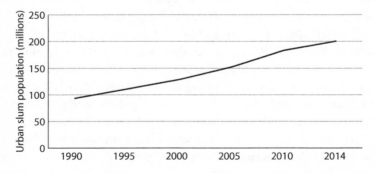

Figure 15.2   Urban slum population at midyear in Sub-Saharan Africa, 1990–2014

Source: Adapted from data in United Nations Human Settlement Programme's Global Urban Indicators Database (2015).

heavily from the Mozambican capital's case, they advance the potential for their reform.

MUNICIPAL OWN-SOURCE REVENUES:
A POLITICALLY CONTESTED BUT REQUISITE REFORM

How urban development, and in particular infrastructure projects, is financed matters for who carries its risks and benefits. Intergovernmental transfers are an important source of revenue for municipalities worldwide, but own-resource revenues also play a key role in financing municipal services. The economic literature gives conflicting theories about whether the local property tax—widely recognized as the most important of own-source revenue at the subnational level—is progressive or regressive (Sepulveda and Martinez-Vazquez 2012; Oates and Fischel 2016). A major shortcoming of such scholarship is that it does not consider the intra-urban scale. For example, Sepulveda and Martinez-Vazquez argue that property tax, as a local government revenue (as opposed to central government revenue), fails the test of the horizontal equity principle because "heterogeneity and different tax bases impose unequal conditions in different jurisdictions" (2012, 180). The capital-tax view, however, allows for the progressive consideration of unequal conditions *within* cities or jurisdictions, given that it largely affects owners of capital throughout an economy. In the context of significant intra-urban heterogeneity in income and wealth—as exists in so many in African cities—this latter view of the property tax as progressive is critical.

Emerging literature on African property tax systems show that the property tax is one of the major untapped revenue sources. Although local government revenues from property taxes on average sit at about 0.42 percent of gross domestic product (GDP) globally, the range between income levels is striking, moving from 0.03 percent of GDP among least developed countries (the majority of which are in Africa) to 0.89 percent of GDP among high-income countries (United Nations Capital Development Fund [UNCDF] and United Nations Department of Economic and Social Affairs [UNDESA] 2016). This difference is even more significant when also considering the GDP differences among country income groups. Fjeldstad and Heggstad (2012) report that revenues from the subnational property tax accounts for less than 0.5 percent of GDP in many African countries, but in many countries, it is much lower than even that. In Mozambique, for example, the property tax (or the *Imposto Predial*

Autárquia, IPRA) is significantly underutilized. In a study of six major cities in the country's central and northern provinces, the IPRA represented only 6.8 percent of total municipal revenues (Boex et al. 2011). In the country's capital, Maputo, the average IPRA collected between 2010 and 2014 represented a slightly higher amount, accounting for approximately 10 percent of local tax revenue (UNCDF and UNDESA 2016).

Updating property valuation and increasing the levels of collected IPRA represent a significant opportunity—and political challenge—for cities like Maputo and others in Sub-Saharan Africa. Maputo's city center is booming with new construction—often luxury buildings including high-rise buildings and new condominium apartments renting for US$6,000 a month (*The Business Year* 2014; Carolini 2017). Yet revenues from the IPRA are underutilized for a few reasons, not least of which is political resistance. First, the updating of cadastral systems in Maputo and other Mozambican cities has been slow (Boex et al. 2011; Weimer 2012; Carolini 2017). The city only issued a declaration legalizing the updating of property values in December of 2010, which also was heavily criticized—despite the fact that the previous update had been several years earlier (*O País* 2011). Maputo's mayor David Simango complained that even with a new digitized registration system launched in 2013, ten thousand of the thirty-six thousand potential IPRA contributors in Maputo had not paid their property tax in 2014 (*O País* 2014).[3]

Second, when the patrimonial or book value of properties is absent, in Mozambique the IPRA is based on self-reported values as a first alternative and on potential market values as a last alternative. This clause allows for individual discretion and creates opportunity for underreporting when formal book values are not recorded. Mozambique's law is not unlike others on the continent in this regard. In fact, Rwanda moved entirely from an area-based property tax valuation system to a system of self-reported market values, generating an extremely low valuation ratio in its capital, Kigali, with significant variation in undervaluations therein (Fjeldstad et al. 2017).

Finally, in Maputo, as in most other cities, legal exceptions from the property tax (IPRA) exist in generous form. Particularly in a city like Maputo—whose city center is dense with both a rich architectural heritage and a recent modernist boom in the built environment—tax exemptions can be devastating for the municipal budget's revenues. Mozambican law indicates that a number of properties are exempt from the IPRA, including buildings used by the government, public utilities, diplomatic missions, museums and educational institutions, buildings constructed using the country's Housing Fund, and buildings of officially recognized nonprofit organizations.[4] Many exempt buildings are concentrated in Maputo's urban core, precisely where real estate market values are also the highest. Equally important for Maputo, newly constructed buildings are exempt from the IPRA for five years (Boex et al. 2011). Like exempt buildings, new construction tends to be concentrated in the high-value city center or coastal neighborhoods; thus, IPRA potential is by the very nature of the law underutilized in the highest-value real estate market in the country. Although exemptions from the property tax are a traditional tool used by city governments around the world to incentivize redevelopment and construction, their use in a context of very low own-source revenues is problematic. In such environments, other mechanisms that recapture the privatization of location-tied benefits, such as a land value capture program or a program for payments in lieu of taxes (or PILOTs),[5] are absent. The result is a significant loss of potential local revenue for the city, and relatedly, the fleecing of an important source to leverage domestic finances for critical infrastructure projects.

To put these figures in perspective, recall that Mozambique emerged from its internal civil war in 1992, and Maputo gained recognition as a financially and politically autonomous city only in 1998. Furthermore, reliable records of the city's budget started later in 2004, after the election of Eneas Comiche as president of the city council (i.e., mayor).[6] As such, delays in updating Maputo's cadastre or property registry system should not be surprising, even more so considering that the status quo favors powerful urban elites who are not paying (or underpay) into the system as of yet. The current property tax system, however, penalizes the urban poor by enabling the perpetuation of untaxed wealth accumulation among the city's higher-income population who own fixed capital assets(i.e., housing) in the city center. In effect, this dilemma facilitates the growth of inequalities in the city between its urban core and rapidly growing periphery neighborhoods, many of which are considered informal or slums where infrastructure delivery is inadequate. Even Maputo's middle-class residents are increasingly being pushed out of the city center by the high-end capture of the city's housing core; instead, they seek affordable shelter in less serviced peripheral or peri-urban neighborhoods (Jenkins 2013). In contrast, the top-end residential real estate market in the city's center is advertised and rented out in U.S. dollars, clearly targeting expatriates working in the private sector, in the international development industry, or in diplomatic missions. Indeed, rental incomes from housing in the city center often provide a significant supplement for homeowners in the city, so much so that an industry of housing brokers emerged to connect well-appointed homes with foreign capital-rich renters.[7]

For these reasons, the rampant evasion or underpayment of property taxes and the slowness of updating the cadastre propagate the city's fiscal dependence on other sources of revenue for urban development projects—including intergovernmental transfers (which are relatively small) and international development aid (which is large relative to other sources). The turn to international aid to finance urban development projects—particularly for key infrastructure—however delimits what taxation scholars globally argue is a key bargaining tool for making political demands. More specifically, as Prichard shows in detailed studies of Ghana, Kenya, and Ethiopia, different but important causal pathways connect taxation with government responsiveness and accountability (2015). Furthermore, the importance of taxation as a financial tool for development is widely supported at an international level, even if it meets with resistance at the local. In the *Addis Ababa Action Agenda* of the United Nation's Third International Conference on Financing for Development, the international community committed "to enhancing revenue administration through modernized, progressive tax systems, improved tax policy and more efficient tax collection . . . including by broadening the tax base and continuing efforts to integrate the informal sector into the formal economy in line with country circumstances" (United Nations 2015a, sec. 22). In its decentralization guide, the United Nations Human Settlement Programme (UN-HABITAT 2009) also acknowledges that "a significant proportion of the financial resources of local authorities should derive from local taxes, fees and charges to cover the costs of services provided by them." (12–13).

Responding to the wide importance afforded to taxation as a financial tool for development, a portfolio of alternative methods for property tax assessments have emerged, including rental value systems, capital value systems, land value systems, and area-based systems (the last of which is used by cities in Mozambique) (Bahl and Wallace 2010; Boex et al. 2011; Norregaard 2013). Ultimately, even if reforms are secured, and both valuation and collection rates rise, the political will of urban leadership will be required to direct investments toward quality-of-life improvements that serve *all* residents. At the very least, a city like Maputo can reconsider the spatial implications of its generous IPRA exemptions to enable a fairer distribution of IPRA inputs between the city's high-market value core, where many exempt buildings stand, and its more peripheral neighborhoods, where a growing number of poorer urban residents seek shelter.

INFRASTRUCTURE DEVELOPMENT: FOR WHOM AND WHAT?

After the 2012 *Declaration on the Program for Infrastructure Development in Africa*, the African Development Bank launched an independent financial entity called the Africa 50 Infrastructure Fund to complement its normal infrastructure finance portfolio and that of other multilateral development banks and private investment funds. Africa 50 targets medium- and large-scale infrastructure development throughout the continent, focusing on energy and transport, although other sectors like telecommunications, water, and sanitation are considered on a case-by-case basis.[8] The fund estimates that the average yearly infrastructure financing need on the continent sits at roughly US$130 billion through 2025. Many such projects are set for urban environments throughout Sub-Saharan Africa. For example, Maputo's urban landscape is changing with a number of significant infrastructure projects in strategic transportation-related projects, as well as basic infrastructure projects in energy, water, and sanitation (Carolini 2017).

Although these infrastructure investments stand to enhance the city's basic services, attention to the details of implementation reveal the complexities involved when accounting for their financial and social costs and benefits. Flyvbjerg (2014) argues that the overestimation of benefits and the underestimation of costs in large-scale infrastructure projects is endemic and can be disastrous for both urban and national wealth. He presents statistical evidence showing that unaccounted-for complexities in major infrastructure projects reveal significant inadequacies of budget and time contingencies that went into initial project plans. In short, development planners dream big but have little grasp—or admit little knowledge—of the actual costs and time required for the execution of major developments or megaprojects. Flyvbjerg's work uses extensive empirical evidence from high-income contexts, but some scholars are examining how infrastructure development, particularly in cities, can wreak havoc on the local public purse and lead to worsening conditions for vulnerable urban populations in other contexts, including China and Ghana. In Nanjing, Wei (2015) shows that the preponderance of projects in development zones meant to enhance industrial development and economic growth have burdened Chinese cities with heavy debts and facilitated corruption. Within the African context, using empirical evidence from more than fourteen thousand basic social infrastructure projects started primarily by local governments in Ghana, Williams (2017) supports the relevance of Flyvbjerg's findings on the miscalculations inherent in infrastructure planning. Roughly one-third of the projects in his Ghanaian study are never finished, a reflection of failed intertemporal bargaining between politicians. Strikingly, he argues that the money spent on noncompleted projects by local governments alone would be enough to fully construct 667 additional three-room schools serving more than seventy-three thousand children in Ghana *every year* (Williams 2017).

Although the underestimation of costs, the heavy burden of debts, and the overestimation of economic benefits provide enough cause for careful consideration of how to better direct infrastructure development to enhance urban prosperity, it is also clear that the distribution of benefits and costs, and particularly the physical implications, of infrastructure projects also demand detailed social accountability. For example, in Maputo, the development of a long awaited Maputo-KaTembe Bridge, which will be the longest suspension bridge in Africa, is displacing and undercompensating affected households (Carolini 2017). The majority of these families are characterized as the urban poor, with both homes *and* livelihoods standing within the planned development sites on either side of the bridge. The bridge is also to be accompanied by a complete redevelopment of the KaTembe District, a rural part of the capital city that is set to witness the development of major tourism facilities, including a golf course, according to developers involved (Carolini 2017). Such plans have been dubbed "fantasy plans" among some leading urban African scholars; they reflect an urban vision that too often ignores the significant urban inequalities such infrastructure and development plans reproduce at best and aggravate at worse (Watson 2014; Cain 2014; Obeng-Odoom 2015; Turok 2012, 2016; Grant 2015). In short, for urban infrastructure development to support African industrialization, broad-based and local support and a wide distribution of project benefits must be part of the plan. This means, for example, that rather than considering displacement an unfortunate but necessary and unavoidable outcome of major urban infrastructure development, public policy makers can do more to enhance alternative planning, augment contingency budgets that include fair compensation for displaced households, and actively seek out and incorporate input from affected households in *initial* phases of infrastructure planning. Such steps could guard against shortchanging the urban poor whose very existence and survival in globalizing African cities is testament to the creative resilience and industriousness they bring to (often informal but important) urban economies. In short, infrastructure development that benefits the wide urban populace calls for good urban planning.

URBAN PLANNING: BUILDING A BETTER
CAPACITY TO SERVE THE POOR

The *New Urban Agenda* emerging from UN-HABITAT's third major orienting conference in 2016 recognizes that "urban form, infrastructure and building design are among the greatest drivers of cost and resource efficiencies, through the benefits of economy of scale and agglomeration and by fostering energy efficiency, renewable energy, resilience, productivity, environmental protection and sustainable growth in the urban economy" (United Nations 2016, 44). In other words, urban planning is cost-efficient development. This is especially the case when significant urban population growth is expected—as it is in Africa's cities. One of the major messages of the UN Millennium Project Task Force on Slums is that planning for the needs of the growing low-income population *in advance* is much cheaper than remedial interventions to upgrade informal settlements (UN Millennium Project 2005). The Task Force estimates that the average cost of providing alternatives to slum formation for Sub-Saharan Africa is US$352 per person, while the cost for upgrading slums is US$528 per person (UN Millennium Project 2005, p.141).[9] Planning for alternative urban futures that adequately incorporate anticipated population growth, particularly of low-income households, requires first that city decision makers are central conductors of urban development (as opposed to national and international actors alone); and, second, that urban-planning capacities to serve the urban poor are enhanced. To this end, a few current efforts to build out professional planning education in Africa are noteworthy and promising.

At a small gathering in Dar es Salaam in 1999, three African urban planning scholars began a professional network of planning programs across universities on the continent (Watson and Odendaal 2012). Today that network, the Association of African Planning Schools (AAPS), includes fifty-five different urban planning programs across Africa and hosts conferences and meetings to discuss current research and exchange ideas on curriculum building for a profession that is still rather small compared with the actual needs for (good) urban planning on the continent.

AAPS's efforts are an important step toward fostering the development of professional urban planners who are well informed and trained about different realities of urban life and planning processes within contemporary African cities. Rather than resting within colonial paradigms of planning, which remain major influences on urban development in so many cities on the continent, member schools in the AAPS are directly contributing to the reform of both planning education and practice by engaging directly with urban residents and local governments in African cities (Watson 2009; Odendaal 2013). Critically, for example, planning curricula in AAPS schools now incorporate training on slum upgrading, given the magnitude of urban populations living in slum conditions on the continent. This turn toward upgrading recognizes the failure of slum-clearance experiences on the continent. The infamous 2005 slum-clearance order in Harare, Operation *Murambatsvina* (or "Drive Out the Rubbish"), for example, is a legacy of old planning laws inherited from the colonial era (Kamete 2009). Such laws have failed to eliminate urban poverty and instead have been commonly used to rationalize uncompensated or forced evictions of thousands of urban households (Watson 2009; Watson and Agbola 2013). New curricula developed within AAPS now recognize the importance of working with—not against—residents in slum neighborhoods to both enumerate households and coproduce plans that envision their upgrading (Watson and Agbola 2013).

Relatedly, at the University of Eduardo Mondlane (UEM) in Maputo, an entirely new master's degree program on planning in informal settlements is now offered by the Faculty of Architecture and Physical Planning (FAPP).[10] The master's degree program's origin is in a capacity-training program started in 2013, supported by the municipal government of Maputo and the World Bank as part of a wider partnership between the two on municipal reforms called *ProMaputo*. That partnership included initiatives centered on institutional development and governance, municipal finance, and service and infrastructure planning and delivery improvement. Capacity training for municipal employees on upgrading informal settlements was envisioned as a mechanism to implement these initiatives in the city. As such, the city government and the World Bank approached the FAPP at UEM to host the training program. UEM expanded the original idea for a capacity-training program by creating a dedicated planning degree in informal settlements upgrading. The two-year program targets municipal professionals through evening classes, online programming, and field research in informal settlements throughout Maputo. The first cohort included thirty-seven students, largely professionals already working in Maputo's city government as well as professionals from the private sector and students from Brazil and Spain. UEM's effort demonstrates the importance of a reformed curriculum that recognizes that informal settlement residents have rights and make important contributions to urban economies. In other words, African planning programs are transforming into realities the high-level international consensus (as articulated in both the Millennium Development Goals and Sustainable Development Goals) on the need to both upgrade slums and create alternatives to new slum formations.

CONCLUSION

This chapter highlights the importance of incorporating the basic needs of the urban poor via three urban development tools that can be reformed to better distribute benefits from Africa's urbanization and economic growth. The wide consensus among scholars of urban planning, urban economics, urban sociology, and urban politics is that development interventions must be broad-based initiatives that explicitly seek out the voice and needs of the urban poor. Too often, however, policies and projects launched in the name of development are disconnected from the realities of implementation in cities that are home to a majority population of the urban poor. Indeed, when more than half of a city's residents are in neighborhoods unrecognized or formally ignored by governments (i.e., informal settlements), then the term "informality" loses its significance. Informality in that context is the norm, not the aberration. Fighting informality with forced evictions, clearance programs, or more subtle means of dispossession in African cities will not foster urban prosperity—quite the contrary, as has been shown repeatedly across the globe. Urban prosperity is instead the product of integrated efforts to enhance the quality of life for *all* urban residents—whether in informal or posh neighborhoods. This means both helping to upgrade the substandard conditions in which many urban residents currently live as well as creating opportunities—through effective urban planning, infrastructure development, and municipal financial reform—for future urban residents (many of whom will be poor) to live and work in dignified conditions. This chapter draws attention to some of the measures African cities and supporting institutions can take or support toward this end, from reconsidering generous tax exemption policies to supporting the capacity development of urban municipal professionals to address the challenges—and opportunities—of working with residents in informal settlements to implement improvements.

NOTES

1. See, for example, the latest Economic Report for Africa from the United Nations Economic Commission for Africa 2017, entitled "Urbanization and Industrialization for Africa's Transformation."

2. The United Nations recognizes slum dwellers as residents living in substandard conditions in regard to housing quality, density, security of tenure, and access to adequate potable water and sanitation; UN Millennium Project, *A Home in the City*, ed. E. Sclar, P. Garau, and G. Y. Carolini (London: Earthscan, 2005).

3. In Mozambique, the national government maintains the property registry system under the authority of the National Tax Authority; see Boex et al., *An Analysis of Municipal Revenue Potential in Mozambique* (Washington, DC, 2011).

4. See Protal do Governo de Moçambique, Descrição Geral, accessed March 31, 2019, http://www.portaldogoverno.gov.mz/por/Empresas/Impostos-e-Taxas/Imposto-Predial-Autarquico-IPRA/Descricao-Geral.

5. Land-value capture has been a significant source of municipal income across Latin America, particularly in Brazil. PILOTs are popular in the United States, allowing cities like Boston to regain much of the tax-income they otherwise lose by law because of the abundance of tax-exempt organizations that own buildings in the city.

6. Interview with municipal official (anonymous) July 6, 2009. Before Comiche's tenure, Maputo's first elected mayor was Artur Hussene Canana, who also had been the appointed mayor before elections were allowed.

7. See, for example, the online brokerage site Aparthotel Mozambique (accessed March 31, 2019, http://www.aparthotelmozambique.com/property-owners/quem-somos/), whose rental listings are in English and quoted in U.S. dollars, whereas its residential supply registration page remains in Portuguese, the official language of Mozambique.

8. See Africa 50, accessed January 28, 2017, https://www.africa50.com/focus-areas/.

9. The UN Millennium Project Task Force's estimates for slum upgrading costs per person in Africa included Sub-Saharan Africa and Egypt.

10. Information about the master's degree program and its origins are from discussions with Professor João Tique, a senior faculty member at FAPP in 2014 and 2015 deeply involved in the program's launch.

REFERENCES

Bahl, Roy, and Sally Wallace. 2010. "A New Paradigm for Property Taxation in Developing Countries." *Challenging the Conventional Wisdom on the Property Tax*, ed. R. Bahl, J. Martinez-Vazquez, and J. Youngman,. Cambridge, MA: Lincoln Institute of Land Policy.

Boex, Jamie; Chimunuane, Ozias; Hassam, Minoz; Hindkjaer, Sven; Raich, Uri, and Bernhard Weimer. 2011. *Um Análise do Potencial da Receita Municipal em Moçambique*. [An Analysis of the Municipal Revenue Potential in Mozambique]. Report Prepared for the Mozambican Ministry for the Coordination of Environmental Action in cooperation with the World Bank: Washington, DC.

Cain, Allan. 2014. "African Urban Fantasies." *Environment and Urbanization* 26 (1): 1–7.

Carolini, Gabriella .Y. 2017. "Sisyphean Dilemmas of Development: Contrasting Urban Infrastructure and Fiscal Policy Trends in Maputo, Mozambique." *International Journal of Urban and Regional Research* 41 (1): 126–144.

Chakrabarti, Anjan, and Anup Kumar Dhar. 2009. *Dislocation and Resettlement in Development: From Third World to the World of the Third.* New York: Routledge.

de Wet, Chris. 2006. *Development-Induced Displacement: Problems, Policies and People.* New York: Berghahn Books.

Fjeldstad, Odd-Helge, and Kari Heggstad. 2012. "Local Government Revenue Mobilisation in Anglophone Africa." ICTD Working Paper 7. Chr. Michelsen Institute (6): 1–34.

Fjeldstad, Odd-Helge; Ali, Merima, and Tom Goodfellow. 2017. "Taxing the urban boom: property taxation in Africa." Chr. Michelsen Institute (CMI) Insight Working Paper, Number 1. March 2017. Bergen, Norway: CMI.

Flyvbjerg, Bent. 2014. "What You Should Know About Megaprojects and Why: An Overview." *Project Management Journal* 45 (2): 6–19.

Grant, Richard. 2015. "Sustainable African Urban Futures: Stocktaking and Critical Reflection on Proposed Urban Projects." *American Behavioral Scientist* 59 (3): 294–310.

Hannan, Sylvia, and Catherine Sutherland. 2015. "Mega-Projects and Sustainability in Durban, South Africa: Convergent or Divergent Agendas? *Habitat International* 45 (P3): 205–212.

Jenkins, Paul. 2013. *Urbanization, Urbanism, and Urbanity in an African City: Home Spaces and House Cultures.* New York: Palgrave Macmillan.

Kamete, Amin Y. 2009. "In the Service of Tyranny: Debating the Role of Planning in Zimbabwe's Urban 'Clean-up' Operation." *Urban Studies* 46 (4): 897–922.

Norregaard, John. 2013. "Taxing Immovable Property Revenue Potential and Implementation Challenges." IMF Working Papers No. 13/129. International Monetary Fund, Washington, DC.

O País. 2014. Mais de metade dos munícipes não pagam impostos. [More than half of municipal residents do not pay taxes] *O País.* August 28, 2014.

O País. 2011. Novo valor do Imposto Predial Autárquico é irregular. [New value of the Municipal Property Tax is Irregular] *O País* February 17, 2011.

Oates, Wallace E., and William A. Fischel. 2016. "Are Local Property Taxes Regressive, Progressive, or What?" *National Tax Journal* 69 (2): 415–434.

Obeng-Odoom, Franklin. 2015. "Africa: On the Rise, but to Where?" *Forum for Social Economics* 44 (3): 234–250.

Odendaal, Nancy. 2013. "Increasing the Relevance of Urban Planning Education in African." Cities. *International Journal of E-Planning Research* 2 (3): 30–37.

Prichard, Wilson, 2015. *Taxation, Responsiveness, and Accountability in Sub-Saharan Africa: The Dynamics of Tax Bargaining.* Cambridge: Cambridge University Press.

Robinson, Courtland. 2003. "Risks and Rights: The Causes, Consequences, and Challenges of Development-Induced Displacement." Occasional Paper. Brookings Institution, Washington, DC.

Sepulveda, Cristian, and Jorge Martinez-Vazquez, J., 2012. "Explaining Property Tax Collections in Developing Countries: The Case of Latin America." In *Decentral-*

ization and Reform in Latin America: Improving Intergovernmental Relations, ed. G. Brosio and J. P. Jimenez. Chetelham: Edward Elgar.

The Business Year. 2014. "Construction Review—Maputo on the Rise." *The Business Year*. Accessed March 31, 2019, https://www.thebusinessyear.com /mozambique-2014/maputo-on-the-rise/review.

Turok, Ivan. 2012. "Securing the Resurgence of African Cities." *Local Economy* 28 (2): 142–157.

———. 2016. "Getting Urbanization to Work in Africa: The Role of the Urban Land-Infrastructure-Finance Nexus." *Area Development and Policy* 1 (1): 30–47.

United Nations. 2015a. *Addis Ababa Action Agenda of the Third International Conference on Financing for Development*. New York: United Nations.

———. 2015b. *World Urbanization Prospects—The 2014 Revision*. New York: United Nations.

———. 2016. *New Urban Agenda*. New York: United Nations.

United Nations Capital Development Fund and United Nations Department of Economic and Social Affairs. 2016. *Strengthening Subnational Finance in LDCs*. New York: United Nations.

United Nations Human Settlement Programme. 2009. *International Guidelines on Decentralisation and Access to Basic Services for All*. New York: United Nations.

———. 2015. Global Urban Indicators Database. Nairobi: United Nations.

United Nations Millennium Project. 2005. *A Home in the City*, ed. E. Sclar, P. Garau, and G. Y. Carolini. London: Earthscan.

Watson, Vanessa. 2009. " 'The Planned City Sweeps The Poor Away . . .': Urban Planning and 21st Century Urbanisation." *Progress in Planning* 72 (3): 151–193.

———. 2014. "African Urban Fantasies: Dreams or Nightmares?" *Environment and Urbanization* 26 (2): 561–567.

Watson, Vanessa, and Babatunde Agbola. 2013. *Who Will Plan Africa's Cities?* London: Africa Research Institute.

Watson, Vanessa, and Nancy Odendaal. 2012. "Changing Planning Education in Africa: The Role of the Association of African Planning Schools." *Journal of Planning Education and Research* 33 (1): 96–107.

Wei, Yehua D., 2015. "Zone Fever, Project Fever: Development Policy, Economic Transition, and Urban Expansion in China." *Geographical Review* 105 (2): 156–177.

Weimer, Bernhard. 2012. "Municipal Tax Base in Mozambique: High Potential—Low Degree of Utilisation." Discussion Paper. German Development Institute, Bonn.

Williams, Martin J. 2017. "The Political Economy of Unfinished Development Projects: Corruption, Clientelism, or Collective Choice?" *American Political Science Review* 111 (4): 705–723.

Antonio Andreoni is senior lecturer in economics at SOAS University of London, research director of the Anti-Corruption Evidence (SOAS ACE) Research Consortium (Department for International Development, DFID), and visiting associate professor of the South African Research Chair in Industrial Development, University of Johannesburg. Antonio led several research projects, including governing financialization, innovation, and productivity in UK manufacturing (Gatsby Foundation); Dancing with Dragons for the South Africa—Towards Inclusive Economic Development Programme (United Nations University World Institute for Development Economics Research); and Political Economy of Skills Development in Africa (DFID). For more than a decade Antonio advised international organizations and governments, including United Nations Industrial Development Organization; International Labour Organization; United Nations Conference on Trade and Development; United Nations Development Programme; United Nations Department of Economic and Social Affairs; United Nations Economic Commission for Africa; World Bank; Organisation for Economic Co-operation and Development; DFID; Deutsche Gesellschaft für Internationale Zusammenarbeit GmbH; African Development Bank; Japan International Cooperation Agency; Tanzanian Ministry of Industry and Trade; South Africa Department of Trade and Industry; Finnish Ministry of Economy and Employment; UK Government Office for Science; Gatsby Foundation; Overseas Development Institute; and Institute for New Economic Thinking. His research in industrial development and policy has appeared in the *Cambridge Journal of Economics, Cambridge Journal* *of Regions Economy and Society, Energy Policy, Structural Change and Economic Dynamics, Oxford Review of Economic Policy,* and *European Journal of Development Research.* Antonio has conducted extensive fieldwork across Africa, in particular Tanzania and South Africa. He holds a doctorate from the University of Cambridge.

Haroon Bhorat is professor of economics and director of the Development Policy Research Unit at the University of Cape Town, South Africa. Haroon's research interests cover labor economics, poverty, and income distribution. Haroon holds a highly prestigious National Research Chair. He is a nonresident senior fellow at the Brookings Institution, a research fellow at the Institute of Labor Economics, and an honorary research fellow at the Human Sciences Research Council. He sits on the United Nations University World Institute for Development Economics Research and National Research Foundation boards. Haroon consults with international organizations, such as the International Labour Organization, United Nations Development Programme, and World Bank, as well as with ratings agencies and emerging market fund managers. He serves on numerous advisory boards and program committees and was head of research for the UN High-Level Panel on the Post-2015 Development Agenda. Haroon was an economic advisor to previous South African presidents and ministers of finance, formally serving on the Presidential Economic Advisory Panel.

Gabriella Y. Carolini is associate professor of international development and urban planning in the Department of Urban Studies and Planning at Massachusetts Institute of Technology (MIT). Her publications and teaching at MIT interrogate how the governance of the financial architecture behind infrastructure projects, such as those in the water and sanitation sectors, matters to the distributional fairness of benefits and the health of urban communities, particularly within Sub-Saharan Africa and Latin America, but increasingly also in North America. Gabriella's work has been published in numerous journals, including the *International Journal of Urban and Regional Research, Urban Studies, Environment and Planning C,* and the *American Journal of Public Health.*

Ha-Joon Chang is director of the Centre of Development Studies and Reader in the Political Economy of Development in the Faculty of Economics at the University of Cambridge. He has published widely on a range of topics, including theories of state intervention, industrial policy, trade policy, technological progress, globalization, and economic development in historical perspective. He was awarded the 2003 Myrdal Prize by the European Association for Evolutionary Political Economy, and the 2005 Leontief Prize by Tufts University.

Luc Christiaensen is lead agricultural economist in the World Bank's Jobs Group. He has written extensively on poverty, structural transformation, and secondary towns in Africa and East Asia. He led the project "Agriculture in Africa—Telling Myths from Facts" and was a core member of the 2008 World Development Report team on "Agriculture for Development." He was senior research fellow at United Nations University World Institute for Development Economics Research in Helsinki, Finland, during 2009–2010. He is an honorary research fellow at the Maastricht School of Management and the Catholic University of Leuven. He holds a doctorate in agricultural economics from Cornell University.

Christopher Cramer is professor of the political economy of development at SOAS University of London. He is a fellow of the Academy of Social Sciences, vice-chair of the Royal African Society, and a former chair of the Centre of African Studies at the University of London. He is chair of the International Scientific Committee of the African Programme on Rethinking Development Economics. His publications include the prize-winning *Civil War Is Not a Stupid Thing: Accounting for Violence in Developing Countries* (2006); *The Oxford Handbook of the Ethiopian Economy* (coedited, 2019); and *African Economic Development: Evidence, Theory, and Policy* (with Oqubay and Sender, forthcoming).

Joachim De Weerdt is a development economist based in Belgium. He is senior lecturer at the Institute of Development Policy at the University of Antwerp and senior research fellow at the Centre for Institutions and Economic Performance at the Catholic University of Leuven. Joachim has lived and worked as an entrepreneur and researcher in Africa for twelve years. In 2002, he co-founded Economic Development Initiatives (EDI), a research institution based in Tanzania, where he served as research director until 2014. During that time, the company grew from a small two-person start-up to one of Africa's most respected research houses with forty core employees and frequently up to one hundred additional project-based staff, operating across East Africa. In 2018, EDI became part of Mathematica, a large U.S.-based policy research company with more than 1,200 employees. Joachim has dozens of scientific articles to his name and has published in top journals in economics and other disciplines.

Isabel Estevez is a doctoral researcher at the University of Cambridge Centre of Development Studies, where her research focuses on the relationships among production-sector strategies, human development, and sustainability. Her recent publications address the role of trade and investment rules in shaping development and global inequality. Isabel has been an advisor and consultant for the Ecuadorian Ministries of Economic Policy, Planning and Development, and Science and Technology.

Lorenzo Fioramonti is deputy minister of education, university, and research and a member of the Chamber of Deputies in Italy. He is currently on leave as professor of political economy at the University of Pretoria (South Africa), where he founded the Centre for the Study of Governance Innovation and was deputy project leader of the Future Africa initiative. He is also extraordinary professor at the School of Public Leadership of the University of Stellenbosch, senior fellow at the Centre for Social Investment of the University of Heidelberg and at the Hertie School of Governance (Germany), and associate fellow at the United Nations University (UNU). Lorenzo is the first and only Jean Monnet Chair in Africa, and also holds the UNU–United Nations Educational, Scientific and Cultural Organization Chair in Regional Integration, Migration, and Free Movement of People. He is the author of more than sixty scientific articles and ten books. His most recent books are *Wellbeing Economy: Success in a World Without Growth* (2017) and *The World After GDP: Economics, Politics and International Relations in the Post-Growth Era* (2017). He blogs at www.lorenzofioramonti.org and is a public speaker on issues regarding new economic paradigms, rethinking development, and responsible business.

Akio Hosono is the current senior research adviser and former director (2011–2013) of Japan International Cooperation Agency Research Institute (JICA-RI). He served in a variety of posts, such as vice president at Tsukuba University in Tsukuba Science City, Japanese ambassador to El Salvador, professor at the National Graduate Institute for Policy Studies in Tokyo, and professor at the Research Institute of Economics and Business Administration at Kobe University. He became a senior advisor at JICA in 2007. His recent publications include "Industrial Strategies Toward a Learning Society for Quality Growth" in *Efficiency, Finance, and Varieties of Industrial Policy* (Columbia University

Press, 2017); *Chile's Salmon Industry: Policy Challenges in Managing Public Goods* (with Iizuka and Katz, 2016); *Development for Sustainable Agriculture: The Brazilian Cerrado* (with Magno and Hongo, 2016). He holds a doctorate in economics from the University of Tokyo.

Bert Ingelaere is assistant professor at the Institute of Development Policy, University of Antwerp, Belgium. His research focuses on the legacy of mass violence and mobility, primarily in Africa's Great Lakes region. He is the coeditor of *Genocide, Risk, and Resilience* and author of *Inside Rwanda's Gacaca Courts: Seeking Justice After Genocide* (2016). His work was awarded the Auschwitz Foundation Prize and the U.S. African Studies Association's 2017 Bethwell A. Ogot Book Prize.

Ravi Kanbur is T. H. Lee Professor of World Affairs, International Professor of Applied Economics and Management, and professor of economics at Cornell University. Ravi's areas of interest are public economics, development economics, and economic theory. He is tenured in the Charles H. Dyson School of Applied Economics and Management, which is part of both the Cornell SC Johnson College of Business and the College of Agriculture and Life Sciences. He is also tenured in the Department of Economics in the College of Arts and Sciences. Ravi served on the senior staff of the World Bank, including as resident representative in Ghana, chief economist of the African Region, principal adviser to the chief economist, and director of the *World Development Report*. He is chair of the board of the United Nations University World Institute for Development Economics Research, cochair of the Scientific Council of the International Panel on Social Progress, member of the Organisation for Economic Co-operation and Development High-Level Expert Group on the Measurement of Economic Performance, past president of the Human Development and Capabilities Association, and past president of the Society for the Study of Economic Inequality.

Moazam Mahmood is professor in economics at the Lahore School of Economics and visiting professor at the Capital University of Economics and Business in Beijing. He was formerly director of research at the International Labour Organization, responsible for producing its annual flagship reports, "World Employment and Social Outlook" and "Global Employment Trends." He is a macroeconomist, having worked on global and regional economic crises over the past two decades.

Takyiwaa Manuh is professor emerita of African studies at the University of Ghana. She served as director at the Social Development Policy

Division of the United Nations Economic Commission for Africa in Ethiopia and as professor of African Studies at the University of Ghana, where she was also director of the Institute of African Studies between 2002 and 2009. She is a fellow of the Ghana Academy of Arts and Sciences. Her research interests include African development, women's rights and empowerment, contemporary African migrations, and African higher-education systems; she has published widely in these areas. She has practiced as a lawyer and is active in the women's movement in Ghana and Africa, and serves on the boards of several international, continental, and national organizations. Takyiwaa has received numerous awards, including the University of Ghana's Meritorious Service Award for 2007, Ghana's Order of the Volta (Officer Class) in 2008, and an honorary doctorate degree from the University of Sussex, United Kingdom, in 2015. She holds undergraduate and graduate degrees in law from the University of Ghana, Legon, and the University of Dar es Salaam, Tanzania, as well as a doctorate in anthropology from Indiana University, Bloomington.

Andy McKay has been professor of development economics at the University of Sussex since 2006. His research interests include issues of poverty and living standards, labor, and agriculture, especially in Sub-Saharan Africa and Asia. He recently led or co-led two research projects examining female labor issues; previously he was actively involved in the Department for International Development–funded Chronic Poverty Research Centre. He is managing editor of the *Review of Development Economics*.

Akbar Noman is a senior fellow and adjunct professor at Columbia University at the Initiative for Policy Dialogue. He has worked at the World Bank, the International Monetary Fund, and the Universities of Oxford and Sussex, and he also served as an economic adviser for the government of Pakistan. His numerous publications include his jointly edited books *Good Growth and Governance in Africa: Rethinking Development Strategies* (2012); *Industrial Policy and Economic Transformation in Africa* (Columbia University Press, 2015); and *Efficiency, Finance, and Varieties of Industrial Policy* (Columbia University Press, 2017).

Ben Orlove is an anthropologist at the School of International and Public Affairs and at the Earth Institute, Columbia University. He has published extensively on environment, climate, and development, including a number of papers on climate, agriculture, and water in Uganda and Burkina Faso. He is a fellow of the American Association for the

Advancement of Science and a recipient of the Presidential Award from the American Anthropological Association. He is a lead author on two reports of the Intergovernmental Panel on Climate Change. He holds a bachelor's degree from Harvard University and a master's degree and doctorate from the University of California, Berkeley.

Simon Roberts is a professor of economics and the founding executive director of the Centre for Competition, Regulation, and Economic Development at the University of Johannesburg. He has worked extensively on issues of industrial development, trade, regional value chains, competition, and economic regulation in Southern and East Africa, advising governments, competition authorities, and regulators. He has testified as an expert witness in a number of major competition cases. Simon has been closely involved in the development of competition law in South Africa and held the position of chief economist and manager of the Policy and Research Division at the Competition Commission of South Africa from November 2006 to December 2012.

Christopher Rooney is a researcher at the Development Policy Research Unit at the University of Cape Town, South Africa. His areas of interest include labor markets, structural transformation, and behavioral economics. He has worked with organizations such as the Department of Labor, World Bank, United Nations Development Programme, the African Development Bank, and the International Labour Organization. He holds a bachelor's degree of science in economics and a master's degree in applied economics from the University of Cape Town, and is pursuing a degree in data science.

John Sender is emeritus professor of economics at SOAS University of London. Earlier appointments include director of the African Studies Centre, University of Cambridge; adviser to Mandela's Presidential Commissions on Labour and on Rural Credit; and economic consultant to the Offices of the President and the Minister of Public Enterprises, South Africa, and to the Federal Democratic Republic of Ethiopia.

Go Shimada is associate professor at Meiji University, visiting scholar at Columbia University, and visiting scholar at the Japan International Cooperation Agency (JICA) Research Institute. Before these appointments, Go was associate professor at the University of Shizuoka, and worked for JICA for more than two decades as senior research fellow. Go has been director of the Trade and Investment Division at the Department of Industrial Development; special assistant to the president; and first secretary, Permanent Mission of Japan to the United Nations. His recent publications include "Inside the Black Box of Japan's Institution for Industrial Policy—An Institutional Analysis of Development Bank, Private Sector and Labour" in *Efficiency, Finance, and Varieties of Industrial Policy* (Columbia University Press, 2017); "Towards Community Resilience—the Role of Social Capital After Disasters" in *The Last Mile in Ending Extreme Poverty* (2015); and "The Economic Implications of Comprehensive Approach to Learning on Industrial Development (Policy and Managerial Capability Learning): A Case of Ethiopia" in *Industrial Policy and Economic Transformation in Africa* (Columbia University Press, 2015). He holds a master's degree in economics from the University of Manchester and a doctorate from Waseda University.

François Steenkamp is a researcher at the Development Policy Research Unit at the University of Cape Town (UCT), South Africa. His research interests include the dynamics and patterns of trade, complexity economics, and structural transformation. François has worked as a lecturer at the UCT School of Economics, where he taught international trade and macroeconomics. He holds a master's degree in economics from the University of KwaZulu Natal and is currently working on his doctorate at UCT, focusing on South African export patterns and their developmental implications.

Joseph E. Stiglitz is a University Professor at Columbia University. He is the cochair of the High-Level Expert Group on the Measurement of Economic Performance and Social Progress at the Organisation for Economic Co-operation and Development, and the chief economist of the Roosevelt Institute. A recipient of the Nobel Memorial Prize in Economic Sciences (2001) and the John Bates Clark Medal (1979), he is a former senior vice president and chief economist of the World Bank and a former member and chairman of the U.S. President's Council of Economic Advisers. In 2000, Stiglitz founded the Initiative for Policy Dialogue, a think tank on international development based at Columbia University. In 2011, he was named by *Time* magazine as one of the one hundred most influential people in the world. He is the author of numerous books, and several bestsellers. His most recent titles are *Globalization and Its Discontents Revisited* (2018), *The Euro: How a Common Currency Threatens the Future of Europe* (2018), *Rewriting the Rules of the American Economy: An Agenda for Growth and Shared Prosperity* (2016), and *The Great Divide: Unequal Societies and What We Can Do About Them* (2016). His latest book is *People, Power, and Profits: Progressive Capitalism for an Age of Discontent* (2019).

Jomo Kwame Sundaram, a Malaysian, writes on economic development challenges. He was an economics professor until 2004 and served as assistant secretary general for economic development at the United Nations from 2005 to 2015. He received the Wassily Leontief Prize for Advancing the Frontiers of Economic Thought in 2007 and authored *Globalization and Development in Sub-Saharan Africa* (2013).

Edlam Abera Yemeru is the chief of the Urbanization Section at the United Nations Economic Commission for Africa (ECA). In this capacity, she leads the development of policy knowledge and tools to support African member states in leveraging the potential of urbanization for accelerated and inclusive growth and structural transformation. Previously, she held research, teaching, and programmatic positions in the field of urban development, including at the United Nations Human Settlements Programme (UN-Habitat) and at academic and research institutes including Addis Ababa University, the University College London, University of Sussex, and the Organization for Social Science Research in Eastern and Southern Africa, Addis Ababa. At UN-Habitat, she led a number of initiatives designed to assist member states in promoting socially inclusive, economically productive, and environmentally sustainable urbanization in Africa and beyond. She has been a coauthor of several editions of UN-Habitat's *Global Report on Human Settlements*, covering issues such as urban safety, security, planning, mobility, and climate change. She has published on urban development in Africa, including most recently in the *Oxford Handbook on the Ethiopian Economy*. Edlam holds an master's degree of philosophy in development studies from the University of Cambridge and a doctorate in human geography from the University of London.

INDEX

Page numbers in *italics* indicate tables or figures.